DEBATING REVOLUTIONS

DEBATING
REVOLUTIONS

Edited by
NIKKI R. KEDDIE

NEW YORK UNIVERSITY PRESS
New York and London

NEW YORK UNIVERSITY PRESS
New York and London
© 1995 by New York University

Library of Congress Cataloging-in-Publication Data
Debating revolutions / edited by Nikki R. Keddie.
p.   cm.
Includes bibliographical references and index.
ISBN 0-8147-4656-X (cloth : acid-free paper)—ISBN 0-8147-4657-8 (pbk. :
acid-free paper)
1. Revolutions.   2. Revolutions—History.   I. Keddie, Nikki R.
HM281.D37   1995
303.6'4—dc20   94-16781
                    CIP

New York University Press books are printed on acid-free paper,
and their binding materials are chosen for strength and durability.
Manufactured in the United States of America
10 9 8 7 6 5 4 3 2 1

CONTENTS

III. Why Communism Fell in the Soviet Union and Eastern Europe

INTRODUCTION

NIKKI R. KEDDIE

Revolutions have been a favorite object for comparative study by scholars, especially sociologists and historians, since shortly after World War II. Revolutions are highly varied and complex events, involving rapid political, ideological, and behavioral changes that normally might not take place in a century, so it is not surprising that comparative studies have had very different points of emphasis. One line of thought, dating to Crane Brinton's study *The Anatomy of Revolution,* concentrates on the similarities in the course of revolutions, especially "great revolutions" like the French, the Russian, and the Chinese. Another school has concentrated on what causes people to revolt. Among concepts stressed by this school are "relative deprivation," a situation in which large numbers of people regard themselves as unjustly treated, and the James Davies "J curve," which sees revolutions as typically occurring when a long period of growth is followed by a sharp downturn. Before World War II, the J-curve idea had already been noted by the historian Ernest Labrousse in relation to the French Revolution.

Another explanation of why revolutions occur can be traced back to the nineteenth-century analysis of Alexis de Tocqueville. In a view somewhat parallel to the J-curve idea, de Tocqueville noted that the French Revolution was partly caused by the presence, not the absence, of reform from the top. The influence on revolution of uneven economic development and of reform from the top can also be found in Russia in 1917, Iran in 1978–79, and in certain other revolutions.

The Marxist view of revolution is another long-standing approach that has become more sophisticated in recent formulations. Basically, this view holds that the mode of production (a combination of technology and the relations of production) develops progressively over time, while political relations are more conservative; those who hold power are unlikely to give it up just because new classes have developed a claim to it. In addition, economic development is uneven, with some classes profiting while others lose out. With time the tension between old political relations and the developing productive forces, expressed in class struggles, becomes acute and often leads to revolutions that may put in power a government more in tune with the productive mode and its newly powerful classes. Marxist or Marxist-influenced scholars, including Christopher Hill, Robert Brenner, Georges Lefevre, Albert Soboul, Eric Hobsbawm, Eric Wolf, and many others have contributed greatly to scholarship about revolution, though only a few like Wolf have written explicitly comparative works on the subject.

Other largely materialist views of the structural causes of revolution have recently been proposed. Theda Skocpol, in her *States and Social Revolutions,* posits that the international relations of states, and particularly the weakening of some states by war, were of great importance in revolutions. Most influentially, Skocpol also argues that states had significant autonomy from classes and other social forces and that ideology was less important in revolutions than has usually been said. Unfortunately for some of Skocpol's theses, the Iranian Revolution broke out at almost the same time as her book appeared. This revolution from the start had a major ideological component and occurred in a state not weakened by war and still apparently strong, which did not support this part of her argument. It was, however, consonant with her central emphasis on the autonomy of the state. This emphasis has remained very influential, as have a number of her other ideas, at least as regards most major revolutions.

Jack Goldstone, whether intentionally or not, guarded against any contemporary falsification of his thesis in his book, *Revolution and Rebellion in the Early Modern World,* which dealt only with the early modern period. Goldstone broke with the usual Eurocentrism (as Skocpol had partly done in stressing China) by discussing both China and the Ottoman Empire along with Western Europe. His main thesis is that the ultimate factor behind early modern revolution was demographic growth, which he sees as having indirectly caused a series of economic and social crises that ultimately led to revolution or rebellion.

Other scholars, in line with recent trends, have stressed the cultural aspects of revolution. Another trend has been to emphasize the uniqueness or chance factors in each revolution and to deny that revolutions are significantly comparable.

What has been said here only scratches the surface of recent theories of revolution. Since World War II, a number of theorists have begun to include discussion of revolutions in third world countries such as Cuba, Nicaragua, and others in Asia, Africa, and Latin America, even before the Iranian Revolution.

The brief overview presented above suggests a central question: What is a revolution? Skocpol and others deal only with major revolutions that are victorious and bring about wholesale social change in entire countries. Goldstone, Charles Tilly, and others deal with movements that others might call revolts. The word "revolution" is generally reserved for a movement that brings about the (violent) overthrow of a government, after which the revolutionary forces take power, at least for a time. Most authors think a major social and/or political-ideological change must also take place for a movement to be called a revolution. A movement that overthrows a government but retains the old forms and ideologies is generally not considered a revolution. Naturally, there are borderline cases; while physical victory is usually a fairly clear-cut phenomenon, significant change as against continuity is often not so easy to distinguish.

This simplified presentation of what a revolution is might be contested by some authors. In addition, new difficulties in defining what revolutions are have arisen in dramatic form since 1978. Until then not only were revolutions generally supposed to occur in states that had undergone various kinds of major crises, usually including financial and international crises, but revolutions were also generally assumed to be led by people with ideologies further to the left than the government in power. Revolutions were also generally thought to involve major mass movements as a prerequisite to overthrowing governments. All of these suppositions changed radically with the combined (though very diverse) experiences of the Iranian Revolution of 1978–79 and the Eastern European and Soviet revolutions of 1989–91.

The Iranian Revolution occurred in a state that was powerful and wealthy and had experienced no major financial or international crises. While some authors stress the weakening effect of such factors as an economic recession and Jimmy Carter's human rights program, the government continued to have overwhelming military, security, and even economic resources. The revolution was primarily led, not by leftists or democrats, but by Islamic revivalists, who also took over the post-revolutionary regime.

While the Soviet and Eastern European states had more serious economic and financial difficulties, which in part reflected their relations with the West and the United States, their revolutions were not characterized by major mass movements. The Soviet revolution was primarily a revolution from above, while the Eastern European overturns occurred mainly because the Soviets, for the first time, made it clear they would not intervene to prevent change. While Eastern European revolutions saw some popular mobilization and more passive support, these were not on the scale previously associated with revolutions. Some people do not refer to the Soviet and Eastern European events as revolutions, but even more clearly than some revolutions they did bring about huge changes in society, economics, government, ideology, and culture. In these senses they were clearly revolutionary.

None of these post-1978 events fits classic patterns of revolution described by most revolutionary theorists, which suggests that the search for general rules or patterns is likely to be a great deal more difficult than some earlier theorists thought.

Is there, for example, any reason to think that nearly all revolutions should conform to one or a few basic patterns, or basic modes of causation? After all, the only thing that seems sure about revolutions to date is that they express a considerable level of discontent with things as they are, and with government as it is. Is there any reason to think that other comparable factors are always, or nearly always, involved in revolution? Although the period since World War II has seen a large number of general theories of revolution, it has also seen telling criticisms of these theories. Thus far, only a few of these criticisms are based on events since 1978. Before that, scholars of the French Revolution and the English Civil War of 1640–48 had begun a revisionist enterprise that rejected generalizing, and particularly class, interpretations of revolutions and that insisted on the particular and nongeneralizable nature of the causation of these two revolutions. (These trends are discussed in the article by Edward Berenson in this volume.)

Without going into the merits of such revisionism, discussed by Berenson, it is possible to say that historians and sociologists tend on such questions to develop their ideas dialectically over time, via theses, antitheses, and syntheses; or, in other terms, theories, revisionist countertheories that often go to an opposite extreme, and, later, synthesizing theories that incorporate the best-grounded and most useful elements of the preceding trends while rejecting what is oversimplified. (Naturally, although the "synthesis" may be more accurate than the previous stages, it is not a final resting point, any more than it was with the original German dialectical philosophers.)

A useful approach is to accept that certain factors may be characteristic of some or most revolutions without expecting them to be present in all. This approach, in part statistical, also accepts that certain revolts and uprisings, including some unsuccessful ones, have more in common with most revolutions than some revolutions, especially atypical ones, have with other revolutions. At the same time, even atypical revolutions are likely to share some characteristics with more "classic" revolutions, even though in other ways they may deviate. In other words, there is an overlap of common factors, but one is unlikely to find major common factors in *all* revolutions, even if one stresses general socioeconomic or political factors.

Some generalizations not stressed by any of the theories mentioned above merit further investigation. One is that major revolutions tend to occur in countries that have begun to enter the capitalist system but have not developed into fully formed capitalist countries like contemporary Western Europe, Japan, and the United States (none of which has experienced revolutions for over a century). Although this is hardly a generalization that differentiates highly revolutionary countries like Iran, China, and Russia from nonrevolutionary ones, it at least could lead scholars to examine why only a certain medium level of "modernization" seems conducive to revolution.

A related generalization might reexamine the social classes most involved in revolutions. Craig Calhoun's works on revolution suggest that in England, as others have suggested for France, industrial workers were far less revolutionary than were classes with a stake in the old regime who felt themselves to be under attack—specifically artisans and peasants. He finds these people ideologically to be "reactionary radicals," which ties them unexpectedly to some of the classes involved in Iran's two twentieth-century revolutions.

Also related to the dearth of revolutions in developed capitalist countries is the fact that democratic countries, which are overwhelmingly capitalist, almost never have revolutions, though they may experience right-wing counterdemocratic movements from the top, as in the case of Weimar Germany and the rise of Hitler. On the whole, however, democracy seems to preclude revolution, perhaps by giving people the feeling that they can influence or change the government by peaceful means.

Another area for comparative study concerns ideology. Both Craig Calhoun and Said Arjomand have found that "reactionary" and/or religious ideologies have been more prominent in a number of revolts and revolutions than most theorists and scholars have believed. More generally, the utopian and Manichean nature of a variety of revolutionary ideologies deserves more study. Few people would risk their lives if they did not expect a far better society—often pictured as a utopian ideal—than the current evil society to result. Revolutions are conducive to utopian expectations and a division of the world into the good and the evil.

The personal character of both "losing" leaders of the old regimes and "winning" leaders of revolutions also merits comparative consideration. Other points that have rarely been compared include the role of women in revolutions. Scholars are finding that upper-class women often had higher status and greater freedom in various societies than either middle-class or popular-class women. This was partly responsible for the limitations put on women's rights by populists in some revolutions, including both the French and the Iranian revolutions. On the other hand, other revolutions brought greater equality for women, and several, like the French revolution, arguably improved women's status in the long run.

Other important comparative issues include the ages of revolutionaries. Recent third world revolutions have occurred in countries with large percentages of young people, many of whom participated in revolutionary movements. Goldstone finds that this was also typical of earlier revolutions. The use and alteration of earlier ideologies, including religious, ethnic, and nationalist ideologies, in revolutions also deserves comparative consideration. There should also be more systematic differentiation between internal revolutions and revolutions of national liberation, like the American and Algerian revolutions.

While most of the chapters in this book treat revolution quite broadly and comparatively, they do not address only the large general questions discussed above. The contributors realize that in a forum stressing debates on a few topics there is space to deal only with a partial selection of possible subjects relating to comparative revolution. This is an indication of the breadth and complexity of questions concerning revolution, which cannot be exhausted in a single book. The articles in this book do, however, add important, novel ideas and proposals to our understanding of revolutions. Nearly all the articles go beyond their particular major themes to shed light on issues important to the broader understanding of revolution.

This book presents a series of chapters first published and debated in the journal *Contention: Debates in Society, Culture, and Science.* In the debating style of *Contention,* a number of later chapters comment on earlier ones. The chapters raise new and sometimes controversial theses regarding revolution in general and several revolutions in particular. Most of them center on three major problems, each of which raises many broader issues. The first concerns whether revolutions can be predicted or understood. The second centers on the evaluation of recent works on revolutions and revolutionary theory, especially Jack Goldstone's *Revolution and Rebellion in the Early Modern World,* but also works by Tim McDaniel, Timothy Wickham-Crowley, Theda Skocpol, and a number of authors writing on the French and

Chinese revolutions. The third concerns the reasons for the fall of the communist system in Russia and Eastern Europe.

CAN REVOLUTIONS BE PREDICTED? UNDERSTOOD?

Nikki R. Keddie's opening chapter, "Can Revolutions Be Predicted; Can Their Causes Be Understood?" starts from the charge that Americans should have predicted the Iranian Revolution of 1978–79 and goes on to question whether most revolutions are in fact predictable. The article argues, partly by analogy from the findings of chaos theory, that small initial changes may lead to large results and that most revolutions cannot be predicted. Revolutions result from complex interactions of circumstances, some of which have close parallels in nonrevolutionary countries, and not all of which can be foreseen. After events occur, however, and all the "might-have-beens" are eliminated, it is possible to understand the chain of events that resulted in revolution. The article also interprets the major causes of the Iranian Revolution.

Timur Kuran's "Why Revolutions Are Better Understood Than Predicted: The Role of Preference Falsification" says that recent events in Eastern Europe, the French Revolution of 1789, the Iranian Revolution, and even the Russian Revolution of 1917 were essentially unpredicted. Kuran points to what he calls "preference falsification" as a key factor leading to the unpredictability of such major events. People will routinely pretend to hold a safer, more acceptable opinion than they actually do. This is true even in the United States, especially on questions of race. For example, more white people told polltakers, and even exit pollers, that they would vote or had voted for David Dinkins or against David Duke than actually had. In more autocratic countries, preference falsification is more acute.

Keddie's reply accepts much of what Kuran says and makes several other points. The most central is that preferences should not be looked on as static and that many, and probably most, people who participated in the Iranian Revolution would not have seen themselves as acutely dissatisfied, to the point of wanting to join a revolutionary movement, a year earlier. This phenomenon adds to the difficulty of prediction.

Jack Goldstone, in response to Keddie's article, says "it is only the failure of area experts and popular wisdom to catch up to this recent work in the theory of revolution that has left most observers astounded by events."

His argument includes a list of his own predictions, and he proposes that area specialists and revolution specialists should work together, which would enable them to predict most revolutions.

Keddie's response reviews the predictions Goldstone says he got right, finding that with one possible exception they are not true predictions of revolutions. The idea of having a revolution specialist and an area specialist work together seems of doubtful utility, as there are not enough of each to cover the world, and, at least recently, revolutions have mostly taken place where they were least expected, and hence were least likely to attract such a team.

Goldstone's "Reply to Keddie" stresses areas of agreement.

INTERPRETING AND COMPARING REVOLUTIONS

Edward Berenson's "The Social Interpretation of the French Revolution" presents the major and radical changes that have occurred in interpreting that revolution during the past few decades. From being interpreted largely in socioeconomic, and often Marxist, terms, the French Revolution has come to be interpreted as a unique, cultural-intellectual-political event, with socioeconomic phenomena being of almost no importance. Partly this is owing to new research, which has shown far less distinction between the bourgeoisie and the nobility than older interpretations posited. But it is also due to the tenor of these times, which stresses cultural, linguistic, and political factors. The leader in this trend is François Furet. Berenson shows how certain aspects of the cultural and political emphasis, such as the stress on undivided autocratic power as a cause of revolution, can contribute to comparative understanding (in this case particularly of Iran and Russia). On the other hand, neglect of social and economic causation leaves out a major area, as shown by Goldstone's insights on demography. What is needed, Berenson believes, is a new synthesis that will incorporate recent writings regarding cultural and political factors while not neglecting economic and social ones, which may in fact help cause cultural and political changes.

John Foran's article, "Revolutionizing Theory/Theorizing Revolutions," discusses three books that have advanced our understanding of comparative revolution, which was first given an impetus in recent times by Theda Skocpol's *States and Social Revolutions*. These three are Jack Goldstone's *Revolution and Rebellion in the Early Modern World,* Tim McDaniel's *Autocracy, Modernization and Revolution in Russia and Iran*, and Timothy P. Wickham-Crowley's *Guerrillas and Revolution in Latin America*. Foran has a favorable view of all three, and is especially enthusiastic about Wickham-Crowley's work, though he notes it is really a study of comparative guerrilla movements. Foran generally accepts Goldstone's emphasis on worldwide population increase as a main, if indirect, factor in revolution. He criticizes Goldstone, however, for his poor understanding of cultural factors, for saying that Europe was more revolutionary than Asia mainly because only Europe had a strong messianic tradition (which existed in the Muslim world), and for rejecting various neo-Marxist and sociological views. McDaniel is praised for a comparative study of modernizing autocracies, but criticized for scanting class, social structure, and culture.

While Foran is primarily positive about Goldstone's theories, Charles Tilly's "The Bourgeois Gentilshommes of Revolutionary Theory" is more critical, noting that Goldstone, like many other contemporary theorists, stresses a single kind of causation for nearly all revolutions, while evidence increasingly shows how much revolutionary causes vary. Goldstone's supposed causal explanation of revolutions is in fact a definition of a revolutionary situation, or a descriptive tautology.

Said Arjomand, in contrast to some of the other writers, in his "Plea for an Alternative View of Revolution" suggests "that we reject Skocpol and Goldstone and look for a better theory." He notes that his own book on the Iranian Revolution stated that it occurred with no defeat, no crisis, and no peasant insurrection, contrary to most generalizations about revolution. And Eastern European events are even more at odds with current theories. Arjomand goes on to present an alternative theory that stresses politics and the state, including the loss of government legitimacy, not stressed by Goldstone or Skocpol.

Jeffrey N. Wasserstrom's essay argues that Goldstone is wrong to suggest that comparativists have much more of theoretical value to say than do area specialists. He cites the comparative interest of the work of François Furet, William Sewell, and Lynn Hunt on the French Revolution, and of three scholars on Southeast Asia. Wasserstrom proceeds to a discussion of his area, China, and tells why he believes neither Skocpol nor Goldstone provides a full enough explanation of China's revolutions. He also states that Goldstone does not adequately treat ideology and culture.

Goldstone's "A Reply to the Critics" responds to Arjomand, Tilly, and Wasserstrom, asserting that his ideas have often been misunderstood and oversimplified. Goldstone states that many historians, having abandoned

Marxist comparative explanations, have also abandoned the search for comparative explanations altogether. Goldstone answers what Wasserstrom says regarding culture and denies Arjomand's claim that he ignores the importance of legitimacy.

Andre Gunder Frank also discusses Goldstone's book and is especially impressed by his inclusion of all Eurasia and of the parallel trends he sees in the entire area. Frank sees Eurasia and Goldstone's discussion of it as part of a world system that he says can be traced back as far as 3000 B.C., which has commonalities owing to worldwide economic cycles, climate, and demography.

THE SOVIET UNION AND EASTERN EUROPE

In "What Was Socialism and Why Did It Fall?" Katherine Verdery sees the disintegration of Communist Party rule in Eastern Europe and its slower unraveling in the Soviet Union as largely rooted in the regimes' failure to carry out their redistributive promises. She attributes this failure to a systemic drive to accumulate power and goods at the center. The resulting tension between promise and performance led to crises of legitimacy that the leaderships, fearful of the political dangers of reform, tried to overcome by borrowing Western capital and technology. Their inability to repay or service loans and to obtain new ones deepened the crisis of regime legitimacy, exacerbated factional divisions in the ruling parties between those who looked to the outside world and those who managed the interior, and worsened dependence on, and collision with, a new, more flexible capitalism.

Thus, as Reginald Zelnik puts it in his supportive commentary on Verdery, the toughest challenge came from the outside. Yet he expresses some doubt about the explanatory power of Verdery's notion that socialism's deadly embrace with capitalism brought about its fall. He asks and requests clarification about whether the system's earlier efforts to resolve its contradictions internally were not equally likely to end in collapse.

Fred Halliday's "A Singular Collapse" also focuses on the international dimensions of the fall of the communist system. Although he thinks that internal factors—stagnation, socioeconomic paralysis, false claims of a more perfect society, loss of confidence in the leadership—played a major part in the collapse, it was not internal pressure alone that counted but also the failure to compete internationally. The inability to rival the West successfully in the third industrial revolution, more so than in the rivalries of the Cold War, made it impossible to ignore, conceal, or solve the system's besetting problems at home and abroad. Magnifying the lack of international competitiveness and its penalties was the role that ideology played in the collapse of communism. Here, cultural challenges, including fashions and images of the good life, were as important as economic or political challenges in explaining why "communism surrendered without a shot."

Daniel Chirot's "After Socialism, What?" notes the decline of socialism even beyond Eastern Europe, in Western Europe and the third world, especially since its fall in Eastern Europe. This fall he attributes largely to the failure, and indeed impossibility, of economic development beyond a certain point in highly centralized economies ruled from the top. Chirot discusses the worldwide implications of this fall, which he sees as mostly negative, with fundamentalism and fascism as likely outcomes in much of the world.

Muriel Atkin, in "The Islamic Revolution that Overthrew the Soviet State," brings together the debate on the fall of communism in the Soviet Union with the one on the perils of predicting revolutions. She notes especially the errors made by specialists in predicting the attitudes of different nationalities in the former Soviet Union. While one well-known specialist wrongly stated that the nationalities would cause no serious trouble and Gorbachev would survive, a whole school of writers led by Alexandre Bennigsen expected Soviet Muslims to be the force that would eventually bring about the dissolution of the Soviet Union. In fact, the Muslim republics were the last and most reluctant to leave the U.S.S.R. and have retained essentially communist leadership the longest.

Even this brief summary indicates that the book's main themes are really closely interconnected. The difficulties of predicting revolution are closely tied to the complexity and variability of revolutions. On the other hand, the book also shows the possibility of disagreement among intelligent scholars. One group tends to find revolutions both closely comparable and, if properly approached, predictable. Others are increasingly impressed by the complexity of revolutions, and, while they may believe that a single factor— whether socioeconomic, political, or cultural—is most determinative, they also believe that other factors can make the difference between a country that has a revolution and one that does not. In this group some feel that revolutions are nonetheless comparable, as they show a number of common features, but few expect every revolution to show them all. Ultimately this volume, which includes some of the most thoughtful current scholars of revolution, shows the pitfalls of oversimplified views of revolution and also the interconnections of social, economic, political, cultural, and feminist approaches to revolutions.

ACKNOWLEDGMENTS

Thanks go to our many anonymous reviewers and especially to associate editors Joyce Appleby and Hans Rogger, who commented on several of the papers and contributed to the introduction. Also very helpful have been staff members and assistants during the period these articles were first published: Eunice Ahn, Houri Berberian, Afshin Matin, Jasamin Rostam, and Ada Shissler.

Thanks also to the publishers of *Contention,* Indiana University Press, and its director John Gallman and journals editor Kathryn Caras who had the vision to be enthusiastic about a new idea in scholarly journals even before it had proved itself. Similar enthusiasm was expressed by the ever-helpful Niko Pfund with regard to publishing this book and *Debating Gender* (forthcoming), also based on *Contention* articles.

Santa Monica, August 1994

PART ONE

CAN REVOLUTIONS BE PREDICTED? UNDERSTOOD?

CAN REVOLUTIONS BE PREDICTED; CAN THEIR CAUSES BE UNDERSTOOD?

NIKKI R. KEDDIE

SHOULD THE IRANIAN REVOLUTION HAVE BEEN PREDICTED?

It is a frequent refrain of the literature on the Iranian or "Islamic" Revolution of 1978-79 that the revolution could and should have been predicted if only more people had found out and heeded what Iranians were thinking. The criticism is widely made of U.S. representatives in Iran that, by the late 1970s, they had renounced all attempts to find out what was going on in the minds of Iranians, and were complacently convinced that nothing could go wrong with the shah's regime. This popular line of argument, which is accurate to the degree that it describes official U.S. ignorance, is found recently in the generally excellent and comprehensive book by James Bill, *The Eagle and the Lion*.[1] The question remains whether, if the Embassy people had not renounced local intelligence functions and had met more people and reported what they were thinking and doing, they would have predicted, even as a reasonable possibility, the Islamic revolution. All the evidence is to the contrary. To take the best control group: U.S. scholars of modern Iran, who were doing research there in large numbers in the 1970s, did not predict anything like the revolution that occurred. This goes across the board for political scientists who interviewed both government and oppositional figures; economists who wrote of serious economic problems; and anthropologists, sociologists, and historians who looked at and listened to many classes of people, urban and rural, including clerics. These scholars, who were inclined to be critical of the shah's regime and not to echo official U.S. support for it, should, if anyone could, have provided predictions of serious trouble, but they did not. They did see that the land reform was helping peasants far less than was claimed, that rural-urban migrants had a hard life, economically and socially, that the oil-based economy was loaded with problems, but much of this was known to be true of a number of other oil-exporting countries, none of which has had a revolution. Nor were the Iranians of various classes seen by scholars predicting imminent revolution. Hence it seems that contact by U.S. intelligence with ordinary Iranians, while it might have made them more critical of the shah's regime, would have been highly unlikely to result in preparations for an imminent crisis, much less a revolution. (In this article, "revolution" covers the whole period from January, 1978 to February, 1979, and not just the final phase, which was predicted by late 1978.)

It is true that with hindsight some persons knowledgeable about Iran now say that they could, had they utilized differently what they knew and saw, have predicted the revolutionary movement. Notable among these is Sir Anthony Parsons, British Ambassador to Iran before and during the revolution. In a very frank, intelligent, and self-critical memoir, Parsons says that his knowledge of the power of the Iranian clergy in earlier revolts and revolutionary movements in Iran should have made him appreciate their power in the late 1970s.[2] This is admirable self-criticism but it appears to go too far. Once again, there were many Iranians and foreigners who knew the history of the Iranian clergy in revolutionary movements in the late nineteenth and early twentieth centuries, but, like Parsons, they failed to use this knowledge to predict a new clerical revolt. Nor is it strange that they so failed. For Iran had been overwhelmingly transformed since 1921 in economic structures, oil income, education, law, and a host of other ways, and the clergy had, in fact and not just appearance, been forced to occupy a greatly reduced role in society. Also, there is no evidence that the clerical opposition, including Khomeini himself, expected to be able to overthrow the shah, at least not without a much longer period of preparation than turned out to be necessary. A few non-Iranians who sided with the religious opposition, like Hamid Algar, came closer to predicting revolution, but did not actually do so.

In sum, although degrees of ignorance varied, virtually everyone was ignorant about the coming revolution — and this includes Iranians of all classes and the best-informed foreigners. Those who criticize U.S. Embassy ignorance have a point when they pinpoint U.S. *policy* failures in Iran. Most notably, had we not helped to overthrow Mosaddeq in 1953, there would almost surely have been no Islamic revolution. But neither the overthrow of Mosaddeq nor our overeager support of the shah was the result of intelligence failures, nor do such failures explain our inability either to predict or react effectively to the Islamic Revolution.

In a situation where, apparently, nobody, however well informed, predicted a successful revolution, one may turn away from the question, "Why didn't anyone think of that," to the question of whether under optimal intelligence conditions the revolution should and could have been predicted by well-informed persons. This inquiry can take us into more basic questions about revolution, historical prediction, and causation.

A fallacy shared by many who think revolutions should usually be predictable is that, since the event is major and involves large numbers of people in a dramatic way, its origins must similarly be visibly massive and distinctive. Big results, it is implicitly thought, must have discoverably big causes. With regard to Iran, a whole series of causes has been noted, including rising and then falling expectations after the 1973 oil price increase and later recession; massive rural-urban migration; cultural alienation; autocracy; hostility to the U.S., and others. Unfortunately, as shown in an interesting book by Henry Munson, most of these causes existed in other countries and did not lead to revolution. They may have been necessary causes of the Iranian revolution, but they were not sufficient causes. The effects of rapidly rising and then plummeting prices of oil were later felt far more dramatically in other countries after 1979 than they were in pre-revolutionary Iran, for example, and in none of them did they cause revolts or revolution.[3] Iran did have some special features, such as the position of its clergy and the dysfunction between autocracy and very rapid and uneven economic change, and one may reasonably say that in Iran causes that were essentially duplicated elsewhere combined with purely local ones to lead to a revolutionary explosion. However, a country about to have a revolution is not necessarily, in ways that can be measured at the time, more revolutionary in appearance than countries that do not have revolutions. Numerous analogies from nature could be made — one pot approaches the boiling point but does not reach it, while another on a slightly hotter flame will boil over, creating a completely different appearance and situation from pot number one.

An important natural analogy appears to come from recent Chaos theory. Some of the experiments that support Chaos theory demonstrate that extremely small initial differences may be translated into huge later differences:

> Tiny differences in input could quickly become overwhelming differences in output — a phenomenon given the name "sensitive dependence on initial conditions." In weather, for example, this translates into what is only half-jokingly known as the Butterfly Effect — the notion that a butterfly stirring the air today in Peking can transform storm systems next month in New York.[4]

A pioneer of chaos theory, Edward Lorenz of M.I.T., in working with a computer-based artificial weather system in 1961, accidently discovered that if he took a shortcut, by typing in three decimal places instead of six, the weather system would deviate increasingly and soon dramatically from his initial system. Translated into the real world, this turned out to mean that a very small initial difference could and often would mean an increasingly large later difference. Right away he thought that long-range weather forecasting was impossible, and later he said that any nonperiodical physical system would be unpredictable.[5] To be sure, not everyone accepts these implications, and many periodic physical processes are predictable by well-tested means, but it seems reasonable to posit that complex human events like revolutions may be more like unpredictable nonperiodic physical processes than like periodic, predictable ones. Also, as noted below, *some* revolutions *are* predictable, and have causes that are large and visible at the time.

A somewhat similar view is now being put forth in evolutionary theory, where it is now widely held that small and intrinsically possible changes long ago could have led to a greatly changed line of evolution, one that would not have led to beings nearly as intelligent and self-conscious as human beings. As Stephen Jay Gould summarizes this argument at the beginning of *Wonderful Life*: "with tiny alterations at the outset [key episodes] could have sent evolution cascading down wildly different but equally intelligible channels . . . that would have yielded no species capable of producing a chronicle or deciphering the pageant of its past."[6] (Logically, different small early changes could equally have led to beings *more* intelligent than we.)

Neither in weather, nor in evolution, nor in revolutions can we totally isolate a point in time and say that this was the initial point leading to the revolution, to the evolution of humanity, or to a hurricane (one of the natural events to which revolutions have been compared). In most cases, however, we can pick out a date or moment, or several days or moments, that relate and lead to different aspects of the phenomenon, and say that for practical analytic purposes this or these are the initial points. With the Iranian revolution one might reasonably choose the overthrow in 1953 of prime minister Mosaddeq with CIA and British help as a starting point. Certain causative factors, however, go back much further — particularly the special role of the Shi'ite clergy. And causation was constantly changing along with current developments, such as the shah's initiation of and reactions to the oil price rise of 1973. Such constant and complex synergistic interactions increase the difficulty of predicting revolutions.

Though Iran differed in a number of ways from other Third World countries, much as all countries differ from one another, there was very little reason to think that these differences would lead to revolution. Autocracy by a widely disliked ruler was hardly unique to Iran; nor was overreliance on oil income; large-scale urban-rural migration; growing income distribution gaps; torture of political prisoners; or popular hostility to dependence on the United States. As noted below, the most crucial different factors in Iran were probably the extreme dissociation between autocracy and both social classes and socioeconomic development; the unique role of Iran's clerical institutions and of leaders with Islamic ideology; and the personality and acts of the shah that helped bring about an extraordinary break between the shah and civil society. Resentment over subordination to foreign powers was also important. That nobody thought that the combination of factors, whether similar or dissimilar to what existed in other countries, was important enough to lead to immediate revolution does not prove that people were blind or stupid, however much many individuals involved may have been so. As in the weather example, relatively small initial differences from other countries could lead to a pattern of increasing deviation from them. Unlike the case of weather, the growth in deviation was much influenced by the actions of individuals, notably, in this case, the shah and Khomeini. Certainly it is difficult to maintain that observers should have predicted the various weak or ill-advised acts by the shah that contributed to the victory of the revolution. As with most revolutions, and analogously to weather and evolution, the deviation from the path of non-revolutionary countries was cumulative and built partly on itself, like a snowball both building and careening increasingly from side to side.

To say this is not to deny a great variety of important structural, economic, and class causes for the revolution, but only to indicate that these were the areas where there were the fewest decisive features differentiating Iran from a number of other countries. These areas provided necessary but not sufficient causation for the revolution, and only became revolutionary in combination with the unique and partly personal factors mentioned above. In saying that the background of the Iranian revolution was not distinctive or dramatic enough to make that revolution predictable I am not saying that all revolutions are equally unpredictable and lack distinctive background causes. To the contrary, while large results can come from what appear to be minor causes, such results can also come from evidently major causes. An obvious example contrasting with the Iranian revolution was the Bolshevik revolution. Here there were a number of causes that people noticed at the time: the contrast between considerable economic development and continued autocracy and lack of political development; a dissatisfied peasantry and working class, with the latter being concentrated in large urban industries; a capricious and unpopular autocracy, and, above all, the continuation of an increasingly murderous and unpopular war. The very fact that Russia had already had two revolutions since 1905 which did not meet its problems suggests the revolutionary situation. Already in 1914 there were widespread militant strikes that some saw as harbingers of revolution, and early wartime national unity soon wore off. There were some predictions of revolutions that came from left, right, and center. The specifics of the two 1917 revolutions were not predicted, but the dangers both to the monarchy and the social order were voiced.[7]

In the case of the Russian revolution and certain other revolutions, there were so many important contributing causes that even had certain causative factors been removed a revolution would very likely have occurred. In the Iranian case, however, one can think of acts by the shah that might have averted revolution. It is not the case that dramatic major events always have dramatic political or structural causes; sometimes yes, sometimes no. (One could call the first category of revolution *over-determined*, even though this is not how Freud or Althusser used the term, and the second category *underdetermined*.) A revolution may be predicted either because there is a general social crisis along with a revolutionary movement, as in the Russian case, or/and because the revolutionaries are very visible and strong, as in China in the 1930s and 1940s, when the Communists held much territory.

Along with the general, and often mistaken, feeling that major events like revolutions should have been predicted, there often goes a cynical view about "20-20 hindsight." Why is it, this criticism goes, that people who were completely wrong about what was going to happen are now convinced that they can explain why things had to happen the way they in fact did? Although skepticism about scholars' or politicians' explanations of events is often in order, it is not true that people who could not predict an event are unqualified to explain it. The processes are entirely different. To take the weather example again, while long-range prediction is now generally considered impossible by scientists, these scientists could, at least if they had enough information, trace back the development of a hurricane to its earlier and calmer stages. Similarly, past evolution may be understood but future evolution cannot be predicted. This relative ease of back-tracing as compared to prediction exists precisely because all the things that might have happened if conditions had been slightly different at various points *did not happen.* It is thus no longer necessary to take into account an infinity of conditions, as would be the case for prediction of long-term weather or revolution. One can deal only with the line of developments that actually occurred, thus greatly simplifying an analysis of the finite, if complex, group of developments that led to the hurricane or revolution. It is true that there remain considerable differences in analyses of revolutions, which is not surprising in view of the differences in social and political outlook of the analysts, but there are also many points of agreement.

None of this provides any consolation for the many people who want their experts to predict things more accurately so they can know more about what will happen in an uncertain world. Our media continue to turn to pundits for prediction despite their inevitably dismal record. Ironically, the media do not demand exact earthquake or hurricane predictions, in part because scientists have the sense not to offer them. It is not only classic revolutions that have not been foreseen, but also such events as the major and quasi-revolutionary developments since the late 1980s in the Soviet Union and Eastern Europe, including the failed coup of August, 1991 and its consequences, or the contrary developments in China, to name only a few cases. To be sure, there are political developments that can be predicted with fair certainty — such as that there will not be a successful coup d'etat in the United States in the next decade, and that either the Democrats or the Republicans will elect our President in 1996. The problem is that such accurate prediction is possible only in situations so stable that nobody doubts the outcome in any case, and hence such statements are not even regarded as predictions for the United States, though their analogs would be risky, and hence would be predictions, for many countries. As soon as one approaches a less stable situation, the overall record of prediction by experts becomes miserable. In general, the more drastic the change, the more prediction is desired, and the less it is possible. There remains in the minds of many, and probably most, people, the idea that if only experts were better informed and more objective they would be able to predict major upheavals. The past record suggests, however, that the more unusual and transforming an event is, the less likely it is to be predicted. The accuracy of prediction is, in other words, inversely proportional to its importance.

Although it is too much to hope that the craze of asking scholars to predict major changes will pass, one may say that some comprehension of our current situation is far more likely to result from understanding its genesis and major elements than from trying to predict violent change. A key to understanding a major event like a revolution is to try to figure out what were the key differences between countries that have had revolutions and those that have not. As suggested above, these differences will not always seem to be of revolutionary proportions, but the *ex post facto* benefits of being able to trace developments back in time in both revolutionary and non-revolutionary countries should make it possible to see what the key factors were in making one country revolutionary and others not.

WHAT DIFFERENTIATED IRAN FROM OTHER MUSLIM COUNTRIES?

All countries differ from one another, as do all individuals. As with the half-full or half-empty glass, one may with equal factual accuracy stress either the similarities of a revolutionary country to non- revolutionary ones or the dissimilarities. History is not neatly quantifiable, and even in the case of weather it is only by isolating parts of the total and not trying to understand the entire complex of weather that a pattern can be meaningfully charted and made to show a measurable course of growing differentiation. In a hurricane as a whole, as in a revolution, we know that the deviation from the norm keeps increasing and is much greater at the end than at the beginning of a process; and it is far more difficult, if not impossible, to chart all the changing factors in their interaction than it is to chart one or two.

For the study of revolution, the question about comparative differences most relevant to causation is: what differences were there between the revolutionary country and non-revolutionary ones that can help to explain the revolution in the former? In the case of Iran in 1978-79, though analysts differ in their views, I would maintain that three major areas of difference were key. These are 1) the evolution of the Shi'ite clergy in Iran, which made a powerful Khomeini and his network possible, 2) the particularities of the shah and the way he ruled, and, 3) probably the most important, the major contradiction between an increasingly autocratic political structure and forced, inequitable, and rapid socioeconomic changes that to some degree alienated all classes in society. All three of these factors interacted and changed over time. Almost surely the third, which affected society as a whole the most, was the most socially disruptive, as is effectively maintained in a comparative study of Iran and Nicaragua by Farideh Farhi and in a book by Mohsen Milani which both recounts and presents a multifactoral and convincing analysis of the revolution.[8] On the other hand, large parts of the structural factor existed elsewhere, and it cannot be taken as the only significant explanation of why Iran was different. Similarly, Iranians' hostility to the Shah's complaisance to foreign powers was a long-term factor that only became revolutionary in the presence of other factors.

To elaborate on the three causes named above:

1) Contrary to a view widely held both by scholars and the public, it was not so much Shi'ism *per se* that was more revolutionary than majority Sunnism, but rather the evolution of Shi'ite institutions in Iran that lent themselves to control by a single powerful revolutionary cleric. Shi'ism, to be sure, had certain revolutionary potentialities, having originated around the figures of Ali and his son Husain, who had both led failed military endeavors to take control of the Islamic community. Also, early Shi'ism and the later branch that came to be known as "Assassins" after their reputed use of hashish, were often militant and rebellious. The majority branch of Shi'ism, the Twelvers, which comprised the great majority of Shi'ites in Iran and the Middle East, however, early developed in a quietist way. The fifth and sixth imams, or leaders, called for accep-

tance of the political rule of existing powers. This continued to be dominant Shi'i doctrine for centuries, and the so-called "disappearance" of the last, twelfth, imam has been plausibly interpreted as a means to avoid having an imam present who might become a center for political loyalties or movements.

It is only when an unorthodox and politicized Twelver Shi'i movement conquered Iran with the Safavid Dynasty in 1501 that Twelver Shi'ism began seriously to reenter the world of politics. In the early Safavid period the clergy were dependent on rulers, but as they built up their own economic and ideological power some of them began to assert the independent claims of the clerical estate. This trend strengthened in the eighteenth century, especially after the Safavids were overthrown in 1722, and many of the clergy moved to their holy cities in Ottoman Iraq and detached themselves from Iranian control. It was in this period that a school of thought became dominant among the clergy which said that every believer must choose one qualified religious jurist to follow (there could be several such leaders at once) and must accept his rulings. It was this, rather than earlier Shi'ite beliefs, that laid the ideological basis for a power over believers by the Shi'ite clergy that had no counterpart among the Sunnis. Indeed it is only among these Shi'ites that one can meaningfully speak of a "clergy" who were necessary to the proper behavior of believers.

Just as important was the economic independence of the Shi'ite clergy. The Shi'ite clergy were able to get recognition of their right to direct collection of religious taxes early in the nineteenth century Qajar dynasty. In Sunni countries, on the other hand, religious taxes came to be increasingly diverted by the government, and governments also asserted growing control over religious endowments, which was far less true in Iran. The eighteenth and nineteenth century location of the main Shi'ite leaders in Ottoman Iraq, outside Iran's control, created a situation more like the long independence of the papacy than like the caesaropapism of Constantinople, Istanbul, or Moscow, where the main religious leadership was located in the empire's capital and subject to close government control.

In the nineteenth century there developed the practice of often having a single religious leader whose word regarding religious law was binding on all believers. In that century there were also a number of developments that encouraged many of the leaders of Iran's informal religious hierarchy to act together in the political realm. These included successful ulama pressure to launch a war against Russia in 1826; ulama activity against the new Babi religion starting in the 1840s; and their joining in a movement to annul the infamous Reuter concession in 1873. On a larger scale were widespread ulama participation in a successful movement against a British subject's tobacco monopoly in 1891-92 and ulama participation in the constitutional revolution of 1905-1911.

The centralization and modernization programs of Reza Shah and his son, Mohammad Reza Shah, lessened the power of the clergy but did not really undermine it. The hierarchical structure and economic independence and strength remained. Hence, the clergy, led by Khomeini, were able to mount a large protest to the shah's White Revolution in 1963. The points most objected to then were land reform, which Khomeini was careful to avoid condemning, but which other clergy, some affected by its provisions, did; votes for women; royal tyranny and subservience to the U.S. When Khomeini refused to stop attacking the government, he was exiled in 1964 to Turkey, whence he went to Iraq from 1965 to 1978, when he was expelled under pressure from the shah. Then he went to France, from where his influence in Iran increased. In Iraq and France he was influenced by more modernist young Muslims like Abol Hasan Bani Sadr and Ibrahim Yazdi.

An important element in leading the revolution and manning post-revolution governments were Khomeini's clerical students. He taught them his evolving ideas that culminated in the view that the clergy should rule directly, an idea new to Shi'ism and Islam. Back in Iran many of these students formed a network that was important before and during the revolution, and several were prominent in secret clerical-bazaar organizations in Tehran.

Related to ulama power was the unusually strong alliance with the oppositional clergy among the merchants and craftsmen of the traditional bazaar economy, who opposed foreign and governmental competition and gave impetus to Iran's main modern rebellious and revolutionary movements. This alliance encouraged ulama participation in most of the mass movements of the past century, and it also initially backed Mosaddeq. Bazaar ties to religious institutions helped create ulama ideology and action, and merchants and reformers acting behind the scenes were often the instigators of key clerical actions. Unlike the situations in some Muslim countries, the bazaar was always overwhelmingly mainstream Muslim, and only a minority were Christian, sectarian, or Jewish.

Thus, in summary form, we may see that the Iranian clergy since 1501 developed a hierarchical organization demanding obedience of believers and evolved ideological positions that emphasized, first, the independence of the clergy and, ultimately, the right of the leading cleric and his followers to rule. They also had more organized ties to the bazaar classes than did ulama elsewhere.[9] While it may be said that this scenario could develop more easily in Shi'ism than in Sunnism, there was nothing in Shi'i doctrine or early organization that necessitated this development. This is indicated by the fact that Shi'ites in most other countries to this day do not have such a hierarchical structure or unified doctrine; to the extent that they have these it is mostly a recent development, influenced mainly by Iran. It is also suggested by numerous Sunni revolts in the past, and by the fact that it was Sunni thinkers in this century who pioneered the idea of an Islamic state, and Sunnis appear to have helped influence Khomeini to put forth this idea as late in his own development as the late 1960s.

This does not mean that Iranian Shi'ism became revolutionary because of some logically necessary evolution of its institutions. Rather, this prior evolution, influenced at every stage by the ambient political and socioeconomic context, helped make a revolutionary development effective. From a subjective viewpoint, Khomeini developed his doctrine because of his conviction that the evil and illegitimate shah, a puppet of the United States and Israel, could and should be replaced by an Islamic government — not because of the evolution of Shi'i institutions and power in Iran. In Sunni Muslim countries similar doctrines had been put forth earlier but they did not have the conditions necessary to effect Islamic revolutions — one may mention Sayyid Qutb in Egypt and Maududi in Pakistan, both of whom called for Islamic government well before Khomeini did. What is different is not the doctrine so much as the objective situation. And a major part of this objective difference concerns the clerical hierarchy of Iran, which, because of its developing organization, doctrine, and ties to an unusually influential bazaar, became an effective instrument for realizing an "Islamic" state as no equivalent force outside Iran could do. Disillusionment with the West and its ideas was also important, but not exclusive to Iran.

This analysis of clerical and ideological development in Iranian Shi'ism is in accord with the insistence on the need to study the changing contexts and outcomes of Islamic ideology expressed so well in Sami Zubaida's book, *Islam, the People and the State*.[10] Like Zubaida, I do not take the prominence of Islam in current Muslim politics as a sign that "Islam" is so different from "the West" that Islamic politics must be a permanent and little-changing feature of the politics of Muslim countries. Modern Islamic politics in Iran and elsewhere are full of modern referents

— the nation-state, parliaments, constitutions, wars to protect national boundaries, and, in post-revolutionary Iran, *raison d'état* justified as overriding Islamic law, and a constantly increasing interventionist government bureaucracy. The importance in Iran (and other Muslim states) until recently of non-Islamic nationalist and even socialist movements and parties suggests that the current Islamist trend is not necessarily a permanent one. And within the clerical government interpretations of Islam keep changing — recently in a more moderate and even partly secular direction.

2) A second major difference between Iran and other Muslim countries concerns the shah and his activities. Although on a world scale the shah was not the most despotic of rulers, if one concentrates on monarchs in the Muslim world one may note that the others have operated much less despotically than the shah. The kings of Morocco, Saudi Arabia, and Jordan have known how to deal, coopt, and even compromise much better than the shah. The shah was encouraged to despotism by a combination of circumstances not duplicated elsewhere: his rescue from Mosaddeq and leftist threats by a U.S. that objectively supported his despotism; large and increasing oil income that obviated concern about taxpayers and encouraged grandiose schemes; almost unconditional military and political support from the U.S.; inheritance from an equally autocratic shah who frightened him but whom he wished to emulate, much like Frederick the Great and his father; and grandiose delusions after the oil price rise about pushing Iran quickly to become one of the world's leading powers via unrealistic and socially disruptive reforms.

These forces leading to royal autocracy were fatally combined with contradictory trends in the shah that undermined that same autocracy. These included his belief, appearing clearly in his final autobiography and in accounts by the British and U.S. ambassadors, that the U.S. and Britain could and would control what happened in Iran, willing him to be overthrown, or, alternatively, saving him. His belief that the U.S. should tell him what to do, and was perhaps plotting against him, based partly on exaggerated extrapolation from a number of actual experiences, helped account for his continual hesitancy to decide on a line of action from 1977 to 1979; for his fears in the face of Carter's objectively weak Human Rights policies; and for his constant appeals to the U.S. and British ambassadors to recommend policies to him.

It seems quite likely that if the shah had acted repressively early in the development of the revolution, say in the spring of 1978, the revolution could have been stopped, at least for some years. The combination of the shah's character with considerations of his illness and his son's coming succession was probably more important than Carter's policies in determining his vacillating response to the revolution. In his recent book analyzing the revolution, Said Arjomand underlines the fact that the army leaders and most followers remained loyal until the end, unusually for a revolution, but the shah refused to use it effectively.[11] And Marvin Zonis stresses the key importance of the shah's personality to his indecisiveness.[12] The shah was neither mentally nor organizationally prepared for revolt and had no plausible policy with which to meet it.

3) The growing contradiction between political autocracy and the socioeconomic forces of change is an area so huge that it is difficult to deal with it in brief compass. Here I will limit myself to listing some of its elements, such as the concentration of virtually all of Iran's modernization or major socioeconomic change into a period of fifty years during which people were uprooted from old homes and ways, often more than once. In the period 1927-1977 were concentrated all of Iran's industrialization, all its modern infrastructure and education, the disarmament and partial settlement of formerly powerful nomadic tribes, the entry of women into public life and the unveiling of many, the modernization of many laws, including sensitive personal and family laws, land reform, reduction in the power of the clergy and the bazaar, rapid population growth, extensive urbanization in rebuilt and expanded cities, and the creation virtually from scratch of modern armed forces and a governmental and state structure. Most of this occurred in accord with royal will; only for a very short period after World War II was there meaningful parliamentary consultation, and parliamentarians themselves did not represent popular will. Groups and classes with grievances were suppressed, not listened to; the suppression after 1953 of oppositional secular political groups gave opportunities to the oppositional clergy and their allies, who could meet in homes and religious buildings and use a code language in which the shah was often represented as Yazid, the Umayyad caliph who ordered the killing of Imam Husain.

It is possible that the overboiling pot might have been cooled had real political participation been allowed and had problems like increasing income gaps or the problems of urban migrants and bazaaris been met, but instead the regime refused to look at the human element of the society it was putting in place and opted to listen to technocrats instead of encouraging participation in change, which might have made it slower but surer.

There is one special feature of this situation that has not received the attention it deserves. That is to explain why the shah, exceptionally among rulers in Muslim lands, ultimately lost the support of all social classes. This was a key factor in the point noted by Arjomand, that the revolution had major reactive or reactionary elements. This factor is explicated in the work done by Amir Farman Farma on comparative counterrevolution, where he notes that Iran had no effective counterrevolutionary force, and attributes this to the fact that the usual counterrevolutionary classes were, in Iran, part of the revolution. The Iranian revolution, in fact, was revolutionary and counterrevolutionary at the same time.[13] This simultaneously revolutionary and counterrevolutionary character is related to the so-called White Revolution of the early 1960s and the shah's reforms of the mid-1970s. In the early 1960s the shah instituted a land reform which, although it helped peasants much less and in a much more uneven way than advertised, did remove big landlords as a class between the shah and the peasants and brought more direct state control over cultivators. It also, along with high birthrates and lowered deathrates, encouraged overrapid rural-urban migration of those with too little land. (Analogies between these reforms and Russia's Stolypin reforms could be instructive.) The bazaaris were discriminated against in favor of large, often partly governmental or officially-tied, businesses. The land reform, the religion corps, and other measures also undermined the power base of the clergy and made them more oppositional, as shown in the clerical anti-White Revolution riots of 1963. The Family Protection Act that brought greater equality for women also aroused clerical wrath. Hence, Iran saw a situation where groups already oppositional, coming from the intelligentsia, new middle class, and workers, were little appeased by growth without political reform, while important groups that had been only partly oppositional became more so — notably the clergy and the bazaaris. Hence classes elsewhere often counterrevolutionary combined with more usually revolutionary classes in opposition to the old regime.

The separation of the shah from all urban social classes increased from the mid-1970s with new "reforms." The creation of a single-party system was unpopular, while a scheme for worker purchase of company shares was widely disliked by both workers and capitalists. A violent and discriminatory "anti-profiteering" campaign that fined and jailed even small businessmen was unpopular, as was the 1977 economic austerity program. And all classes were united in disliking subservience to the United States and ties to Israel.

This point can also be elaborated in a different way. In the language of contemporary social thought, the Iranian state was highly autonomous, meaning not necessarily that it was more politically dictatorial than a number of others, but that it increasingly acted without significant accommodation to, or consideration of, the major social classes and groups. A recent book by Mark Gasiorowski recognizes that the appearance of this autonomy coincided with the White Revolution. As he writes:

> The year 1963 can be regarded as the one in which a highly autonomous state was finally established in Iran. The modern middle class was greatly weakened. . . . The traditional upper class had already lost most of its influence . . . the land reform program . . . soon essentially destroyed this class. The Iranian bourgeoisie remained weak and subservient to the state . . . The industrial working class had not been able to exert much influence over the state since the collapse of the Tudeh party. Similarly, traditional middle- and lower-class elements . . . had also lost their main sources of influence over the state by the end of 1963.[14]

The government from 1963 to 1977 also engaged in harsh suppression of all oppositional groups and their leaders. This helped turn some oppositionists to guerrilla groups and others to radical and often underground Shi'ite networks. Although the autonomous state was for the moment very strong, it spawned an opposition dedicated no longer to reform but to overthrow and a complete change in the nature of the state. There are dialectical ironies and contradictions in this, as in other aspects of the Iranian revolution. The U.S., in establishing a complaisant client state, most dramatically in the 1953 overthrow of Mosaddeq, but also in its encouragement of reform from above under Kennedy and Carter and in its heavy sales of arms and training of security forces, helped create a state that had little incentive to democratize or to heed the interests of its people. What was apparently a strength became a fatal weakness. And the shah, by suppressing all the more visible reform groups, encouraged the development of a revolutionary opposition and particularly that part of it that was hardest to root out — the clerical and Islamic radicals. Both a U.S. policy less obsessed with a grossly exaggerated Soviet menace to Iran (which was what made the U.S. give the shah whatever he wanted) and an Iranian state willing to make some political compromises and to listen to at least some of its class and political opponents might have brought about a state more stable even if less ostentatiously potent.

The divergence between governmental policies and the needs of society grew rapidly after 1953; and it produced increased discontent and helped produce the revolution. A combination of long-term U.S. cliency, strong since the U.S. backed Mosaddeq's overthrow, and increasing oil income, enabled the shah to act with growing disregard for the needs and interests of his people. It also fed his delusions of grandeur, leading him to grandiose programs without roots in Iranian reality.

BIG AND SMALL DIFFERENCES: PREDICTABILITY AND UNPREDICTABILITY

It may seem that the above discussion of Iran's special features, which emphasizes their importance and unique character, contradicts my earlier claim that Iran's revolution was not predictable, but this is not so. First, some of the features noted above had parallels in other Muslim countries: many kinds of modernization were more sudden and thorough in Ataturk's Turkey (although Ataturk's position and popularity were more solid than the Pahlavis'); family law reform was very common, as were basic change in education, modernization of the economy with socioeconomic dislocations, and even land reform. There have also been major elements of autocracy and lack of political participation in many countries. Such elements become revolutionary only with the proper conjuncture, and it was because of this that I put the more distinctive elements of the nature of the clergy and of the shah first. These elements turned out to be important but their importance could not, on the basis of past experience of human history, have been so accurately assessed in advance as to lead to predictions of revolution. There was nothing in the experience of Iran or any other country to make one think that a cleric could effectively lead either a revolution or a subsequent government. Nor can we suppose that if a Khomeini-like figure appears somewhere else that he will be likely to lead a successful revolt. Similarly, many of the shah's faults and foibles were well known, but there was no reason, based on what people knew of past human or even Iranian events, to think that the shah would have to face a revolution and would prove lacking when he did so. One strong friend and adviser, like Asadollah Alam who counselled force in 1963, might have made some difference. Even the shah's crucial loss of support in all social classes could not have been assessed at the time in the same way as it was once it became operative *during* the revolution.

Another difficulty in predicting the outcome of a lengthy revolution like the Iranian is that its outcome was largely determined by the complex interaction of events during a long revolutionary period. Even if we take only one variable in events between the first protests by intellectuals in late 1977 and Khomeini's accession to power in early 1979, we may begin to appreciate the complexity of such a revolution. During a revolution as many politically crucial decisions may be made in a month as are normally made in a decade, and each such decision may alter the overall complexion of events. (In a country like Iran, in fact, as many mass political activities occurred in some weeks of the revolution as had occurred in the previous 25 years.) To schematize this reality we may isolate one variable — decisions by the shah and his regime — and posit a simple binary situation: either the shah (or his regime; it matters little) made the decision he in fact did or he did not make this decision. The negative clearly opens a range of alternative possibilities, but we will simplify and reduce these to two for each decision.

To specify the elements of this abstract model, we can point to key regime decisions in 1977 to liberalize; to allow opposition statements; not to crack down on liberal protests, and so forth. In January, 1978, there was the key royal decision to publish a scurrilous attack on Khomeini, which led to the first in a year-long cycle of demonstrations, and then came decisions for the limited force used against the ensuing demonstrations. There were also various acts of further liberalization in the spring and summer and their very partial reversal with the declaration of martial law late in 1978. The bloody repression of a mass demonstration in the fall was another key decision, as was the decision not to try to use the armed forces in a massive way at any other time.

Alternative decisions at any point would have affected the total situation, sometimes significantly. Even with a simple doubling of alternatives that often had three or more possibilities, it takes a comparatively small number of decisions to reach a million alternatives by February, 1979 from regime decisions alone. (If one follows the clever example of camera manufacturers in saying 2x64=125, it takes just twenty such binary decisions to reach a million; with accurate arithmetic it takes slightly fewer.)

When one adds in such variables as popular movements, the paralyzing strikes of late 1978, and acts by major foreign players, one will

Figure 1

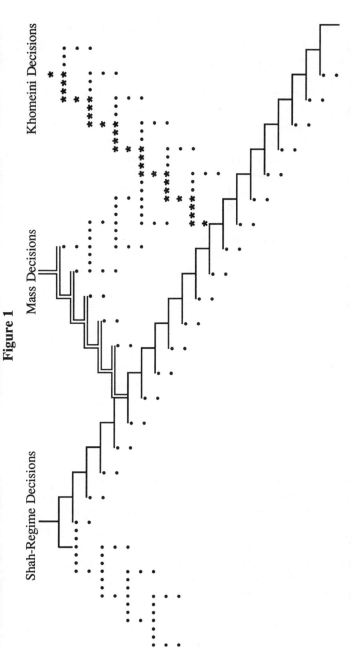

This is a highly schematized figure, as the three dimensions above are not exhaustive, and these dimensions were constantly interacting. Each of the three groups, if it operated independently and made only simply binary yes or no decisions, after twenty (20) such decisions would reach a million alternatives. In interaction, the alternatives would reach into the billions or trillions.

quite soon get to billions of possibilities. Some of these would have led to substantially different outcomes, and almost surely only a minority would have led to substantially the same outcome.

I do not, however, believe that in the real world there were billions or millions of different paths that could in fact have been taken. I do not believe that here were hundreds such paths or tens, or even two. As I believe that all phenomena arise from prior phenomena — something that used to be called causation — my personal belief is that events could only have taken the path they did take. (This belief, which some would call determinism and which it would take too long to argue here, is not a prerequisite to following the rest of my argument, which would not be essentially different even if history might have taken a number of courses different from the one it did. A belief in the real possibility of numerous different courses, in fact, should *increase* the difficulty of predicting historic events.) Each development or decision had one or more reasons why it occurred that the other possibilities lacked. The problem is that these reasons were often and necessarily invisible to contemporaries, and might even have been trivial or accidental in relation to larger forces (as the shah's illness was caused, but was an accident in relation to general historical forces). Hence, a combination of complex interactions and the impossibility of predicting many individual events multiplies the difficulties of predicting long-lasting revolutions and their outcome. Once they have occurred, however, it is possible to eliminate all the roads not taken and to study the forces behind what actually occurred. Thus we can get a reasonably comprehensive picture of the causes and evolution of a revolution that was far too complex and had too many plausible possibilities to be predicted in advance.

A further conclusion, perhaps uncomfortable for liberals, is the old de Tocqueville one about troubles arising not when things are getting worse but when they are getting easier. To this can be added a modified "J-curve" view, that revolutions are likely to arise when people experience a downturn in a previously improving situation.[15] Without separating out the economic and political elements of such statements, I would note that doses of political liberalization after long political repression often lead to demands for more change, as was seen in Eastern Europe. Hence, the optimistic Human Rights agenda may seem unappealing to many dictators, not only because it limits their direct powers, but also because it may put their regimes at risk. In the contemporary world neither liberalization from above nor overthrowing autocracies seems to be a recipe for meeting the fundamental structural and economic problems affecting many groups in society, however. Today more serious thought, whether in or regarding Iran or Eastern Europe, must be given to how to change structures with the active input and participation of the population if useful changes are to occur. Specifically, liberalization undertaken from above without considering the actual priorities of the main social groups is unlikely to meet these groups' demands. The common Western assumption that a *specific* overall human rights and democratization agenda will meet local needs and grievances everywhere is unlikely to be true in any particular case. Governments, whether before or after a revolution, might be better advised to consult with their subjects and their representatives and to ensure their serious input in any reform program. This, of course, may require both a good faith aim of achieving popular goals and a freedom of action in face of vested interests, and these are rarely present. And today exclusivist national, religious, and ethnic doctrines greatly complicate solutions to socioeconomic problems.

To date the Iranian revolution is unique in its accession to power of a traditional religious group with a reconstructed traditional-modern ideology. With the benefit of hindsight we can trace many of the causes of this unique revolution. Its very uniqueness as well as the key role played by the personalities of Khomeini and the shah, in addition to structural causes in part familiar in many countries, militated against anyone's predicting it, as did the difficulty of prediction of any such unusual event, whose later phases were heavily dependent on the complex interaction of its early ones.[16]

NOTES

Earlier versions of this paper were given as a George Antonius lecture at M.I.T. and for the Center for Comparative History and Social Theory, U.C.L.A. Thanks for the comments of participants, especially Ali Banuazizi and Philip Khoury, and for those of Perry Anderson.
1   James A. Bill, *The Eagle and the Lion: The Tragedy of American-Iranian Relations* (New Haven and London: Yale University Press, 1988).

2   Anthony Parsons, *The Pride and the Fall: Iran, 1974-79* (London: Jonathan Cape, 1984), pp. 134-37.

3   This point is made as part of the comparative study by Henry Munson, Jr., *Islam and Revolution in the Middle East* (New Haven and London: Yale University Press, 1988), pp. 111-12.

4   James Gleick, *Chaos: Making a New Science* (New York: Penguin Books, 1987), p. 8.

5   Gleick, *Chaos*, Ch. 9 "The Butterfly Effect," pp. 9-32.

6   Stephen Jay Gould, *Wonderful Life: The Burgess Shale and the Nature of History* (New York and London: W. W. Norton & Company, 1989), p. 15.

7   See Leopold H. Haimson, "The Problem of Social Stability in Urban Russia, 1905-1917," in Michael Cherniavsky, ed., *The Structure of Russian History: Interpretive Essays* (New York: Random House, 1970), pp. 341-80, and Hans Rogger, "The Question Remains Open," in Robert H. McNeal, ed., *Russia in Transition, 1905-1914: Evolution or Revolution?* (New York: Rinehart and Winston, 1970), pp. 102-09.

8   Farideh Farhi, *States and Urban-Based Revolutions* (Urbana: University of Illinois Press, 1990); Mohsen M. Milani, *The Making of Iran's Islamic Revolution: From Monarchy to Islamic Republic* (Boulder, Colorado: Westview Press, 1988). Earlier books on the revolution include Shaul Bakhash, *The Reign of the Ayatollahs: Iran and the Islamic Revolution* (New York: Basic Books, 1984); Hossein Bashiriyeh, *The State and Revolution in Iran* (New York: St. Martin's Press, 1984); Nikki R. Keddie, *Roots of Revolution* (New Haven: Yale University Press, 1981); and Gary Sick, *All Fall Down: America's Tragic Encounter with Iran* (New York: Random House, 1985). On the revolution's background see Ervand Abrahamian, *Iran: Between Two Revolutions* (Princeton: Princeton University Press, 1982; and Fred Halliday, *Iran: Dictatorship and Development* (New York: Penguin, 1979). There is a vast participant and scholarly literature on the revolution, some of which is cited below.

9   On the political evolution of the Iranian clergy, see Nikki R. Keddie, ed., *Religion and Politics in Iran* (New Haven and London: Yale University Press, 1983); Juan R. I. Cole and Nikki R. Keddie, eds., *Shi'ism and Social Protest* (New Haven and London: Yale University Press, 1986); Said Amir Arjomand, *The Shadow of God and the Hidden Imam: Religion, Political Order, and Societal Change in Shi'ite Iran from the Beginning to 1890* (Chicago: University of Chicago Press, 1984); Shahrough Akhavi, *Religion and Politics in Contemporary Iran: Clergy-State Relations in the*

Pahlavi Periods (Albany: State University of New York Press, 1980); Michael Fischer, *Iran: From Religious Dispute to Revolution* (Cambridge: Harvard University Press, 1980); and Hamid Algar, "The Oppositional Role of the Ulama in Twentieth-Century Iran," in Nikki R. Keddie, ed., *Scholars, Saints, and Sufis: Muslim Religious Institutions in the Middle East since 1500* (Berkeley: University of California Press, 1972), pp. 231-256.

10   Sami Zubaida, *Islam, the People and the State: Essays on Political Ideas and Movements in the Middle East* (London and New York: Routledge, 1989).

11   Said Amir Arjomand, *The Turban for the Crown: The Islamic Revolution in Iran* (New York and Oxford: Oxford University Press, 1988), p. 120.

12   Marvin Zonis, *Majestic Failure: The Fall of the Shah* (Chicago: University of Chicago Press, 1991).

13   Amir Farman Farma, "A Comparative Study of Counter-Revolutionary Mass Movements during the French, Mexican, and Russian Revolutions with Contemporary Application," (D. Phil diss: Politics, Oxford University, Oxford, 1990), chap. vi. I have not seen this dissertation but have heard its analysis of Iran as a conference paper at Harvard's Middle East Center, 1989.

14   Mark J. Gasiorowski, *U.S. Foreign Policy and the Shah* (Ithaca: Cornell University Press, 1991), p. 187.

15   I have not tried here to evaluate the numerous theories of revolutionary causation, though I have been influenced by some of them. For criticism of Davies's "J Curve" and other "volcanic" theories of revolution see Rod Aya, *Rethinking Revolutions and Collective Violence: Studies on Concept, Theory, and Method* (Amsterdam: Het Spinhuis, 1990). Other recent works relevant to my argument include Mehran Kamrava, *Revolution in Iran: The Roots of Turmoil* (London: Routledge, 1990); Misagh Parsa, *Social Origins of the Iranian Revolution* (New Brunswick: Rutgers University Press, 1989); Jack A. Goldstone, "Revolutions and Superpowers," in Jonathan R. Adelman, ed., *Superpowers and Revolution* (New York: Praeger, 1986); *idem*, "Theories of Revolution: The Third Generation," *World Politics* 32 (April, 1980), 425-443; Theda Skocpol, *States and Social Revolutions: A Comparative Analysis of France, Russian, and China* (Cambridge: Cambridge University Press, 1979); *idem*, "Rentier State and Shi'a Islam in the Iranian Revolution," *Theory and Society* 11 (May 1982), pp. 265-304; and responses in that same issue by Nikki R.

Keddie, Walter Goldfrank, and Eqbal Ahmad; and J. Gugler, The Urban Character of Contemporary Revolutions," *Comparative International Development*, xvii, 2(Summer 1982), 60-73. The most original recent comparative book is Jack Goldstone, *Revolution and Rebellion in the Early Modern World* (Berkeley: University of California Press, 1991), which is relevant to contemporary revolutions. The Iranian works above give less importance to ideology and the clergy than I. I agree with the primary stress of many works on states and socioeconomic conditions and think there is something to Goldstone's largely demographic argument. His view that early modern Ottoman and Chinese movements were less "revolutionary" than Western ones because only the West had a linear and millenarian view of history is, however, wrong. Sunni Islam early on incorporated a messianic mahdi. Numerous Sunni messianic revolts looking to a millennial outcome occurred down to modern times. The cyclical Ibn Khaldun was atypical.

16   The October 1991 hearings on Robert Gates, George Bush's nominee to head the Central Intelligence Agency, remind me to stress that I do not believe that everyone's predictions are equally mistaken. Wrong, ideological analysis results in wrong predictions of even *non*-revolutionary trends that could have been foreseen. Most scholars of Iran knew the shah faced widespread discontent and that his type of rule could not outlive him, while the CIA focussed on a grossly exaggerated Soviet menace and at the shah's request renounced contact with the opposition, whom they considered unimportant.

WHY REVOLUTIONS ARE BETTER UNDERSTOOD THAN PREDICTED:

THE ESSENTIAL ROLE OF PREFERENCE FALSIFICATION: COMMENT ON KEDDIE

TIMUR KURAN

Scholars disagree about a lot of things, so there is nothing unusual about the numerous controversies that shroud the fall of communism. What is remarkable is our near-perfect agreement on a major aspect of this collapse, namely, that it caught the world by surprise. The evidence happens to be overwhelming that virtually no one expected communism to collapse throughout Eastern Europe in a matter of months, or that this could happen with very little bloodshed. Among the stunned were aging party bosses and young dissidents, the CIA and the KGB, top statesmen and experienced diplomats, eminent journalists and seasoned academic specialists.

This was not the first revolution of global significance which was unanticipated. As Tocqueville observed more than a century ago, pre-revolutionary documents contain no evidence that the French Revolution was foreseen. In the years and months leading up to July 1789 no one, in France or elsewhere, seems to have anticipated the momentous events that lay ahead.[1] The Iranian Revolution of 1978-79 is a more recent case in point. In her essay on the predictability and explicability of revolutions, Nikki Keddie presents telling evidence that the monarchy's collapse came as a surprise to the demonstrators who sealed its fate, to local and foreign observers, to the Shah and his entourage, and even to the Ayatollah Khomeini.[2] It is worth noting that until a few weeks before his triumphant return to Tehran, Khomeini was telling his close associates that the Shah would probably succeed in extinguishing the fire that had engulfed his regime.[3]

Keddie cites the two Russian Revolutions of 1917 as examples of overturns that were not entirely unpredicted.[4] It is true that both the French Revolution and Russia's own revolution in 1905 had sensitized the Tsar's supporters and opponents, as well as independent observers, to the possibility of another revolt. It is also true that many segments of the population had grievances against the regime. The peasants were hungry for land, urban workers felt underpaid, and soldiers hated the harsh conditions of military service. But the case should not be overstated. First of all, the potential revolutionaries were divided. Second, in the decade before 1917 the incidence of strikes was minuscule compared to the preceding decade.[5] And third, the war had generated a wave of pro-Tsarist, nationalist sentiment. Accordingly, both friend and foe of the Tsar considered the army a reliable protector of the regime. In 1848, many people reasoned, Bismarck had averted a revolution in Germany by retaining the support of the army. Why should Bismarck's strategy not work for the Tsar?[6]

Lenin's remarks in the early days of 1917 were revealing. He told an audience in Switzerland that older men like himself would not live to see Russia's great explosion.[7] (We may safely assume that he was not thinking of August 1991.) Lenin's pessimism was shared by other opponents of the regime, including leading Bolsheviks and Mensheviks stationed in Russia.[8] Nor did independent observers show more foresight. As the demonstrations that would overthrow the Romanov dynasty got underway, many diplomats in the capital retained confidence in the Tsar's ability to hold onto his power. Just three days before the Tsar's fall, the British Ambassador cabled London: "Some disorders occurred to-day, but nothing serious."[9]

Such facts leave me unconvinced that Russia provides a valid counterexample to the proposition that major political overturns catch the world by surprise. If there *are* revolutions that were truly anticipated, where is the evidence? It is not enough to identify a "contrast between economic development . . . and lack of political development," or "a dissatisfied peasantry and working class," or "a capricious and unpopular autocracy," or "an increasingly murderous and unpopular war."[10] Many countries featuring some, even all, of these conditions manage to avoid revolution. Moreover, predictions of revolution are made routinely throughout the world in countries featuring social tension, and the vast majority of these predictions turn out to be false. To establish retrospectively that a certain revolution was anticipated, it is essential to demonstrate the following: (a) that the prevalence of the correct predictions was above the norm, and (b) that these predictions were held in unusually high confidence.

The data necessary to resolve the case of 1917 to everyone's satisfaction are probably unavailable. Yet it would be easy to secure broad agreement on the claim that the revolutions I have mentioned — the French, the Russian, the Iranian, and the East European — all surprised large groups of people, including key players and very knowledgeable observers. Anyone who reviews the literature on these revolutions would also agree that there is no shortage of explanations for them. Literally thousands of books present a huge array of reasons why the French Revolution should have occurred. Other revolutions, too, have generated vast numbers of explanations, at least some of them quite plausible. We thus face a puzzle. How is it that revolutions easily explained in hindsight were practically unforeseen? Why do eminently knowledgeable people with everything to lose or gain from revolution fail routinely to see where events are headed?

Having attempted in a series of papers to answer these questions systematically,[11] I find much in Keddie's article that is insightful and valuable. But there are significant differences between our two approaches, and I believe that readers will find it useful to see these spelled out. It is my hope that the present remarks will stimulate further debate. The significance of the paradox in question cannot be overstated, for it bears on the limits of social knowledge. Theorizing on these limits has not been a popular pursuit in the social sciences, where a widely shared, though seldom articulated, view holds that more and more research, driven by ever more sophisticated techniques, will render every facet of the social order perfectly knowable. As a number of distinguished writers have suggested, ignoring these limits can become a serious obstacle to the advancement of human knowledge.[12] It can fuel endless controversies on matters that can never be settled, shifting attention away from the questions to which social scientists can make socially useful contributions.

Keddie's basic explanation for the unpredictability of social revolutions goes as follows. Political players routinely encounter situations offering a choice of actions or reactions, and every individual selection leaves its mark on the path of social evolution. With multitudes of political players making decisions every day, the number of possible future paths reaches into the "billions" even over a very short time span. These paths will lead in all sorts of directions. Consider a government decision to crack down on demonstrators. This decision may generate a chain of reactions which, months or years later, will leave society governed very differently than if the decision had been to let the demonstration proceed without interference. We cannot predict infallibly how political actors will respond to particular situations. Yet *small* differences in their choices can generate, through chains of further choices, *large* differences in social outcomes. It follows that our ability to forecast the course of social evolution is quite limited. A decision that escapes our attention today may set the stage for a massive explosion several years down the road.

This logic offers some clues as to why regime changes happen so very suddenly, catching everyone off guard. It collides, however, with Keddie's point that some revolutions are more predictable than others, and also with her more general claim that prediction is relatively easier in some societies and contexts. As examples of predictions that can be made with "fair certainty," she forecasts that "there will not be a successful coup d'etat in the United States in the next decade" and that "either the Democrats or the Republicans will elect our President in 1996." But what distinguishes the United States from Egypt, Iran, or Poland — all countries where near-term political instability is within the realm of possibility? If there are countless paths open to each member of this trio, so too, countless paths are open to the United States. After all, American political actors make a huge array of decisions every day, and some of these may set in motion socially significant chains of reactions. Keddie's argument leaves unclear the determinants of differences in predictive confidence. What, precisely, is special about the United States? When we look toward the end of the millennium, why are we more confident about forecasting stability in the United States than about predicting the nature of Iran's government?

My own work addresses these questions through a model that focuses on interdependencies among the decisions of political actors. Specifically, I recognize that on any given issue (for instance, trade liberalization, the status of Jerusalem, or the regime's legitimacy) a person has a *public* preference and a *private* preference. When the two differ the individual is engaged in *preference falsification*. To take the simplest formulation, let the former represent what he chooses to reveal to others;

and let the latter be known only to himself.[13] A person's private preference on a given issue is influenced, in practice, by the social processes that determine *public opinion*, whose constituent elements are the public preferences of society's members. For our purposes here, however, we can take private preferences and their evolution as given, focusing on the formation and transformation of public opinion. Even a cursory description of these processes will yield key insights into the puzzles outlined above.

One determinant of a person's public preference is his private preference. A person who despises the prevailing regime is more likely, holding all else constant, to join an anti-government rally. Another determinant is the set of benefits and costs associated with alternative public-preference options. If the likely price of joining the rally is a stint in jail or ostracism by one's peers at work, the prudent course of action may be to remain on the sidelines, even to cheer the security forces to leave no doubt as to where one has chosen to stand. The benefits and costs in question depend on the choices made by others. If only a handful of people are demonstrating, with everyone else supporting the regime, the cost of participation is likely to be much higher than if hundreds of thousands are already in the streets.

In any society where the regime's legitimacy is under challenge, individual members will differ in their *revolutionary thresholds* — the circumstances under which they are prepared to switch political sides. Variations in private preferences are sufficient to generate a distribution of thresholds, as are variations in sensitivity to social pressure. Under a very wide class of situations, the threshold distribution will generate more than one self-sustaining distribution of public preferences. In other words, public opinion will feature *multiple equilibria*. One or more of these equilibria may harbor revolutionary implications for the prevailing social order. But if such equilibria exist, this will not necessarily be known, because revolutionary thresholds are not common knowledge.

A major implication is that cognitive, economic, and social processes may be making it ever easier to spark a revolutionary bandwagon without anyone's sensing this. Society may come to the brink of a massive social explosion with everyone continuing to believe that it is quite stable. Once this point has been reached, a small, intrinsically insignificant event will suffice to put in motion a revolutionary bandwagon. This bandwagon will catch everyone by surprise, including the very individuals whose actions got it rolling.

When a revolution occurs, long-repressed grievances burst into the open. Moreover, people who were relatively content with the old regime embrace the new one to avoid being stigmatized and persecuted as potential counterrevolutionaries. They pretend that their support for the old regime was never genuine, that it involved preference falsification motivated by self-preservation. In the process, they make the toppled regime appear even more vulnerable than it actually was. And they make it doubly easy for scholars to concoct plausible explanations. So it is that historians produce multitudes of explanations for revolutions that no one had predicted. This paradox is rooted, I submit, in preference falsification. Before a revolution, preference falsification conceals the potential for a successful revolt. After the fact, it masks the factors that were working against change.

One must distinguish between the speed of a political overturn and its unpredictability. The source of the former is the *interdependence* of public political preferences. That of the latter is *imperfect observability* of the determinants of these preferences. These determinants are not equally unobservable in every context or in every society. Where people are relatively open about their feelings, thoughts, and aspirations, impending changes may be foreseen.

It is tempting to infer that major political changes are predictable in well-functioning Western democracies, where the right to express unpopular views, no matter how outrageous, is protected by laws. It is certainly true that in the West enemies of democracy generally enjoy and exercise the right to speak. They happen to be vastly outnumbered by citizens genuinely content with the basic elements of their political system. This is why one can assert confidently that the American government is unlikely to be overthrown in the 1990s, that a popular uprising against the two centuries-old American system is highly unlikely. By no means, however, is preference falsification absent from American politics. Many important matters are deemed highly sensitive and considered off-limits to open, frank, truthful discussion.

One such issue involves racial inequality. The fear of being branded a racist is so strong that on matters with an obvious racial dimension people routinely lie about their feelings even to pollsters. It is revealing that in elections where race or racial policy is a factor, the margin of error tends to be enormous in both pre-election polls and exit polls. On the eve of the 1989 mayoral election in New York, polls gave David Dinkins, a black candidate, leads between 14 and 18 percentage points. Exit polls showed him leading by six to ten points. His actual margin of victory was only two points.[14] And in the 1990 U.S. Senate election in Louisiana, the incumbent Democrat was predicted to beat David Duke, a former Grand Wizard of the Ku Klux Klan who based his platform on opposition to affirmative action, by an overwhelming margin. Some experienced organizations projected that Duke would garner no more than 25 percent of the vote. Yet he won 44 percent, including 60 percent of the white vote.[15] Even the exit polls were way off, suggesting that people who voted for Duke would not even admit this to a pollster whom they would never see again.

If my argument is correct, the United States is poised for a dramatic swing in public opinion on racial issues. As the above examples show, a wide gap exists between *private opinion*, which aggregates private preferences, and its public counterpart. More precisely, the potential exists for an explosion of public discontent concerning the prevailing racial policies. The timing of such a backlash cannot be predicted, because, once again, the relevant threshold distribution is practically invisible. Moreover, unforeseeable changes in economic conditions or international affairs could diminish white frustration or rechannel it toward foreigners.

It is important to recognize why my model points to instability. Given the interdependencies among people's public preferences, gaps between private and public opinion suggest the possibility of a *latent bandwagon* that unknown changes might push into motion. With regard to the American system of governance, American private opinion appears rather similar to public opinion, so we have no reason to expect a hidden potential for revolt against the regime. By contrast, on the issue of race — which touches on taxes, welfare, education, crime, and more — preference falsification is rampant, so a dramatic political overturn is a very real possibility.

As far as I can tell, Keddie's model does not yield a systematic method for distinguishing between social stability and instability, or for identifying degrees of predictability. Having forecasted that the two-party system of the United States will remain in place through the 1990s, she goes on to suggest that "such accurate prediction is possible only in situations so stable that nobody doubts the outcome," with the qualification that analogs of this prediction would be "risky" in respect to many other countries.

But why, precisely, are predictions riskier with regard to some countries or contexts than to others? What accounts for variations in predictability? If the social sciences are to have a realistic agenda, we must develop a systematic, coherent answer. Biologists recognize their own limits because Darwin's theory of evolution demonstrates simply and powerfully how small environmental or biological changes can generate large changes in the ecological balance. Social scientists will stop confusing explanation with prediction only when they become acquainted with equally sound mechanisms that establish the boundaries to social knowledge. Until such mechanisms are identified, developed, diffused, and widely accepted, accounts of our terrible record at social prediction, however well documented, will continue to fall on deaf ears. Just as the intellectual community's failure to anticipate the Iranian Revolution had no perceptible impact on thinking about Eastern Europe, accounts of this latest momentous surprise could leave the social sciences untouched.

NOTES

1   Alexis de Tocqueville, *The Old Régime and the French Revolution*, trans. Stuart Gilbert (Garden City, New York: Doubleday, 1955; orig. French ed., 1856).

2   Nikki R. Keddie, "Can Revolutions Be Predicted; Can Their Causes Be Understood?" *Contention* 2 (Winter 1992): 159-82.

3   Shaul Bakhash, *The Reign of the Ayatollahs: Iran and the Islamic Revolution* (New York: Basic Books, 1984), p. 45.

4   Keddie, "Can Revolutions Be Predicted," 164.

5   William Henry Chamberlin, *The Russian Revolution, 1917-1921*, vol. 1 (New York: Macmillan, 1935), pp. 62-63.

6   Martin Malia, *Comprendre la Révolution Russe* (Paris: Éditions du Seuil, 1980), ch. 1, and pp. 92-93.

7   Leonard Schapiro, *The Russian Revolutions of 1917: The Origins of Modern Communism* (New York: Basic Books, 1984), p. 19.

8   Schapiro, *The Russian Revolutions of 1917*, p. 39; and Chamberlin, *The Russian Revolution*, vol. 1, p. 73.

9   Chamberlin, *The Russian Revolution*, vol. 1, p. 76.

10   Keddie, "Can Revolutions Be Predicted," 164.

11   Timur Kuran, "Sparks and Prairie Fires: A Theory of Unanticipated Political Revolution," *Public Choice* 61 (April 1989): 41-74; Kuran, "The East European Revolution of 1989: Is It Surprising that We Were Sur-

prised?" *American Economic Review* 81 (May 1991): 121-25; and Kuran, "Now Out of Never: The Element of Surprise in the East European Revolution of 1989," *World Politics* 44 (October 1991): 7-48. A related theme is addressed in Kuran, "Cognitive Limitations and Preference Evolution," *Journal of Institutional and Theoretical Economics* 147 (June 1991): 241-73.

12   Friedrich A. Hayek, "The Pretence of Knowledge" (Nobel Memorial Lecture, 1974), in his *New Studies in Philosophy, Politics, Economics and the History of Ideas* (Chicago: University of Chicago Press, 1978), pp. 23-34; and Jon Elster, *The Cement of Society: A Study of Social Order* (Cambridge: Cambridge University Press, 1989), especially pp. 1-16.

13   For greater precision and generality, see Timur Kuran, "Private and Public Preferences," *Economics and Philosophy* 6 (April 1990): 1-26.

14   *New York Times,* November 9, 1989, A1, B14. See also Phillip Thompson, "David Dinkins' Victory in New York City: The Decline of the Democratic Party Organization and the Strengthening of Black Politics," *PS: Political Science and Politics* 23 (June 1990): 145-48.

15   Patrick Thomas, "The Persistent 'Gnat' that Louisiana Can't Get Out of Its Face," *Los Angeles Times,* October 14, 1990, M1.

Response to Kuran

NIKKI R. KEDDIE

Timur Kuran's interesting comment, along with his articles on the unpredictability of revolutions, which I read only after writing my article, raises questions for social science theory that go beyond what I was attempting to do, and in some cases beyond what I am capable of doing. Regarding what he says on the unpredictability of the Russian Revolution he may have good points, but the fact remains that some observers did predict revolution, and they predicted it more than anyone did for Western countries. My main point here, however, was to indicate that some revolutions are predictable and predicted. If one rejects Russia, one can look to situations where the revolutionary forces controlled territory and armed forces before their country's situation was considered a revolution, such as China or Cuba. In those countries revolutionary success was widely predicted once significant territories came under the control of revolutionaries. It is true, as Kuran states, that many predicted revolutions do not occur, but I would be surprised if the number of predictions for such countries equalled those for China or Cuba. My main point in this regard was that most revolutions are neither predicted nor predictable, and in this Kuran and I are in agreement.

I also agree with the thrust of much of what he goes on to say, though I would put it somewhat differently. In countries with wide latitudes of free expression, which are usually quite synonymous with democratic political systems, people express their opposition to regimes quite openly, they vote, they organize open and often effective protest movements, and mass revolutions do not occur. On the other hand, reactionary coups do sometimes occur, as seen in the rise of Mussolini, Hitler, the Greek colonels, and others. This indeed raises serious questions about how I define a society like the U.S. (or Great Britain) as stable, and exceedingly unlikely to experience either revolutions or coups in the next decade. As a historian who only dabbles in social science concepts and very rarely speaks of models, I do not feel obligated to find a social science answer to this question, although I would welcome attempts by others. It appears to me that the answer is probably more historical and contextual than social scientific. It would go along the lines of saying that countries like the U.S. and Great Britain have already experienced more than two centuries without revolutions or coups, and that changes both in their power elites and in public opinion have found a large measure of expression in government without any need for coups or revolutions. In one sense, stability feeds on itself; most Americans or Britons would probably express basic satisfaction with their long-tried systems, and think that even terrible hardships could be dealt with either by electoral politics or by mass movements like those in America for trade unions in the 1930s or Civil Rights in the 1960s, or Britain's long history of influential reform movements. I do not predict that this will always be the case; the predictions in my article did not go beyond the twentieth century. Clearly, in the long term, some degree of general economic wellbeing is also tied to stability.

In continental Europe even countries now democratic have undergone more revolutions, wars, changes in constitution, and coups than have the U.S. and Great Britain, and many may still regard these as legitimate ways to change things. This is even more true in Eastern Europe and in countries outside Europe and the U.S., which have neither long democratic traditions nor, in most cases, high or relatively egalitarian living standards.

Kuran's contrasting of public and private preferences, especially in repressive countries, is very important, but I have a point to add. This is the significance of the bandwagon or snowballing effect which makes many people who had borne difficulties without feeling massively aggrieved come to feel so aggrieved and join in mass protest movements once they reach a certain size. Hence, even a totally honest poll of what Iranians, Russians, or Chinese felt and thought shortly before their revolutions might not have revealed massive dissatisfaction or revolutionary sentiment. This is confirmed by the social scientists and anthropologists who talked with Iranians shortly before their revolution. There were, however, important expressions of dissatisfaction and concern among nearly all classes, and such views should have been taken seriously beyond scholarly circles. The voices in East-Central Europe and the ex-Soviet Union who are either looking for nationalist or religious solutions to their growing difficulties or long for a return to a strong regime that will restore economic well-being should also be taken seriously. In the Cold War, much as in the U.S. campaigns in Panama and Iraq, there is a tendency by the U.S. government and most of the public to be satisfied with victory without trying to help ensure that what follows is not as bad or worse than what went before. The open wounds in East-Central Europe, the ex-U.S.S.R., Iraq, and Panama, not to mention many other societies, are evident enough to make it predictable that most of these are unstable societies that are unlikely soon and without outside help to develop economies and governmental forms that will meet the economic needs and political aspirations of their citizens. Where specifically there will be coups or revolutions remains unpredictable, but we should not need such predictions to manifest our concern as well as our understanding that parliamentary forms and free markets are not a simple recipe for healthy and prosperous societies.

PREDICTING REVOLUTIONS:

WHY WE COULD (AND SHOULD) HAVE FORESEEN THE REVOLUTIONS OF 1989-1991 IN THE U.S.S.R. AND EASTERN EUROPE

JACK A. GOLDSTONE

In 1989-1991 Communist Party regimes that had deeply penetrated society and had been institutionalized for generations came apart. Could this — or other revolutions, like those in the Philippines in 1986 or in Iran and Nicaragua in 1979 — have been predicted? I believe, with certain qualifications, the answer is yes. A huge amount of research on the nature and origins of revolutions has been done since the mid-1970s. Pioneering and once-dominant work by Chalmers Johnson, Ted Robert Gurr, Samuel Huntington, and Charles Tilly was improved upon by Theda Skocpol and S.N. Eisenstadt. Further modifications have been made by myself and by writers on specific revolutions of the last two decades.[1] Cumulatively, these works led to a considerable reevaluation of what revolutions are, and how they are caused. I believe it is only the failure of area experts and popular wisdom to catch up to this recent work in the theory of revolution that has left most observers astounded by events.

The proof of any recipe for predictions is in the eating. I apologize for self-indulgence, but let me offer a sampling of my predictions. In 1985, in drafting a paper on "Superpowers and Revolutions," I observed that Marcos's regime in the Philippines faced a situation much like those in the

U.S.-supported regimes in Iran and Nicaragua in the 1970s, and that his regime was unlikely to last more than a few years.[2] In 1986, in planning a reader on revolutions, I insisted that my publisher include a chapter dealing with the Hungarian and Czech uprisings of 1956 and 1968. I argued that I expected more uprisings in Eastern Europe before the book exhausted its first edition; we could then add an update on recent uprisings in Eastern Europe in the next edition. The chapter was included, and I am now at work on the updated chapter.[3] In a newspaper interview in February 1990, at a time when the Bush administration was ignoring Boris Yeltsin and trying to shore up Mikhail Gorbachev, I predicted that Gorbachev was on his way out and would likely be out of power within a few months.[4] That prediction was correct, though premature — it was not until eighteen months later that Gorbachev lost power.

Turning to predictions of *non*-revolution, I argued in a lecture at the University of Arizona in early 1990 that Saddam Hussein's regime in Iraq was likely to remain secure, and that U.S. hopes that he would be overthrown by his own people were delusory. Earlier, in May 1989, as demonstrations were unfolding in Tiananmen Square, I predicted in the *Los Angeles Times* that the demonstrations would mark a turning point in Chinese history, but not bring immediate radical change; even if a more liberal leadership came in "the key points of contention — the pace of reform . . . will remain. It may take months or years before this is fully resolved." Earlier, in 1985, as the largest wave of riots since Sharpeville rocked South Africa and predictions were rife of impending revolution, I argued in the *Chicago Tribune* that although South Africa was eventually bound to change to cope with an increasingly integrated labor force, the government was in no danger of revolution.[5]

I should note one major failed prediction. In early October 1989, when demonstrations in East Germany were beginning and police clashed with demonstrators in Leipzig and other cities, I predicted in a lecture that no revolution in Germany was imminent. I believed that although Germany was in a revolutionary situation, it retained the largest and most loyal police forces in Eastern Europe and that Erik Honecker was ruthless enough to use them. I anticipated that Poland, Hungary, Czechoslovakia, and even Russia would see a fall in the power of the Communist Party, which would leave Honecker isolated, and only then would East Germany's government shift. I was wrong. For reasons noted below, Gorbachev felt he had to prevent Honecker from using the force he was prepared to use.[6] The result was the rapid unravelling of East Germany's communist regime. In this case, not atypical for revolutionary predictions, the *situation* in East Germany in October 1989 was close to a revolutionary one. The intervention of a single influential individual (Gorbachev), who could have acted differently, pushed the situation over the precipice of revolution before it would have otherwise reached that point.

Thus two quick conclusions: First, it is not impossible to predict, within a range of a year or two, forthcoming revolutions or non-revolutions. Second, attempts to predict the exact month or day of a revolution are fruitless. This is because individual (or accidental) interventions can delay or accelerate the transformation of a potentially revolutionary situation into an overt revolutionary struggle. What *can* be done, and this is my meaning when I speak of "predicting" a revolution, is to identify states that are moving rapidly toward a revolutionary situation, so that if trends continue unchecked a revolution is highly likely to break out when a triggering or accelerating event occurs.

IS PREDICTION OF MAJOR SOCIAL UPHEAVALS IMPOSSIBLE?

Three arguments are adduced by Nikki Keddie and Timur Kuran to suggest that such predictions as I have offered are generally impossible.[7] Keddie's first argument is from recent experience of experts' predictive failures. Keddie's second argument, and that of Kuran, are based on considerations of observation; both argue, with slightly different emphases, that the information needed to predict a revolution is unobtainable, even by experienced and expert observers, due to the nature of social change and political behavior.

Keddie first notes that despite claims of hindsight, "nobody, however well informed, predicted a successful revolution" in Iran prior to its occurrence in 1979.[8] A similar argument could be made regarding events in 1989 in Eastern Europe: a wide array of area experts, local elites, and journalists with deep knowledge of the countries concerned totally failed to foresee the coming political upheaval. Faced with massive expert failure, one may well argue that a few individual claims of successful foresight, such as I have offered above, are insignificant. Just as people who win at roulette or call the stock market right might simply be lucky gamblers, despite their claims at having a sophisticated predictive system, so too any political crisis will have some people betting both ways, so that whatever happens *someone* will be right, even if they have no superior knowledge or theory. Keddie's claim deserves consideration; if in most recent major revolutions the vast majority of experts could not see them coming, perhaps there *is* something in the nature of revolution that precludes prediction.

I believe Keddie is pointing to a real phenomenon. The failures of area experts to foresee recent upheavals are painful and glaring. But the explanation may be rooted in an inability of *area experts* to predict revolutions, due to inherent limits in their training, rather than in any inherent unpredictability of revolutions. Area experts, after all, are *not* experts in revolutionary processes; they are experts in the current structure and past history of a society. An expert in analyzing the dynamics of the Soviet Politburo may be untrained for and incapable of analyzing the dynamics of social movements or ethnic nationalism. Similarly, an expert on Iranian society might be familiar with the groups opposed to the Shah, and with the deficiencies of the Shah's development policies. But unless that expert is also versed in the art of revolutionary coalition building, or the relationships between economic development, state revenues, and political instability, the expert may be unable to convert that information into useful predictions regarding a revolution. In short, area experts have rarely studied the process of revolutionary development in sufficient depth, or in a sufficient variety of situations, to recognize the signs of a revolutionary situation in their society when they see them. They may be aware of the relevant facts for analyzing instability without being aware of their implications; or they may be aware of facts relevant to the ordinary working of their societies, yet unaware of signs that extraordinary events are in train. Area specialists who have spent years studying a stable society may thus be unprepared accurately to analyze that society once it becomes unstable.

To take Keddie's example of Iran, Islamic specialists had never before seen a radical religious revolution against a secular state; thus such specialists would have had a hard time conceiving the dynamics of such an event, much less foreseeing it. Islamic specialists would have lacked historical models to turn to for help with forecasting. However, students of the English Puritan Revolution of 1640 are quite familiar with the phenomenon of a radical religious revolution against a secular state; a comparative revolutions expert might thus have had a better grasp of the possibility of upheaval in Iran in the late 1970s than most Iran specialists, who lacked a familiar point of reference. Combining the skills of the area specialist and the expert on revolutions *per se* is probably necessary to predict revolutions. Expecting area specialists by themselves to evince such foresight may be unreasonable.

In sum, if war is too important to leave solely to the generals, then so too one may say that the stability of key areas of the world is too important to leave solely to the area specialists. The failure of area experts to predict recent revolutions is real. However, that failure is arguably chiefly a result of the way we train and utilize area specialists. Such failure does not prove that experts in the development of revolutionary situations and area specialists, working together, could not do far better.

The other two arguments *do* deny this possibility. In effect, these arguments claim that even an expert on revolutions, provided with all the relevant data that area experts could obtain, is helpless to predict whether a given revolution will ensue.

Keddie's second argument makes an analogy from chaos theory. Certain natural systems, such as the weather, cannot be predicted much in advance because tiny shifts in conditions which are too innocuous to measure can later produce dramatic changes in system behavior. If social systems are like weather systems, then they too are fundamentally unpredictable except over short and local time frames; we simply cannot predict how small perturbations, such as the acts of individuals, might produce massive system-wide swings in social behavior.

In regard to revolutions, this means that two states could look similar with regard to everything we can measure, yet one state may differ in some tiny way that leads to revolution, while the other avoids it. Thus "a country about to have a revolution is not necessarily, in ways that can be measured at the time, more revolutionary in appearance than countries that do not have revolutions."[9] Keddie therefore argues that revolutions such as the one in Iran in 1979 must be explained by showing how various factors, which may have been present in many Islamic states that did not experience revolutions, could "become revolutionary only with the proper conjuncture" of other factors that were unique to Iran and whose significance is apparent only with hindsight.[10] If this is true, then no general theory could have been used to predict the Iranian revolution — or most other revolutions for that matter.

Things get even worse over time. If at any one time a small unmeasurable difference in initial situations may lead to divergent outcomes for apparently similar states, then the problem of prediction multiplies rapidly when we realize that revolutions are not single events but processes, in which outcomes are "largely determined by the complex interaction of events during a long revolutionary period."[11] Over the course of this process, small changes in some variable might send the whole nation's trajectory tumbling down an alternate pathway. During the years of revolutionary mobilization and struggle so many opportunities arise for small events to shift the trajectory of political development that there is no way for a causal analysis at any one time to predict events or outcomes a significant time later.

Keddie is correct that no simple list of causes X,Y,Z, . . . can predict a revolution. Yet this does not make prediction impossible. It only means that predictions based on a simple enumeration of particular causes, assumed to be the same for all revolutions, will fail. Indeed, a variety of authors have observed that no simple set of prior socioeconomic conditions is consistently correlated with revolution,[12] and the broader truth that simple linear models of causation will generally fail has been pointed out for a variety of contexts by such scholars as Charles Ragin and Andrew Abbott.[13] What is needed to predict revolutions is a conjunctural, process-based theory of revolution.

Is such a theory possible? It is just that kind of theory I have been working to develop over the past few years.[14] In *Revolutions of the Late Twentieth Century* I wrote that one should focus "on causal *processes* and on how revolutions develop over time rather than on individual causes or specific events," and that "[t]he analyst seeking to assess the likelihood of revolution [should attend to] the *interaction* of such trends with the existing structure of a particular society, and whether this interaction is creating, in conjunction, the conditions whose combination leads to state breakdown."[15] More simply, if revolution is an unfolding process, an analyst seeking to predict revolution should aim to monitor how far that process has progressed. The specific causes that hinder or favor such progress may be particular to various cases and may be hard to measure or foresee. But knowing which factor has pushed the process forward is more important for explanation than prediction. If one observes a society moving rapidly down a trajectory that leads to revolution, then one can say that unless the situation gravely changes, revolution will grow more likely. And if one can observe that a society has already moved far down that trajectory, then one can predict that revolution will ensue, barring some sharp reversal of the situation. These predictive conclusions can be made simply from knowing what the trajectory toward revolutions looks like, even without knowing exactly what causes are pushing a society down that trajectory. This is a bit like saying that if you observe a safe falling from the sky, you can predict that it will do major damage unless some radical intervention occurs even if you have no idea what caused the safe to fall — the trajectory and not the cause is the key to predicting what will ensue. Similarly, with the right theory, one can observe a society careening toward revolution, even though further after-the-fact detective work might be needed to determine the particular causes that launched the society in that direction.

Such a conjunctural process model of revolution lies behind the predictions described at the beginning of this paper. In brief, the model argues that a society is careening toward revolution when there arises a *conjuncture* of three conditions: (1) the state loses effectiveness in its ability to command resources and obedience; (2) elites are alienated from the state and in heightened conflict over the distribution of power and status; and (3) a large or strategic portion of the population can be readily mobilized for protest actions. When any of these factors is weak or absent, revolution is unlikely; when all are present and strong, revolution is very likely. Movement from the former situation to the latter constitutes movement along the trajectory from stability to a revolutionary situation.

As formulated, this model says nothing about the *causes* for movement along this trajectory. The empirical investigations in my books revealed a varied stock of causes. It was a surprising finding, conveyed in *Revolution and Rebellion in the Early Modern World*, that the combination of sustained population growth with the agrarian economies and traditional bureaucratic states common to early modern Eurasia consistently produced the conjuncture of revolutionary conditions just described. Thus early modern Eurasia experienced "waves" of revolution and rebellion that followed waves of population growth. However, I do not mean that population growth is *the* cause of revolutions. It happened to be a significant element in the early modern period in producing revolutionary conjunctures. In *Revolutions of the Late Twentieth Century* my co-editors and contributors discovered that recent revolutions show a wider variety of causes capable of moving societies toward revolution. Failed state policies and cultural conflicts, as well as fiscal problems, social mobility, urbanization, and economic decline, can all contribute critically to a revolutionary conjuncture. Analyzing revolutions does not depend on identifying a particular fixed characteristic set of causes — there is none. Instead, analyzing revolutions depends on understanding the process of revolution and being able to track its trajectory in diverse cases.

This theory is quite different from the physical science model of a predictive theory, described by Hempel,[16] in which the use of a theory is essentially identical for explanation and prediction. In this process model, the two uses of the theory are distinct. To *predict* revolution one needs only to ask whether conditions in a particular country are moving simultaneously toward a growing ineffectiveness of the state, alienation of elites, and rising potential for mass mobilization. To *explain* revolution one must seek out the specific causal factors — some of which may be unique, or only clear with hindsight — that produced these revolutionary conditions. One must ask *why* state effectiveness declined, elites became alienated, and populations became prone to mobilization. Prediction thus requires only monitoring current trends while explanation requires causal tracing; these are different tasks, requiring different data and perhaps different skills. Most theories of revolution, which treat revolution as an event due to particular causes or social structures, cannot — as Keddie rightly claims — be used for prediction. Only a theory that starts from the assumption that revolution is a developing process, which can be brought on or hindered by a variety of causes, is capable of being used for *both* explanation and prediction.

Monitoring the conditions leading to revolution is not a trivial task. It may take the skills of top area experts to detect whether a state is losing effectiveness, whether elites have a basis for alienation from the state, and whether the potential for popular mobilization is increasing. Thus area experts remain critical to predicting revolutions. However, the most fruitful basis for prediction is collaboration between area specialists and specialists in revolutionary processes; each brings knowledge and skills that are an indispensable part of being able to perceive and track the development of political crises.

Below, relying on data and publications produced by area specialists, I show how this conjunctural process theory could have been used to predict the collapse of communist power in the Soviet Union. I also show why area experts, to the extent that they remained guided by older theories, would have had difficulty foreseeing this event.

Before that, I will consider the second strong argument against predicting revolutions, made with exceptional clarity by Timur Kuran. Kuran's is also an argument from observational limits, concerning *concealed preferences*. In this argument, as in Keddie's, a revolution cannot be predicted because two societies which both appear stable may in fact be quite different in unmeasurable ways. Kuran's innovation is to note that the difference may not be in a minor, semi-invisible factor, or an issue whose importance only becomes clear in retrospect. Rather, Kuran focuses on a major, vital factor — people's attitudes toward the regime. Kuran notes that key elites or popular groups may act as though they fully support the current regime when in fact their support is contingent or feigned. If the regime falters in some economic, political, or other policy, people may then rapidly switch loyalties. As a few elites or popular groups become active and the state is seen to be ineffective, other groups may become overt in their opposition to the state in a cascading, snowballing fashion, leading to revolution. Unfortunately, according to Kuran, no observer can tell before the event the difference between a state whose supporters will rally to its defense in times of difficulty and a state whose supporters will swiftly desert to a revolutionary alternative. This is because it is to the advantage of key elites and popular groups to act as though they are supporters of a regime so long as the regime is intact and powerful. A society with highly contingent support will thus appear, to an observer, identical to a society with genuinely enthusiastic support. The difference will only become apparent if both states run into difficulties; the latter will survive, while the former will collapse with a speed and thoroughness that will startle observers. The sudden, unexpected collapse of communist regimes in eastern Europe gives strong support to Kuran's views. The general implication of preference falsification is that there is always the possibility of an "invisible difference" between otherwise similarly appearing societies that renders one susceptible to rapid collapse while the other is stable. Thus, predicting which societies are vulnerable to revolutions is not possible.

I concede that Kuran is correct about observing preferences; there is no way to penetrate people's "real" feelings, and given the strategic advantages to showing support for a regime, there is no way to know the tenacity or evanescence of such support. Nonetheless, the work of the contributors to *Revolutions of the Late Twentieth Century* argues that it is possible to identify objective conditions that *do* lead to tenacity or evanescence of support for a regime.

Popular mobilization potential, for example, depends in part on the kind of structural factors noted by Skocpol — do popular groups have the autonomy from conservative elites, and a framework for community action, that will allow mobilization? Such structures are commonly found in villages, urban working communities, and religious networks.[17] In addition, mobilization potential depends on the existence of popular grievances against states and elites — are the state and/or elites increasing exactions beyond commonly accepted limits? Are opportunities for work, housing, marriage, and social mobility declining? Are wages and nutrition falling and/or mortality rising? Are popular groups in increasing conflict with the state or elites over cultural/religious standards and practices? Is state or elite corruption giving rise to increasingly manifest inequalities and injustices? When such objective conditions for grievances are increasing, and structures conducive to mobilization are in place, we may conclude that popular mobilization potential is rising, *even if support for the regime appears strong and unaffected.* On the other hand, if such objective conditions for grievances are slight or absent, or the structural conditions lacking, then popular mobilization is unlikely.

Such vague terms as "rising" and "slight" suggest that precise measurement of the objective conditions for popular mobilization potential is difficult. This is true, but need not undermine our ability to predict revolutions. For it is the general pattern of revolutions, past and present, that popular mobilization to rectify grievances depends not so much on the precise level of discontent as on the existence of political opportunities to act effectively against the regime.[18] Thus to predict revolution it is not critical to measure with great precision the degree of popular discontent or opposition to the regime. It is enough to ask whether the structure and grievances that create mobilization potential are significantly present. If so, popular action is liable to follow when political opportunity arises, and the type of sudden "snowballing" explosion of overt popular action against the regime that Kuran describes will arise. Thus it becomes more critical to examine the other elements of the revolutionary conjuncture that create that opportunity: state effectiveness and elite alienation.

Fortunately, observations of state effectiveness and elite alienation are not nearly as limited by Kuran's argument as is popular discontent. State effectiveness depends on having fiscal resources adequate to state policies, on retaining strong nationalist and cultural credentials for authority, and on commanding loyal and disciplined coercive forces (in the long term, loss of the first two factors generally results in loss of the third). A number of observable factors — losses in war, large and unmanageable state debts, high inflation, failed development policies, recourse to extraordinary taxation, conflicts with cultural elites, ineffective military forces, problems with foreign allies — are signs of decreasing state effectiveness.

How elites respond to such conditions is also critical. Elites may respond simply by seeking a change in personnel or policies — this is the normal course in modern democracies, and in many traditional states. They may respond by seeking to shore up a regime if it is "working" for them. But elites may also decide that the only solution is to change the regime's structure. How is such alienation to be observed? First, elites may be secure enough to manifest their opposition openly. Alienation of the intellectuals was seen by de Tocqueville as obvious prior to the French Revolution; Crane Brinton found it in several other revolutions.[19] Alternatively, if elites are dependent on the regime, they also may find it necessary to conceal their true preferences for change. In this case, as with popular mobilization, we must seek both structural conditions that facilitate action and grievances that motivate it.

The key structural conditions for effective elite opposition to the regime are networks and resources. Elites must be able to communicate and organize in forums not under control of the regime; these may be formal, as in legislative or religious assemblies, or informal, as in salons and county associations. Elites must also have control of essential technical skills, manpower, or capital that can be used to give leverage against the regime. The objective conditions for grievances are varied, but again there are many observable signals that herald elite alienation: is the regime failing to maintain the society's international prowess and standing, hence undermining the prestige of its elites? Are opportunities to maintain elite status, wealth, and power being undermined, either by competition from new groups or by a deterioration in economic conditions? Is the state attacking elite prerogatives, increasing its demands on elites, reducing elites' economic rewards or access to power and status? Is state policy or corruption favoring a few individuals at the expense of broader elites? Is state coercion being used against elites in a manner that violates expected "elite" treatment?

Any complex society has varied elites; regimes can generally abuse some elite groups if others are favored who provide a secure base of support. Revolution becomes likely if several elites who have the resources for opposition also experience the objective conditions for grievances and form a multi-elite (e.g., bureaucratic/military, merchant/cleric, bourgeoisie/ noble/intelligentsia) coalition that opposes the regime.

In sum, even granting Kuran's argument that direct observation of popular (and sometimes elite) discontent is impossible, a basis still remains for analyzing the likelihood of revolution. This is in part because precise measurement of popular discontent is not a sound or necessary basis for predicting revolution; what is needed is seeing whether substantial popular discontent with the regime is likely, *and* whether such discontent is combined with declining state effectiveness and elite alienation.

I believe that all three of these factors can be monitored through the observable signs I have described. Indeed, the multi-factor nature of the conjunctural process model, and the multiple signs given for tracking each factor, provide a buffer against the need for precise measurement. If *all* three factors can be detected, each though multiple signs, then whether these signs are of modest or great magnitude is not important; a revolutionary situation has arrived, and the regime's repressive response is the most important determinant of how soon a revolution will break out. On the other hand, if one or two factors is missing, and cannot be detected by any of the objective signs mentioned above, then it is highly likely that a revolutionary situation is not developing, and whatever problems the society is experiencing — e.g. inflation, corruption, rising inequality — the regime (though not necessarily its personnel or policies) will survive.

Let us now consider how earlier theories of revolution misled observers of the U.S.S.R., and how the conjunctural process theory of revolution could have provided stronger insight into the development of a revolutionary situation in 1989-91.

CHANGING EMPHASIS IN THE THEORY OF REVOLUTIONS

Theorists of revolution agree that revolutions involve at least two components — a populace motivated to rebel, and a state too weak to resist popular action. But theorists have differed greatly over which component is primary. The current generation of political leaders, commentators, and journalists received their schooling in a period when the dominant theories of revolution stressed popular action, or bottom-up efforts, as the key to revolution. Theories of "peasant revolution" were sought to account for the communist revolutions in Russia, China, and Vietnam. This bottom-up viewpoint was codified in a series of books in the 1960s and 1970s that capped a generation of bottom-up theorizing. Ted Robert Gurr's *Why Men Rebel* offered a persuasive account of popular frustration caused by unmet aspirations as the motive force of revolutions. Samuel P. Huntington's

Political Order in Changing Societies similarly stressed popular frustration, although it focussed on the need for political participation as a source of desires for change. Chalmers Johnson's *Revolutionary Change* cited systemic dysfunction as the key to revolutions, but argued that such dysfunction worked by creating a search for new ideologies, leading to popular mobilization against the state. Neil Smelser's *Theory of Collective Behavior* similarly traced revolution to popular groups being increasingly drawn to value-oriented movements that opposed the state. And Charles Tilly's provocatively titled *From Mobilization to Revolution* argued that mobilizing and organizing popular groups was the prerequisite for revolutionary conflict.[20]

Although all these authors conceded that popular frustration alone would not lead to a successful revolution, which required the vulnerability of the state, all agreed that the first stage of revolution was mounting popular unrest. Thus, in looking for coming revolution, popular unrest and mass mobilization should have been the early warning signs. With these signs absent, leaders and commentators schooled in a bottom-up view of revolution were amazed that revolutions could have broken out in East Germany, Czechoslovakia, Hungary, Romania, and the Soviet Union. For in all these cases, prior to 1989 there were no signs of popular unrest, no mass mobilization. Such opposition to the state as was visible consisted of a handful of brave dissidents, most of whose activities had been curtailed by time in prison or exile. Kuran's theory is a valid and valuable explanation of why so many observers were surprised: they were looking for signs of something — popular rejection of the communist regimes — that people had every reason to conceal until the last moment when the decay of these regimes was suddenly apparent to all.

Yet there is another tradition in the analysis of revolution, a top-down tradition that stresses changes in the strength of the ruling regime as the key to stability or change. Again, this view grants that popular grievances are necessary to a revolution. But instead of beginning with popular action, this view stresses that international pressures or domestic economic change may cause a state's power to decay. As this happens, state leaders and elites may come into conflict, and rulers may frantically try to reform the state to hold onto power. Such internal conflict and frantic reform reveals the weakness of the state and invites restless elites to press for further changes. Competing elites may then seek to gain popular support for change, support that is more readily forthcoming as the old regime visibly crumbles. In this view, the dismantling of the old regime starts at the top, produced by state leaders and social elites who perceive the old order as decaying. Popular mobilization and the expression of grievances follows, and only explodes into the open when the decay of the old regime is fully apparent to all. De Tocqueville may be credited with the first full expression of this view, in his work on the French Revolution, where he stated:

> Louis XV did as much to weaken the monarchy and to speed up the Revolution by his innovations as by his personal defects, by his energy as by his indolence. . . . During his entire reign Louis XVI was always talking about reform; . . . in fact, he gave an impression of merely wanting to loosen [the regime's] foundations and leaving to others the task of laying it low. Some of the reforms he personally put through . . . prepared the ground for the Revolution not so much because they removed obstacles in its way but far more because they taught the nation how to set about it.[21]

More recently, Theda Skocpol elaborated a theory of revolution in which state-centered, or top-down, problems initiate the process of revolution.[22] Skocpol examined the French, Russian, and Chinese revolutions and argued that international pressures, particularly military competition or incursion, revealed weaknesses in the Old Regime states. State leaders, attempting to remedy those weaknesses, came into conflict with political, economic, and social elites. Such conflicts further weakened or paralyzed the government, creating the opportunity for popular groups to mobilize and express their grievances. When popular groups acted on those grievances at the same time that states were weakened and elites were in conflict, the result was massive state breakdown leading to revolutionary change.

Skocpol's book was hailed as a major improvement on earlier theories of revolution. Skocpol broke new ground by offering a truly *conjunctural* theory of revolutions. That is, although Skocpol emphasized the role of the state to distinguish her work from prevailing "bottom-up" theories, there was in fact no one leading cause of revolution in her work. Instead, several structural causes — a state facing competition from stronger states, an autonomous political elite with leverage against the state and the ability to resist taxation and block state policy, and a peasantry with autonomy from direct supervision and a collective framework for mobilization — had to combine to create a revolutionary situation.

Despite this advance, Skocpol's theory too had difficulties with prediction. Skocpol described her theory as a "social-structural" theory, which identified certain structures that made states especially vulnerable to revolution. Though these structures were effective for explanation in Skocpol's particular cases, they did not predict others. When the Iranian revolution occurred (ironically in the same year that Skocpol's book was published), the limits of Skocpol's theory as a general guide to revolution were apparent. The Shah of Iran did not face competition with stronger states — Iran was at peace and by far the strongest military power in its region. Nor did Iran have autonomous elites with leverage against the state like the members of the French *Parlement* or Chinese scholar-officials; the key elites in the Iranian revolution, the clergy and bazaar merchants, could not influence state policy and had to mobilize popular groups against the Shah from outside the state structure. Finally, peasants played virtually no role in Iran's revolution. In short, although Skocpol's state-centered approach to understanding revolution was illuminating for Iran, her particular social-structural theory of revolutions was not. The theory also does little to help explain the anti-Communist revolutions of 1989 — peasants again were not significant; elites were not autonomous, but dependent on the state; and only the factor of external (Cold War) competition with stronger states has relevance to these revolutions. The social-structural theory developed for the "classic" revolutions of France, Russia, and China, provided little help in foreseeing the events of 1989.

In the last few years a movement away from structural causes toward a process model of revolution has developed. Robert Dix, James DeFronzo, Tim McDaniel, Matthew Shugart, Farideh Farhi, Valerie Bunce, Jeff Goodwin, and Timothy Wickham-Crowley have all emphasized the creation of revolutionary situations in Central America, Latin America, Iran, and eastern Europe.[23] My *Revolution and Rebellion in the Early Modern World* tried to develop a conjunctural, process-based model of revolution that would be applicable to societies with a wide range of social structures, from early capitalist England to Imperial China. Still, that volume focused on peasant societies and thus stressed causal factors germane to such societies, particularly population growth. For the Soviet Union in the 1980s, this factor was irrelevant or of secondary importance; population growth was crucial only in the central Asian states and some urban centers.

Revolutions of the Late Twentieth Century, co-edited with Ted Robert Gurr and Farrokh Moshiri, further developed the process model.

That volume still emphasized a top-down view in which a state crisis of authority, when abetted by elite alienation and popular mobilization potential, creates a revolutionary situation. However, it argued that a wide variety of state failures — economic, environmental, cultural — can precipitate a crisis of state authority. Moreover, we found that even elites closely tied to the state can suffer alienation if state failures affect their ability to attain status, income, and influence, and even modern urban populations have the potential to act in support of revolution. In sum, in this work, it is not a particular kind of state, or of elite, or of popular group, that is necessary for revolution. Instead, in *any* kind of state, among any elites, and any kind of population, what mattered was the *relationships* among and within the state, elites, and general population.

Also, my co-editors and contributors discovered that even the "accidental," triggering events that seem to give revolutions their unpredictable nature fell into a recognizable pattern. Once a state entered a revolutionary situation — that is, when state effectiveness was declining, elites alienated, and populations liable to mobilization — the state's repressive response determined whether revolution was likely to occur rapidly or be delayed. If the state could isolate its opponents from the general population and confront them with ruthless repression then stability could be retained, at least for several years. However, if repression could not focus on a limited group and was erratic or inconsistent, repression acted to forge an anti-regime coalition that made rapid revolution more likely. The regime's ability to command and direct repression thus become paramount in determining, once a revolutionary situation has arisen, whether revolution is imminent or not.

This account offers a very different set of guidelines for predicting revolutions than either the "bottom-up" theories that stress apparent popular mobilization or structural theories such as Skocpol's, which stress a particular constellation of social-structural characteristics. Instead, following Keddie's and Kuran's injunctions, this theory seeks to follow revolution as an interactive process that can occur in a variety of different structural settings, and seeks to examine conditions that will shape even currently unexpressed preferences.

Given the limits of available theories of revolution, it is not surprising that analysts were unable to anticipate the events of 1989. However, I believe the latest developments in revolutionary theory offer substantial advances. Indeed, I believe that with such theory in hand, the breakdown of the communist state in the Soviet Union could have been foreseen.

THE ORIGINS OF STATE BREAKDOWN IN THE SOVIET UNION

As suggested, let us focus attention on three issues: First, was the Soviet state losing effectiveness in a manner visible to state leaders and Soviet elites? Second, were elites of the Soviet state and society discontented with the status quo, and coming into heightened conflict in response to such problems? Third, were popular grievances (i.e., objective hardships or deterioration in living standards, not expressions of discontent) evident that could provide a potential basis for mobilization of the populace? If the answers to all three questions are yes, then I would argue that the revolution in the U.S.S.R. is not only comprehensible, it could have been foreseen.

In assessing the effectiveness of the Soviet state, it is useful to begin from Michael Mann's argument that there are four types of power — economic, ideological, military, and political.[24] Until roughly 1970 the Soviet state showed success on all four counts; but thereafter all four bases of Soviet power steadily decayed, with that decay accelerating after 1985.

After its costly victory in World War II, the Soviet regime scored numerous economic triumphs in the next twenty-five years. Steady industrial growth rates of over six percent per annum established modern industrial societies throughout Soviet territory.[25] The U.S.S.R. rose to world leadership in output of oil, steel, and other basic industrial goods. In space and nuclear technology, the U.S.S.R. became one of two superpowers.

Militarily, for three decades after World War II the U.S.S.R. and its allies kept NATO and the U.S. on the defensive throughout the world. The Berlin Wall and Cuban missile crises in the 1960s, though seen as western victories, were defensive victories that only slightly limited Soviet gains from its increased control of East Germany and Cuba. In Vietnam, the U.S. suffered a costly defeat at the hands of Soviet-supported opponents. The U.S. was powerless to prevent Soviet armies from maintaining communism in Hungary in the 1950s, in Czechoslovakia in the 1960s, and in Afghanistan in the 1970s. Soviet automatic rifles, tanks, and jet fighters challenged U.S. arms manufacturers for dominance on the battlefield and in world arms markets.

Ideologically, America's civil rights battles, student movements, anti-poverty campaigns, and intervention abroad gave the world the impression of a capitalist society that was racist, oppressive, imperialistic, and fostered poverty. In contrast, the socialist ideology of the Soviet Union, which appeared free of unemployment and discrimination and had led Russia's rise in a few short decades to challenge American power, had enormous international appeal. In 1975, when the U.S. withdrew in defeat from Southeast Asia, America's capitalist ideology seemed weak. In Angola and Mozambique, Egypt and Syria, Cuba, and even in Western Europe, communist ideology seemed to be gaining influence.

Politically, the Communist Party under Khrushchev and Brezhnev gradually normalized and extended its control of Soviet society. The police state and mass gulags under Stalin were replaced by extensive, but more light-handed, political authority, which operated as much by favoritism and incentives as by coercion and terror. Political opposition was reduced to a few thousand dissidents, while political allegiance was gained from silent millions who benefitted from the extension of industrial amenities and services. From 1958 to 1971, Soviet infant mortality was halved, from 40.6 to 22.9 deaths per thousand.[26]

From 1975, however, conditions in all these domains changed. Economically, Soviet productivity faltered. An economy geared to producing heavy industrial commodities could not make the adjustment either to the next industrial generation of microcomputer technology, nor to the provision of diversified consumer goods and services.[27] By 1975, society's ability to absorb basic industrial commodities had been met. What was needed were cars and light trucks, plastics, and more sophisticated alloys and castings. Thus in the late 1970s the Soviet economy poured enormous resources into basic investment, but with less and less growth in output. Manufacturing and agriculture stagnated, and the U.S.S.R. became more dependent on production and trade of raw materials. Annual industrial growth per annum fell from 6.5 percent in 1961-1970 to 5.5 percent per annum in 1971-75, and then to 2.7 percent in 1976-80 and 1.9 percent in 1981-85.[28] In 1955, 28 percent of the U.S.S.R.'s exports to Western Europe had been manufactured goods. By 1983, as a result of shortages in the U.S.S.R. and the inferiority of Soviet manufacturers, that had fallen to 6 percent.[29] Shortages of consumer goods and housing increased sharply. No more houses were built in the U.S.S.R. in 1984 than had been built in

1960, despite a substantially increased population; thus the stock of housing relative to the population "actually decreased by 30 percent" over these years.[30]

Militarily, after 1975 the tide of Soviet influence and effectiveness receded. Vietnam and Cuba became burdens, rather than outposts for further expansion in Asia and Latin America. Egypt threw off its Soviet alliance, leaving a badly defeated Syria as the U.S.S.R.'s main Middle East ally. Most critically, when the communist regime in Afghanistan faced an internal rebellion in 1979, Soviet troops were confidently dispatched to defend it. But ten years of unsuccessful warfare later, Soviet troops withdrew from Afghanistan, leaving the rebels in control of the countryside (they captured the capital three years later). In a striking parallel to America's experience in Vietnam, Soviet withdrawal in 1989 marked the most dramatic military failure in Soviet history.

Ideologically, the failure of socialism was most marked in the environmental arena. Capitalism had been castigated as an economic system that exploited and ravaged its workers for the sake of profits for the few. The U.S.S.R. claimed to operate with the workers' welfare as its chief aim. Yet the explosion of the Chernobyl nuclear power plant, and the reaction of the authorities, exploded these claims.

The Chernobyl disaster led to a total radiation release perhaps eighty times that of the Hiroshima or Nagasaki explosions.[31] Nonetheless, Soviet authorities made no announcement to people in the regions affected by fallout, advocated no precautions. Party leaders ordered schools, shops, and workplaces to remain open, while sending their own families away. May Day parades went on in Kiev (whose 2.4 million residents lived only 75 miles from the reactor site) while radiation plumes were still spreading overhead. As the extent of the disaster slowly became clear, western radio reports increasingly conflicted with the reassurances from Soviet authorities. As the truth gradually became known in the U.S.S.R. it became clear to Soviet citizens that the regime had been encouraging them to feed their children with contaminated foods, and left them uncertain about the safety of their homes. The myth that they lived in a society chiefly concerned with workers' welfare vanished, replaced by a cynical reevaluation of the "authorities."

Moreover, Chernobyl was just the tip of the iceberg of an environmental disaster that had begun to come to light. Radioactive wastes, chemical effluent, fertilizer and pesticide misuse, and poorly designed and managed irrigation schemes have left much of the U.S.S.R. and eastern

Europe an ecological nightmare, encompassing some of the most dangerously polluted lands on earth and wreaking destruction of habitats and
resources (such as the shrinkage of the Aral sea and the disappearance of
the Volga sturgeon fishery) on an unprecedented scale.

The bottom line of ecological disaster was a reversal of the progress
that had been made in health care and mortality. From its low point in
1960/61 to 1975/76, the Soviet death rate increased thirty percent. Infant
mortality, which had steadily fallen to 22.9 per thousand in 1971, swiftly
rose (according to Soviet official statistics) by almost half, to 31.1 per
thousand by 1976.[32] Things then deteriorated even further. By 1980-81,
adult life expectancy had fallen four full years from 1964-65, from 66 to
62 years.[33] By 1987, the Soviet health minister admitted that infant
mortality in the U.S.S.R. ranked no better than 50th in the world, after
Barbados and the United Arab Emirates.[34]

Shortages of medical supplies contributed to the decline of public
health. As Field notes, "the health service, as constituted at the end of the
1980s, [was] indeed in such poor shape that it help[ed] to undermine the
legitimacy of the Gorbachev regime."[35] Increasing numbers of industrial
accidents, as workers suffered with worn-out machinery and deteriorating
mines and factories, probably also contributed to greater mortality.

As public health and mortality sharply deteriorated while Party
officials evaded responsibility and shielded themselves, any ideological
claims of the superiority of socialism, or its greater regard for the working
man and woman, provoked anger rather than assent.

The alienation of diverse elites grew rapidly as the trends discussed
above became evident; indeed they were most evident to Party leaders and
middle-level and provincial elites. As J.F. Brown noted, "the communist
ruling elite . . . began to lose confidence in its ability to rule, and more to
the point, to lose the willingness to use the means to retain its rule."[36]
Among middle-level and provincial elites, the change in attitudes —
though varied through millions of individual experiences — could be
summed up by the disgust of Leonid Teliatnikov, chief of the Chernobyl
Nuclear Plant Fire Station at the time of the accident. Learning of the way
in which the population was not informed or evacuated, he told the journal
Smena "I felt sick in my soul and ashamed that I should belong to the same
Party as these people . . . I stopped respecting many city leaders."[37]

Gorbachev, sharing this sense that the Party and its regime needed
to be reformed, thought the way to overcome entrenched conservative
interests was to encourage the population to make apparent the shortcom-

ings of Soviet society, and hold guilty authorities responsible. Thus his policy of *glasnost* was developed as the essential precursor to restructuring, or *perestroika*.

Glasnost, however, led as certainly to state breakdown in the Soviet Union as the policy of the French Crown two centuries earlier when it invited peasants, bourgeois, and nobles throughout France to meet in local assemblies to discuss the problems of the nation and elect representatives to the Estates General. Once a far-reaching debate on the problems of the U.S.S.R. was encouraged by the authorities, they could neither set the terms of that debate, nor resist the demands for solution of pressing problems that followed. Given an opening, the intelligentsia who had earlier faced a hard choice between conforming to, or opposing, the regime leapt at the chance to highlight a myriad of problems that had previously been concealed. The vast range of problems that came to light, and conflicts between conservative and reformist elites over their solution, led to policy paralysis. With inaction and waffling from the central authorities, local and regional grievances quickly blossomed into demands for greater autonomy, and then into national separatist movements.

Glasnost thus put Gorbachev in an untenable position. Once he decided that the policy of covering up errors would lead to further decay, it was clearly necessary to expose faulty state policies. Seeking to undermine party conservatives, Gorbachev encouraged people to demand responsibility, support the intelligentsia, and encourage popular representation. But when such actions unleashed increased opposition, Gorbachev could not suppress that opposition without handing power to conservatives and silencing future complaints against the system's faults. In eastern Europe in particular, armed intervention to suppress autonomy in Poland or East Germany would dash Gorbachev's hopes for increased autonomy and support for his reforms from Soviet society. Gorbachev had little hope but to attempt to keep ahead of the wave of popular discontent he had aroused, hoping to ride it to greater power and further reform.

But Gorbachev's insurmountable problems quickly became clear in his efforts peacefully to buy, rather than force, reform, for Gorbachev literally bankrupted the Soviet state. Printing rubles to underwrite massive promises of raises and investment for key sectors of the economy, he swelled the currency dramatically. The state budget deficit, stable at 15-18 billion roubles per year in 1980-1985, suddenly rose to 90 billion roubles per year in 1988-89.[38] The stiff inflation that followed further undermined the legitimacy of Gorbachev's government.

Given the marked deterioration of health, life, environment, and economy in the Soviet Union, the intensification of popular grievances after 1975 requires no comment. What is remarkable is the extent to which Western observers refused to believe that this deterioration existed.

The sharp rise in infant mortality was evident to Western demographers, who suggested that its steep rise in the 1970s indicated fundamental problems in the Soviet system.[39] But imported consumer goods on display in Moscow (often purchased with borrowed funds) gave foreign observers a sense that the regime was meeting consumer needs. The drabness and disrepair of East Berlin was often contrasted with the liveliness of West Berlin. But some observers downplayed the import of this distinction, assuming that modern factories lay behind pockmarked walls and that contented workers lived in crumbling tenements. Speaking of East Germany, but using words applicable to the entire Soviet bloc, Amos Elon noted that when "Eduard Reuter, head of Daimler Benz, returned from his first thorough tour of East German industrial installations he is reported to have said that the problems there could only be resolved by bulldozers." Elon further observed that "Many now wonder at the apparent willingness of so many governments and 'experts' in the West over the years to swallow as a fact the myth of East Germany as the 'eleventh' industrial world power. The one successful public relations coup of the East German regime — a regime otherwise so disreputable — was to make so many people believe in the myth."[40]

By the late 1980s the deterioration in the economy, environment, and credibility of the Soviet Union and its government were manifest. The conditions for the Soviet state to unravel from the top down, unleashing elite and popular discontent, were too far advanced to be reversed. Gorbachev's attempt to undermine Party conservatives could only remove the remaining props of the regime, not overcome its manifold deficiencies.

To be sure, a Tiananmen-type solution was certainly possible in East Germany, and was conceivable in the U.S.S.R. The difference was Gorbachev, whose calculation that avoiding repression would aid his efforts at reform led to an inaction that permitted modest rebellion to grow swiftly into revolution. What does this mean for revolutionary prediction and explanation? As stated above, it means that although a conjunctural analysis can tell when a state is weak and facing a revolutionary situation, it cannot predict whether accident or an individual's actions will intervene to slow down arrival of a revolutionary crisis, or to rush it forward. Past cases do reveal that in such situations, frantic efforts at reform coupled with erratic or inconsistent repression generally hasten the development of revolutions. In other words, Gorbachev's overconfidence that he could control the situation and initiate massive reforms without repression was wrong, and a historically and theoretically alert adviser could have told him he was taking risks which would likely lead to his overthrow. But no political sociologist could "predict" that Gorbachev would be so overconfident. What *could* be predicted was that the U.S.S.R. had arrived by 1989, as argued above, at a revolutionary situation that would either entail massive repression or the breakdown of Soviet and Party authority. Once it became clear that Gorbachev intended to continue with frantic reform and eschew massive repression, the fairly rapid breakdown of Soviet rule could be readily foreseen.

CONCLUSION

Area experts and past theories of revolution have failed in predicting recent major revolutions. However, given the limits of area expertise and the focus of dominant theories of revolution on popular agency or particular kinds of state structure, neither of which forms a sound basis for analysis of revolution, such failure is not surprising and is not grounds for rejecting the possibility of prediction. The actions of key individuals can influence whether an overt revolution will occur sooner or later, but can not undo overall conjunctural dilemmas. Understanding revolutions as the product of a conjunctural process is the key to predictive success.

NOTES

Portions of this paper were presented at the 1991 Benjamin Lippincott Symposium, "Democracy and Markets in Central Europe," Department of Political Science, University of Minnesota. My thanks to the participants for their helpful comments.
1   For a summary of the development of revolutionary theory through the work of Johnson, Huntington, Gurr, Tilly, Skocpol, and Eisenstadt, see Jack A. Goldstone, "Theories of Revolution: The Third Generation,"

World Politics 32 (April, 1980), 425-443. For more recent work, see note 23 below.

2   Jack A. Goldstone, "Revolutions and Superpowers," in *Superpowers and Revolution*, ed. Jonathan Adelman (New York: Praeger, 1986), 38-48. Adelman insisted on deleting the most strongly predictive passages, describing them as speculation. He has publicly admitted his regrets (at the 1989 American Political Science Association Meetings), and will substantiate the prediction.

3   Jack A. Goldstone, ed., *Revolutions: Theoretical, Comparative, and Historical Studies* (San Diego and New York: Harcourt Brace Jovanovich, 1986).

4   *The Davis Enterprise*, February 4, 1990, p. A-9.

5   "For China, the Revolution of Modernization is Just Beginning," *Los Angeles Times* May 24, 1989, Sec. II, p. 7; "S. Africa: No revolution yet," *Chicago Tribune* September 16, 1985, Sec. 1, p. 11.

6   J. F. Brown, *Surge to Freedom: The End of Communist Rule in Eastern Europe* (Durham, NC: Duke University Press, 1991), 145-146.

7   Nikki R. Keddie, "Can Revolutions Be Predicted; Can Their Causes be Understood?" *Contention* 1 (Winter 1992): 159-182; Timur Kuran, "Now out of Never: The Element of Surprise in the East European Revolution of 1989," *World Politics* 44 (October 1991): 7-48.

8   Keddie, "Can Revolutions Be Predicted," 161.

9   Ibid. 161.

10   Ibid. 175.

11   Ibid. 176.

12   Mark Lichbach, "An Evaluation of 'Does Economic Inequality Breed political Conflict' Studies," *World Politics* 41 (July 1989): 431-470; T.R. Gurr, ed., *Handbook of Political Conflict* (New York: Free Press, 1980).

13   Charles Ragin, *The Comparative Method* (Berkeley and Los Angeles: University of California Press, 1987); Andrew Abbot, "Transcending General Linear Reality," *Sociological Theory* 6 (Fall 1988): 169-186.

14   Jack A. Goldstone, *Revolution and Rebellion in the Early Modern World* (Berkeley and Los Angeles: University of California Press, 1991); Jack A. Goldstone, Ted Robert Gurr, and Farrokh Moshiri, eds., *Revolutions of the Late Twentieth Century* (Boulder, CO: Westview, 1991).

15   Jack A. Goldstone, "An Analytic Framework," in *Revolutions*, ed. Goldstone, Gurr, and Moshiri, 37, 41.

PREDICTING REVOLUTIONS 63

16   C. G. Hempel, "The Function of General Laws in History" *Journal of Philosophy* 39 (January 1942): 35-48.

17   On villages, see Theda Skocpol, *States and Social Revolutions* (Cambridge: Cambridge University Press, 1979); on urban working communities, see Craig J. Calhoun, *The Question of Class Struggle* (Chicago: University of Chicago Press, 1982); on religious networks, see J. P. Van Vugt, *Democratic Organization for Change: Latin American Christian Base Communities and Literacy Campaigns* (New York: Bergin and Garvey, 1991).

18   Skocpol, *States and Social Revolutions*; Charles Tilly, Louise Tilly, and Richard Tilly, *The Rebellious Century 1830-1930* (Cambridge, MA: Harvard University Press, 1975).

19   Alexis de Tocqueville, *The Old Regime and the French Revolution*, trans. Stuart Gilbert (New York: Doubleday, 1955); Crane Brinton, *The Anatomy of Revolution*, rev. ed. (New York: Vintage, 1965).

20   Ted Robert Gurr, *Why Men Rebel* (Princeton: Princeton University Press, 1970); Samuel P. Huntington, *Political Order in Changing Societies* (New Haven: Yale University Press, 1968); Chalmers Johnson, *Revolutionary Change* (Boston: Little Brown, 1966); Neil Smelser, *Theory of Collective Behavior* (New York: Free Press, 1962); Charles Tilly, *From Mobilization to Revolution* (Reading, MA: Addison-Wesley, 1978).

21   Tocqueville, *The Old Regime*, 188.

22   Skocpol, *States and Social Revolutions*.

23   Robert Dix, "Why Revolutions Succeed and Fail," *Polity* 16 (1984): 423-446; James DeFronzo, *Revolutions and Revolutionary Movements* (Boulder, CO: Westview, 1991); Tim McDaniel, *Autocracy: Modernization and Revolution in Russia and Iran* (Princeton: Princeton University Press, 1991); Jeff Goodwin, "Colonialism and Revolution in Southeast Asia: A Comparative Analysis," in *Revolution in the World-System*, ed. Terry Boswell (New York: Greenwood Press, 1989), 59-78; Farideh Farhi, *States and Urban-Based Revolutions: Iran and Nicaragua* (Urbana and Chicago: University of Illinois Press, 1990); Matthew Sobart Shugart, "Patterns of Revolution," *Theory and Society* 18 (1989): 249-71; Valerie Bunce, "The Polish Crisis of 1980-1981 and Theories of Revolution" in *Revolution*, ed. Boswell, 167-188; Timothy P. Wickham-Crowley, *Exploring Revolution: Essays on Latin American Insurgency and Revolution Theory* (Armonk, NY: M.E. Sharpe, 1991).

24   Michael Mann, *The Sources of Social Power, Vol. I* (Cambridge: Cambridge University Press, 1986).

25   W. W. Rostow, "Eastern Europe and the Soviet Union: A Techno-logical Time Warp," in *The Crisis of Leninism and the Decline of the Left: The Revolutions of 1989*, ed. Daniel Chirot (Seattle: University of Washington Press, 1991), 62.

26   Christopher Davis and Murray Feshbach, *Rising Infant Mortality in the USSR in the 1970s* (Washington, D.C.: U.S. Department of Commerce, 1980), 3.

27   Daniel Chirot, "What Happened in Eastern Europe in 1989?" in Daniel Chirot, ed., *Crisis of Leninism and the Decline of the Left: The Revolutions of 1989* (Seattle: University of Washington Press, 1991), 3-32.

28   Rostow, "Eastern Europe," 62.

29   Anders Aslund, *Gorbachev's Struggle for Economic Reform*, expanded ed. (Ithaca, NY: Cornell University Press, 1991), 19.

30   Abel Aganbegyan, *Inside Perestroika: The Future of the Soviet Economy*, trans. Helen Szamuely (New York: Perennial/Harper & Row, 1989), 228.

31   Viktor Haynes and Marko Bojcun, *The Chernobyl Disaster* (London: Hogarth Press, 1988), 44.

32   Davis and Feshbach, *Infant Mortality*, 2-3.

33   Vladimir G. Treml, "Drinking and Alcohol Abuse in the U.S.S.R. in the 1980s," in *Soviet Social Problems*, ed. Anthony Jones, Walter Conner and David E. Powell, eds. (Boulder, CO: Westview: 1991), 126.

34   Mark G. Field, "Soviet Health Problems and the Convergence Hypothesis," in Anthony Jones, ed., *Soviet Social Problems* (Boulder: Westview Press, 1991), 79.

35   Field, "Soviet Health Problems," 79.

36   Brown, *Surge to Power*, 3-4.

37   Haynes and Bojcun, *Chernobyl*, 51.

38   Aslund, *Gorbachev's Struggle*, 190, 192.

39   Davis and Feshbach, *Infant Mortality*; Nick Eberstadt, *The Poverty of Communism* (New Brunswick, NJ: Transaction Books, 1988).

40   Amos Elon, "In a Former Country," *New York Review of Books* 39 (April 23, 1992), 36.

RESPONSE TO GOLDSTONE

NIKKI R. KEDDIE

Jack Goldstone's essay maintains that if others had absorbed recent advances in the theory of revolution they could have predicted recent revolutions. Goldstone is, in large part, debating my article on predicting revolutions in *Contention*, I, 2.[1] After listing some theorists of revolution, including himself, he says, "I believe it is only the failure of area experts and popular wisdom to catch up to this most recent work in the theory of revolution that has left most observers astounded by events." He then gives examples from his own predictions to show that contemporary theory enables us to predict revolutions.

To take Goldstone's examples in order: he begins with the most relevant one, saying that in a 1985 draft he wrote that Marcos's regime was unlikely to last more than a few years. Unfortunately, Goldstone's editor made him omit the prediction. The printed version compares Marcos's strengths and weaknesses with some twentieth century dictators who were overthrown, and Goldstone may be granted a majority hit on this unpublished prediction.

The other examples are doubtful. Goldstone in 1986 insisted on including a chapter in a reader on revolutions on the Hungarian and Czech uprisings, as he expected more such risings. Others also expected more uprisings; what they did not expect and what is at issue is a sudden collapse. Expecting uprisings is not predicting revolutions. Then, eighteen months before Gorbachev's fall, Goldstone predicted Gorbachev would probably be out of power in four months. Many people, including myself, predicted Gorbachev's fall, orally or in writing (some with better timing than

Goldstone), but this is far from predicting revolution. Today some are predicting Yeltsin's fall and the fall of various other world leaders, but this is not prediction of revolution unless it says so explicitly, even though some falls could be part of a revolution.

Goldstone's predictions of non-revolution are barely germane, especially as nobody, to my knowledge, argues that non-revolutions are unpredictable. Elementary statistics show that people will do better when asked to predict countries that won't have revolutions than ones that will, as the vast majority of countries do not have revolutions, especially within a brief period. We may imagine a group of informed social scientists drawing up a list of the world's fifty most unstable, potentially revolutionary countries. We then ask each to predict those likely to have revolutions in the next five years. The one most likely to do best or nearly best is the one who says "none of them." This is because few countries have revolutions in any short period (with the domino-toppling of Eastern Europe the only exception), and also, those who name countries that will have revolutions are bound to get some wrong. The person who says, "none" may be 100% right, and even if there are two revolutions, past experience suggests that nobody will name just those two. The person saying "none," even if five of the fifty countries have revolutions, will be 90% correct, while I know of nobody who predicted two or more revolutions correctly. (There are different ways the percentages can be figured, but the point remains.)

Predicting that revolutions will not occur is going with the probabilities and is much more likely to turn out right than is predicting that they will. The particular predictions of non-revolution given by Goldstone do not change this. Nobody I talked to said there would be revolution in China or South Africa at the times he mentions, nor do I remember this being a dominant view in the press or media. As for Iraq, Goldstone writes as if the U.S. was simply an observer, when it was in fact a major player, which could have united with rebellious forces in the country to topple Saddam Hussein. Predicting the U.S. would not do this would have been right, but what Goldstone says is that "U.S. hopes that he would be overthrown by his own people were delusory." In 1991 the U.S. clearly wanted a coup from within the elite, and actively worked against a popular overthrow. Finally, Goldstone notes "one major failed prediction," when he said in October, 1989, that no revolution in East Germany was imminent.

Goldstone's correct predictions of non-revolution achieved 75%, which, given the good odds noted above, is unremarkable. Regarding the subject under debate, predicting revolutions, his *only* self-cited prediction of a revolution (in a period of history when revolutions were unusually numerous) is the case of Marcos. Even though there is no written record of this prediction to show how it was phrased, we will grant this as a real prediction. *One* correct prediction of a revolution by *one* leading representative of a group said to have developed theories allowing revolutions to be predicted is hardly an overwhelming demonstration of that proposition.

From his argument thus far Goldstone concludes, "it is not impossible to predict, within a range of a year or two, forthcoming revolutions or non-revolutions." I will ignore predicting non-revolutions, which, given the odds, is easy, and deal only with predicting revolutions. In my article I pointed to situations where prediction was possible, chiefly those where a series of major destabilizing forces and oppositional movements was evident, as perhaps in pre-1917 Russia, or those where strong revolutionary forces were on the ground and visible, as in pre-victory Cuba and China, where some people did predict revolutionary victories considerably in advance. Goldstone on the whole does not distinguish between such situations and those that, in my view, make most revolutions unpredictable. I should have added another factor that makes some revolutions predictable, namely, having a series of closely related countries that are influenced by the same factors (most often coming from abroad). The obvious case is East-Central Europe in 1989, where the crucial impetus to revolt was given by Gorbachev's renunciation of the Brezhnev doctrine allowing Soviet military intervention. After this it became possible for Eastern Europeans successfully to revolt; there was a "domino effect" of revolts in each place influencing the next, and some people no doubt predicted further successful revolts after the first ones occurred.

Hence, I agree that some revolutions can be predicted, but think these are in a minority. As Goldstone thinks such prediction possible overall, if recent revolutionary theory is used, I will ask him the only question that has probative value: where in the next five years will there be revolutions? (Like him I use "revolution" only for movements with some mass involvement that take over the state and change its nature in some basic way.) Though it will take time to finish this experiment, I hope he takes up the challenge to demonstrate the accuracy of his position. I might even offer some hints of countries in major trouble or conflict, such as Algeria, Iraq, and Cuba. In Algeria dissatisfaction and crisis are widespread. As both internal crisis and the oppositional Islamists are very visible, it could fall into my category of countries where revolution could be predicted, unlike Iran and the Soviet Union, and hence it might be predicted even by people who had never heard of Goldstone or Keddie. Iraq and Cuba similarly have such evident "proto-revolutionary" features that, were Goldstone to choose only the three countries named it would be unclear whether his view, mine, or neither was being vindicated. He should ideally pick countries that meet his criteria but not mine.

Alas Goldstone, a few lines after telling us predications are not impossible, guards, whether intentionally or not, against the possibility of his (or anybody's) being proven wrong, no matter how many bad predictions they make. He says, "What *can* be done, and this is my meaning when I speak of 'predicting' a revolution, is to identify states that are moving rapidly toward a revolutionary situation, so that if trends continue unchecked a revolution is highly likely to break out when a triggering or accelerating event occurs." Ah, yes, "if trends continue unchecked" "a revolution is highly likely"; there are the rubs that make the proposition circular, unfalsifiable, and without predictive value. Let us say, to use a conceivably revolutionary country, that J. Doe should predict a revolution in Algeria within the next few years, and that it does not occur. Doe can always find changes in major trends (trends always change in various ways and degrees) to explain why the revolution did not occur. Doe may even be right, but there is no way we can know for sure, and R. Roe, perhaps from the fifth or ninth wave of revolutionary theorists, is bound to dispute him/her/it and give a different interpretation. Doe can quote Goldstone that prediction only means that revolution is highly likely, not that it will actually occur. In some ways the proposition boils down to: "If forces that generally lead to revolutions continue to grow in country X it will very likely have a revolution; if they don't it probably won't." While in this form or in Goldstone's the proposition is not useless, it does not take us far on the path of prediction.

In Goldstone's wording, there is one part of the statement that could be falsifiable and hence of some scientific value. The statement assumes that we can identify states that are moving rapidly toward a revolutionary situation. If Goldstone is right he should be able, given his truly vast knowledge of the world, wide reading, and extraordinary intelligence, to give us a list of states in the world that are moving rapidly toward a revolutionary situation. If states not on this list undergo a revolutionary crisis in the near future there is something wrong with the means of identification. There is also something wrong with the theory if the relationship between states picked and actual revolutions is weak. A predictive formula that does not predict is not of much use. On the other hand if the list of countries in, or moving toward, a revolutionary situation that I hope Goldstone provides does come up with, say, 50% that actually have revolutions, and not more than one revolution comes soon in a country off the list, then we may say that Goldstone's theory probably has a value. (Though we cannot rule out the possibility that his intelligence, knowledge, and good luck might be more responsible than his theories for this good outcome. And we are allowing a high level of misses.)

Goldstone next says that recent revolutions have not been predicted because their countries have been studied almost exclusively by area specialists rather than also by specialists in revolutions. Taking the example of Iran, he says that Islamic specialists had never seen a radical religious revolution against a secular state, but that students of the English Puritan Revolution of 1640 are familiar with this phenomenon. "The combination of skills of the area specialist and the expert on revolutions . . . is probably necessary to predict revolutions." If this is necessary we might as well give up, as it is impossible to imagine the mechanism by which it could have come about in the case given, Iran. For it to have occurred, someone, say by early 1977 to give the revolution specialist some months to bone up on Iran, would have had to decide that revolution was likely in Iran. This, however, is just the point at issue: no Iran specialist or revolution specialist or anyone else who wrote on Iran did think this, and since there aren't hundreds of smart revolution specialists around willing to be assigned to all countries on the off-chance they might have a revolution, it is impossible to imagine why a good revolution specialist would then have taken up a study of Iran. For the revolution person to have done so, someone must have predicted that revolution was likely, which they did not and could not have done. For a revolution specialist to move in, someone must already have made the prediction that is the central point at issue. This could not have worked for Iran or the Soviet Union, the examples Goldstone gives. It could only be tried in places where some people are predicting that revolution is likely; once Goldstone gives us this list we may hope that he or another specialist goes to work on these countries in order to give us more detailed predictions. But the key prediction on the serious possibility of revolution has to be made *before* the entry of the revolution specialist that he sees as crucial to such predictions. Once again the implications are circular.

There are additional problems with Goldstone's remarks on Iran summarized above. With regard to the helpfulness to understanding Iran of scholars who know the English revolution of 1640 (many of whom would not accept his description of it as "a radical religious revolution against a secular state") there are doubts. The special thing about the religious revolutionaries in Iran is not that they were religious, a phenomenon common to many revolts, but that they were led by a top member of the established religious hierarchy and by his followers in that hierarchy. They were, to use common if inexact terms, orthodox believers leaning to fundamentalism, not partly heterodox figures to the left of the religious establishment, as was the case in England and in many other religious revolts. The virtually unprecedented nature of an orthodox clerical-fundamentalist-led revolution and its myriad differences from what happened in seventeenth century England makes it doubtful that even if those who knew the English revolution had turned their minds and research to Iran, they would have predicted revolution there.

This seems confirmed by the fact that a number of Iran scholars before 1978 had considerable interest in comparative revolution, including European revolutions, such as Ervand Abrahamian, Said Arjomand (then working on a relevant dissertation), Ahmad Ashraf, Farhad Kazemi, and myself. None of us saw a major parallel to England in 1640 any more than specialists on that revolution or on comparative revolution did. Nor do most scholars say now that these revolutions were so similar that more knowledge of the first one would have helped us predict the second. Partial parallels were later drawn by Arjomand to many religiously (and non-religiously) led revolts of left and right.[2] But Arjomand sought out these revolts after experiencing the Iranian revolution; it would have been amazing for someone who knew earlier about all these revolts, each of which resembled the Iranian revolution only partially, to have predicted that revolution on the basis of this knowledge.

There was, however, one country known to Iran specialists where members of the religious establishment had before 1978 had leadership roles both in a major revolution and in lesser rebellions and uprisings. This country was — Iran. There several leading members of the clerical hierarchy had important roles in the revolution of 1905-11, which gave Iran a parliamentary constitution, and they had also been important in a successful rebellion in 1891-92. A revival of clerically-led mass protest occurred in 1963, when a major movement was led by Ayatollah Khomeini, who was exiled in 1964 but continued to be influential. Iran scholars were hardly unaware of the continued importance of this tradition: its pre-1978 discussion in major books and articles by Ann Lambton, Hamid Algar,

Shahrough Akhavi, Michael Fisher, Richard Cottam, Marvin Zonis, myself and others may be mentioned.[3] This, along with a knowledge that Iran since 1890 had had several revolutionary or rebellious movements, was more relevant than knowledge of seventeenth century England. It was not inexperience with comparable revolts and rebellions that hindered the Iran specialists, but the intrinsic obstacles to prediction of Iran's revolution. Briefly, the evident strength and prosperity of the Iranian state, including a strong international position and good relations with all the world's major powers, along with the weakness of organized opposition before 1978 made revolution seem highly improbable, even though many of us wrote that Iran faced more trouble and discontent than the U.S. government expected.

Goldstone's following point that a model saying what a society moving toward revolution looks like may be more useful to prediction than are older more static models of prerevolutionary conditions may be true. Goldstone, however, implies a universal validity for his model that can be claimed only by greatly stretching the evidence. A society is careening toward revolution, he says, if all three of certain conditions are met, and "when any of these factors is weak or absent, revolution is unlikely." Condition (1) is that "the state loses effectiveness in its ability to command resources and obedience." To take the case of Iran: just before the first big rising in January, 1978, the state had not, in any normal sense of the term, lost effectiveness as defined. Condition (2) is "elites are alienated from the state and in heightened conflict over the distribution of power and status." Elites were alienated in Iran, though probably no more so than in many other countries. For the sake of discussion I will concede point 2, as the main problems arise from points 1 and 3. Point (3) is that "a large or strategic portion of the population can be readily mobilized for protest actions." In Iran, as in many dictatorships, this proposition has no operational meaning before the revolution actually began, at which point we are no longer really talking about prediction. In most dictatorships little or no mass mobilization takes place, and so we do not know if a large or strategic portion of the population could be mobilized under different conditions. Once such mobilizations do occur, as they did in Iran in 1978, it is possible to predict a revolution that had already begun and such predictions were made in Iran in 1978. But had we used the Goldstone model in 1977, we would have had to say that revolution in Iran was very unlikely.

Goldstone goes on, "To *predict* revolution one needs only to ask whether conditions in a particular country are moving simultaneously toward a growing ineffectiveness of the state, alienation of elites, and rising potential for mass mobilization." We could add to my request for a list of countries on the path to revolution a request for how they fit this three-element model, but the first list alone will suffice.

Goldstone, possibly anticipating the problem with mobilization under dictatorships, says that mobilization potential depends on popular grievances that can be summarized as social, economic, and cultural. When objective conditions for grievances are increasing and structures for mobilization exist, "we may conclude that popular mobilization potential is rising, *even if support for the regime appears strong and unaffected.*" This helps little: today the kinds of grievances Goldstone lists exist in most countries and subregions in the world. Worldwide economic trends affect most of the world's population negatively and other grievances scarcely need listing here; most of these, fairly or not, are blamed on existing governments. To be more specific we can move to the second part of Goldstone's statement, that "structures conducive to mobilization are in place." I would like from him one more list — of countries where such structures are in place, which then might have revolutions if his points one through three are fulfilled, and of countries where they are not in place, so they should not have revolutions. Offhand, if I have any understanding about what structures being in place means, I would expect developed and democratic countries to have more such structures than poor and autocratic ones, but this matters little to the basic point, which is that such statements have no meaning unless fleshed out by examples that within a few years prove accurate.

In elaborating his point on state effectiveness, Goldstone says, "A number of observable factors — losses in war, large and increasingly unmanageable state debts, high inflation, failed development policies, recourse to extraordinary taxation, conflicts with cultural elites, undisciplined or ineffective military forces, problems with foreign allies — are signs of decreasing state effectiveness." Iran would have scored very high on the *non*-revolutionary side of most of these, with only partially failed development policies and conflicts with cultural elites on the revolutionary side. Nearly everyone said in 1977 that the Iranian state was strong, and Goldstone's list would not have ranked it nearly as weak as it would many other states.

I will skip the remaining part of Goldstone's article, concerning new theories of revolution and his analysis of the Soviet case, both because I found this analysis far superior to the first section, with many good insights, and because others are more competent to comment on it. However good his analysis of the Soviet case is, it cannot prove the predictability of revolution, because Goldstone's theory of predictability and his current analysis of the Soviet Union could have influenced one another (indeed it would be strange if the Soviet case did not influence contemporary theories of revolution); because retrospective predictions are far easier than real predicting; and because one case or even several cases cannot prove a universal theory. One case can, however, disprove a theory that claims universality, which is why I felt free to concentrate on Iran.

Even if Goldstone's theory had perfectly fit the Soviet, East European, and Iranian cases (which it does not), it would not prove its ability to predict future revolutions. Just as generals are always said to be fighting the last war, so revolutionary theorists, generalizing from past revolutions, are prepared to predict the last revolution. But just as the Iranian and East European revolutions differed significantly from past revolutions, so are future revolutions likely to differ from them, even though there will be some similarities.

Goldstone's formulation also downplays international factors, even though he stresses them in other writings about contemporary revolutions. His process model appears here to lead him to omit crucial international forces and to discuss mainly internal ones. Regarding international forces, take Iraq as of this writing (September, 1992): the country is in many ways in crisis, and there is very strong and active opposition to the government among the majority of the population comprising the Shi'a and the Kurds (not to mention opposition in central Iran). Yet whether there is a successful overthrow of Saddam Hussein and the creation of a new type of government appears to depend more on U.S. policy than on the forces Goldstone names. If this seems a singular example we can turn to East-Central Europe where, as suggested above, the most important single factor in the successful overthrow of regimes was Gorbachev's abandonment of the Brezhnev doctrine; without that we could have had continued ineffective opposition with occasional risings for a long time. In Iran, Carter's Human Rights program (or rather the perception of it by the shah as precluding certain internal security measures and involving possible abandonment by the U.S.) was one important factor in the revolution's victory. Such factors are not spelled out in Goldstone's predictive model.

The model also slights the role of individuals. It is possible that had the shah moved forcibly against demonstrators in the spring of 1978 the movement would have been limited to a short series of mass demonstrations rather than becoming a revolution. Goldstone says different acts by Gorbachev could have delayed revolution for a time; but it is sometimes possible for an individual to determine whether a revolution occurs. The changing policy of key foreign states and the often unpredictable role of important individuals fit awkwardly if at all into the three-point scheme. This may be one reason why Goldstone puts caveats around his promise of prediction; but if a predictive theory mostly fails to predict it is not very useful.

There are cases where one may predict that revolution is very possible, such as those with large and visible revolutionary forces, or those where governments have been undermined by foreign developments like the collapse of the Soviet Union. Many revolutions, however, have crucial causes that cannot be distilled from past experience. They occur in new conditions and have largely new patterns. This is true of the main revolutions that have occurred since 1978, the Iranian and the Eastern European. The Iranian revolution, while having some causes similar to earlier revolutions, was unusual in arising in a largely strong and wealthy state, and was unique in bringing to power leaders of a traditional orthodox religious hierarchy. The Soviet and Eastern European revolutions were unique in involving the collapse of a major power and its social system from within, caused by both internal and external factors. These revolutions were not predicted and it is not surprising that they were not.[4] The history of possible types of revolution is not played out, and more surprises are in store.

As for Goldstone's model, it would look better if it could result in at least a 50% score in actual predictions of actual revolutions rather than in impressive, but hardly uniquely impressive, retrospective discussion. Retrospective prediction is easy and only serves to underline the old saying that may be paraphrased as: It is predictions that concern the future which are difficult. Only by checking all of our statements about the future of any phenomenon against that future when it comes can we know anything about the degree of accuracy we may expect of predictions.

Finally, I have not spent so much time and space answering Goldstone because I care a great deal about the predictability of revolution. The world has hundreds of more important and consequential problems. It is important, however, that scholars employ careful reasoning and logic if we are to increase our understanding of the world. Hence it is worthwhile to deal seriously with a serious and important scholar like Jack Goldstone in the hope that debate can lead to greater clarity of thought.

NOTES

1   Nikki R. Keddie, "Can Revolutions Be Predicted; Can Their Causes Be Understood?," *Contention* 1 (Winter 1992): 159-182.
2   Said Amir Arjomand, *The Turban for the Crown: The Islamic Revolution in Iran* (New York: Oxford University Press, 1988), chap. 10.
3   Several works were written or planned and researched before 1978 concerning religious politics. Among them, Ann Lambton, Hamid Algar, and I wrote several articles on relations between the clergy and politics, including revolution, in the past century. See especially Hamid Algar, "The Oppositional Role of the Ulama in Twentieth-Century Iran," and Nikki R. Keddie, "The Roots of the Ulama's Power in Modern Iran" in Nikki R. Keddie, ed., *Scholars, Saints, and Sufis* (Berkeley: University of California Press, 1972). Among books see Shahrough Akhavi, *Religion and Politics in Contemporary Iran* (Albany: SUNY Press, 1980); Michael Fischer, *Iran: From Religious Dispute to Revolution* (Cambridge: Harvard University Press, 1980) (both researched and largely planned before the revolution); Hamid Algar, *Religion and State in Iran 1785-1906* (Berkeley: University of California Press, 1969); Nikki R. Keddie, *Religion and Rebellion in Iran* (London: Frank Cass, 1966) and *Iran: Religion, Politics and Society* (London: Frank Cass, 1980). Also having relevant material on the clergy and politics are Richard Cottam, *Nationalism in Iran* (Pittsburgh: University of Pittsburgh Press, 1964) and Marvin Zonis, *The Political Elite of Iran* (Princeton: Princeton University Press, 1971).
    Perhaps because I had written a lot on the importance of clergy-led politics (and also because people seem to long for predictions), many people have repeated to me the mini-myth that I had predicted (in one version "everybody knew that" I was the only person in the world who had predicted) the 1978-79 revolution. This myth, voiced by respected Middle East specialists, makes me especially wary of reported but unverifiable past predictions.
4   Although Goldstone does not make this argument, others have told me that the Soviet overturn was predicted by Randall Collins, in *Weberian Sociological Theory* (Cambridge: Cambridge University Press, 1986) or by Zbigniew Brzezinski in *The Grand Failure: The Birth and Death of Communism in the Twentieth Century* (New York: Scribner, 1989). What each in fact predicted, based on causation different from one another and

also from that stressed by Goldstone or any theorist of revolutions, was a gradual decline and fall of the Soviet Empire, probably to culminate in the twenty-first century. While these predictions were much closer to what happened than were those of most analysts, they were not very close. (As I don't think the Soviet overturn was predictable, this is not a criticism, though I do not in fact agree with most of the analysis in either book.) A different scenario of a future end of the Soviet Union as coming from the growth in size and opposition of Muslim populations is analyzed by Muriel Atkin in this issue. As Atkin notes, the Muslim republics were, in fact, the last and most reluctant to leave the Soviet Union, and they retain more ex-communist leaders than do non-Muslim republics.

REPLY TO KEDDIE

JACK A. GOLDSTONE

Nikki Keddie's generous and spirited response points to exactly the right issues. Let me agree forthrightly with her main jibe — I have not proved that revolutions can be systematically predicted.

Yet that was not the goal of my essay. I first sought merely to overcome Keddie's substantial arguments that such prediction was, in many cases, flatly impossible. Second, I attempted to make a plausible case that advances in the theory of revolutions should allow us to predict revolutions far better than recent failures would suggest.

Regarding these contentions, I seem to have been at least somewhat successful. Keddie has not sought to maintain her arguments that predicting revolutions is generally impossible. Nor has she argued with my contention that the theory of revolution has changed, and that such changes *should* improve our ability to forecast revolution. What Keddie has maintained is that such improvement has yet to be demonstrated by a conclusive scientific test. To that I agree, and her challenge — that I select a number of societies and make predictions — is a fair one. I am now seeking the resources (research assistants and collaborators with area expertise) to put my ideas about predicting revolutions to the test.

If I disagree violently with Keddie about any issue, it is her overly kind opinion that I myself have the knowledge to do a multi-nation test with historical depth and accuracy. It took me ten years to research *Revolution and Rebellion in the Early Modern World*. If I am to perform the kind of test Keddie quite rightly demands, performing a comparative examination of a half-dozen or more nations in sufficient depth to be accurate, but with sufficient swiftness that completion of the analysis will be timely enough for prediction, I will have to collaborate with area specialists. The natural sciences have long ago adopted this mode of research — multi-researcher teams incorporating theorists and empirical experts who pool their talents for testing theories. I believe the sooner the social sciences move toward this model the better; my co-edited volume *Revolutions of the Late Twentieth Century* is an attempt to show what can be done in this vein.

Keddie not only lays out the kind of testing that needs to be done for such a theory, she also lays out conditions for its application. These deserve attention, for a predictive theory is useless if it cannot be effectively applied to real cases. Keddie raises three issues in this regard: (1) Will revolution specialists be called in to examine cases if they are not already seen to be headed for revolution? (2) Can such a theory ever be falsified, if revolutions can be headed off by a "change in trajectory?" and (3) Can any theory developed to explain past revolutions predict the possibly quite different revolutions of the future? Let me address these in turn.

As a practical matter, revolution specialists are indeed called in to examine states long before they are evidently in a revolutionary condition. The reason is not that the U.S. is concerned about revolution in general, but that because before investing heavily in aiding a foreign state, or building substantial facilities there, it is prudent to ask whether that state is stable. Companies investing in specific countries routinely undertake such risk analysis; so too does the U.S. It is true that we usually only call in a doctor once the patient is sick; on the other hand, if the "patient" is a horse about to run a race on which we will place a heavy bet, we may well call in a specialist to examine the "patient" to make sure that we have not overlooked some hidden problem.

My ability to have anticipated Marcos's fall resulted from just such a consultation. In 1984, I briefly took part in a routine, low-level analysis by government area specialists examining the Philippines. To our surprise, we readily found clear signs of a changed political "trajectory." During the 1970s, the rural guerilla movement led by the New People's Army (NPA) had been stable, and Marcos' opponents among the Philippines' traditional landed political elites had been hopelessly divided by factional feuds, leaving Marcos reasonably secure. However, by the mid-1980s growing economic difficulties in the Philippines resulted in greatly increased recruitment of peasants to the NPA. Far more ominously, the

Philippines' army was unable to curtail the increased level of NPA activity. Instead, the growing challenge of the NPA revealed gross corruption and indolence within the army, which itself was showing divisions between "political" leaders content to simply collect rewards from Marcos and do nothing, and "reform" leaders who wanted to professionalize the army, improve its performance, and act decisively against the NPA. While the split in the army was growing, Marcos's traditional elite opponents were burying their differences and uniting against him, galvanized by the assassination of Benigno Aquino the previous year.

The split in the army and greater unity among anti-Marcos elites were not yet *overwhelming*; however, the marked change in direction from the situation in the 1970s was clear to area specialists. We agreed that if these trends continued, Marcos would face calls for his ouster from both the reform elements in the army and the traditional political elites, as both these elite groups were threatened by the growth of the NPA movement. If these elites turned on Marcos jointly, the small crony circle around him would be unable to defend him. Moreover, if popular groups hurt by the economic downturn joined these opposing elites, the forces arrayed against Marcos would be overwhelming.

In short, it appeared to us that Marcos's traditional tactics of dividing his elite opponents and holding off rural rebellion were failing; unless some sudden and unanticipated change of direction occurred — a major upswing in the economy, or a new falling-out among Marcos's opponents, neither of which seemed at all likely — the forces against Marcos would grow to be *overwhelming* in just a few years. At that time, these low-level discussions were ignored, as U.S. officials who were long-time friends of Marcos refused to believe that his position had radically changed since the 1970s. However, such trends did continue, and the expected result followed.

The question of whether such predictions can be falsified, of course, depends on having such predictions precisely specify the trends on which revolution depends. The value of a theory, after all, is to tell *which* of the infinite number of ongoing trends is significant. In the above example, the prediction rested on two primary trends — the weakening of the Philippine economy, which fueled NPA growth and divisions in the army over how to deal with this; and growing unity among traditional elite opponents of Marcos, which gave political effectiveness to the opposition. If Marcos had managed to retain power for another decade, while both these trends persisted, the theory would be incomplete at best, and completely useless at worst. Thus, Keddie's suggestion that *any* trend change could be pointed at to "save" the theory is not correct. When the theory is tested, it must spell out precisely which trends must continue for the prediction to hold.

Moreover, it is necessary to spell out precisely which variables should be measured, and by what scale, to follow these trends. Keddie is correct that my remarks about declining state effectiveness are sufficiently vague that there is room to differ about how well they apply to Iran, although I would argue that *in combination*, significant inflation, rising debts, severe and widespread conflicts with elites, and problems of U.S. interference with Iran's repressive actions against internal opponents added up to serious state difficulties. In *Rebellion and Revolution in the Early Modern World* I did offer scales for measuring the key trends leading toward revolution, and was able to graph — in a testable, falsifiable manner — the conjunction of forces leading to revolutionary situations in seventeenth-century England and eighteenth-century France. I have not offered a similarly exact analysis for Iran, and Keddie is right to remain skeptical about whether this revolution could have been foreseen. Such skepticism can only be dispelled, and a useful predictive theory obtained, when rules for operationalization of the key variables are provided. I acknowledge this task remains, and Keddie makes clear its vital significance.

As to whether the future will be radically different from the past, I confess that my reading of history suggests certain constants in human nature and political systems that will be sustained. Until such a day as states can control all members of a society directly (perhaps by electronic implants) and dispense with elites to carry commands and gain obedience, states will need loyal and effective elites to maintain their rule. Until individuals can obtain all public and personal services through private providers, and dispense with states to ensure their rights, liberty, and justice, individuals and their organizations will hold states accountable for certain conditions in their societies. And until all societies have developed institutions for stable, peaceful changes in government leaders and their policies at the insistence of the politically active population, conflicts among the state, dissatisfied elites, and popular groups will continue to raise the risk of revolution. I thus believe that attention to the relations among states, elites, and popular groups will continue to be a valid basis for explanation (and prediction) of revolutions into the foreseeable future. The specific *causes* that disrupt these relations may change, but I believe such changes can be accommodated by a process theory of the development of revolutionary situations.

In sum, Keddie's response generously accepts the possibility of a predictive theory of revolutions. Yet she correctly insists that such a theory must be tested against multiple cases with clear predictions before it can be given credence. Moreover, precision in specifying and operationalizing the trends to be examined to assess the risk of revolution is necessary if such a theory is to be applied. Keddie notes that my theory has not yet met those conditions for Iran, or for other contemporary and future revolutions.

To those claims I accede, and welcome the call for a more precise formulation of my theory, including rigorous testing. I appreciate Keddie's efforts to clarify exactly what is lacking, and her demonstration that much remains to be done. I look forward to taking up her challenge.

PART TWO

COMPARING AND INTERPRETING REVOLUTIONS

THE SOCIAL INTERPRETATION OF THE FRENCH REVOLUTION

EDWARD BERENSON

For much of this century social interpretations of the causes of revolution were such a staple of historical and social scientific writing that when Alfred Cobban set out to challenge that mode of analysis some thirty years ago, he could do little more that substitute one social interpretation for another. In his effort to debunk the prevailing Marxist view of the French Revolution, one that defined 1789 as the work of a triumphant bourgeoisie, he succeeded merely in finding a new revolutionary class. For Cobban the bearers of revolutionary upheaval were not a rising bourgeoisie but a declining cadre of middling bureaucratic *officiers*.[1] Cobban's revolution was still a bourgeois social revolution, only his bourgeoisie was, if anything, anticapitalist and wedded to a bloated state apparatus.

Although Cobban was himself unable to dislodge the social interpretation, he inspired a generation of historians who would succeed in doing so beyond his fondest dreams. By the late 1970s a "revisionist" account of the origins of 1789 challenged the very notion that the French Revolution had important social and economic roots. Under the brilliant leadership of François Furet, the revisionists have shifted the search for the origins of 1789 to the realms of politics, culture, ideology, and language.[2]

During roughly the same period of time, the early 1960s through the 1980s, the historiography of the English Revolution has undergone a similar transformation. The notion that the events of the 1640s expressed the triumph of a rising capitalist bourgeoisie over a declining feudal aristocracy has been emphatically put to rest. So too have other, non-Marxist, social interpretations; the English Revolution is now widely seen as a largely political and ideological phenomenon with religious conflict between Puritans and Anglicans playing a major role. For some historians of 1640, the critique of social origins of the Revolution has been extended to question whether any significant long-term causes can be discerned at all. These revisionists maintain that the English Revolution was the result of incompetent leadership at the top and a series of accidents and miscues that compounded each other and snowballed out of control.[3]

Work on the Chinese Revolution has undergone a similar shift. Many of the field's most prominent historians now downplay the importance not only of class conflicts between landlords and peasants in explaining Mao's victory but of other structural aspects of Chinese rural society as well. They also reject as inadequate the notion that it was largely the superior organizational and military power of the Communist party-army that sealed its victory over the Guomindang. And they dispute the idea, first advanced by Chalmers Johnson, that the Communists' skill in harnessing the peasantry's nationalist reactions against the Japanese invasion ultimately enabled Mao's party to reign supreme. All of these once-dominant interpretations of the origins of the Chinese Revolution appear to have succumbed to withering empirical attack; no widely-accepted picture of any kind — much less a social interpretation — remains intact.[4]

The challenge to the social interpretation of major world revolutions has been so all-encompassing that it is worth devoting some detailed attention to how this intellectual transformation came about. I will focus on the French Revolution not only because it is the one I know best but because its historiography has been so influential.[5] It is especially curious that what began with an assault against the Marxist interpretation soon evolved into an attempt to dismiss all socio-economic views. There has been some effort recently to redress this balance, but to the extent that these works neglect the role of culture and ideology in preparing the way for revolution they fail to convince. What is needed, it seems to me, is a new form of social interpretation that sees social phenomena as mediated by language and embedded in cultural contexts that must be understood in their own right.

In many ways, Cobban's assault against the Marxist interpretation of the French Revolution was more polemical than empirical, but those he inspired turned en masse to the archives and to the plentiful statistics originally collected by the Old Regime's scrupulous bureaucrats. The revisionists used those statistics to challenge the notion that eighteenth-century France was a society divided by social class and consequently that class could have been a decisive factor in causing the French Revolution. What these empirically-minded historians of the 1960s and 70s found was a nobility that looked quite bourgeois and a "bourgeoisie" that wanted nothing more than to be noble.

In particular, historians on both sides of the Atlantic came to the conclusion that wealth had become more important than seigneurial or "feudal" privilege in eighteenth-century society and that nobles every-where managed their properties with an eye to making a profit. Noblemen administered their estates shrewdly and carefully; they also invested heavily in mining, metallurgy, colonial trading companies, land-clearing and speculation enterprises, banking, and tax-collection operations of all kinds. Eighteenth-century nobles sold their timber in an increasingly lucrative market, and they had become adept in marketing grains and wine. As Robert Forster wrote in an influential study published in 1960, the nobility adhered "to the so-called bourgeois virtues of thrift, discipline and strict management of the family fortune."[6]

It also turned out that, contrary to the widespread beliefs of both Marxist and liberal historians, the nobility did not hold a monopoly over fiscal privilege. The great non-noble traders of France's mercantile centers enjoyed tax exemptions larger than those of most titled aristocrats.[7] Further complicating the picture was the finding that a substantial portion of the eighteenth-century nobility had only recently bought its way out of the middle class. For the most part, wealthy commoners did so by purchasing one of France's 4,000 or so offices in the royal bureaucracy that conferred hereditary nobility on the owner or his family. From the middle of the eighteenth century until 1789, Louis XV and XVI granted some 6,500 ennoblements, swelling the aristocratic ranks to the point that by the late 1780s between one quarter and one third of all noble families had achieved their status within the past fifty years.[8] Clearly, the nobility of Old Regime France was anything but a closed caste. It constantly received new mem-bers recently promoted from the bourgeoisie.

This widespread desire for noble status, of course, says a great deal about the middle class of the eighteenth century, a group whose values and mode of living differed from those of aristocrats much less than historians have traditionally believed. For the Old Regime bourgeoisie, wealth was not an end in itself or a means of creating new and more abundant resources through productive investment; it was a ticket into the realm of honor and status that titles represented. The enormous cost — and meager returns — of these offices makes it clear that wealthy members of the Old Regime bourgeoisie were willing to sacrifice lucrative business and investment opportunities for noble status alone. The average position required payment of more than 50,000 *livres*, or enough to feed, house, and clothe 200 rural families for a year.[9]

A central conclusion, therefore, of this revisionist research is that far from the two distinct and mutually hostile classes of Marxist lore, the nobility and bourgeoisie of the Ancien Régime look more and more as though they were a single social group. It is easy, of course, to exaggerate this convergence; there clearly was an enormous social difference between a nobleman with a million acres of choice land and a middling lawyer with a handful of clients. Still, the elite sections of both groups seemed to grow increasingly alike as the eighteenth century wore on, and their similarity creates insurmountable problems for the historiographical tradition that focused on class struggle.

Not only were the nobility and bourgeoisie alike in socio-economic terms; historians increasingly found that they resembled each other culturally and intellectually as well. In some ways, the nobility seems to have been more "bourgeois" than the bourgeoisie. Based on an extensive reading of the nobility's *cahiers de doléances*, statements of grievances requested by the King in 1789, the prominent French historian Guy Chaussinand-Nogaret showed that aristocrats had steeped themselves in the philosophy of the Enlightenment, traditionally considered a bourgeois ideology. The *cahiers* revealed spokesmen for the nobility as deeply hostile to the Bourbon monarchy and eager to establish a representative government in which the talented would be free to rise to the top. Noblemen, of course, saw themselves as comprising that talented group. Still, in the months before the revolution began, they advocated the rudiments of a liberal state, one that protected the individual's natural rights. Influenced by the ideas of Locke and Montesquieu, they took these positions in an effort to reduce the monarchy's power to impose taxes and rule without their consent.[10]

Meanwhile, the bourgeois *cahiers de doléances* were, if anything, less "enlightened" than those of the nobility. On the whole, however, there seems to have been a remarkable ideological convergence between the groups during the years before the Revolution began. Some of the reasons for this commonality stem from the associations and activities of what Jürgen Habermas has called the expanded "public sphere" of the eighteenth century. In this sphere, individuals whose ancestors had confined their ideas to the private realms of manor and court now came together to express themselves openly in what came to be known as "public opinion."[11]

The institutions that permitted such expression began modestly with salons in the relative privacy of the home, but they soon moved outward into cafés, academies, lodges, and clubs. These emerging forums of public opinion exhibited a certain egalitarianism by including educated — and generally well-to-do — members of both nobility and bourgeoisie.[12] In these settings, individuals within the two groups developed political philosophies and ideological perspectives that cannot be distinguished by class. The Enlightenment discourse shared by all the fellows of these associations — whether noble or bourgeois — combined with their common status as owners of propertied wealth, made them into a largely unified elite. Differences of status that continued to divide members of the noble and non-noble elites paled in comparison to the divisions *within* the nobility between wealthy proprietors and modest squires and within the bourgeoisie between owners of large landed estates and middling merchants.[13]

These conclusions make clear that, leaving aside the peasantry, the significant divisions of eighteenth-century French society existed not between a nobility and bourgeoisie, but *within* each of those misnamed and somewhat anachronistic categories. The interests and ideas of the well-to-do and well-educated, noble and non-noble alike, increasingly converged, while those of the middling and lower echelons of the two groups grew further apart. Colin Lucas has found that declining members of each category, especially members of the lesser nobility and bourgeois office holders, were particularly pinched economically in the 1780s; they increasingly felt excluded from the elite circles occupied by members the wealthy nobility and prosperous middle class.[14] The petty nobility and middle bourgeoisie, Lucas maintained, were the two groups most strongly opposed to the government during the political crisis of the later 1780s. Their mounting mutual hostility as well as their resentment against those above them did much to polarize the political situation in 1789.

The conflicts surrounding these lesser categories of the nobility and bourgeoisie appear to open the possibility of a modified social interpretation based on class, namely that the revolution was caused, at least in part, by the antagonism of these groups to each other and to the crown. The problem is that there is no evidence that members of either middling group helped to spark the revolution in the fall of 1788.

Historians widely believe that the revolutionary momentum began in September 1788 when opposition erupted against the Parlement of Paris's decree that the Estates General should be convened according to its organization forms of 1614, the last time this medieval representative body had met. Traditionally, the Estates had been divided into three separate chambers, one for each of the three orders of the realm: the Clergy, Nobility, and the Third Estate or commoners. It was this structure, one that confined the commoners to just one-third of the votes, that the Parlement sought to maintain. Although there was little opposition to calling the Estates General, the Parlement's attempt to revive its medieval character evoked considerable dissent: the Third Estate was much larger, richer and more powerful than it had been in 1614. To give its members only one-third of the vote in an assembly convened to resolve the state's fiscal impass seemed, at least to some, grossly unfair.

Georges Lefebvre and others associated with the Marxist school maintained that opposition to the announced structure of the Estates General marked the beginning of a bourgeois revolution, the event that made 1789 a social revolution. The nobility may have opened the revolutionary door by forcing the king to revive the Estates General, Lefebvre wrote, but it was the bourgeoisie that actually made the upheaval happen by demanding the "doubling of the Third." The forms of 1614 should, they declared, give way to a more modern representative body in which the Third Estate would control half of the votes.

The problem with this argument is that members of the bourgeoisie were not the exclusive, or even principal, leaders of the effort to double the Third. In a powerful critique of Lefebvre, Elizabeth L. Eisenstein showed that according to the historian's own evidence, "a loose coalition of men *drawn from all three estates* provided the initial impetus for the protest movement [against the Parlement of Paris]."[15] Those most prominent in the effort to ensure equal representation for the Third Estate came from the Second, or noble, Estate. They included, in the words of Lefebvre himself, "great noblemen [such as] the duc de La Rochefoucauld-Liancourt, the marquis de La Fayette, the marquis de Condorcet, and certain [aristocratic] members of the Parliament, Adrien du Port, Hérault de Séchelles, Le Pelletier de Saint-Fargeau." Other leaders Lefebvre identified included wealthy bankers like the Labordes, a family linked by marriage to the high nobility, as well as eminent academicians such as the lawyer Target and "jurists and writers of note."[16] Without realizing he was doing so, Lefebvre identified as the originators of the so-called bourgeois revolution that very unified noble and non-noble elite that had taken shape earlier in the eighteenth century.

It seems, then, that what had begun as an aristocratic protest movement consonant with traditional institutional forms was transformed into something far more radical by leading members of a cross-class elite. Men as wealthy and powerful as these were unlikely to have been moved primarily by social and economic grievances. The ideological commitments forged in the academies, philosophical societies, and Masonic lodges of the late Enlightenment must have played a central role in moving this convergent group of titled aristocrats and bourgeois barristers to demand equal representation for commoners. In their view, the Estates General ought to be constructed anew.

The overall thrust of the historiographical developments summarized above is compelling and difficult to refute, so much so that one of the few remaining unapologetically Marxist historians of the Revolution, George Comninel, accepts virtually all of them.[17] Still, the solidity of the new consensus, not to say orthodoxy, raises the question of why there was a revolution at all. If it is no longer possible to separate the nobility and the bourgeoisie into two antagonistic classes locked in struggle, then what could have caused such an unprecedented upheaval? Surely events of that magnitude do not happen by accident. The efforts of the past dozen years or so to answer this question have shifted the search for the causes of the French Revolution first from the social to the political realm and then from the political to the cultural, ideological, and linguistic one. These developments have produced a rich and complex literature, much of it shaped by the vaunted "linguistic turn" of the past half-dozen years.[18]

François Furet has been the guiding intellectual light in this turn to the political and ideological; in his own massive body of work and the volumes he has inspired, his questions now stand at the center of research and debate on the origins and meaning of 1789. In particular, Furet and his followers have been interested in discovering what it was about the political culture of the Old Regime that made the revolution — and especially the Terror — possible. Whereas most republican and Marxist historians of the past century have avoided this two-year period of revolutionary radicalism and violence — or sought to explain it away — Furet has made the Terror a fundamental concern of his work. For him, "the central enigma of the [Revolution] was its egalitarian and democratic radicalism." What, he wants to know, were the origins of this unprecedented phenomenon and why did the revolutionary leadership find it so difficult to control?[19]

One key result of Furet's focus on the Terror has been to diminish the reverence for the Revolution that had long been central to its historiography. Scholars now view leaders of the Revolution, especially the most radical among them, far more critically than at any time since the mid-nineteenth century. And the violence and suffering associated with these events are no longer swept under the rug. Donald Sutherland has argued that the revolution produced so much hardship that it must be seen as creating as its mirror image a counterrevolution more widespread and more powerful than most students of 1789 have been willing to admit. Revolution and counterrevolution were inextricably linked, each shaping the other with disastrous consequences for liberal and libertarian ideals.[20]

In distancing themselves emotionally from the leaders and ideology of 1789, historians have registered in scholarly form their own disillusionment with revolution itself. The Soviet invasions of 1956 and 1968 along with Krushchev's critique of Stalinism tarnished for a great many intellectuals much of the Russian Revolution's remaining luster; revelations about the Great Leap Forward and the brutality of Mao's Cultural Revolution did much the same thing for China. It has been a long time, moreover, since many western intellectuals believed in the promise of Fidel's Cuba, and few are unaware of the evils Khomeini has wrought. Furet has made quite explicit the connection between his distaste for Bolshevism and his critique not only of the Marxist interpretation of 1789, but of attempts to explain away the Terror as the revolutionaries' understandable response to war and counterrevolution.[21]

Not surprisingly, scholarly treatments of twentieth-century revolutions have expressed these emotional and ideological developments all the more. Joseph W. Esherick has written recently that the Chinese Revolution "was not a Liberation, but (for most) the replacement of one form of domination with another."[22] The historiography of the Soviet Union has taken a similar turn, as have many western accounts of Third World revolutions and movements for national liberation. For France, some historians have gone so far in this effort to demythologize the Revolution as to find virtually nothing of merit at all. Simon Schama notoriously suggests that the revolutionaries' terrorist zeal created the political and ideological precedents for the totalitarian regimes of the twentieth century and even of the Holocaust itself.[23]

Although Furet may have inspired Schama, he is not as resolutely hostile to the Revolution as his best-selling colleague in the United States. Furet's position is far more nuanced: for him the Revolution is both the precursor of Soviet absolutism and the founding stone of France' democratic republic, a regime firmly in place since the 1870s. It was Tocqueville's view, and Furet's as well, that the French Revolution created the ingredients for both kinds of regimes, though Furet, like his mentor, devotes far more attention to the democratic despotism revealed so starkly in the Terror.[24]

That event, Furet suggests, following the now-classic argument of his mentor, recapitulated in revolutionary form the work of the Old Regime's absolutist monarchy. In the seventeenth and eighteenth centuries, the Bourbon kings destroyed or rendered politically impotent the intermediary institutions — parliaments, assemblies, the Church — that might have mediated and moderated the increasingly centralized monarchical authority. By the 1780s, only the decrepit shells of these once-powerful aristocratic bastions stood between the people and the state. No one possessed any more power than anyone else, and thus no one could stand up to the crown. Absolutism had produced a democratic despotism in which the equality of condition had robbed the nobility — and the people it was their duty to protect — of the institutions that once had given them political liberty.

The Revolution, according to Furet, did much the same thing by vesting absolute authority in those who claimed to speak for the people and depriving individuals of the ability to speak for themselves. It too became a democratic despotism built on a radical equality of condition. These absolutist tendencies, Furet writes, were inherent in the Revolution right from the beginning: not merely the Bourbon monarchy, but the entire political culture of the Old Regime had prepared the way.

The argument for how it did so is enormously complex; its contours extend beyond politics and culture to ideology, discourse, and the rise of public opinion.[25] For Furet, the key political factor is France's undivided sovereignty, its absolutist power lodged wholly in the king. In this undiluted royal prerogative France differed fundamentally from England, where sovereignty was divided between king and parliament and between the two houses of parliament itself. Individual British subjects possessed political power, some far more than others, and public policy emerged from the play of competing interests and from the power of certain individuals and groups to shape the decisions of state.

In France, by contrast, few centers of power existed outside Versailles, and those that did were weak. The prevailing philosophy of government, moreover, held that the king alone represented the whole of the realm and all power was concentrated in and emanated from him. By the eve of the Revolution, the French polity had been steeped for two centuries in this form of sovereignty; its government and people knew nothing else. Although there was one group of revolutionaries who advocated a British-style government, the overwhelming majority of those who set out in the summer and fall of 1789 to devise a new political system could conceive of sovereignty only as "one and indivisible." The revolutionaries were, of course, not about to reinvest that undivided power in the king, so they gave it over to a single assembly in what was to be a unicameral parliament. In doing so, Furet maintains, leaders created a new form of absolute power in the Constituent Assembly, an institution that would not only devise a new constitution but govern without checks and balances.

The Assembly would rule, moreover, according to the absolutist idea that sovereignty necessarily expressed itself in a single voice; it did not emerge from the competition of interests and the clash of individual centers of power. Thus, by clothing the old concept of undivided sovereignty in revolutionary garb, the leaders of 1789, men who saw themselves as breaking radically with the past, nonetheless adopted "a concept of political sovereignty that owed its characteristics to absolutism: now the people took the place of the king, but it was the same place; pure democracy was substituted for absolute monarchy. Just as in the old sovereign power nothing was left to anything that was not the monarch, so nothing was granted in the new one to anything that was not the people, *or supposed to represent the people*."[26]

Furet's concluding phrase is crucial, for it suggests how a new form of despotism could arise from a revolutionary system whose architects, despite all their innovative intentions, were creatures of the Old Regime. If all power was vested in a unified people, and a particular group achieved success in its claim to represent the people, then that group could exercise absolute control. But why did this revolutionary idea of sovereignty assume a unified people? Why, that is, did the revolutionary sovereign, like the absolutist sovereign, necessarily have to express itself in unison?

The answer, according to Keith Baker and Mona Ozouf, is that given the absolutist context of Old Regime thought, the radically democratic philosophy of Rousseau carried far more weight than the liberal and corporatist views of Montesquieu.[27]

What the revolutionaries learned from Rousseau, Furet and his colleagues maintain, was that in the ideal political system each individual would express not his own particular interests but the general interest; what would emerge from a genuinely democratic consultation was the general will, not a collection of individual desires competing for recognition. Rousseau believed that the English system of representative parliamentary government inhibited the expression of this general will, for that system necessarily divided people into factions that could express only particular interests. Representation thus rendered unity impossible; only a system of direct democracy in which all citizens enjoyed perfect equality could allow the general will to emerge.

Rousseau's philosophy, therefore, was egalitarian but not individualist. It emphasized the common good over individual liberty and stressed that sovereignty ought to be united in the service of a single general will. In this interpretation of Rousseau, the parallels with Old Regime sovereignty are obvious; Rousseau is merely the other side of the absolutist coin. What was dangerous, according to Furet, about the popular Rousseauianism he believes to have been prevalent on the eve of 1789 was its illiberal cast. Once in power, the revolutionaries found it all too easy to submerge individual freedom, little valued during the Ancien Régime, beneath the putative claims of the common good. From here the slope was slippery indeed. Those who exercised political power — and therefore, Furet adds, rhetorical power — would be in a position to define the common good in a way that excluded large numbers of people. Lacking the guarantees of individual rights, the excluded individuals would find themselves vulnerable to arbitrary rule and ultimately to terror itself.

As an historian trained in the national tradition, I am hesitant to apply insights from one revolution's historiography to analysis of another. Still, some of Furet's ideas and approaches may well prove useful for the study of certain other revolutions.[28] In particular, the phenomenon of undivided sovereignty, the monarchy's monopolization of power and decision-making authority, might be an aspect of political culture that makes a society vulnerable under certain circumstances to state breakdown and revolutionary upheaval. Because such societies lack potent intermediary institutions and fail to provide positions of genuine, as opposed to ceremonial, power for members of the elite, their governments can find themselves paralyzed by problems that a more flexible system might be able to solve, or at least muddle through.

In late eighteenth-century France, it wasn't, as Jack Goldstone suggests, just the growing intra-elite competition for scarce government positions and the elites' allergy to higher taxes that helped unravel the state.[29] The wider problem is that the absolutist monarchy had deprived itself of the political institutions and culture of state-elite cooperation that might have allowed influential noblemen and commoners to share not just the glories of power but the burdens and responsibilities of governing. The existence of a parliament in which wide sectors of the elite enjoyed a significant voice in public affairs might have made it possible to reform the fiscal system and thereby prevent the state from falling apart. Essentially no one in 1788 or even 1789 — not even the future regicides — wanted the monarchy to collapse. Thus, given well-functioning institutions and a political culture of shared responsibility, Louis XVI might have been saved, despite all of the demographic and economic pressures Goldstone's remarkable discussion of the French Revolution chronicles so well.

Such a system of shared political power and responsibility might also have avoided the alienation of intellectuals, a problem Tocqueville gives significant, albeit exaggerated, importance.[30] For Tocqueville, one of the most troubling aspects of the Enlightenment period was the lack of institutions that might have enabled "men of letters" to contribute to political life, directly or indirectly, through vital representative bodies. Such institutions, he maintained, would have moved the *philosophes* to moderate their utopian and revolutionary views by enabling them to work for practical measures of reform. Tocqueville doubtless goes too far in concluding from these observations that intellectuals played a key causal role in bringing down the Old Regime. But it remains likely nonetheless that France's system of undivided sovereignty offered political thinkers little incentive to adapt their ideas to the immediate situation and eschew all-embracing revolutionary schemes.

These reflections on undivided sovereignty are relevant perhaps to analyses of the Russian and Iranian Revolutions, among others.[31] In Russia of the late nineteenth and early twentieth century, not unlike France of the late eighteenth, the Czar's monopoly of political power and the consequent exclusion of the elites doubtless contributed to the regime's inability to undertake essential reforms or even to enlist needed support in moments of crisis. Clearly, the existence of undivided sovereignty did not cause the Russian Revolution, nor did it equal military conflict or peasant discontent in importance. Still, without it, everything from the conduct of the First World War to the government's response to internal opposition may well have been very different.

A similar case can be made for the Shah's Iran. By the late 1970s Mohamad Reza Pahlavi had made his regime extremely vulnerable through his ruthless effort to deprive the country of institutions that might have mediated among the state, the Islamic clergy, and the mass of the population. John Foran's discussion of revolutionary theory in *Contention*, 5, suggests as well that Iran's undivided sovereignty alienated the country's intelligentsia and created a nightmare version of the men of letters on whom Tocqueville blamed much of the French revolutionary radicalism. Commenting on Tim McDaniel's *Autocracy, Modernization, and Revolution in Russia and Iran* (1991), Foran writes that the Shah's policies "cut the intelligentsia off from society; the intelligentsia became oppositional, though dogmatic and rigid, highly sectarian and polarized."[32]

Beyond the phenomenon of undivided sovereignty and the old regime political culture it spawned, Furet's discussion of the ways in which that culture shaped the leaders of revolution and the political systems they established may be relevant to the situations in Russia and Iran as well. Just as France's Jacobins, born and raised under Bourbon absolutism, rallied after 1789 to Rousseau's singular general will, so the Bolsheviks, unaccustomed to individual liberty, embraced the absolutism of an omnipotent Party-state. Likewise, the Iranian revolutionaries ousted an authoritarian Shah only to replace him with a theocratic dictatorship. In Russia and Iran, as in revolutionary France, there were those who advocated more liberal regimes; but in all three cases the prevailing political cultures conspired with surrounding military and socio-economic circumstances to exclude them from power.

In making these claims about the significance of political culture I mean only to add this phenomenon to the complex mix of revolutionary causation, not to downplay the role of socio-economic and demographic factors. Unfortunately, Furet and his collaborators do not appear to share this interest in keeping the social interpretation alive. The full extent to which Furet's ideological and philosophical inquiries have departed from the once-dominant socioeconomic approach can be seen in a recent volume entitled *A Critical Dictionary of the French Revolution*.[33]

Written for the most part by Furet and Ozouf (there are about a dozen other contributors as well), this thousand-page work provides a revealing overview of the Furet position on the origins and meaning of 1789. The *Critical Dictionary* is as significant for what it ignores as for what it includes. Missing are virtually all the major social groups that contributed to the Revolution or felt its effects: the nobility, clergy, bourgeoisie, peasants, artisans, and women. The *Dictionnaire*, moreover, includes no studies of the *longue durée*, no history from the bottom up, no concern with everyday life and popular culture, and nothing about the production of grain, subsistence crises, or the economy in general, save for some brief entries on taxes, *assignats*, and nationalized land. It is as if the *Annales* school had never existed. Even anthropological history, fashionable in France and elsewhere since in mid 1970s, finds no place in this volume. There is virtually no mention of rituals and symbolic representations, or the meanings expressed by clothing, gestures, and the human body itself. In the effort to break with the Marxist social interpretation, Furet *et al.* have created a history with the society, economy, and popular culture left out.

But these omissions are hardly inadvertent; it is not as though Furet and Ozouf know nothing of the social, economic, and cultural history written during the past fifty years. Indeed, Ozouf has published a brilliant anthropological history of the revolutionary festivals.[34] The aim of the *Dictionnaire* seems almost to display the extent to which the historiography of the Revolution has been reoriented toward politics, language, ideology, and political philosophy over the past decade. Furet devotes nearly half of his *Dictionnaire* to ideas in general and to the particular notions of a privileged cadre of historians and philosophers: Burke, Fichte, Kant, Jaurès, Michelet, and Taine.

With all this attention to philosophy and philosophers it is no wonder that so much has been left out. One of the most unfortunate omissions is a discussion of the recent — and highly interesting — feminist analyses of the origins and meaning of the French Revolution. In some ways the new feminist work runs parallel to Furet's in its emphasis on the nullification of individual rights, in particular the rights of women. Joan B. Landes, among others, has shown that aristocratic women of the Old Regime possessed a certain power and standing that the male leaders of the French Revolution took away and then refused to extend to any other women.[35] Before 1789, women who inherited noble estates not only could administer them in their own names, but in some regions they enjoyed the right to vote in local and regional assemblies that such property conferred. As late as 1661, aristocratic women could still be given titles of nobility in their own right, and they exercised the prerogatives of their rank by sitting as members of the *parlements* that dispensed justice under the Old Regime. Dozens of noble women retained seats in various provincial *parlements* until the eve of the French Revolution itself.[36]

Such privileges accrued, it need be said, only to a tiny minority, but a considerably larger group of prominent women enjoyed extensive informal power and influence in what Landes, borrowing from Habermas, calls the "absolutist public sphere" of the late seventeenth and eighteenth centuries.[37] This sphere consisted largely of urban salons organized and animated by aristocratic women. In these salons intellectual figures, writers, gentlemen, high government officials and other members of the urban elite came together for conversation and conviviality in a setting distinct from the much more restricted and hierarchic life of the royal court. All conversation revolved around the female *salonière* or hostess, who in animating her salon established standards of dress and comportment that her mostly male guests were expected to observe. Thus, in founding these intimate theaters of social and intellectual life, women of the Old Regime not only created an arena of public experience that had never existed before, they made themselves the cultural arbiters of an emerging polite society of cultivation and taste.

Such female prominence, Landes maintains, began to annoy many of the male writers and Enlightenment thinkers who congregated in the woman-centered salons. These men of letters came to associate the *salonières* with the royal mistresses and confidants, the ladies in waiting and female conspirators, whom "enlightened" men widely believed to exercise undue power at court. In the hands of Jean-Jacques Rousseau, the prophet of virtue, purity, and modesty for women, this protest against the aristocratic woman's cultural and political power became a critique of the Old Regime itself. French society and politics were corrupt, Rousseau maintained, because they had become effeminate. Such was not the case, the *philosophe* added, in republican Geneva whose all-male clubs Rousseau depicted as bastions of virility in which "conversation becomes less polished, [but] reasons take on more weight."[38]

By condemning the absolutist monarchy for empowering women and emasculating men while praising the republic for its grave masculine

reason, Rousseau did much, Landes argues, to shape the later discourse
and action of the French Revolution.[39] After 1789, and especially after
1792 when the republic was declared, revolutionaries set out to eliminate
all remnants of an aristocratic culture they believed to be decadent and
corrupt. They resolved to replace an effeminate monarchy of artifice and
ornament with a virile republic of virtue and reason. To do so, the
revolutionaries undertook to banish women from all public life.

In 1793, the Revolution's Jacobin leaders dissolved political organizations composed mainly of women and then banned women from
attending any political meetings at all. That same year, Olympe de
Gouges, author of the "Declaration of the Rights of Woman," was sent
to the guillotine for supposed acts of treason, while another early
feminist, Théroigne de Méricourt, was publicly whipped.[40] In 1795,
women were even forbidden to sit in the visitor's gallery of the National
Convention, and after a violent demonstration in which women were
prominently involved, the Convention singled them out for a special
kind of punishment, namely confinement to the home: "Be it decreed
that all women . . . found in the streets, gathered in groups of more than
five, will be dispersed by armed force and arrested until public calm is
restored."[41]

This was the harshest, most repressive side of the Revolution's
treatment of women, the most negative consequence of the desire to keep
women from the public sphere. But there was another side to this
"privatization" of women, one that was much more positive. For even as
revolutionary leaders consigned women to the home, they joined with
feminists in declaring that women had something of unique importance to
do there. The role of women in the new revolutionary order was to produce
the virtuous and patriotic citizens who would people it. Women, especially
women of the middling classes, were exalted for their status as "republican
mothers," for the crucial part they would play in nurturing and educating
the Republic's new-born citizens.[42]

There are no simple conclusions to be drawn from a consideration
of 1789 that pays due attention to women and feminist analysis. On the
one hand, Landes and others are surely right to say that the Revolution —
especially when the Napoleonic Code is taken into account — did little in
the immediate to foster women's rights. But on the other, its ideals of
liberty and equality as well as the political participation — albeit mostly
male — encouraged by the Revolution did much to inspire the feminist
movements of the nineteenth century and to convince large numbers of

women that no democracy was worth its name if it excluded half the human race.

Regardless of how one views the French Revolution's effect on women, the new feminist historiography of 1789 and other works sensitive to gender suggest what might be attempted for other revolutions.[43] Although Timothy Wickham-Crowley takes note of the extent to which women have become involved in recent Latin American movements, and other commentators have referred to women's participation elsewhere, the comparative study of revolutions has largely ignored gender.[44] In part this absence reflects the structuralist tendencies of many of its practitioners, scholars who appear to believe that the actions and beliefs of the revolutionary contenders can be safely left to "area specialists" and narrative historians. Clearly, structuralism has its limits; in John Foran's words it "needs to be supplemented with more attention to the perspectives and outlooks of the varied social forces that engage in revolutions."

These forces certainly include women, whose role in revolutions has been anything but passive. Historians and social scientists need to look in detail at the parts women played in revolutionary movements and examine the extent to which they shaped a movement's overall goals. Analysts ought as well to consider whether women emerged as independent actors in a given revolution and the circumstances under which women tend to strike out on their own. We need to know how male and female revolutionaries viewed one another and how those perceptions shaped their respective conceptions of the task ahead.

It is not enough, of course, merely to study the roles and ideology of women in revolution; we must, as Lynn Hunt and a few others have done, take gender as a category of analysis.[45] Is it common for old regimes to be dismissed, as in the French case, for being effeminate while revolutionaries credit themselves with restoring the country to seriousness and virility? And do such gendered commentaries help us better understand the causes and outcomes of the upheaval in question? Hunt shows how the art and literature of eighteenth-century France both registered the decline of the King's paternal authority and helped to undermine it.[46] Her "family romances" in which fathers are emasculated or killed and brothers take their place, did not, of course, cause the French Revolution in any direct sense; but they did help strip the King of his all-important standing as the nation's paterfamilias and deprive him of the legitimacy that might have prevented his state from falling apart.

Useful as well is an analysis of the ways in which the symbols of revolution are gendered. Maurice Agulhon has found that liberty and the other moderate virtues of 1789 found representation in female form, especially as Greek goddesses. But when it came to the supposedly higher stages of the revolution, stages characterized, as Hunt puts it, "by the force and unity of the people," the imagery was unambiguously male: Hercules wielding his club.[47] I suspect analogous forms of symbolism might be found in the Russian Revolution and its aftermath and that analysis of their gendered meaning could enrich our understanding of the causes and outcomes of that event. It seems likely, moreover, that the Chinese Revolution exhibited some gendered narratives of its own; Jeffrey Wasserstrom's essay in *Contention*, 7, announces a forthcoming paper entitled "Was There a 'Family Romance' of the Chinese Revolution?"[48]

As the French historiography makes clear, there is much exciting work to be accomplished on women and gender; the new emphasis on culture offers hope that more of it will be done. A revitalized social interpretation can do the same by including women as a key category of analysis and by gendering the traditional sociological classifications of peasants, artisans, nobles, and bourgeois. It will be useful to know how female members of each group compared in their behavior and ideas to the males.

Important as well will be the effort to assess the extent to which a revolution affected women differently from men. This question is complex; as we have seen, the French Revolution appears in the short run to have set a great many women back, whereas from the perspective of the late nineteenth century its legacy is far more positive. Something similar can be said of the French Revolution as a whole. For despite the evils of the Terror, the counterrevolution, and the deprivation of women's rights, no analysis of 1789 can be wholly convincing if it neglects to explain how its constellation of actors and ideas managed nonetheless to bequeath to future generations and to people around the world not only the desire for political liberty and social equality but the belief that both could be achieved. Nor can any discussion of 1789 that omits its social origins do full justice to the event. One irony of the historiographical debate is that William Doyle, one of those who argued most convincingly for a largely political interpretation, has recently urged us to remember that the cultural and political underpinnings of the Revolution took shape in a context of social and economic change. The development of salons, clubs, academies, and literary societies, Doyle writes, required the existence of **growing** numbers of educated French men and women who possessed the leisure to engage in political and philosophical debate. Only an expanding economy could account for France's widening reading public, and the reasons and implications of this expansion need to be taken into account.[49]

At the same time, we must recognize that if economic expansion constituted the whole of the story, a revolution would have been unlikely. Something else must have been occurring in French economic and social life to create the potential for widespread discontent. It is here that Jack Goldstone's recent work makes a pivotal contribution. His *Revolution and Rebellion in the Early Modern World* (1991) possesses the great virtue of explaining how the French economy could have expanded significantly in the eighteenth century while creating the conditions of possibility for revolution. That he does so without resorting to discredited Marxist ideas about a rising bourgeoisie or to J-curves of frustrated expectations represents a major achievement. Nor does he consider it enough to demonstrate that France failed to expand as fast as England or that the French economy experienced growth but not development; such a scenario is commonplace in world history and hardly the stuff of revolution. What Goldstone managed to do is show the extent to which demographic pressures and the troubles they provoked made economic gains pale by comparison.

Like England in the seventeenth century, France in the eighteenth experienced a surge in population that endangered virtually every aspect of its fragile agrarian society. According to Goldstone, the demographic upswing that began in earnest around 1730 had by the end of the century threatened food supplies, fueled the peasantry's traditional hunger for land, raised prices and rents, lowered real wages, and fostered a variety of conflicts within the elite. The demographic growth produced a youthful population with a propensity to rebel, and perhaps most damaging of all, it evoked an inflation that overwhelmed the state's inflexible system of taxation and left the monarchy perpetually short of funds.[50]

France's inflationary spiral, Goldstone writes, resulted from the inability of the country's agricultural output to keep pace with its steady population growth. The supply of food, therefore, lagged behind demand, leading to higher prices for consumers. This development harmed the growing number of peasants who possessed too little land to ensure their subsistence, but it failed to increase prices and rents fast enough to allow more than a few of the most prosperous landowners to keep ahead of inflation. As individuals and families were forced to spend more of their income on basic subsistence needs, less remained for other kinds of purchases, especially since the prices of manufactured goods stayed relatively high owing to overseas demand and rising urban incomes.

As a result, the great majority of rural dwellers found themselves in difficult economic circumstances. The commercial and manufacturing sector, by contrast, had become fairly robust by the latter decades of the eighteenth century, a time when the agricultural economy virtually ceased to grow. The relative value of farm output, therefore, lagged considerably behind that of trade and industry, creating a certain prosperity among large-scale merchants and manufacturers that contrasted with a widespread penury in the countryside.

Beyond the difficulties of food supply and high grain prices, this imbalance between the agricultural and commercial-industrial sectors led, Goldstone convincingly shows, to a seriously underfunded royal treasury. Goldstone's discussion here is pivotal to our understanding of why the state ultimately dissolved and ranks among the most important of his many contributions. Inflation, he writes, had driven the state's expenses sharply upward, but the French tax system, tied as it was to the country's tepid agricultural economy, proved incapable of increasing revenue fast enough to match the rising governmental costs. Taxable farm incomes grew too slowly to meet the king's mounting needs, especially since many of the largest growers enjoyed significant tax exemptions as holders of noble seigneuries.

These agricultural exemptions were not, however, the worst of the problem. Thanks to long-standing agreements between the crown and France's major municipalities, merchants and manufacturers enjoyed fiscal privileges more significant than those cherished by a great many noble lords. These urban exemptions were particularly damaging to royal finances, for they denied the state revenues from the most vital sector of the economy. The problem became particularly acute in the last third of the eighteenth century, when the costs of two overseas wars and a series of harvest failures raised the state's revenue requirements all the more. By that point the contrast between an expanding commercial-industrial realm and a stagnating agricultural one was greater perhaps than ever before. Thus, at the moment when the government most needed to raise its revenues, the sector that provided the bulk of them was least able to pay. Prevented from adequately taxing the expanding commercial-manufacturing enterprises, the king had no alternative but to increase borrowing and attempt to boost taxes on the land.

By taking both these steps, the crown worsened its fiscal plight owing to the added cost of debt service while doing little to shore up its political support: in an age of inflation, rural elites clung to their tax exemptions with particular zeal. Had the King been able to raise taxes on industry to the level prevailing in England, Goldstone maintains, he could have avoided the fiscal crisis of 1787-89. What prevented Louis from doing so were a series of political and perceptual constraints. Goldstone does a good job of outlining — if not explaining — the former but mentions the latter, perhaps more crucial, constraints only in passing. We learn that all major towns were exempt from the *taille*, the basic tax of the realm, but not why the crown found it impossible to abolish those exemptions even in a period of dire need.

To give such an explanation would have required Goldstone to delve into the culture and ideology of the Old Regime, phenomena he wants to dismiss as nothing more than bit players on a stage dominated by material forces. That he fails to enter this realm and thereby to support a crucial part of his argument reveals the limits of his predominantly materialist approach. To observe the crucial non-material forces at work we can turn to William H. Sewell, Jr., who shows that the very foundation of the Old Regime rested on an ideology that "pictured society as a set of privileged corporate bodies held together by the supreme will of a semi-sacerdotal king."[51] The privileges residing in each of these bodies constituted, as Sewell puts it, "a set of laws peculiar to itself."[52] The role of the monarch was to blend all of these separate private entities, each with its own particular rules, into a unified state. Without his central control, the kingdom would inevitably dissolve into a corporate war of all against all as each individual body sought to maintain its privileges against the variety of rival claims. The state could not exist, therefore, without a monarch of undisputed power, for all the institutions of the realm depended upon that power to preserve the order they each needed but were unable by themselves to produce.

This necessary dependence on the King granted him absolute power, but only in theory. His position at the pinnacle of the corporate state depended on the maintenance of the form of society it implied and with it all the privileges that each body enjoyed. To deprive them of the very privileged status it was his duty to protect would destroy his raison d'être and undermine the foundation of his power. Moreover, since the ideology of Enlightenment opposed the existence of corporate privilege, any effort on the King's part to compromise it would make him appear to side with the enemy. It was difficult in the extreme, therefore, for the Crown to do away with the municipalities' long-standing privileges, even as bankruptcy loomed.

Heightening this ideological obstacle to raising taxes on cities and the merchants and manufacturers who worked there was a perceptual problem that itself had ideological roots. As Goldstone himself notes, the physiocratic thought so influential among reformers and government bureaucrats alike held that all the nation's wealth resided in the land. Since Louis XVI's leading economic advisors largely shared this belief, they were unlikely even to perceive that taxing commerce and manufacture could help solve the state's fiscal crisis. Land was where the potential revenues lay; there was little sense in taxing anything else. It was ideology, then, both corporate and physiocratic, that prevented the monarchy from raising taxes on industry and trade, dooming it not only to fall into bankruptcy but to alienate rural dwellers by proposing heightened taxes on them. If Goldstone is correct in saying that higher levies on French industry "would have allowed the Crown to avoid the fiscal crisis of 1787-1789" (p. 208), then the ideological forces that prevented the state from raising those taxes were central to the regime's ultimate collapse. Ideology, therefore, played a major role in causing the state breakdown that led to the French Revolution itself.

Like the older social interpretations that Goldstone's book does so much to supersede, it too cannot stand alone without taking account of the crucial cultural and ideological forces at work. Ideology does not come into play, as Goldstone claims, only after the Revolution has already begun; it is present all along as crucial to any understanding of how and why 1789 came about. Attention to culture and ideology helps explain why members of the noble and non-noble elites came together as a single class in the years before 1789; why the monarchy failed to surmount the fiscal crisis of the 1780s; why liberal government proved so difficult to achieve; and why women's rights took a turn for the worse after 1792. Discussion of politics and ideology, moreover, reveals the extent to which the existence of undivided sovereignty can make states vulnerable — given severe social and economic grievances — to breakdown and collapse. Just as it makes little sense, therefore, to dismiss social interpretations in favor of purely political and ideological accounts, so do social interpretations appear hollow, even mechanical, if they fail to give culture and ideas due causal weight.

NOTES

1   Alfred Cobban, *The Social Interpretation of the French Revolution* (Cambridge: Cambridge University Press, 1964).

2   Furet's most important works include *Interpreting the French Revolution* (Cambridge: Cambridge University Press, 1981 [1978]); *Revolutionary France, 1770-1880* (London: Blackwell, 1992 [1988]); *A Critical Dictionary of the French Revolution*, with Mona Ozouf (Cambridge, MA: Harvard University Press, 1989 [1988]); *The French Revolution and the Creation of Modern Political Culture*, ed. with Mona Ozouf (Oxford: Pergamon Press, 1989).

3   For a superb analysis of the evolution of the English historiography, see Robert Brenner, *Merchants and Revolution: Commercial Change, Political Conflict, and London's Overseas Traders, 1550-1653* (Princeton: Princeton University Press, 1993), postscript. The principal revisionist works include: Conrad Russell, *The Origins of the English Civil War* (London: Macmillan, 1973); *Parliaments and English Politics* (Oxford: Clarendon Press, 1979); and *Unrevolutionary England, 1603-1642* (Hambledon: Hambledon Press, 1990); Kevin Sharpe, ed., *Faction and Parliament: Essays on Early Stuart History* (Oxford: Clarendon Press, 1978) and "The Personal Rule of Charles I," in *Before the English Civil War*, ed. Howard Tomlinson (New York: St. Martin's Press, 1984). See also the interesting review article by John Kenyon, "Revisionism and Post-Revisionism in Early Stuart England," *Journal of Modern History* 64 (December 1992): 686-99.

4   See Edward Friedman, Paul Pickowicz, and Mark Selden, *Chinese Village, Socialist State* (New Haven: Yale University Press, 1991); Philip C.C. Huang, "The Paradigmatic Crisis in Chinese Studies: Paradoxes in Social and Economic History," *Modern China* 17, 3 (July 1991): 299-341; Mark Selden, "Yenan Communism Reconsidered," forthcoming in *Modern China*, Spring 1994; Lyman P. Van Slyke, "Rethinking the Chinese Revolution," forthcoming in *Modern China*, Spring 1994.

5   Virtually all the papers given in a recent UCLA conference on the Chinese Revolution referred to the historiography of 1789 and especially to the work of François Furet. See the forthcoming issue of *Modern China*, Spring 1994. In addition, a great many of the essays published in *Conten-*

tion refer to the French Revolution even though they are mostly devoted to revolutions elsewhere in the world.

6   Robert Forster, *The Nobility of Toulouse in the Eighteenth Century* (Baltimore: Johns Hopkins University Press, 1960), quoted in William Doyle, *The Origins of the French Revolution* (New York: Oxford University Press, 1980), p. 17. I am indebted here to Doyle's lucid analysis. See also George V. Taylor, "Types of Capitalism in Eighteenth-Century France," *English Historical Review* 79 (1964): 478-97; D.M.G. Sutherland, *France, 1789-1815* (New York: Oxford University Press, 1986), pp. 16-19.

7   Betty Behrens, "Nobles, Privileges and Taxes in France at the End of the Ancien Régime," *Economic History Review* XV (1962-63): 451-75.

8   Sutherland, *France*, 17.

9   Sutherland, *France*, 17.

10   Guy Chaussinand-Nogaret, *The French Nobility of the Eighteenth Century: From Feudalism to Enlightenment* (Cambridge: Cambridge University Press, 1985 [1976]); Denis Richet, "Autour des origines idéologiques lointaines de la Révolution française: élites et despotisme," *Annales E.S.C.* 24 (1969): 1-23.

11   See Jürgen Habermas, *The Structural Transformation of the Public Sphere: An Inquiry into a Category of Bourgeois Society* (London: Polity Press, 1989 [1962]), (French trans. 1978). For Habermas, the public sphere was necessarily bourgeois; French and American historians of the Revolution and its origins have dropped the adjective. See Dena Goodman, "Public Sphere and Private Life: Toward a Synthesis of Current Historiographical Approaches to the Old Regime," *History and Theory* 31 (1992): 1-20.

12   Daniel Roche, *Le siècle des Lumières en province. Académies et académiciens provinciaux, 1680-1789* (Paris: Mouton, 1978).

13   On divisions within the nobility, see Jean Meyer, *La noblesse bretonne au XVIIIe siècle* (Paris: S.E.V.P.E.N, 1966). For the bourgeoisie, see L.R. Berlanstein, *The Barristers of Toulouse in the Eighteenth Century* (Baltimore: Johns Hopkins University Press, 1975).

14   Colin Lucas, "Nobles, Bourgeois, and the Origins of the French Revolution," *Past & Present* 60 (1973): 84-126.

15   Elizabeth L. Eisenstein, "Who Intervened in 1788? A Commentary on *The Coming of the French Revolution*," *American Historical Review*, Oct. 1965: 80. Emphasis added.

16   Georges Lefebvre, *The Coming of the French Revolution* (Princeton: Princeton University Press, 1947 [1939]), pp. 52-53, quoted in Eisenstein, "Who Intervened," 81.

17   George C. Comninel, *Rethinking the French Revolution* (London: Verso Press, 1987).

18   On the linguistic turn, see John F. Toews, "Intellectual History after the Linguistic Turn: The Autonomy of Meaning and the Irreducibility of Experience," *American Historical Review* 92 (October 1987): 879-907.

19   François Furet, "A Commentary," *French Historical Studies* 16, 4 (Fall 1990): 793.

20   The most important statement of the centrality of counterrevolution is Sutherland, *France, 1789-1815*. See also Jacques Solé, *Questions of the French Revolution* (New York: Pantheon, 1989 [1988]).

21   See François Furet, "The Revolutionary Catechism," in *Interpreting the French Revolution*.

22   Joseph Esherick, "Rethinking the Chinese Revolution: Ten Theses," forthcoming in *Modern China*, Spring 1994.

23   See Simon Schama, *Citizens* (New York: Knopf, 1989).

24   Furet elaborates this view most fully in *Interpreting the French Revolution*, part I. Tocqueville's long-neglected argument forms the basis of his *Old Regime and the French Revolution* (New York: Doubleday, 1955 [1856]).

25   In advancing this position, Furet enjoys the company of several talented colleagues: Mona Ozouf and Ran Halévy among others in France, and Keith Baker in the United States. See their respective contributions to the two key volumes of conference papers edited by Keith Baker, *The Political Culture of the Old Regime* (Oxford: Pergamon Press, 1987) and Colin Lucas, *The Political Culture of the French Revolution* (Oxford: Pergamon Press, 1988). See also, Keith Baker, *Inventing the French Revolution* (Cambridge: Cambridge University Press, 1990). For an interesting analysis of the conference that led to the volume of 1987, see Jack R. Censer, "The Coming of a New Interpretation of the French Revolution," *Journal of Social History* 2 (Winter 1987): 298-309.

26   Furet, "Commentary," 801. My emphasis.

27   Keith Baker, "Fixing the French Constitution," in *Inventing the French Revolution*; Mona Ozouf, "L'opinion publique," in *The Political Culture of the Old Regime*, ed. Keith Baker.

28   Jeffrey Wasserstrom, a China specialist, joins me in finding works having to do with the ideology and political culture of eighteenth-century

France useful for the comparative study of revolutions other than France. See his article, "Bringing Culture Back in and Other Caveats: A Critique of Jack Goldstone's Recent Essays on Revolution," *Contention* 3, 2 (Winter 1994).

29   Jack Goldstone, *Revolution and Rebellion in the Early Modern World* (Berkeley: University of California Press, 1991), chapter 3.

30   Tocqueville, *Old Regime*, part III, chapter 1.

31   On Russia and Iran, see Said Amir Arjomand, "Plea for an Alternative View of Revolution," *Contention* 2, 2 (Winter 1993): 171-84. His argument is consonant with the one I suggest here.

32   John Foran, "Revolutionizing Theory/Theorizing Revolution: State, Culture, and Society in Recent Works on Revolution," *Contention* 2, 2 (Winter 1993): 65-88.

33   I am indebted here to Claude Langlois's excellent discussion of the nature and structure of Furet and Ozouf's *Dictionnaire* in "Furet's Revolution," *French Historical Studies* 16, 4 (Fall 1990): 766-76.

34   Mona Ozouf, *Festivals and the French Revolution* (Cambridge, MA: Harvard University Press, 1988 [1976]).

35   Joan Landes, *Women and the Public Sphere in the Age of the French Revolution* (Ithaca: Cornell University Press, 1988).

36   Landes, *Women and the Public Sphere*, 122; Steven C. Hause, *Women's Suffrage and Social Politics in the French Third Republic* (Princeton: Princeton University Press, 1984), pp. 3-4.

37   Landes, *Women and the Public Sphere*, ch. 1.

38   Jean-Jacques Rousseau, "Letter to M. d'Alembert on the Theatre," quoted in Landes, *Women and the Public Sphere*, 87-88.

39   Landes, *Women and the Public Sphere*, chs. 4 and 5.

40   Claire Goldberg Moses, *French Feminism in the Nineteenth Century* (Albany, NY: SUNY Press, 1984), p. 13; Hause, *Women's Suffrage*, 5.

41   Quoted in Moses, *French Feminism*, 14.

42   On the concept of "republican motherhood," see Landes, *Women and the Public Sphere*, 129-38. See also the lucid discussion in Bonnie Smith, *Changing Lives: Women in European History Since 1700* (Lexington, MA: D.C. Heath, 1989), pp. 103-16.

43   Other important works beyond those already cited include Lynn Hunt, *Politics, Culture, and Class in the French Revolution* (Berkeley: University of California Press, 1984); Hunt, *The Family Romance of the French Revolution* (Berkeley: University of California Press, 1992); Jane

Aubray, "Feminism and the French Revolution," *American Historical Review* 80 (1975): 43-62; Sara E. Melzer and Leslie W. Rabine, eds., *Rebel Daughters : Women and the French Revolution* (New York: Oxford University Press, 1992); Darline Gay Levy, Harriet B. Applewhite, and Mary D. Johnson, eds., *Women in Revolutionary Paris, 1789-1795* (Urbana: University of Illinois Press, 1979); Olwen Hufton, "Women in Revolution, 1789-1796," *Past & Present* 53 (1971): 90-108.

44   On Wickham-Crowley, see John Foran, "Revolutionizing Theory," 78-85.

45   See Joan Wallach Scott, "Gender: A Useful Category of Historical Analysis," in Scott, *Gender and the Politics of History* (New York: Columbia University Press, 1988).

46   Hunt, *Family Romance*, esp. chapters 2 and 3.

47   Hunt, *Politics, Culture, and Class*, 98; Maurice Agulhon, *Marianne into Battle: Republican Imagery and Symbolism in France, 1789 to 1880* (Cambridge: Cambridge University Press, 1981 [1979]).

48   Wasserstrom, "Bringing Culture Back In," fn. 17.

49   William Doyle, "Reflections on the Classic Interpretation of the French Revolution," *French Historical Studies* 16, 4 (Fall 1990): 746-48.

50   These comments represent a necessarily abbreviated abstract of an argument Goldstone elaborates over the course of a chapter nearly 180 pages long. See *Revolution and Rebellion*, chapter 3.

51   William H. Sewell, Jr., "Ideologies and Social Revolutions: Reflections on the French Case," *Journal of Modern History* 57, 1 (1985): 62.

52   Sewell, "Ideologies and Social Revolutions," 62.

REVOLUTIONIZING THEORY/THEORIZING REVOLUTIONS:

STATE, CULTURE, AND SOCIETY IN RECENT WORKS ON REVOLUTION

JOHN FORAN

JACK A. GOLDSTONE, *REVOLUTION AND REBEL-LION IN THE EARLY MODERN WORLD* (Berkeley, Los Angeles, and Oxford: University of California Press, 1991)

TIM MCDANIEL, *AUTOCRACY, MODERNIZATION AND REVOLUTION IN RUSSIA AND IRAN* (Princeton: Princeton University Press, 1991)

TIMOTHY P. WICKHAM-CROWLEY, *GUERRILLAS AND REVOLUTION IN LATIN AMERICA. A COMPARA-TIVE STUDY OF INSURGENTS AND REGIMES SINCE 1956* (Princeton: Princeton University Press, 1992)

A reading of recent works on revolutions suggests that we may be entering a period of major advances in methodological, historical, and conceptual terms. Even as ideologists of the right proclaim the end of history, and activists on the left bemoan the harsh realities of the post-Cold War, post-Gulf War New World Order, a new cohort of scholars is emerging to rethink past struggles in fresh ways. The present essay will assess the state of the field through a focus on some key works that collectively illustrate this new thinking, although in differing ways that allow us to highlight some breakthroughs and identify remaining challenges in the sociology of revolution.[1]

Jack A. Goldstone's study of state breakdown across the early modern world, Tim McDaniel's reflections on autocratic modernization in Russia and Iran, and, most recently, Timothy P. Wickham-Crowley's comparative analysis of successful and failed guerrilla insurgencies in Latin America[2] all advance the project of elaborating a better theory of the causes, processes, and to some degree, outcomes, of major revolutions in world history (the knotty problem of defining a revolution has prompted many answers; I am satisfied with Theda Skocpol's combination of mass participation in a project that alters both polity and society as the distinctive criteria of a major, or "social" revolution[3]). Though Goldstone possesses the skills of a demographer, Wickham-Crowley the techniques of a statistician, and McDaniel the craft of a historian, all three write in the general genre of comparative macrosociology and display formidable sociological powers. All likewise create their theories inductively, though of course in engagement with other approaches, and this is what makes their contributions exciting blends of theory and history.[4] Among them they cover a span of more than three centuries, and geographical zones ranging from Europe to Asia, the Middle East to Latin America. Along the way, each proposes a distinctive perspective on the causes of social revolution, and all engage with the complex relationships among state, society, and, increasingly, culture, that characterize much of the new thinking in the human sciences of the last two decades. Through interrogation of the strengths and weaknesses of these projects, the contours of the new ferment in this field will emerge more clearly.

1.

Jack Goldstone's *Revolution and Rebellion in the Early Modern World* is a work of breathtaking scope and ambition which develops a truly novel take on the causes of state breakdown in seventeenth- and eighteenth-century Europe and Asia. In the sociology of revolution, where the basic number of possible approaches is actually quite small, this is no mean achievement in itself. "State breakdown" refers to political crises involving simultaneous loss of legitimacy by the sovereign, elite competition, and popular unrest. Since such crises may be resolved in various ways, they are not necessarily the same as thoroughgoing social revolutions (which entail changes in economy, state, elites, and political cultures). Goldstone asks: Why did early modern states experience cycles of state breakdown in the mid-seventeenth, late eighteenth, and mid-nineteenth centuries, with stability from 1660 to 1760? And why were the causes of state breakdown similar across Europe and Asia, yet their outcomes different in long-run political and economic terms?

The answers, Goldstone argues, lie largely in the long-term, cyclical interactions of demographic growth with social, economic, and political institutions. His key causes:

> Put simply, large agrarian states of this period were not equipped to deal with the impact of steady growth of population that then began throughout northern Eurasia, eventually amounting to population increases in excess of the productivity gains of the land. The implications of this ecological shift went far beyond mere issues of poverty and population dislocation. Pressure on resources led to persistent price inflation. Because the tax systems of most early modern states were based on fixed rates of taxation on people or land, tax revenues lagged behind prices. States thus had no choice but to seek to expand taxation. This was all the more true as population increases led to the expansion of armies and hence to rising real costs. Yet attempts to increase state revenues met resistance from the elites and the populace and thus rarely succeeded in offsetting spiraling expenses. As a result, most major states in the seventeenth century were rapidly raising taxes but were still headed for fiscal crisis (24).

Elites began to scramble for a limited number of positions, while rural and urban popular classes suffered declining real wages. The result: state breakdowns involving bankruptcy, elite rebellions, and popular uprisings based on ideologies of rectification and transformation.

From this it should be clear — and Goldstone takes pains to signal this — that the model is not one of demographic determinism, but rather "a demographic/*structural* analysis" (xxvi, emphasis in the original): Demography's impact on institutions is the key, not demographic trends alone. Far from any simple Malthusianism, which Goldstone criticizes sharply, this perspective investigates the *linkages* between population growth and a wide variety of political and economic developments, some examples of which we will trace below. The model's claims are buttressed in two key ways not usually found together in studies of revolution — the construction of sophisticated quantitative measures and careful comparison of cases. The former is accomplished through elaboration of a "mass mobilization potential" concept showing the combined effects of declining real wages, urban growth, and increasing youthfulness of the population, and a "political stress indicator" capturing state fiscal crisis, elite competition, and the mass mobilization potential of the population. The case studies argue that over the time-span of about a hundred years — three generations — these measures peaked on the eve of the revolutions in 1640 England and 1789 France. They are therefore plausible underlying long-term causes of these state breakdowns (if not actually predictive of the events themselves or their outcomes, as Goldstone realizes). This framework is then applied across a wide range of historical cases, spanning early modern Europe and parts of Asia, where Goldstone's preferred strategy is to note similarities (state breakdowns) in differing contexts (geographic, economic, cultural). The result is a vast research canvas on which to work: "By confronting the historical details and demonstrating previously unrecognized connections between them, comparative history makes its mark" (60). And so Jack Goldstone does.

To get a flavor of this enormous project, we may look at the arguments made about the two main cases, England and France. Goldstone neatly summarizes the historiography of the two cases (64ff., 170ff.), noting that in each case older, Marxist analyses focused on long-term causes (in particular, the dislocating consequences of the growth of capitalism through enclosures and world trade), and revisionists have chipped away at this received wisdom to the point where both revolutions are now sometimes seen as the result of fortuitous combinations of short-term bad luck and mismanagement, chance crises of multiple unrelated causes. Goldstone seeks to appropriate the Marxist emphasis on long-term causes (of a different kind), *and* to re-link these two cases with larger trends across Europe and Asia. Whigs and Marxists see the period from 1500 to 1830 in England as one of "continuous progress" — either toward parliamentary autonomy or capitalist development; Jack Goldstone sees instead cyclic social pressures, with population increase propelling social change from 1500 to 1640, state breakdown in the 1640s and 1680s followed by population and political stability through 1750, in turn followed by more conflict from 1750 to 1832. The relevant sequences of causal processes for

Goldstone went something like this: In the century leading up to the state breakdown of the 1640s, population doubled, the number of gentry tripled, and prices rose five-fold. The Tudor and Stuart monarchies would have needed twelve times their original revenues to keep up with inflation in real terms. Mounting debt led Charles to alienate Scotland and Ireland with revenue schemes, precipitating rebellion overlaid with religious differences. Internally, meanwhile, old elites lost ground as the number of aspirants grew; the Crown could not come near to providing adequate patronage to the sons of old groups and newcomers alike, and localities grew heavily factionalized, as measured by cases of civil litigation, university enrollments, and candidates for parliament. Rising grain prices and falling real wages hurt artisans and shopkeepers. In the midst of these structural pressures, people of the "middling classes" turned to Puritanism as "a cure for social ills" (129): it provided a "culture of discipline," sobriety, and morality in the face of disorders, helping a cross-class alliance unite against the Crown. The state collapsed in the 1640s, devolving into a revolution that was "in part a religious, in part a constitutional, and in part an economic conflict" (145). Its long-term causes, for Goldstone, were the impact of population growth on wages, prices, inflation, elite competition, fiscal crisis for the state, and popular living standards. The crisis of 1688 was contained, on the other hand, due precisely to reduced social mobility and urban growth, stable prices, and rising real wages.

The template provided by England is then tested against other cases, especially France. Here Goldstone enters the list against the Marxists from Soboul to Brenner; the revisionists, led by Furet; and Theda Skocpol, whom he criticizes on a number of points: France was not lagging behind England economically nor was it defeated in war, intra-elite conflict is not explained, and urban unrest is underrated. Goldstone notes that the French population increase of thirty percent from 1700 to 1789 was not faster than in England, Germany, or Russia, but France was more densely populated to begin with. He sorts out the great debate on whether eighteenth-century France was rich or poor by noting that the economy grew quite modestly overall, with dramatic gains in manufacturing and overseas trade offset by a stagnant agriculture. Louis XIV's absolutism was predicated on state expansion rather than on the kind of transformation that England had managed; he needed a prosperous peasantry to keep it afloat and a stable-sized elite. Instead, after 1760, his successors encountered a fiscal crisis as the new non-agricultural wealth could not be taxed, inflation took off, and population growth put pressure on elites. Contra Brenner,

Goldstone notes that most peasants were cash tenants or wage laborers rather than small-holders, and he documents their growing land hunger and vulnerability to price and wage rewards with a careful regional and ecological analysis. Peasants, town-dwellers, and elites alike could not comprehend the fiscal crisis of 1787-89, blaming the state for price rises and shortages. The Enlightenment began as a reformist movement, but it took on a more radical resonance with the failure of the monarchy to cope with the crisis in 1788 over the composition of the Estates-General, and the revolution was on.

Goldstone's model of state breakdown is extended through comparisons involving a number of other cases of early modern, bureaucratic monarchies presiding over agrarian economies. He argues that the Ottoman empire and China were subject to the same overall processes as France and England, and were no less revolutionary in the outcomes of their crises (the jelali revolts and Ming/Ching transition respectively); indeed, they experienced more social structural and political transformation than did their more celebrated Western counterparts. In this way Goldstone deflates exaggerated claims about the extent of change in England and France, and restores to the Asian empires a more balanced view of their trajectories of change than some Western historians have accorded them. Other cases that come in for some attention include those of Meiji Japan, and France, England, and Germany in the nineteenth century. His primary conclusion is that "*the periodic state breakdowns in Europe, China, and the Middle East from 1500 to 1850 were the result of a single basic process. . . .* The main trend was that population growth, in the context of relatively inflexible economic and social structures, led to changes in prices, shifts in resources, and increasing social demands with which agrarian-bureaucratic states could not successfully cope" (459, emphasis in original).

Before I proceed to a critique, one final area of the book is worthy of note. While the model emphasizes material factors in state breakdowns, culture and ideology come to the fore in explaining state reconstruction and revolutionary outcomes. In surveying debates on the role of ideology in the French Revolution, Goldstone notes that Soboul, following Marx, saw the Enlightenment as pro-bourgeois; Furet sees the ideology of the revolution as a veil obscuring true motives; Sewell admits that the Enlightenment did not cause the breakdown but that it deepened the crisis into a revolution; while Skocpol "prefers to emphasize structural constraint over ideological autonomy, holding that political, economic, and social conditions limit which ideologies can succeed" (429). Goldstone sees the resolution of these debates in sorting out the differing roles of ideologies at different phases of a revolution. In the prerevolutionary period, perceptions accumulate that something has "gone wrong," engendering calls for rectification of the old regime or for its transformation into a new order. In the course of revolution, attempts are made to unite diverse class coalitions around slogans such as "Peace and Land" in Russia, "Somoza must go" in Nicaragua, or "Down with the Shah" in Iran. Calls for redistribution by lower orders may be papered over by elite appeals to nationalism, which lead (sometimes through a period of terror) into the outcome/reconstruction phase. Ideology is also invoked to account for divergent outcomes among cases: the English and French Revolutions challenged monarchies to the core; the monarchies survived, but absolute power was limited. In the Ottoman empire and China, there were political and economic changes but "little further innovation, and their societies stagnated" (454). Counter-Reformation Spain, too, was "throttled by state-enforced *cultural conformity*, whereby states increased their domestic authority at the expense of future vitality" (454, emphasis in original). France and England stand out by their high levels of "ideological tension," so "their postbreakdown states did not harden and stagnate, but instead showed a continuing dynamic evolution" (454).

As with any rich and provocative work, there is much here with which to take issue. We might begin with issues raised by the treatment of culture just discussed. Goldstone's pragmatic/realistic conception of radical ideology as a common sense response to political and economic dislocation is a fair first approximation of an approach to the problem, but one which is ultimately a bit mechanical in relating ideas to social structural processes. It likewise centers largely on elite activities, acknowledging little role for ordinary citizens to play in shaping political culture. His attempt to blend material and ideological factors into a single analysis is also admirable, but he largely violates his own prescription, separating out the two kinds of factors by downplaying the cultural in the causation of state breakdowns, and the material in their outcomes. Modernizationist assumptions color the comparison of East and West, where the crucial factor appears to be the West's "eschatological view of history, rooted in the Judeo-Christian tradition" (446); are we to believe that culture prevented China, Spain, and the Ottoman empire from meeting the challenge of world capitalism? Apparently we are, for in a sweeping final chapter we are told that "The success of the West lies in a combination of two factors, both of which emerged in complex and gradual fashion: personal freedom based on toleration, broad civic participation, and protection of individual rights; and capitalist economic organization" (485). This prescription for success is then extended as an invitation to the Third World as an alternative to revolutions which rarely achieve their goals. This too seems to lose sight of the variable effects of capitalism in time and space, and to lay the blame for underdevelopment on cultural differences. A more effective approach might have been to relate the material to the cultural at *all* phases of the process, for *all* cases.

In parallel fashion, the extended debate with Marxist explanations that runs through the text sometimes misses opportunities for fruitful combination. Goldstone emphatically rejects the revisionists' destruction of long-term causal models of revolution, but is equally determined to distance himself from neo-Marxist alternatives. In this he is not always unambiguously successful. He is brilliant, for example, in showing, contra Barrington Moore and Richard Lachman, that the cause of landlessness in pre-1640 England was not the enclosure movement, but population increase and subdivision among male heirs (70-73). The Marxist interpretation is not, however, entirely displaced by showing that it was debt, economic misfortune, and market processes rather than the fraud and violence of enclosures that forced increasing landlessness (the *outcome* is as important as the cause). He then shows that the rural rebels of the period were landless squatters and artisans rather than the dispossessed copyholders and yeomen, but again, what Marxist would be surprised to find lower-class rebels? He takes Wallerstein to task by noting that it was the domestic grain trade that made English farmers richer, not the world market, and that Wallersteinian world-system theory would predict a revolutionary crisis around 1590. But if Goldstone is entitled to a time lag before his processes take effect, isn't Wallerstein? Contra Perry Anderson, Goldstone sees a long alliance rather than antagonism between London financiers and the Crown, arguing that it was only a shorter-term falling out in the 1620s and 1630s that led to the split. Again, a compromise seems more in order than a polarization of perspectives. His resolution of the debates on the French economy is a textbook example of what dependency theorists call dependent development (growth within limits benefitting some and disadvantaging many); his argument that Europe was not feudal after 1400 *or* capitalist before 1850 is consistent with a neo-Marxist modes of production approach. It is ultimately interesting (and curious) that while Goldstone is so perceptive in tracing the impact of economics and markets, he doesn't think readily in terms of classes. In each case above, telling points are made, but Marxist/class analysis is not thereby refuted decisively; in the end it might be more satisfactory to bring the two orders of explanation — Goldstone's and the neo-Marxists' — together.

To return to the core framework of the model, demography is put to very effective use (the example of enclosures is but one of numerous elegant and powerful demonstrations of its utility), but is population in fact an "independent variable"? Goldstone explicitly cautions that his is not a one-cause model, that it is the interaction of population with institutions that is key: "Where institutions are different, as the case of Tokugawa Japan clearly shows, population stability rather than growth can lead to crisis" (468). Yet if both growth and stability can lead to crisis, how central is population as a cause? Moreover it is curious that population growth had the same impact in so many places at once — why did population grow in so many different countries at the same time? The theory may be plausible in specific places at specific times (England in the 1640s, France in the 1780s), but population growth ought to be largely a national issue, especially given the emphasis here on context. Multiple, conjunctural causation is likely at work in the different cases: for example, late eighteenth-century England experienced population growth due to higher fertility, while France's is attributed to lower mortality. This undermines somewhat the search for cycles and patterns. Some of the "mechanical" quality of the argument is perhaps due to the drawing of metaphors and analogies from biology and geology (state breakdowns as earthquakes, the "fractal" properties of social structure, and the like). The model is suited to explain the seismic build-up of pressures, but not the precise moment or form of the eruptions that later occur (or even their inevitability). This is recognized by Goldstone himself (174), but to make the course of revolution then hinge on "the contingent and particular details of each crisis" (468) doesn't help the student of revolution very much. In sum, structural analysis, of which Goldstone shows himself a master, cannot provide the whole story.

If there is much to criticize, there is much to praise in *Revolution and Rebellion in the Early Modern World*. Admirable in its sweep and vision, as much at home with demographic as economic and political analysis, the book does alter the way future scholars will think about past events. It will stand as a synthesis of major proportions, and a storehouse of provocative leads and arguments.

2.

Tim McDaniel's *Autocracy, Modernization, and Revolution in Russia and Iran* brings the empirical focus into the modern era, serving as a bridge between Goldstone's early modern cases and Wickham-Crowley's contemporary Latin American ones. The book's emphasis on just two cases allows for an in-depth treatment of each and an agile weaving back and forth between them: McDaniel's goal is "not simply generalization, but also insight into each concrete case through contrast, a kind of dialogue of theme and variations" (15). The framework for this tale is provided by McDaniel's key concept of *autocratic modernization*. "Autocracy" invokes not any personal dictatorship, but traditional ones based on theoretically unlimited power unchecked by parties (even pro-regime ones), mass mobilization, institutions, official ideologies, or law. "Modernization" refers to "the period of attempted transition to a mature industrial society, with its new social groups and classes" (6). The two main world-historical cases combining both these features into autocratic modernization — Tsarist Russia and Pahlavi Iran — ended in revolutions, posing a puzzle for macrosociological analysis: What makes autocratic modernizers vulnerable to social revolution? This in turn allows McDaniel to search the deep background of the causes of the two revolutions, in a way that expands the relevant causal time frame to several decades, a bit like Goldstone, rather than the shorter-term crises often stressed by other theorists of revolution (such as the resource mobilization approach of Charles Tilly and others, which he criticizes for its emphasis on sudden breakdowns rather than persistent crises).

What are the mediating links in this argument? Modernization of the economy generally tends to widen barriers between state and society, thereby undermining state legitimacy. Autocratic regimes further undermine social stability by weakening groups in society and closing off channels of participation in the polity. Autocratic modernization differs from Barrington Moore's notion of reactionary capitalism as a route to the modern world in Japan and Germany because it dispenses with strong and legitimate elites and doesn't buttress hierarchical relations among classes. It also differs from modernizing one-party dictators such as Stalin or Ataturk who claim legitimation through a party and forge stronger links with society. Personal autocracy can "work" in earlier stages of modernization, as in the cases of Peter the Great and Reza Shah in our two countries, but is characteristically weaker later in the industrialization process; more institutionalized dictatorships may work better then, as in the Soviet Union or Meiji Japan, but may themselves prove unable to develop further later (1989 in Eastern Europe). The central paradox of this model of development in its various types is that strong states have trouble transforming weak civil societies. In a nice extension of Theda Skocpol's work McDaniel notes that the absence of intermediate formal organizations such as legal parties, unions, and other associations weakened the state's capacity to modernize the economy, while the presence of informal, sometimes underground, associations provided effective solidarity and cultures of resistance.

The core argument of the book is that "through their sponsorship of social modernization [Nicholas II and the Shah] undermined the traditional rationale upon which autocratic rule was based and created a hybrid social and political model satisfying neither conservatives nor modernizers" (89). In the state, conflicting views led to policy immobilization both in the administrations and in the rulers themselves (this despite the differences between Nicholas's passive style of rule and the shah's hands-on approach). In the absence of independent institutions in civil society (due in large part of course to state repression), the monarchs attempted to transform both industry and agriculture, failing especially in the countryside where they only stirred up expectations in Russia and touched off migration to the cities in Iran. Social elites were weakened in each case: The Russian gentry was bound to the state and industrialists had no political clout (with the liberalism of each hardened by the 1905 revolution), while the Iranian landed elite was neutralized, and bazaar merchants and the ulama attacked politically even as they maintained some economic standing. Both regimes stifled the private initiative they needed for development with the result that no economic elite would stand by the state in the crises or emerge as leaders after the revolutions.

Culture plays a lesser role in this narrative than economy and polity, but is meditated upon in some interesting ways. McDaniel is interested in how societies *function*, in how economy, polity, and culture interact in the process of autocratic modernization. He asks: "Is an ideology conceivable that reconciles autocratic authority and popular participation, tradition and progress? . . . Is there any way to make arbitrary personal authority compatible with modern social institutions and class relations in convincing ways?" (52) For the cases at hand McDaniel's answer is no, despite the nicely observed point that previous autocratic rulers endowed the two states with a kind of repertoire of historical memories and experiences on which to draw. Though the shah, for example, saw himself as a populist, nationalist, divinely sanctioned monarch, these legitimation claims were not accepted by the people. Rapid modernization and autocratic repression cut the intelligentsia off from society; the intelligentsia became oppositional, though dogmatic and rigid, highly sectarian and polarized, and in the end personalistically organized around a leader. The contrasting outcomes — socialism and Islamic theocracy — notwithstanding, he argues that Russian Marxism and Iranian Shi'ism shared some deep traits: utopian visions and practical politics, elitism, dualism, an emphasis on knowledge, chiliasm, claims to universality, the role of consciousness and martyrdom. His position on causation is that neither structural factors nor ideology are determinant on their own.

Let us begin our critique of McDaniel's synthesis with a look at the relative weight accorded state, society, and culture. McDaniel's project is sympathetic with the goal of Skocpol and others of bringing the state back in: "The analysis presupposes that the nature of political authority is one of the fundamental determinants of the traits and outcomes of any path of development, which cannot therefore be reduced to economic or class variables alone" (70). The project is admirable but the critique works both ways: The book's focus on the state makes it hard to evaluate other potential elements of a theory of revolution. We simply don't learn enough about the other forces at play — international markets and foreign investors, lower-class struggles, local capitalists, etc. — to tell if the commonalities between Russia and Iran do in fact explain their revolutions. The emphasis on the state's role in the Russian economy (114ff.) is contradictory because the conclusion reached is that the state was too weak to regulate and define the economic sphere. To say of the democratic opening of 1941-53 in Iran that "Domestic social and political affairs became highly confused. . . . Political life lost its coherence" (58) is to take the autocrat's point of view! There is, indeed, no discussion of the alternative to autocratic modernization attempted during the Mussadiq government of 1951-53. The core concept of autocratic modernization itself also raises some logical and historical problems: Was the shah really committed to the reforms he sponsored? If he had been, maybe autocratic modernization would have worked or evolved into a real constitutional monarchy. Of course, then it wouldn't have been autocratic anymore.

The correlate of the extensive interest in the state is a relative lack of attention to issues of class and social structure, ideology and culture.

Aside from some reflections on Russian workers, the only class that gets systematic attention in these pages is elites like the Russian nobility or the Iranian ulama. In the Russian case we find class polarization, rather the opposite of Iran's coalition of disparate groups, which becomes an "all-national movement," with all groups making a contribution but only the ulama seen as decisive. In place of class, for the Iranian case, McDaniel substitutes more informal urban associations: religious schools, sufi brotherhoods, neighborhood, tribe, craft, profession, kinship. There are suggestive but empirically vague passages on the fragility of social bonds, with a compelling vision of the surrealism of social life that implies the aimlessness, anomie, and ultimately irrationality of actors.

Despite a chapter devoted to "Cultures of Rebellion," this topic too is scanted. The exercise of comparing Russian Marxism and Iranian Shi'ism is too ideal-typical and reductive, missing the *varieties* of Islam — democratic, liberal, militant, radical, fundamentalist and conservative — that coexisted in Pahlavi Iran. Nor should culture be reduced to religion, for there were important secular trends, again of several hues, at work in the Iranian case. All of this reflects the exaggerated role ascribed to the ulama in the making of the revolution, an error of interpretation made in a number of works on Iran, and perhaps due to the fallacy of reading *backward* from the Islamic outcome. Again by remaining at the level of formal — especially elite — ideologies, we never quite catch sight of the millions of actors who made these revolutions, or their grievances and motives for doing so.

Lurking behind some of these problems one finds, perhaps, a set of core assumptions tangled up with the effort to appropriate useful elements of the 1960s modernization paradigm. McDaniel makes a contribution to an improved neo-modernization approach with his careful attention to phases of development, historical specificity and variation, and the interrelated consequences of the economic, political, and cultural spheres of society. He avoids modernizationist misconceptions by telling us for example that "The concept *traditional* . . . does not imply immobility or stagnation" (141), referring instead to pre-industrial groups who come under pressure in modernization processes. But he can still cover insights on legitimation ideologies with jargon on diffuseness versus specificity. In the debate between Teodor Shanin, who sees tsarist Russia as a developing society, and Alexander Gerschenkron, who implies it could have become another Germany, McDaniel sides more with Shanin but stops short of embracing "dependent development" as a concept preferable to modernization. Yet much of the data — for example, the existence of land hunger and poverty alongside rising per capita grain production, agricultural productivity, and peasant purchasing power — constitutes an almost textbook illustration of the way dependent development is treated by sophisticated practitioners such as Fernando Henrique Cardoso and Enzo Faletto. Behind some of these difficulties one can discern the problems of reading in the older secondary literature on Iran. Thus McDaniel accepts conventional views that the period from the seventeenth to nineteenth centuries is entirely one of "decadence and decay" (24), or that the Qajar period from 1800 to 1925 was essentially a static one of decline. In the end, 1970s Iran is described in terms that make it sound more "traditional" than 1900 Russia.

The book's most valuable contribution lies in its extensive analysis of the contradictions of autocratic modernization, which is a neat combination of political economy and regime types of the two cases. The comparisons drawn here are provocative, if not always compelling. McDaniel modestly doesn't attempt to build a theory of the causes of revolutions; indeed, he seems to think this a fruitless goal given the role played by fortuitous events and more fundamentally, I think, his deep respect for historical specifics. The result is the missing of some possible cases for comparison, notably Mexico under Porfirio Diaz and perhaps Somoza's Nicaragua. The search for a multi-causal *theory* requires consideration of multiple cases, including failures, a task carried out in the final study under consideration here.

3.

Timothy Wickham-Crowley's *Guerrillas and Revolution in Latin America. A Comparative Study of Insurgents and Regimes since 1956* represents a sociological tour de force — ambitious theoretically, sophisticated methodologically, and wide-ranging empirically. Going far beyond his earlier journal article treatments of aspects of this project, he here tells his whole story on a grand scale. In his own words, "We wish to understand why the Cubans and Nicaraguans won, why several guerrilla movements garnered substantial support yet failed to proceed to victory, and why guerrillas in several instances failed badly to obtain any support whatever from the populace, failing militarily as well" (51). Wickham-Crowley compares over two dozen Latin American cases from 1956 to 1990, with methodological forays into Boolean algebra and truth tables, ecological analysis of different regions, districts, and municipalities within countries, and considerable use of quantitative techniques, which is rare (Goldstone aside) in the sociology of revolution.

Theoretically, Wickham-Crowley rejects the monism of one-sided approaches for a kind of multiple "triangulation" of perspectives that could bear on his topics. This means not only arguing for a multi-causal model of revolution, but also acknowledging conjunctural causality — the recognition that different causes may produce the same result (e.g., peasant rebelliousness, discussed below). Drawing on Charles Tilly, Jeffery Paige, James Scott, and Theda Skocpol as precursors in the study of revolutions, he also ranges widely into the work of other heroes: Peter Berger, Robert Merton, and Max Weber among them. In the end, he goes well beyond each, eclectically (in a positive sense) picking up hints from all manner of sociologists, psychologists, journalists, historians, and revolutionaries. While believing — somewhat obviously — that peasant support is crucial to the success of rural guerrilla movements, he notes other factors too — military power, popular (urban) support, and weak regimes (each with plural determinants). Wickham-Crowley makes use of both macro- and micro-sociological types of data to build his own theory inductively out of the comparison of two "waves" of guerrilla insurgencies in Latin America: from the Cuban revolution of 1956-58 to the failed rural *focos* in Colombia, Venezuela, Peru, Guatemala, and Bolivia of the 1960s, and from the Sandinista victory of 1977-79 to the failures or ongoing struggles afterwards in El Salvador, Colombia, Guatemala, and Peru. Along the way, there are neat tests of competing theories about focos, building popular support, that outside aid is decisive, that U.S. intervention explains defeats, or that weak regimes always fall. Rather than strictly refuting each of these, he finds most of them possess some, but only partial, explanatory value.

Wickham-Crowley's own view is that revolutions proceed in two stages: First, a nucleus of usually middle-class urban intellectuals forms, and then peasants are recruited. His comparative investigations point to a set of favorable conditions for revolution:

> . . . revolutionaries came to power in Latin America from
> 1956 to 1990 only when a rural-based guerrilla movement
> secured strong peasant support in the countryside and
> achieved substantial levels of military strength; if that

movement also faced a patrimonial praetorian regime (a.k.a. *mafiacracy*), then it was structurally pressured to seek, and succeeded in securing a cross-class alliance against the patrimonial dictator who, lacking the social bases of support to resist such an alliance, in the end fell to a national resistance; under such conditions the United States tended to withdraw support from the dictatorship because of the symbolic and social pressures exerted by the constitutionalist and electoral symbols under which the revolutionaries and their more moderate allies united (318).

Thus, the class and regime parallels of the Cuban and Nicaraguan cases, the only two resulting in successful social revolutions, are teased out: Both exhibited patterns of incohesive or conflictual upper classes, small or disorganized middle classes, weak party systems, non-professionalized armies, widespread corruption and repressive rule under Batista and Somoza. Both resulted in cross-class oppositions to the common dictatorial enemy, astutely led by radical revolutionaries who toned down their messages to build internal and external support (280). Long sections are devoted to the particulars of each case, as well as their commonalities, and students of either one will find items of interest here (157-192 on Cuba, 261-284 and elsewhere on Nicaragua).

The absence or failure of revolution is ascribed to three possible combinations of these same factors. 1) Guerrillas with some popular support could not overthrow electoral democracies or collective military dictatorships regardless of whether these regimes enjoyed U.S. support (which can range in form from military to economic to political assistance). This pattern is found in a dozen cases ranging from Venezuela, Guatemala, and Colombia in the 1960s to Argentina, Peru, Uruguay, and El Salvador in the 1970s and 1980s. 2) Guerrillas lacking peasant support faced strong regimes with U.S. backing in another ten cases and failed even more decisively, most notably in Che Guevara's Bolivian foco in 1967. 3) Patrimonial regimes, with or without U.S. support, did not fall in the absence of guerrilla attempts in another five cases, including Nicaragua in the early 1960s, Paraguay under Stroessner, Haiti under the Duvaliers in the 1960s, and Panama under Noriega (i.e. it took direct U.S. intervention to topple him in 1989). Guerrillas in both waves failed when peasant support was weak or the regimes they faced were elected and could thereby retain urban supporters. In some cases failure to unite forces also contributed to defeat. In El Salvador, both class structure and regime type differed from Nicaragua, and the result has been a prolonged class war rather than an all-class revolution. Sendero Luminoso's limited success in Peru (on which some critical comments below) is traced to its "utter sectarianism and sheer 'orneriness' " (298). The point of these comparisons is to reinforce the argument that a particular conjuncture of causes must be present to produce success; in their absence, various routes lead to failure.

These findings, and the emphasis on rural guerrilla warfare, raise further questions, and in particular, "What makes peasants revolutionary?" as Theda Skocpol once asked. Wickham-Crowley's foray into the thickets of this debate shows him at his most judicious, theoretically pluralistic best. The contending perspectives include Jeffery Paige's thesis that different agrarian structures give rise to different types of collective action; James Scott's view that economic dislocations threaten peasants' moral economy; Samuel Popkin's rejoinder that peasants respond out of self-interest rather than any moral economy; and Skocpol's brief that peasants are always discontented, revolting only when pressures build and they possess solidarity or are free from landlord control. Wickham-Crowley tests the Scott-Paige debate most carefully, and turns up cases where neither fits. He extends Paige's thesis on revolutionary migrant workers and sharecroppers to include squatters, and Scott by looking at whether peasants have literally been losing ground: both moves capture a few more cases, but not all. He also treats the theories as complementary, rather than antagonistic: peasant dislocation (Scott) may lead to a migratory labor force (Paige). In the end Wickham-Crowley concludes that three different routes account for all his cases of rebellious peasantries: 1) conducive agrarian structures (those with a high proportion of migrant workers, sharecroppers, and squatters) combined with dislocations in areas of pre-existing guerrilla-peasant linkages, 2) conducive structures and a historically rebellious peasantry, and 3) a historically rebellious peasantry and pre-existing links (93-125, 305-309).

These last routes suggest another important piece in the puzzle — the role played by culture. For Wickham-Crowley, this is measured in two ways — noting the presence of historically rebellious regions within a country, and assessing how social networks facilitate solidarity. It is not fortuitous that the Cuban revolutionary stronghold of Oriente witnessed slave revolts in 1812, 1827, 1843, and 1849, or that the wars for independence (1868-78 and 1895-98) were largely fought in the mountains of this economically backward bandit region. In Nicaragua, the Sandinistas were strongest in the same rural areas as Sandino had been, the city of León boasted a legacy of struggle against the Somozas, the indigenous communities in Monimbó and Subtiava had long histories of self-administration and revolted against the Spanish in 1811-12. In Peru today, Sendero Luminoso uses pre-Columbian myths as do the Guatemalan revolutionaries in the Mayan highlands. Social networks play mobilizing roles both through formal organizations such as parties, universities, and guilds, and patron-client ties, kinship, friendship, and shared ethnicity — all can help or hinder guerrillas in forging alliances with peasants. Thus the community level of micro-processes plays an important role. Though he treats the media not in his discussion of culture but rather under the heading of building a situation of revolutionary dual power, it is in fact also another element of popular/political culture: both Castro and the Sandinistas stand out in their ability to gain access to the national and international media, and were successful in conveying moderate, consensus-building messages. In each of these ways culture is explicitly or implicitly invoked to account for the success and failure of guerrilla insurgencies.

Wickham-Crowley spends more time systematically analyzing the roles of specific actors than either Goldstone or McDaniel, and this considerably enriches his analysis. In addition to the peasantry already discussed above, he devotes some — if less — attention to urban actors, noting the propensity of students, youth, professionals, and the educated middle and upper classes generally to emerge in leadership roles. This is accounted for by various devices: universities as total institutions (Goffman), as autonomous, protected spaces and refuges during dictatorships (Barrington Moore), the self-image of Latin American students historically as "saviors of society" (cf. Blumer), the generational experience of the Cuban revolution (following Mannheim), and youth as a psychologically distinctive stage of the life cycle (Piaget). The role of marginal elites (an echo of both Goldstone and Skocpol) is noted in the origins of most of these movements in dissident offshoots of existing political parties. Regimes and armies come in for extensive analysis as well: The vulnerabilities of personalized military rulers (a type termed "mafiacracies") are dissected, and the various ways in which armies cohere or collapse constitute a significant sociological contribution often neglected in other studies. Nor are gender and ethnicity absent from this analysis: the "striking expansion" (215) of women in more recent movements in El Salvador, Peru, and Nicaragua is attributed to the regional rise of feminism and the shift in strategy from shorter-term insurgencies to prolonged popular wars.

The vicissitudes of the gradual turn of many Afro-Cubans against the Batista dictatorship, and the more striking indigenous roles in the post-1970 insurgencies in Peru and Guatemala, where recruitment was often done in local languages and Quechua and Mayan peasants reached local leadership positions, are carefully documented as is the relative quiescence of the indigenous western highlands of El Salvador, traced to the long-term effects of the repression there in the 1930s.

In turning to criticism, it is still certainly possible to find problems in what is an outstanding book on revolutions. We may begin with its theoretical object, which is in fact guerrilla insurgencies, not social revolutions. That is, the focus on guerrillas as armed fighters means that "real" revolutionaries are reduced to those bearing arms, and this downplays the roles played by many other groups in the events as of secondary importance. To study the causes of social revolutions, and to work out a theory thereof, one would need to expand analysis beyond the two cases that make it into this book: Cuba and Nicaragua could be supplemented, even in the Latin American context, by Mexico 1910-20, Bolivia 1952, Chile 1970-73, Grenada 1979-83, and Guatemala from 1944 to 1954 (arguably a more revolutionary period than the 1960s or 1980s), plus, importantly, Iran on a world-scale. But if the historical limits of the study preclude the first two cases and its geographical demarcations the last, then the electoral origins of events in Chile and Guatemala are obscured from view by the emphasis on revolutions as wars. The result, then, is a theory of the causes of guerrilla insurgencies more than social revolutions per se.

Related to this is the question of who makes revolutions, and the role played by class in them. Wickham-Crowley does see that urban actors are central, but peasant/guerrilla struggles still define what is a revolution for him. After a good analysis of the students and other urban middle classes in the opposition to Batista, he concludes that "the strongest supporters of the revolutionary cause were the peasants of the sierras of Oriente Province" (190), a statement of assertion in light of what he has just said, but understandable given his emphasis on "active recruits, not just passive sympathy" (191). The Cuban working class and upper class saw some members support both Batista and the opposition; rather than concluding that workers "as a class . . . largely remained outside the struggle until the very end" (188), why not conceptualize these groups as classes *split* in their loyalties? Sometimes, too, the measures of activism seem crude, as in the argument that the sheer increase in numbers of university students enrolled has something to do with their radicalism in key cases (220). This, like Goldstone's arguments on elite competition and population density, seems too mechanical. Likewise, the analysis of specific cases is sometimes a bit static: Classes are assessed before the revolution, but there is not always adequate attention to what was happening to them, or their actions in the revolution. This neglect of the roles played by diverse class actors has consequences at the national level of characterizing the coalitions as cross-class ones: "Cross-class" need not mean "no-class" as is sometimes suggested; there is still need for class analysis of such coalitions. Mexico and Bolivia are acknowledged as class-based "populist" "explosions" of the masses, but Nicaragua and Cuba are not so characterized. We are told that "it will not do to suggest that the Nicaraguan revolution was an urban revolution" (210), which is correct. But neither "urban" nor "rural" nor "*guerrilla*" is the best adjective, and while "cross-class" is better, "multi-class and populist" might be better still. Behind an aversion to Marxian class analysis, there is also a lack of attention to economic developmental processes: We are told that Cuba under Batista was "one of the four or five most developed nations in Latin America, and the most developed tropical nation in the world" (166), but this startling fact is never given any central analytic importance. Development trajectories and their impact on class formation thus drop out of the running as relevant causal variables. In the end, social structure, for Wickham-Crowley, is seen in terms of typologies (à la Paige's agrarian structures) rather than as a set of relationships, and perhaps because of this, along with a taste for quantifiable data, we have less insight than we would like into the economic conditions or political cultures that shape it.

This question of perspective colors the treatment of culture as well. Wickham-Crowley is neither particularly hostile *nor* sympathetic to the movements under study; there is a corresponding omission of the human element among the structures — the consciousness of participants remains opaque, as do the consequences of the outcomes for them (to be fair, Goldstone omits this even more). The most significant weakness of the treatment of culture is the substitution of *markers* for analysis of content or causal role. So, for example, we are given lists of organizations and loci of historically rebellious areas rather than focused meditation on the content of ideologies or the question of *why* given areas have histories of revolt. *How* is culture at work in these cases? Noting the moderation of Castro's messages to the Cuban and world publics in 1957-58 does not tell us what in those messages resonated to the various groups in society engaged in the struggle. We learn that social networks transmit messages of legitimation and opposition in a number of cases but little about how and why these messages were effective in mobilizing the population. Sendero Luminoso's sectarianism is seen as evidence of the political rather than cultural obstacles to revolution (it would seem to be both at once, for the fervent quality of support for Sendero also provides testimony to the power as well as the limits of political culture).

The theory of Latin American revolutions adumbrated in this volume is now, I think, the best we have. Its strength lies in its range of coverage and flexibility of explanation. The case and variable approach used here (discussing multiple cases in serial form with respect to key causal factors) inevitably suffers by yanking complex events out of their historical and full contextual setting to make focused comparisons. The alternative strategy — to discuss each case holistically in its own turn — would lose the analytic power of the matched comparisons achieved here, but it might also permit other, underacknowledged factors to emerge into full causal significance. Among the book's omissions we have already noted some key comparative instances of attempted social revolution in Mexico, Bolivia, Guatemala, Chile, and Grenada, and attention to various aspects of economy, culture, and class structure. To this list we might add the world-system as a context for shaping social structure (U.S. aid and its sometimes withdrawal is not the whole story here). The attempt to underpin the several sources of peasant support with Weber's four ideal-types of social action (310) seems an arbitrary and purely formal exercise. Finally, some criticisms can be registered in the interpretation and prediction of the ongoing cases: it is suggested that the 1991 negotiations between the FMLN and government in El Salvador represent a defeat for the rebels, but given the record of failure documented in the book and the factors making success unlikely (regime type, U.S. aid, etc.) it could just as well be interpreted as a relative success. Sendero's ultimate demise is predicted in Peru; according to the theory, the 1992 Fujimora coup may increase Sendero's chances, but the group's narrow social base and radical message portend continued failure. Time will tell, but a Sendero victory would falsify the theory to some degree.[5] All of these criticisms duly noted, *Guerrillas and Revolution in Latin America* will stand as a superb book on revolutions, and deserves to reach a wide audience of area specialists, macrosociologists, and yes, revolutionaries.

4.

The social science study of revolutions is markedly advanced by the works reviewed here. Each pushes the state of the art a bit beyond the point where Theda Skocpol carried it in the late 1970s. Each does this with theoretical innovation, methodological verve, and the empirical depth provided by a focused concentration on sets of cases not previously grouped together. Characteristic weaknesses in current theorizing have also emerged through this assessment: Structuralism needs to be supplemented with more attention to the perspectives and outlooks of the varied social forces that engage in revolutions. However conditioned they may be by forces larger than themselves, and to which they may be partially blind, their contribution is of co-equal importance to that of structure. As Teodor Shanin has cautioned us:

> Social scientists often miss a centre-piece of any revolutionary struggle — the fervour and anger that drives revolutionaries and makes them into what they are. Academic training and bourgeois convention deaden its appreciation. The "phenomenon" cannot be easily "operationalised" into factors, tables and figures. . . . At the very centre of revolution lies an emotional upheaval of moral indignation, revulsion and fury with the powers-that-be, such that one cannot remain silent, whatever the cost.[6]

Of crucial importance to this project is the better integration of understandings of how culture, in its range of meanings from collectively shared values to explicit ideologies, becomes effective in the causation, course, and outcomes of social revolutions, a project which is barely begun in the present literature on the subject. Related to this is the whole issue of agency: Answering the question of who makes revolutions and why requires a sharper conceptualization of social structure, including its gendered and racialized dimensions along with class, and how these complex structures change over time. Only in these ways do we begin to get truly clear of structuralism's limitations.

The ultimate question of *causality* is difficult indeed: Making inferences about the causes of social processes is a tricky business. Are we to accept population, autocratic modernization, or the constellation of factors facilitating guerrilla success as the final word? The present essay must answer in the negative, noting just the conflicting claims advanced by the fine studies under discussion here. A new theory might emerge if their insights are integrated with the critical considerations advanced throughout this essay. In answer to Nikki Keddie's question, "Can Revolutions be Predicted; Can Their Causes be Understood?",[7] while revolutions are never predictable (humans may controvert theories that "determine" their actions, as Anthony Giddens has noted), their causes can perhaps be "understood," if in doing so we do not lay claim to theoretical closure. For students of revolution — let alone the revolutionaries of the future — this is a large enough challenge to try to meet.

NOTES

1   The texts chosen for extensive commentary here were selected on the basis of their theoretical ambitiousness and coverage of a range of important cases in time and space. Several others could have been chosen, notably John Walton, *Reluctant Rebels. Comparative Studies of Revolution and Underdevelopment* (New York: Columbia University Press, 1984), and Farideh Farhi, *States and Urban-Based Revolutions: Iran and Nicaragua* (Urbana and Chicago: University of Illinois Press, 1990). I discuss them in a more comprehensive (but less in-depth) review essay: "Theories of Revolution Revisited: Toward a Fourth Generation?," forthcoming in *Sociological Theory*, 11, 1 (Spring 1993).
2   Jack A. Goldstone, *Revolution and Rebellion in the Early Modern World* (Berkeley: University of California Press, 1991); Tim McDaniel, *Autocracy, Modernization and Revolution in Russia and Iran* (Princeton: Princeton University Press, 1991); Timothy P. Wickham-Crowley, *Guerrillas and Revolution in Latin America. A Comparative Study of Insurgents and Regimes since 1956* (Princeton: Princeton University Press, 1992).
3   See Theda Skocpol, *States and Social Revolution. A Comparative Analysis of France, Russia, and China* (Cambridge: Cambridge University Press, 1979), pp. 4-5.
4   Other recent contributions to the literature remain on the plane of theorizing per se without the extensive empirical testing that I feel makes the present works significant: See, in particular, Rod Aya, *Rethinking*

Revolutions and Collective Violence. Studies on Concept, Theory, and Method (Amsterdam: Het Spinhuis, 1990), for some rigorous conceptual ground-breaking, and Michael S. Kimmel, *Revolution. A Sociological Interpretation* (Philadelphia: Temple University Press, 1990), for a systematic literature review of the field up to the early 1980s. Aya makes a good conterpoint to the works discussed here, which he would, I think, have been pleased to survey, as they avoid a number of the pitfalls he cautions against.

5   The September 12, 1992 capture of Sendero leader Abimael Guzmán alters the political equation, but not our assessment of the theory.

6   Teodor Shanin, *The Roots of Otherness: Russia's Turn of the Century*, volume 2: *Russia, 1905-1907, Revolution as a Moment of Truth* (New Haven and London: Yale University Press, 1986), p. 30.

7   Nikki R. Keddie, "Can Revolutions be Predicted; Can Their Causes be Understood?," *Contention*, 1, 2 (Winter 1992): 159-182.

THE BOURGEOIS GENTILSHOMMES OF REVOLUTIONARY THEORY

CHARLES TILLY

Monsieur Jourdain, Molière's *bourgeois gentilhomme*, rejoiced when the trickster-savants who were fleecing him announced that for all his life, unknowing, he had been speaking an exotic language: prose. Theorists of revolution are making a similar discovery, but with less joy; they have long thought they were dealing with a singular phenomenon and have tried to use a singular language in talking about it, but little by little they have begun to recognize variability as the essence of revolution. I mean singular chiefly in its first dictionary version ("being only one; separate; individual; *sui generis*"). In the cases of crime, collective protest, and revolution, however, analysts often dip into the second version as well: "deviating strongly from a norm; rare; extraordinary." Both versions serve us badly.

Models of crime, collective protest, and revolution as *sui generis* and deviant — as singular — are cracking under the weight of criticism and evidence. Our better theorists are conceding in their footnotes the multiplicity and variability of these social processes while often continuing to focus their main texts on singularity. As this symposium amply illustrates, theorists of revolution therefore have trouble seeing what is revolutionary about their own theories. After almost two centuries in which singular models of revolution have prevailed, today's theorists are finally recognizing that revolution is not a singular phenomenon, could not in principle be a singular phenomenon, is therefore inexplicable in terms of necessary and sufficient conditions, yet is quite regular and intelligible in its behavior. Muriel Atkin, John Foran, and Jack Goldstone, if not André Gunder Frank, rightly call attention to the variable conditions under which different sorts of revolutionary processes occur. Still they hold stubbornly to a singular vocabulary: the unique, necessary, and sufficient conditions for revolution. Current general discussions of revolution, including those in this issue of *Contention*, explode from their own contradictions before sinking back into confusion.

The study of revolution is not the only zone of the human sciences in which singular models have recently been collapsing. Consider an analogy to theories of memory. For centuries, students of human memory thought they were dealing with a singular process, despite disagreeing furiously as to whether that process was the physical marking of tissue, the alteration of an electrical field, the hooking together of "nerves," the depositing of ideas in an array of other ideas, or something quite different. Even specialists in brain physiology, misled by the ways in which lesions destroy memory, long supposed that some single structure or location controlled a unitary process of recollection. To be sure, distinctions such as those between conscious and unconscious, recall and recognition, implicit and explicit memory, or long-term and short-term memory acknowledged the phenomenon's complexity, but did not abolish the hope for a singular model of its operation, a sort of covering law in which different forms would simply turn out to be special cases.

The more neuroscientists and cognitive psychologists have delved into the ways that organisms retain and respond to traces of earlier experiences — into memory — the more they have recognized the deep variability of those ways. This does not mean they have abandoned the search for a coherent theory. It means the desired theory will concern variation among memory's many forms. The theory will surely feature recurrent mechanisms (current candidates being the activation and deactivation of highly specialized neurons), but in varying combinations, sequences, and outcomes. It will explain why memory sometimes appears sharp, sometimes dull; why some details are easy to recall, others difficult; why youthful memories often remain powerful in old people whose memories of recent events are evanescent; why some people remember numbers with extraordinary precision, while others can call up pungent recollections of smells.

A similar recognition is beginning to dawn on students of revolution. From Alexis de Tocqueville to Theda Skocpol, theorists of revolution generally insisted on offering singular models, specifying the invariant conditions under which revolutions were likely to occur, often adding invariant sequences and standard outcomes in the style of Crane Brinton or Pitrim Sorokin. Vis à vis previous theorists, newcomers commonly adopted one or both of two strategies: a) criticizing a previous conditions-and-sequence scheme only to promulgate an ostensibly improved version of the same scheme and/or b) identifying a case that the previous scheme did not fit, then introducing new variables to accomplish that fit. In grappling with the Iranian revolution, which inconsiderately started in the publication year of *States and Social Revolutions*, Skocpol herself dramatized the contradiction between the attempt to identify general conditions for revolution via large-scale comparative history and the formulation of an argument stressing the influence of state structure — a variable social phenomenon, if ever there was one — on the character and outcome of revolution. The constant and the variable fit together badly.

Jack Goldstone's two recent books display the same contradiction, his *Revolution and Rebellion in the Early Modern World* insisting on the generality of a singular model, his *Revolutions of the Late Twentieth Century* (and the welcome extension of its conclusions in his essay for this symposium) glorying in the systematic variability of conditions for revolution. In *Revolution and Rebellion*, Goldstone's own singular model concerns the effect of "pressure," especially demographic pressure, on resources, which he sees as driving 1) commodity prices, 2) state fiscal distress, 3) elite competition, and — with additional assistance from urban growth, declining real wages, and youthful age structure — 4) mass mobilization. Such pressures, according to Goldstone, produce state breakdowns, which under some ideological conditions generate revolutions. Goldstone's summing up those factors in a single Political Stress Indicator declares clearly that one unusual configuration of conditions, and only one, causes revolutions; the model allows variability only in the relative weights of the conditions.

That Andre Gunder Frank wants to paint Goldstone's passing use of cyclical arguments onto his own vast canvas of world history should not distract us from the essential: Goldstone's theory links revolution to state breakdown, and thence to political stress. Despite his emphasis on the similarity of demographic conditions in early modern Europe and Asia and his claiming of the near-simultaneity of geographically separate state breakdowns as support for his theory, Goldstone is clever and observant enough to avoid attaching his central model to one phase or another of the world economic cycle.

Frank's appropriation of Goldstone rushes past a crucial distinction. Goldstone is careful to treat seventeenth-century England, China, and Anatolia as separate "cases" responding to common causes (chiefly demographic) whose exact connections he leaves discreetly undecided; they could well be due to fluctuations in global climate or, *à la rigueur*, to epidemic disease. Goldstone certainly does not argue that Chinese political breakdowns caused European breakdowns, or vice versa. Frank, on the other hand, wants to establish the ancient existence of a single tightly-connected world system, for which subjection to common climatic cycles or even linkage through epidemics would be unconvincing evidence in most analysts' eyes, if not necessarily in Frank's. Tight connection surely entails interaction and mutual influence.

Recent theorists of revolution including Skocpol, Goldstone, and Foran have generally stated their arguments in an ambivalent manner, pronouncing for singular models in their programmatic statements while actually paying great attention to variation in their detailed analyses. Goldstone only makes his model work beyond the initial seventeenth-century cases by treating his enumeration of "pressures" as a set of variable conditions that produce different sorts and degrees of state breakdown. He cannot, for example, resist applying his arguments to the miscellaneous European mobilizations of 1848, where he employs his model specifically in the explanation of regional variation within Germany — a thoughtful move, but one that is utterly incompatible with his initial claim to be discovering repetitive "robust processes" in history. A robust process, for Goldstone, is "a sequence of events that has unfolded in similar (but neither identical nor fully predictable) fashion in a variety of different historical contexts" (*Revolution and Rebellion*, p. 57). For Germany in 1848, however, Goldstone abandons the analysis of similarities in the path to revolution for a discussion of how the politics of different regions and social classes varied as a function of the degree of Goldstonian stress under which they lived at the time. He slides like a trombone from similarities to differences.

Goldstone's essay in this issue confirms his *glissando* from the old note to the new. On the one hand, the "conjunctural" model he states here, unlike the population-pressure model of *Revolution and Rebellion*, is essentially tautological. The three conditions ("the state loses effectiveness in its ability to command resources and obedience"; "elites are alienated from the state and are seeking fundamental change"; "a large or strategic portion of the population at large can be readily mobilized for protest actions") constitute a definition of a revolutionary situation, which is in fact what the rest of the paper undertakes to analyze; Goldstone later declares, after all, that

> although a conjunctural analysis can tell when a state is weak and facing a revolutionary situation, it cannot predict whether accident or an individual's actions will intervene to slow down the impending arrival of a revolutionary crisis by months or years, or to bring it rushing immediately forward.

In short, we cannot predict revolutionary outcomes, only predict revolutionary situations, and the factors we use to predict them are . . . the very defining elements of revolutionary situations! Tautology reigns.

Definitional tautologies can be quite useful. My own model of a revolutionary situation (as distinguished from a revolutionary outcome) incorporates a tautology similar to Goldstone's; it stipulates that a revolutionary situation has three elements: 1) the appearance of contenders, or coalitions of contenders, advancing exclusive competing claims to control of the state, or some segment of it; 2) commitment to those claims by a significant segment of the citizenry; 3) incapacity or unwillingness of rulers to suppress the alternative coalition and/or commitment to its claims. The stipulation does not, however, constitute an explanation of revolutions, or even of revolutionary situations, but a convenient specification of what we must explain. The *explanation* of a revolutionary coalition's existence, for example, lies in the realms of political mobilization, inter-group solidarity, and political opportunity, while the explanation of support for revolutionary coalitions lies in the realms of accumulated collective grievances, within-group solidarities, and citizen-state relations. No harm in Goldstone's tautology, then, once he recognizes that it does not constitute an explanation, but a specification of variable features of revolutions that require explanation.

Following up his collaborative work *Revolutions of the Late Twentieth Century*, in fact, Goldstone moves decisively to the analysis of variability. Now we find him declaring that:

> a wide variety of state failures — economic, environmental, cultural — can precipitate a crisis of state authority. More-

over, we found that even elites closely tied to the state can suffer alienation if state failures affect their ability to attain status, income, and influence goals, and even modern urban populations have the potential to act in support of revolution. In sum, in this most recent work, it is not a particular kind of state, or of elite, or of popular group, that is necessary for revolution. Instead, in *any* kind of state, among any elites, and any kind of population, what mattered was the *relationships* among and within the state, elites, and general population.

Which is, I submit, what such analysts of variability among revolutionary phenomena as Jeffery Paige, John Foran, Jeff Goodwin, Timothy Wickham-Crowley, Matthew Shugart, and Theda Skocpol herself have been saying for some time, without quite recognizing the conclusion to which the reasoning leads: Abandon singular models, recognize the continuity between revolutionary and non-revolutionary political processes, try to identify the general mechanisms that make a difference to political processes, seek to examine and explain variability. Move over, Monsieur Jourdain; you have company.

PLEA FOR AN ALTERNATIVE VIEW OF REVOLUTION

SAID AMIR ARJOMAND

I. ON JACK GOLDSTONE AND RELATED MATTERS

On the question of the predictability of revolutions, I find myself in almost complete agreement with Nikki Keddie's clearly and effectively stated criticism of Jack Goldstone's position. I would simply note that Goldstone's strongest point, which would perhaps have emerged more clearly without the self-aggrandizing throat-clearing at the beginning of his article, is that the process of revolution is autonomous and has its own predictable dynamics, whatever causes might have set it in motion. The course and consequences of this process can therefore be foreseen without monitoring myriads of particular decisions. However, if an "area expert" may be permitted to pronounce on such a weighty theoretical matter, the point is not new; it was made by the first exponent of the natural history of revolutions, Lyford Edwards, in 1927.[1] The significance of Kuran's contribution lies in his demonstration that it is not possible to detect what Edwards called "preliminary" and "advanced" symptoms of revolution because of the way preferences are falsely expressed — and the more so the less democratic and open the regime. It is true that Goldstone, drawing on Skocpol, amplifies the account of the revolutionary process by bringing in the state. The problem is that the addition of the state does not make the process any more predictable. Was Louis-Philippe's prompt resignation that triggered off the European revolutions of 1848, or were the Shah's vacillations in 1978, predictable from "state ineffectiveness"? The same consideration applies to Goldstone's attempt to amplify the revolutionary process by drawing on Tilly's ideas about mobilization. How would one assess the strength of mobilizational resources to pit against state effectiveness in a society prior to a revolution? Could one find societies where people have fewer than two feet to use as resources in demonstrations, or do not live in communities and other social networks? In any event, Goldstone's own attempt at demonstrating the feasibility of predicting the revolutionary process in the second part of his article inspires little confidence, as his *ad hoc* enumeration of the alleged causes of the collapse of the Soviet Union has little systematic bearing on the interactive revolutionary *process* as outlined in *Revolutions and Rebellions in Early Modern Europe*.

I will return to this point in the second part of my article. But before leaving the issue of prediction, let me just move from logical to pragmatic considerations. Looking at Islam in the Soviet Union, Muriel Atkin in this issue shows how widely off the mark actual and highly respected predictions of revolution can be. I see no harm coming to any sociologist of revolution for having the humility to learn from that area expert's warning on the pitfalls of academic prediction.

Andre Gunder Frank and John Foran lavish praise on Goldstone's book as a major achievement in the study of revolution. My assessment of that work, presented in a review article elsewhere, differs drastically from theirs.[3] Frank's article contains a number of interesting statements on matters other than revolution. However, I have little sympathy for his subtext, which I take to be that we should give up the analysis of the dynamics of revolution — or for that matter any other "local" phenomenon — for the study of the Kondratieff cycles in world economy since 3,000 (or even 5,000) B.C. I would rather stick to the study of the local dynamics of revolutions, and Goldstone should be given credit for doing so, as should Foran in his survey of recent works in the study of revolutions.

For Foran, as for Goldstone, Theda Skocpol's *States and Social Revolutions* is the intellectual breakthrough that marks the beginning a new phase in the theory of revolution. It made possible the subsequent theoretical strides presented in three recent works by Goldstone, McDaniel, and Wickham-Crowley. Foran's treatment of Goldstone is primarily expositional, and he pays no attention to the nature of evidence and empirical support adduced by Goldstone for his propositions. I have examined Goldstone's treatment of evidence in considerable detail, and found it unsatisfactory.[4] Unlike me, Foran accepts Goldstone's factual assertions at their face value. But, as the author of an article on the fall of the Safavid empire in Iran which begins with a quotation from a contemporary (eighteenth century) *History of the Late Revolutions of Persia*,[5] Foran should at least have noticed that *that* Eurasian revolution — and the fall of the Safavids in 1722 has at least as much claim to be considered a revolution as the disturbances in the Ottoman empire in the mid-seventeenth century which did *not* result in the overthrow of the dynasty — falls into the period of Goldstone's demographic and therefore political "stability."

Foran next turns to Tim McDaniel's interesting comparison of the Russian and Iranian revolutions. As I have pointed out elsewhere, McDaniel's work has many merits, but it is not really a book about *revolution*.[6] It rather reverts to the older concern of Barrington Moore's with paths of modernization. This may be good for other reasons, but does not enhance our understanding of revolution. McDaniel does assert that autocratic modernization breeds revolution. Focusing on revolution, however, would further require emphasizing similarities between Russia and Iran other than "autocratic modernization," and would have brought out the importance of such factors as the political culture of the intelligentsia and their alienation from the state. Nevertheless, McDaniel's formulation has the merit of pointing to the indispensability of a typology of political regimes for explanation of revolution, and of thus drawing our attention to a dimension missing in Goldstone's demographic-processual model, namely the autonomy of political institutions. I have not read the last and most recent book discussed by Foran, Timothy P. Wickham-Crowley's *Guerillas and Revolution in Latin America*, but it appears to share the same merit. Furthermore, its adoption of "conjunctural causality" — the recognition that different combinations of causes can produce the same outcome — suggests a step in the right direction in the study of revolution.

Overall, however, I do not share Foran's irenic disposition and cannot bring myself to accept his spirit of synthesis and reconciliation. I consider such old-fashioned virtues of theory as economy, simplicity, elegance and parsimony important, and would rather reject a theory I find inadequate than blunt its distinctness by reconciling it with some other perspective in order to get a comprehensive, synthetic theoretical mush. I therefore propose that we reject Skocpol and Goldstone, and look for a better theory. Such a theory should accommodate at least some of the distinctive features of each revolution — and as Keddie points out, each revolution has certain unique features that cannot be predicted by any general model. It would be a theory that does not claim any precise predictive value, but whose explanatory value can nevertheless be tested *ex post facto*. And what better field to test the alternative theory than the former Soviet Union and Eastern Europe since 1989?

II. THE EASTERN EUROPEAN REVOLUTIONS AS A TEST CASE FOR ELEMENTS OF AN UNFASHIONABLE THEORY OF REVOLUTION

In concluding my book on the Islamic Revolution in Iran, I made the following observation:

> The Shah's regime collapsed despite the fact that his army was intact, despite the fact that there was no defeat in war, and . . . despite the fact that the state faced no financial crisis and no peasant insurrection. Where does all this leave the usual generalizations about revolutions? Mostly in the pits.

And if you looked down to the bottom of the pits into the footnote, you would find Skocpol's fashionable theory which, for Foran, marks the beginning of a new era in theorizing about revolution. Another point contra Skocpol was made on the same page:

> the collapse of the political order in Iran demonstrates that there is more to a system of authority than coercion. There is also the normative factor of legitimacy. What brought the Pahlavi regime down was not the disintegration of its army but rather its loss of legitimacy and a massive nationwide campaign of civil disobedience.[7]

With the remotely possible exceptions of financial crisis, the Eastern European Revolutions run even more clearly counter to Skocpol's theory than did the Iranian revolution a decade earlier. Similarly, Goldstone admits that the case does not fit his demographically-based theory. Nevertheless, he proceeds with his litany of economic ills, nuclear fallout and rising infant mortality rates in the Soviet Union prior to its collapse. This amounts to an *ad hoc* explanation in extraneous terms of a case that does not fit the most distinctive feature of Goldstone's theorizing, namely its demographic fundamentalism, just as Skocpol's *ad hoc* explanation of the Iranian revolution was extraneous to her structural theory.[8] This is not to deny the significance of Skocpol's contribution to the theory of revolution, which consisted in her emphasis on the autonomous role of the state. This recognition of the autonomy of political institutions, which is considerably subverted by Goldstone's "materialism," is undoubtedly a positive step, but one that does not go further than positing a reified notion of the state. What is more to the point, however, is that her theory does not fit the cases of Iran and Eastern Europe any more than Goldstone's. Instead of trying to buttress these fashionable but unfit theories, I would like to offer an alternative one, which I would claim captures some important features of East European revolutions. The alternative I am offering focuses on the character and normative foundations of political order, which are denied autonomy by Goldstone.

The elements of this alternative theory are drawn from my current comparative study of revolution and counter-revolution. From that study, I will take the two structural ideal types, or models, of revolution, and a fundamental distinction between revolutions with and without ideology — the great divide being the French Revolution which generated the modern myth of revolution as an apocalyptic event. The two structural models rest on two fundamental relationships: 1) the well-known relationship between revolution and centralization of power, and 2) the much less widely recognized one between revolution and enlargement of the political community.

The first is more familiar and more modern. In this modern type of revolution, a centralized state is already in place. In fact, revolution takes the form of the disintegration of the authority of the state, and the collapse of the established political order at the center. Crucial to this collapse of the system of authority is, to use Plato's words, "the outbreak of dissension in the ruling class."[9] The progressive sapping of the authority of the old regime is central not only to de Tocqueville's analysis of the French Revolution, but also, on close reading, to Trotsky's analysis of the Russian Revolution of 1917.[10] De Tocqueville showed how the growth of the centralized bureaucratic state dissolved the group solidarity necessary for routine concerted political action, and thus caused periodic revolutionary explosions that paralyzed the state temporarily. I will call this model the Tocquevillian ideal type of revolution.

My other model is much older, and can be found in societies *without* centralized states as well. Aristotle considered the restriction of access to political power a major cause of revolutions. Oligarchies and aristocracies are prone to revolution because of those they *exclude* from the political society. Impoverished members of the governing class become revolutionary leaders; the regime is undermined by persons who are wealthy but excluded from office; and sedition arises when the circle of government is too narrow and "the mass of a people consists of men animated by the conviction that they are as good as their masters in quality."[11] Revolution enlarges the political community by broadening membership and political rights. Among the moderns, Pareto's theory of revolution comes closest to Aristotle's idea. Put simply, the theory is as follows: If access to the political class is blocked to energetic and resolute individuals from the lower classes, a revolution is likely to occur.[12] In this situation, socially upwardly mobile individuals who are excluded from power develop into a revolutionary counter-elite and eventually seize power. These considerations provide me with my second model, which I will call the Aristotelian-Paretian ideal type of revolution. In a forthcoming book, I try to demonstrate that the Aristotelian-Paretian integrative model of revolution fits the revolutions of the ancient and medieval world very well.[13] Furthermore, the English, the French, and the mid-nineteenth nationalist revolutions all had their integrative aspect, as did the revolutions of national liberations in the twentieth century, which set up new political communities under native elites.

The most striking feature of the Eastern European political systems of the Soviet Union and Eastern Europe, to belabor an obvious point, was the great concentration of power in the political structure, the overcentralization of the party-state, which is the focal point of the Tocquevillian model. The second important, and equally obvious, feature of these regimes was that the Communist Party constituted the political society, and there was no meaningful political enfranchisement of the nominal citizens. The party was the oligarchy that restricted access to various levels of political power, and excluded a large and constantly growing number of educated people from the political community. This feature made the regimes of the Eastern block prone to revolution according to our Aristotelian-Paretian model. Last but not least, the East European revolutions were preceded by what has been described as a "collective crisis of faith,"[14] but is better characterized as the first example in world history of a complete collapse of a world religion *from within*.[15] Let me dwell briefly on each of these three points:

(1) *Collapse of the Soviet monolith:* Revolutionary situations occur because of the disintegration of central authority. With this disintegration of central authority, other forms of legitimate authority, including those

with hitherto shadowy existences come to life and assume greater importance. These include both formal political institutions, such as parliament,
and non-political, academic, and professional ones whose authority is
extended into the political sphere in emergency.

In a work published over a decade ago, a Lithuanian emigre social
scientist recognized the importance of these alternative structures of
authority as a kind of "second pivot" for transition from totalitarianism.[16]
The significance of the *perestroika* reforms of 1988 lies precisely in the
creation of such a second pivot, notably in the form of such institutions as
the All-Union Congress of People's Deputies, and the putting of life into
the Russian Supreme Soviet, and so forth. This second pivot quickly
became the institutional frame of reference in which "the outbreak of
dissension" within the Soviet political elite occurred. The Soviet elite
became divided, and some apparatchik of the republics crossed the line to
the opposition within this framework.

Constitutions shape political institutions and are therefore more
than scraps of paper;[17] and the fact that Lenin had in theory divided the
monolithic power structure under control of the Bolshevik party into a
federation of nominally sovereign republics that were increasingly staffed
by indigenous cadres made it possible for the Soviet bureaucracy to split
along republican lines seventy years later, and for the paper republics
suddenly to come to life and embark on assiduous legislation.[18] The formal
institutional arrangement was embodied in the constitutions in which the
dissidents, based on a variety of non-political institutions or informal
gatherings, and the Soviet republican apparatchiks, for whom sovereignty
meant real power, could find points of common interest and form the
political coalitions that carried out the dismantling of the Soviet Union.[19]

(2) *The enlargement of the political community:* The consolidation
of the revolution of 1917 meant the destruction and/or bureaucratic subju-
gations of those organs of civil society that had been the agents of the
revolutions of 1905 and 1917 — namely, the institutionalized Zemstvos
(assemblies) and the spontaneous Soviets (councils). At the same time, the
Communist Party of the Soviet Union became a closed oligarchy. In
Stalin's words, "the party has become in all respects like a fortress, the
gates of which are opened only to those who have been tested."[20] Com-
pleting the process underway since World War II, Khrushchev fully opened
the gates of the fortress and presided over a significant influx mainly of
working class representatives into the party. This influx continued under
Brezhnev: the party became something of a "lazy monopoly," and its

"proletarianization" continued. Gorbachev's goal for the restructuring and enlargement of the political society required controlled opening of the party as well as the working out of linkage between it and the new resuscitated political institutions. During the *perestroika*, various attempts at controlled enlargement of the political society failed, including proposals for preserving factory constituencies alongside residential ones.[21] In the end,

> Gorbachev destroyed the system, and he did so by fatally
> weakening the Communist Party. . . . [&] failing to replace
> it with a meaningful institutional substitute.[22]

The result, as we know, was the crumbling from within and collapse of the imposing but hollow Soviet monolith in a way highly reminiscent of de Tocqueville's description of the collapse of absolutism in France, which has helped my own understanding of the collapse of the centralized and equally hollow structure of the Shah's state in Iran.

Let us look more closely at the integrative dimension of the East European revolutions. Three points are worth mentioning: (1) the opening up of the political community was the major motive of the oppositions everywhere; (2) the challengers who "wanted in" were the intelligentsia, and the political elite whose monopoly they wanted to break were the political class and their cooptees, who came predominantly from the working class; and (3) the clash of citizenship and nationality as competing criteria for membership in the newly constructed political communities is at the root of the tragic paradox of the East European revolutions against the communist oligarchies.

During 1988 the dissident movement in the Soviet Union, like their counterparts in other East Europe countries, began to attack the central tenet of Marxism-Leninism - namely, the monopoly of the Communist Party. Gorbachev himself did not contemplate the abolition of the one-party system, and as late as October 1989 would dismiss the radicals' proposal to abolish the monopoly of the Communist Party as rubbish. Yet he was forced to go along and introduced the same proposal himself, and the Amendment of Article 6 of the Soviet Constitution in March 1990 disestablished the Communist Party. By then, the Communist Party was already disestablished (and/or had changed its name) as the first major step in the velvet or constitutional revolution in Czechoslovakia, and in Hungary and Poland.

What did the composition of the Communist Parties look like in the late 1980's, and who were the challengers who wanted in, and were advocating the political enfranchisement of civil society? Brezhnev's "proletarianization" policy was meant to confirm "the claim that Soviet authority is derived from the people."[23] The working class background of the political elite and the sub-elites was a source of ideological legitimation for the communist regimes. It was particularly important given the non-democratic character of the selective cooptation process. In Poland in 1970 under Gierek, and in Czechoslovakia after 1968, a similar process of "proletarianization" had occurred, while in Rumania under Ceausescu, recruitment of some of the peasants into the cadres performed a similar ideological, legitimatory function.[24] Here are some arresting statistics: there was of course a large measure of self-reproduction among cadres. This apart, workers constituted 63% of the new Communist Party of Czechoslovakia between 1971-1976. In Hungary in 1985, 40% of the party members were workers. In their congress in 1989, the proportion of working class delegates had dropped to only 9%. In the Soviet Union worker deputies quota at its peak in 1985, when Gorbachev came to power, was 44.5% of the total (compared to 30.7% from the intelligentsia).

Who were the challengers? The intelligentsia: former premier Mazowiecki in Poland, the Presidents of Czechoslovakia, and Hungary, the mayors of Moscow and St. Petersburg, are obvious examples. And just one particularly salient statistic: in Hungary's 1989 party congress 90% of delegates were intellectuals (compared to 9% workers).

A particular feature of the East European revolutions is neverthe-less explainable in terms of our second general model in that it derives from the clash of two principles of political integration. Citizenship and nationality have emerged as two contradictory bases for membership in the newly enlarged political societies after the East European revolutions. Citizenship and nationhood are alternative principles of political integra-tion. The latter principle is in fact disintegrative in the multi-national, multi-ethnic context of Eastern European and Eurasia. The Austro-Hungarian and Ottoman empires disintegrated after the first World War and the Russian empire was the only territorially contiguous empire to survive. One of the most striking failures of the Communist regimes, in the Soviet Union, Czechoslovakia, Rumania and elsewhere, was the failure to foster the notion of citizenship and a sense of collective identity on the basis of membership in the nation-state as a socially constructed political community. The consequence of this failure has been the breaking up of the Soviet empire and various nationality problems in other East European countries which were part of the Ottoman and/or Hapsburg empires.

(3) *Loss of Legitimacy:* We now come to the factor I consider the most important cause of the collapse of Communism but which has no place whatsoever in Skocpol's and Goldstone's theories, namely its complete loss of legitimacy. A political order is a system of authority which may be upheld by coercion but also requires legitimation. Loss of legitimacy therefore makes it vulnerable by undermining what Weber called its "validity" (*Geltung*).[25] Given the non-democratic nature of communist regimes, the validity depended less on popular support than on the faith of their administrative staff. Loss of faith on the part of the members of the Communist parties has been universally acknowledged.[26] This is not to say that popular support for the regime was not eroded. It obviously was; and Poggi is right in identifying the economic cause of this erosion:

> While [the Soviet-type] state is committed to economic
> success, it is doomed to economic failure, at any rate insofar
> as its economic performance is measured against that of
> advanced capitalist economies . . .

The economic failure that came to light in the 1980's therefore was devastating:

> because for too long. . . . the Soviet state had sold itself to
> its citizens by promising to catch up with and overtake the
> standard of living of advanced capitalist countries.[27]

To my mind, this amounts to saying that it was not the economic crisis *per se* as much as its devastating impact in undermining the ideology and legitimacy of the Communist regimes that accounts for their collapse. Economic success was necessary for the validation of the Communist faith; economic failure therefore devastated it, as the worldly faith lacked the safety valves of the world religions.

(4) *The Distinctive Feature of the East European Revolutions in World History:* The striking feature of the loss of legitimacy of the East European regimes is the utter devastation of the very idea of *ideology*, on which it was based. The opponents of the regime rejected the idea of ideology, and ideological politics alongside the totalitarian culture. To live with them was, to use Havel's (1978) famous phrase, to "live within a lie."[28] It is significant that as its last act on September 5, 1991, the Congress of People's Deputies of the Soviet Union issued a Declaration of Human

Rights that included the following proviso: "There should be no state ideology made incumbent upon citizens."[29] Not only does this vehement rejection of ideology makes the East European revolutions revolutions without ideology — which is by no means unprecedented, especially in pre-modern times — but it also gives them a pronounced *anti*-ideological, indeed dystopian, character. This last stunning feature of the East European revolutions does make them unique in world history.

The current revolutions in Eastern Europe suggest that the era of chiliastic revolutions may have come to an end for the foreseeable future with the Islamic revolution of 1979 in Iran. What we are witnessing with the current Eastern European revolutions are revolutionary changes in the political order which fit both the state-centered Tocquevillian and the integrative Aristotelian model, and yet are not only revolutions without ideologies, but are products of a distinct anti-ideological impetus. The modern myth of revolution as the salvation of mankind, which produced its cycle of ideological revolution, has played no role in them.

Max Weber noted in the preface to *Ancient Judaism* that modern revolutionary ideology is rooted in the Judeo-Christian Islamic world religions of salvation. Islam is the youngest of these; and Mohammad saw his prophecy as the final revelation, and the Seal of Prophecy. Will the intensely ideological Islamic revolution in Iran turn out to be the Seal of Revolutions in the apocalyptic sense? The East European revolutions suggest an answer in the affirmative. If so, coming revolutions will be closer to Aristotle's more limited and political conception than to the modern myth of revolution as dressed up by Marx. But whatever type of revolution the future may hold in store for us, there is no excuse for ignoring the typological and teleological diversity of revolutions, any more than for neglecting the primacy of political factors in vain, positivistic pursuit of predictive models.

NOTES

1   Lyford P. Edwards, *The Natural History of Revolution* (Chicago: University of Chicago Press, 1970).

2   Timur Kuran, "Why Revolutions are Better Understood than Predicted," *Contention*, 1.3 (1992), and the articles cited therein.
3   "A Demographic Theory of Revolution; or, Sociology as Sorcery?" *Contemporary Sociology*, 21.1 (1992), pp. 3-8.
4   *Ibid.*
5   John Foran, " The Long Fall of the Safavid Dynasty: Moving beyond the Standard Views," *International Journal of Middle East Studies*, 24.2 (1992), pp. 281-304.
6   See my forthcoming review in *Theory and Society*.
7   *The Turban for the Crown. The Islamic Revolution in Iran* (New York: Oxford University Press, 1988), p. 191.
8   Theda Skocpol, "Rentier State and Shi'a Islam in the Iranian Revolution," *Theory and Society* (1982).
9   *The Republic*, ed. F.M. Cornford (Oxford at the Clarendon Press, 1941), p. 262.
10   This similarity is stressed in Arthur Stinchcombe, *Theoretical Methods in Social History* (New York: Academic Press, 1978).
11   *The Politics of Aristotle*, ed. E. Barker (New York: Oxford University Press, 1962), p. 221.
12   Vilfredo Pareto, *Oeuvres Completes*, XII, *Traité de Sociologie Generale* (Geneva: Librairie Droz, 1968), p. 1305.
13   *Revolution and Counter-Revolution in World History*, forthcoming, University of Chicago Press. In Vol. 1 the following cases are covered: the revolution that unified the Mesopotamian city-states on the basis of the idea of universal monarchy *ca* 2350 B.C., the revolution that instituted democracy in Athens around 500 B.C., a series of revolutions in ancient Rome which integrated first the whole of Italy, and then the whole empire into the political systems of the Roman city-state, Mohammad's integrative revolution in Arabia, and the 'Abbasid revolution in 750, which was Islam's integrative revolution in that it systematically opened membership in the political community to non-Arabs.
14   Giuseppe Di Palma, "Legitimation from the Top to Civil Society: Politico-Cultural Change in Eastern Europe," *World Politics*, 44, 1 (1991), p. 49.
15   I owe this characterization to Ernest Gellner; for his own statement see his "Nationalism in the Vacuum," in Alexander J. Motyl, ed., *Thinking Theoretically about Soviet Nationalities* (New York: Columbia University Press, 1992).

16   Alexander Shtromas, *Political Change and Social Development: The Case of the Soviet Union* (Frankfurt: Verlag Peter Lang 1981), cited in Geoffrey Hosking, "Roots of Dissolution," *New York Review of Books*, January 16, 1992, p. 34.

17   See my "Constitutions and the Struggle for Political Order: A Study in the Modernization of Political Traditions," *European Journal of Sociology*, 33, 4 (1992), pp. 39-82.

18   Alexander J. Motyl, "Russian Hegemony and Non-Russian Insecurity: Foreign Policy Dilemmas of the USSR's Successor States," *The Harriman Institute Forum*, 5, 4 (December 1991), p. 1.

19   Geoffrey Hosking, "Independent Political Movements in the USSR since 1985," lecture delivered on February 5, 1992, as reported in *At the Harriman Institute*, 5, 5.

20   Cited in Kenneth Jowitt, "Gorbachev: Bolshevik or Menshevik," in Stephen White et al., eds., *Developments in Soviet Politics* (Durham, N.C.: Duke University Press, 1990), p. 217.

21   Ottorino Cappelli, "Comparative Communism's Fall. The First Phase: The 'Intelligentsia Revolution' of 1989-1990," *The Harriman Institute Forum*, 3, 6 (June 1990), pp. 5-6.

22   Motyl, *op. cit.*, p. 3.

23   Seweryn Bialer, *The Stalin Successors. Leadership, Stability and Change in the Soviet Union* (Cambridge: Cambridge University Press, 1984), p. 181, cited in Cappelli, p.2.

24   Istvan Deak, "Survivors," *The New York Review of Books*, March 5, 1992, p. 48.

25   Max Weber, *Economy and Society*, ed. & trans. G. Roth and C. Wittich (University of California Press, 1978), p. 31.

26   See especially, Di Palma, *loc. cit.*

27   Gianfranco Poggi, *The State: Its Nature, Development and Prospects* (Stanford, CA: Stanford University Press, 1990), pp. 168-169.

28   Cited in context in Jeffrey C. Goldfarb, "Post-Totalitarian Politics: Ideology Ends Again," *Social Research*, 57, 3 (1990), p. 539.

29   Cited in John N. Hazard, "Soviet Law Takes a Fresh Breath," *The Harriman Institute Forum*, 5, 6 (February 1992), p. 5.

Bringing Culture Back In and Other Caveats:

A CRITIQUE OF JACK GOLDSTONE'S RECENT ESSAYS ON REVOLUTION

JEFFREY N. WASSERSTROM

Jack Goldstone's excellent 1980 *World Politics* survey of the development of what he termed the first "three generations" of studies of comparative revolutions demonstrated that he could write with considerable insight about the strengths and weaknesses of other theorists.[1] Now, just over a decade later, his reputation as an original thinker is also firmly established, thanks in large part to his ambitious 1991 study of *Revolution and Rebellion in the Early Modern World*, which has recently received glowing reviews in journals such as *Sociological Theory* (where Randall Collins calls it "surely the best work on revolutions yet produced") and *Contention* (where Andre Gunder Frank hails it as a "marvelous book").[2] In the space of roughly a dozen years, in sum, Goldstone has become an influential voice in the multidisciplinary debate on revolutions and established himself as a leading spokesperson for what we might call "fourth generation" comparativists.[3]

There is thus good reason why we should take him very seriously indeed when he makes programmatic statements about the predictability of and roles that cultural factors play in the revolutionary process, topics that he addresses in recent essays written for *Contention* and *Theory and Society*.[4] And as someone with an abiding interest in comparative history, whose publications have tended to focus on either Shanghai student movements of a key revolutionary era (1919-1949) or the Chinese protests of 1989 (one of the "non-revolutions" about which Goldstone claims in *Contention* to have made an accurate prediction), I read both of these pieces with great interest.[5] Unfortunately, this experience proved a troubling one. I came away from Goldstone's *Contention* piece feeling that he had misrepresented what exactly has confounded so many scholars about recent upheavals. My reaction to his *Theory and Society* essay on ideology was that he had not gone nearly far enough in stressing the importance of cultural factors. The pieces also left me feeling generally uneasy about Goldstone's vision of the direction in which revolutionary studies should be moving.

     The main purpose of this essay is to elaborate upon these three areas of concern, but in doing so I begin by focusing on a somewhat different issue: the distinction that Goldstone draws between "area experts" (a group in which he would, presumably, place me) and "theorists" (such as himself) in his contributions to *Contention* (both his original essay on prediction and his reply to Nikki Keddie's insightful critique of that piece).[6] This is actually not as much of a digression as it seems, since Goldstone's attitude toward this distinction affects the way he handles issues relating to prediction, culture, and the future of revolutionary studies. Thus, for example, in his *Contention* pieces, Goldstone outlines a model for studying and preparing to predict social upheavals, in which "empirical experts" and "theorists" would work together in a particular way.[7] And his *Theory and Society* essay is in part a response to specific scholars working on individual countries, who have criticized Theda Skocpol (one of Goldstone's teachers) for underestimating the significance or distorting the meaning of the cultural or ideological dimensions of particular revolutions.[8]

AREA EXPERTS AND THEORISTS

     The most basic problem with his discussion of "area experts" and "theorists" is that he acts as though the distinction were clearcut. His original *Contention* piece opens and closes with the claim that a key reason that the events of 1989-91 took so much of the scholarly world by surprise, was that area experts had failed to realize that the "dominant theories of revolution" of the past (with their emphasis on "popular agency or particular kinds of state structure") had become obsolete, since being "improved upon by Theda Skocpol" and other third generation comparativists, whose sophisticated conjunctural models of state breakdown had in turn been further refined by scholars such as Goldstone himself.[9] In other parts of his *Contention* pieces he also refers to "area experts" (who focus exclusively upon the "current structure and past history of a society" and "are *not* experts in revolutionary processes") and "theorists" (who are generalists versed in such things as "the art of revolutionary coalition building" and "the relationships between economic development, state revenues, and political stability") as clearly divisible groups.[10]

Andre Gunder Frank seems to have a similar distinction in mind, when he writes that we should be prepared to hear parochial complaints from "(s)pecialists [who], as always, will exhibit their jealousy of outsiders' comparative analysis and generalists' broader scope, not to mention Goldstone's better analysis of their own material, by saying that it is not that way in their own backyard."[11] To Goldstone's credit, he never describes the situation this indelicately. He admits that "to predict revolutions" it is "probably necessary" to combine "the skills of the area specialist and the expert on revolutions *per se*," and that area experts should play a role in the grand collaborative projects he sees as holding out the best hope for advances in revolutionary studies.[12] These projects would (as in the "natural sciences") involve "multi-researcher teams incorporating theorists and empirical experts" who would "pool their talents" to test the latest theories and make predictions.[13]

What is wrong with treating area experts and theorists as two distinct groups of scholars? The most obvious flaw is that, as Goldstone is well aware, some of the most important theoretical breakthroughs in the study of revolutions have been made by people deeply concerned with the "current structure and past history of a society." Within what he calls the first "two generations" of major theorists, for example, we find such hybrid scholars as Crane Brinton, Charles Tilly, and (in my own geographical "area") Chalmers Johnson. When constructing their comparative models, each of these important figures drew upon detailed knowledge of (and encounters with primary documents relating to) an individual revolution.

One could argue, of course, that the situation changes once we reach the era of "third" and "fourth" generation models. After all, neither Skocpol and Goldstone nor other key figures such as Ellen Kay Trimberger and Timothy Wickham-Crowley have been identified with the study of a single country. And one can claim that this is no accident, but rather the natural result of two interrelated (or should I say "conjunctural") developments: the fact that "third" and "fourth" generation models stress the importance of factors (such as state strength and population growth) that can be studied (and quantified) without immersion in specific languages and cultures; and the fact that so many key members of these generations have been trained in a discipline (sociology) that has tended to put much less emphasis upon regional expertise than, say, history (Brinton's discipline).

It is, however, one thing to show that those whom some sociologists describe as the key contemporary revolutionary theorists are not specialists in the "current structure and past history of a society," and quite another to prove that people who have the credentials to be considered "area experts" have stopped making important theoretical contributions relating to revolutions. I am quite ready to concede that "pure" comparativists have done some of the most valuable work on revolutions during the past two decades, but I do not find the attempts that Goldstone and others have made to present the development of revolutionary theory as a unilinear "evolution" toward a particular type of state-centered conjunctural paradigm convincing.[14] Extremely sophisticated theoretical work, which is either explicitly comparative or has clear relevance for students of a wide range of revolutions, continues to be done by scholars whose starting point is an individual country's history. And, it is worth noting, many of these scholars are quite critical of some features of both the "bottom-up" and unsystematic works Goldstone considers passé, *and* the type of studies he views as representing the current state-of-the-art.

The easiest way to illustrate this is to look briefly at recent work on revolution by people who might be called French "area experts." Although François Furet's *Interpreting the French Revolution* contains relatively few explicitly comparative comments, it describes a single revolution in so insightful and theoretically suggestive a fashion that it seems narrow-minded to say that he should not be treated as a major theorist.[15] William H. Sewell, Jr.'s 1985 essay on revolutionary ideology, which the author modestly presents as a French area specialist's response to Skocpol's *States and Social Revolutions* but is in fact a major theoretical statement, is an even better case in point. In this piece, Sewell builds upon Furet's forays into semiotics to argue for a "structural" interpretation of the French Revolution that places ideological struggles and changes at the center of the model. He then concludes with some insightful comments on how the approach he outlines in relation to France might be used to help refine our understanding of revolutionary change in Russia and China.[16] Lynn Hunt's *Politics, Culture, and Class in the French Revolution* is another impressive and theoretically innovative work on France that combines an interest in the symbolics of power with close attention to social factors, and her recent discussions of the political implications of revolutionary familial imagery also have important theoretical and comparative implications. Hunt has explored some of these herself in discussions that link French developments to roughly contemporaneous Dutch and American ones, but I argue elsewhere that the themes she addresses are ones to which scholars working on revolutions occurring in very different times and places should also start paying attention.[17]

I have intentionally started out with examples relating to France to avoid being accused of parochial "backyardism," but students of the French Revolution are not the only ones to cross the area expert/theorist divide of late. Scholars working on Mexico, Iran, or any number of other places could be mentioned to illustrate this, but I will confine myself here to citing the work of three scholars whose work focuses on East or Southeast Asia. One is Elizabeth J. Perry, who has used the case of North China peasants to raise doubts about the idea that the existence of local traditions of rural rebellion are *necessarily* advantageous to Communist organizers interested in fomenting peasant revolution. Another is James C. Scott, who has used analysis of the Vietnamese countryside as a starting point for theoretical works that make very different claims about the dynamics of peasant revolution. A third is Prasenjit Duara, whose work on the "cultural nexus of power" and "state involution" in China engages with a number of ongoing theoretical debates. Duara's critique of Skocpol's assumption that "the state must weaken before a revolutionary condition can develop" is, for example, something that comparativists would do well to take seriously.[18]

The authors cited above have not explicitly set about constructing metatheoretical models of revolution. Some would probably even express discomfiture with the very notion that the problem of "revolution" can be discussed effectively in "singular" terms, a theme Charles Tilly addresses in a provocative response to Goldstone's essay on prediction. Arguing that the image of revolutions as singular events (in the dual sense of being "*sui generis* and deviant") is "cracking under the weight of criticism and evidence," Tilly says we should put more emphasis in future on the "variability among revolutionary phenomena" and the "continuity between revolutionary and non-revolutionary political processes." The works of some of the area expert/theorists cited above would certainly support his claims.[19] This emphasis upon variability as well as comparability hardly constitutes sufficient grounds to deny them the right to be treated as serious "theorists" of revolution, however, unless we are ready to define that title so narrowly that it ends up losing all meaning. Just as Goldstone claims that "the stability of key areas of the world is too important to leave solely to the area specialists," theorizing about revolution is too important to leave to the constructors of metatheoretical models.[20]

I would not try to argue that all area experts are as theoretically sophisticated as those cited above. I would even grant that scholars who "have spent years studying a stable society" tend to be out of touch with the development of new ideas concerning revolution, and that there are area experts working on revolutions who have little interest in comparative and broadly theoretical issues of any sort.[21] This said, serious engagement with comparative and theoretical issues relating to revolution is not all that rare among area experts who work on countries that have either experienced major upheavals in the past, or are routinely treated as potential sites of future unrest, and many of the specific countries Goldstone refers to in his essay on prediction (including China, the Soviet Union, and South Africa) fall into one of these two categories.

My own experiences as a graduate student help illustrate this point, since I was trained in just the sort of programs that would seem on the surface to be geared toward turning out narrowly focused area experts. Despite the fact that my master's degree is in a geographically defined field (Regional Studies: East Asia), and my doctorate is in a discipline known for frowning on explicitly comparative work (history), throughout my graduate career I encountered a string of professors (including Hue Tam Tai, Elizabeth Perry, Lynn Hunt, and Frederic Wakeman, Jr.) who insisted that I place my research on Chinese protests within the context of ongoing comparative and theoretical debates. This meant that, when I was preparing to write my dissertation, I took it for granted that I needed to relate my findings to both previous studies of Chinese student movements *and* to relevant works by scholars whose main interest was not China *per se*. It also meant that I viewed it as the natural course of things when, in the thesis and subsequent works, I ended up drawing inspiration of one sort or another from a broad array of comparative and theoretical studies, including those of non-China specialists such as Clifford Geertz, Steven Lukes, Natalie Davis, Richard Schechner, and Mona Ozouf.[22]

I cannot say just how "typical" my admittedly eclectic approach is, but my sense from reading other publications in my particular field is that there are at least a fair number of area experts who are equally interested in comparative and theoretical issues. A quick glance at recent essay collections dealing with modern Chinese history, such as *Chinese Local Elites and Patterns of Dominance*, would seem to confirm this. This volume grew out of a multi-disciplinary conference involving political scientists, historians, and anthropologists interested in China and a specialist in the history of French elites, and the introductory and concluding essays by the book's editors place Chinese data into a variety of comparative and theoretical frameworks. The end result is a book that is based on solid area expertise but also draws on, engages with, and/or raises doubts about claims made in works by people as diverse (and as far removed from Chinese studies) as Lawrence Stone, E.P. Thompson, S.N. Eisenstadt, and Pierre Bourdieu.[23]

THE PROBLEM OF PREDICTION

Even if I have managed to convince the most skeptical of comparativists that not all area experts are parochial empiricists, two of the basic questions Goldstone raises in *Contention* remain unanswered. First, have regional specialists trying to predict (and make sense of) contemporary crises paid relatively little attention to the specific kinds of conjunctural theories of revolution Goldstone champions? And, if this is true, has this been the main reason we have been confused by recent events? My argument below is that these questions should be answered respectively "yes" (but not necessarily for the reason Goldstone assumes) and "no" (at least on the basis of current evidence).

Before I elaborate on these answers, I should note that in this section I plan to stay within the confines of my academic "backyard." One reason for doing this is that previous contributors to *Contention* have already expressed their skepticism concerning Goldstone's general approach to predictive issues in what seem to me sensible ways. Another is that the comments concerning China that Goldstone makes in his *Los Angeles Times* article of May 24, 1989 (which he cites in his original

Contention piece) prove on inspection to be so problematic, that focusing on them will give me plenty of opportunity to make my own reasons for skepticism clear.

Having tipped my hand concerning my attitude toward Goldstone's specific predictions, I need to backtrack and look at his claim that relatively few area specialists have adopted the kind of approach to revolution advocated by "third" and "fourth" generation comparativists. I think that this claim is basically true, but I do not think it is because we have all been out of touch with new developments in revolutionary theory, or because we have remained staunch defenders of the "once-dominant" competing models Goldstone describes as the main alternative to the conjunctural approach. Some China specialists (including, no doubt, some of those to whom the media routinely look for predictive guidance) certainly have been unaware of (or unreflectively resistant to) new models. There are other China specialists, however, who have read and been very impressed by certain features of works by scholars such as Skocpol and Goldstone, yet have remained uneasy about their general approach to revolution.

Generalizing from discussions I have had with various colleagues in Chinese studies, I would say that there are two somewhat different sources of this uneasiness, which prevents us from embracing the new conjuncturalism wholeheartedly. The first is disagreement with specific descriptive or comparative comments concerning "our" country (to use one favorite stylistic device of area experts) made by particular theorists. The second is a vaguer sense that (to use the equally favored area expert device of quoting a regionally specific colloquialism) the new models of revolution just do not quite "scratch where it itches."

Some specific complaints about how "our" country is handled may indeed be treated as the kind of "not-in-my-backyard" parochialism at which Frank scoffs, but others cannot be dismissed so easily. Skocpol's treatment of "international pressures" as a variable is a case in point. While few of us would question her claim that such pressures did indeed contribute to the fall of the *anciens régimes* of France, Russia, and China, the notion that France's "(r)epeated defeats in wars" fought abroad and "competition from England" was comparable in any meaningful way to China's being carved up by foreign imperialist powers seems problematic to many whose work focuses on Chinese history. Admittedly, she distinguishes between international pressures being "strong" in the case of early twentieth-century China and only "moderate" in that of late eighteenth-century France, but this hardly does justice to the contrast.[24]

More important than this type of specific complaint is a more general one relating to the emphasis that "third" and "fourth" generation theorists tend to place on the breakdown of old regimes and the construction of new states. Even if most of the general claims these theorists make about the causes and eventual outcomes of revolutions are right, we are often left feeling that their models do not provide much help in answering the questions that bother us most about the Chinese Revolution. This failure to "scratch where it itches" is again easiest to illustrate with reference to Skocpol's work.

The main limitation of *States and Social Revolutions*, for me at least, is simply that it sheds too little light on the most perplexing aspect of the Chinese Revolution — its long, and often tortuous, course. Skocpol's careful narratives of the French, Russian, and Chinese revolutions stress the beginning and end of each story at the expense of their middles (the revolutionary process itself). The result is that her book provides China specialists with very sophisticated analyses of questions (such as how and why the Qing Dynasty collapsed) for which we already had fairly satisfactory answers. It is much less helpful where the question of why the Qing's collapse did not simply lead to a change of dynasties, or why (if the creation of a new kind of governmental system had to take place) the process by which that new system came into being was so protracted. Skocpol's focus on the state helps sharpen our understanding of one set of key comparative issues, in other words, but it leads her to pay too little attention to what is in many ways the most intriguing comparative question of all: If social revolutions are "*rapid*, basic transformation of a society's state and class structures," why does she have to deal with a thirty-eight year period in the case of China (1911-1949), as opposed to a four year one for Russia (1917-1921) and a thirteen year one for France (1787-1801)?[25]

Jack Goldstone's recent writings seem intended, at least in part, to make up for precisely these shortcomings of Skocpol's model. Thus, for example, he claims in *Contention* that he and his collaborators have begun to integrate a concern with "process" back into the study of revolutions, and that this is one of the reasons that recent work is more helpful than Skocpol's when it comes to predicting contemporary crises.[26] In his *Theory and Society* piece, meanwhile, Goldstone addresses the question of why some state crises lead to revolutions when others end with the creation of new regimes that are only slightly different from their predecessors. For an upheaval to turn into a revolution as opposed to merely a coup or rebellion, he argues, there must be " 'marginal' elites who want not only to seize power but also to change the principles that they feel originally relegated them to marginal status." The culture must also contain "an eschatological element that can be utilized to cast the political struggle as a final end to the Old Regime, to be followed by the emergence of a new, more virtuous society."[27]

There is much for students of the Chinese Revolution to admire about these and other modifications Goldstone makes to Skocpol's basic framework, which was itself already impressive in many ways. The treatment of demographic factors in *Revolution and Rebellion* fits in well with some recent studies of late Qing China (1644-1911), for example, and Goldstone's emphasis on the importance of cities is also welcome, at least to those of us who have become convinced that urban unrest played a crucial part in many stages of the Chinese Revolution. This said, "fourth" generation comparative works such as his still do not provide completely convincing answers to the following question: Why was the collapse of the Qing followed by such a long and chaotic period, during which a complete reversion to the previous political status quo was impossible, and yet those attempting to establish new orders seemed destined to fail?

Goldstone's specific arguments relating to "process" and "ideology" would seem to provide useful leads to pursue, but following these leads proves difficult. How, for example, are we supposed to apply to the Chinese case his argument that a "ruthless" and tightly focused repressive strategy can allow a regime to stave off revolutionary change for "several years," while "inconsistent" repression makes "rapid revolution more likely"?[28] Imperial policies during the years leading up to 1911 were certainly inconsistent, but (if we assume that revolutions end with the establishment of relatively stable new state structures) the events that followed were not played out in anything like a "rapid" fashion. If 1949 is chosen as the important ending point (as Skocpol suggests), then the process is very long indeed. But if we break up the Chinese Revolution into a series of interconnected revolutions, and say that the first one ended when the Nationalists took power in 1927, this just creates a new problem of protraction. The Nationalists were ruthless and focused in their attempts to repress the Communist Party (CCP), but Goldstone's suggestion that such behavior can buy a regime "several years" of stability is not terribly helpful in this case. In the end it took a full twenty-two years for the Nationalists to fall, even though the factors that trigger state crises were present from the moment the new regime took power.

Goldstone's discussion of ideology, in which he identifies Marxism as the brand of eschatology that broke China from its cycle of rebellion, also proves problematic on close inspection. If we want to use the notion of eschatology to solve the problem of protraction, then we need to assume that there was no guarantee that the fall of the Qing would actually lead to a true revolution until the CCP and its particular brand of millenarianism appeared on the scene in 1921. The difficulty is that, as Yuan Shikai's abortive attempt to install himself as an emperor in 1916 showed, the possibility for a complete return to the old order had ceased to exist *before* the CCP had even been founded. As the late Joseph Levenson pointed out so eloquently decades ago, despite its incompleteness and the tendency of its leaders to invoke dynastic imagery, the Revolution of 1911 did succeed in "draining" the old Imperial institutions of the "monarchical mystique" from which they gained their power.[29]

The preceding pages help explain why China specialists have been hesitant about embracing the approach of "third" and "fourth" generation comparativists, but is Goldstone justified in claiming that his model would have helped us do a better job in 1989? I have no argument with him concerning the fact that China specialists (including myself) were unprepared to come to terms quickly and effectively with many aspects of the events of that year, and I think that as a field we have a great deal to learn from that experience.[30] Neither his *Los Angeles Times* article nor his *Contention* pieces has convinced me, however, that we would have been less perplexed by 1989 if we had looked to his theories for guidance.

There are two basic problems with his predictions concerning recent Chinese events. The first has to do with the way he presents the issue, which implies that area experts thought that China was heading for "immediate radical change" but he knew better. Some China specialists swept up in the exhilaration of the events may have assumed that we were witnessing a full-blown revolution that would end in the creation of a new political order, but this was by no means a general feeling. That the Chinese regime came as close to crumbling as it did; that the authorities waited well over a month before resorting to force; that the occupation of Tiananmen Square failed to simply peter out in May; that the regime's campaign of repression was as brutal as it was — all of these things were more surprising to many of us than the fact that a harsh crackdown ultimately put an end to the movement.

A much bigger problem with Goldstone's predictions about China is that it turns out that much of what he actually wrote in his *Los Angeles*

Times op-ed piece was so vague as to be essentially meaningless, or has since turned out to be wrong.[31] For example, although in *Contention* he describes the Chinese events of 1989 as one of the "non-revolutions" he predicted, Goldstone began his *Los Angeles Times* piece by comparing the occupation of Tiananmen Square to the "taking of the Bastille," a comparison that might reasonably lead one to look for a series of interconnected events ending in radical transformation of some sort. He does recommend patience at one point, reminding his readers that "1789 marked the beginning, not the end of the French Revolution." Hence "it may take months or years" before the basic contradictions that precipitated the crisis of 1989 are "fully resolved," according to Goldstone, and in this interim period "recurrent demonstrations, further divisions in the government and armed forces, attempted coups and increased violence are all likely."

There are many ways for Goldstone to use his own theories to explain why so few of these "likely" events have taken place during the last several years of comparative social calm in China. The regime's policies of repression, for example, have certainly been of the "ruthless" variety that he argues can delay a revolutionary outcome. Although there is undoubtedly some validity to points such as these, and I share Goldstone's conviction that China is bound to experience new outbursts of popular unrest in the future, as divisions within the elite relating to the pace and scope of reform continue to facilitate these expressions of discontent, on balance his predictions concerning the Chinese crisis simply do not seem particularly prescient or unusual. The notion of 1989 as a counterpart to 1789 would undoubtedly please some of the protesters, who were quite conscious of the bicentennial of the French Revolution, but for this analogy to be defended we would have to make special allowances once again for the protracted nature of Chinese revolutionary processes. The best we can hope at this point is that someday the protests that broke out in Beijing and most of China's other cities in 1989 may be seen as equivalent to the abortive Russian revolt of 1905, i.e., as an outburst that set the stage for (but was not part of the immediate chain of events leading up to) the fall of an authoritarian *ancien régime*.

In dismissing Goldstone's claim to special predictive powers, I do not want to imply that I was fully prepared for the Chinese events of 1989, but I cannot resist mentioning one prediction I *almost* made during a talk on the evolution of the Shanghai student protest repertoire that I delivered in early April as part of a Berkeley symposium. When I reached the part of the talk that dealt with the tendency for Chinese protesters to turn certain types of rituals (such as funerals and officially sponsored mass gatherings) into theatrical expressions of dissent, and to hold demonstrations on particular kinds of politically significant dates, I thought about slipping in a reference to the likelihood that students would take to the streets on the upcoming anniversary of the May 4th Movement. The May 4th Movement has special meaning for the CCP (which claims that the anti-imperialist protests of 1919 laid the groundwork for the party's birth), as well as for students and intellectuals (who view the whole "May 4th era" of the late teens and early twenties as a time when the intelligentsia's commitment to patriotism and cultural enlightenment was manifested). Since discontent was running high on college campuses, and the CCP could hardly insist that no public gatherings be held on the seventieth anniversary of a date that had such an important place in its own mythology, it seemed logical to suggest that something dramatic would happen on May 4. In the end, I never said anything about the upcoming anniversary date during my talk, and when I was proved "right" I did not have an editor to blame (as Goldstone did when he was forced to strike his prediction about Marcos), since I had done the censoring myself.

Tempting as it would be to end the story there, it seems only fair to ask just how "right" I actually would have been? One small problem with my prediction was that the first protests of 1989 actually took place more than two weeks before May 4. I could easily dismiss this as a minor point. After all, those protests occurred during funeral marches honoring Hu Yaobang, and I had explicitly put events mourning the dead and holidays celebrating past achievement in the same category in my talk. In addition, information soon came to light that some students had indeed been planning to hold major demonstrations on May 4, so that Hu's unexpected death may simply have moved the timetable up a bit.

There is a bigger problem with my "almost prediction," however, which is simply that I had no idea that the protests I thought might occur would grow into a mass movement of such enormous proportions. This was clear from the one prediction I put on paper. In late April of 1989, I filed a dissertation on pre-1949 student movements, which contained a hastily added off-hand comment to the effect that the protests taking place as I wrote were unlikely to end up either as widespread or as important as the great mass movements of the Republican era described in my thesis.

In light of my own checkered career as a prognosticator, I should say that I find Goldstone's willingness to remind us of his *Los Angeles Times* article refreshing. Many people who make predictions that turn out

168   JEFFREY N. WASSERSTROM

to be even partially inaccurate do all they can to encourage people to forget that they ever made them. This has certainly been my tendency: one reason I worked so hard to get my dissertation turned into a book after June 4, 1989, was that I knew that if I did so people would be less likely to read the predictive comment in my thesis. It would probably be better, however, if we were all as willing as Jack Goldstone to remind our colleagues of predictions that did not quite turn out right.[32]

CULTURAL FRAMEWORKS AND THE STUDY OF REVOLUTIONS

The final points I want to bring up have to do with Goldstone's view of ideology and culture, and his notion that comparative work on revolutions should be done by teams made up of theorists and empirical experts. I should begin by noting that I agree with Goldstone on two basic points: that an interest in ideas and symbols needs to be reintegrated back into models of revolutionary change; and that the problems presented by revolutions are so complex that collaborative projects may well be the best hope for the future of the field. Where I differ with him is on some key specifics.

Let me begin with some comments concerning his treatment of ideology and culture. Reviewers are certainly right to note that Goldstone pays more attention to ideological variables in *Revolution and Rebellion* than Theda Skocpol does in *States and Social Revolutions*. It is also clear from his recent essays that Goldstone thinks that, by breaking the revolutionary process into stages and arguing that ideology can be a particularly important variable in the period that follows the fall of an old regime, he has successfully dealt with the kinds of problems relating to culture that Sewell and other scholars highlighted in early critiques of Skocpol's book.[33]

Even some of those reviewers who have greeted Goldstone's work most enthusiastically have, however, found fault with his treatment of ideology. They have noted, for example, that when he deals with culture, Goldstone focuses almost exclusively on elite as opposed to popular culture. Some have also described his division between materially-driven regime breakdowns and ideologically-driven processes of state construction as a bit too neat and schematic.[34] An even bigger problem, it seems to me, is that Goldstone is only partially successful in his effort to solve the general definitional and conceptual problems relating to ideology that Sewell described in his 1985 critique of Skocpol. Goldstone is not quite ready to follow Sewell's suggestion that theorists of revolution stop viewing ideology primarily in terms of formally espoused schools of thought, and treat it instead as something that is "anonymous, collective, and . . . constitutive of social order."[35]

Goldstone's unwillingness to treat ideology as "constitutive of social order" is clear in his *Theory and Society* essay, which begins with the claim that "it is increasingly agreed that ideological factors may promote, but do not produce, the breakdown of Old Regimes." Goldstone goes on to argue that it "is chiefly *after* the initial breakdown of the state . . . that ideology and culture play a leading role."[36] He then fleshes out these opening statements on the following pages, by describing the centrality of "material and social forces" in precipitating state crises, and looking at the way in which "ideology and culture develop a momentum of their own" after the "institutional constraints of the Old Regime have collapsed."[37] These arguments suggest that, while Goldstone is willing to admit that the *States and Social Revolutions* model gives too little attention to cultural variables, he has not really come to terms with Sewell's claim that "social orders" are structured by and dependent on ideologies.

Sewell's critique, though published before the latest wave of revolutionary upheavals took place, is in some ways even more persuasive now that they have occurred. This is because, to make sense of the differing courses that events took in China and Eastern Europe, we need to place ideological factors (in Sewell's sense of the term) at or near the center of our analysis. One of the biggest mistakes made by those China specialists and journalists who thought that radical change was imminent in 1989, was to overestimate the extent to which the CCP's claim to legitimacy had been compromised before the June massacres took place. Fascinated by "democratic" slogans and icons, and tending to ignore or downplay their culturally specific connotations, analysts paid too little attention to the fact that protesters also relied heavily upon symbols (the "Internationale," May 4th, Chairman Mao) that the CCP itself had helped to sacralize. It is also important to note that throughout April and May most protesters were not calling for an end to Communist rule, but rather insisting that leaders live up to the CCP's own ideals, so that the "Revolution" (which, in the rhetoric of students and officials alike, was generally treated as an unfinished sacred quest) could be put back onto its proper course. In some cases, protesters undoubtedly turned to officially sanctioned symbols, practices and rhetoric for pragmatic reasons (i.e., to make it harder for the authorities to repress their actions), but it now seems clear that in April and May the CCP's ideology had not yet lost its power to shape the thinking of even those associated with dissident movements, nor had official symbols lost their power to inspire awe. In contrast to Eastern Europe, where (to modify Levenson's phrase) the draining of the ruling elite's mystique preceded the outbreak of popular unrest, in China it was the bloodshed of early June that (like Russia's "Bloody Sunday" of 1905) stripped the regime's symbols of what Clifford Geertz refers to as their "numinous" quality.[38]

The argument presented above does not contradict Skocpol's claim that a simple theory of legitimation cannot explain how it is possible for a state to "remain quite stable" even after suffering a "great loss of legitimacy," since this is exactly what has happened in China since 1989.[39] My argument is an attempt to show that, if we want to come to terms with recent crises, we need to find a more sophisticated understanding of how, in each stage of the revolutionary process, political legitimacy and cultural hegemony are asserted, contested and redefined. Said Arjomand's *Contention* response to Goldstone provides some valuable suggestions concerning how this might be done, even though he also falls into the trap of treating "ideology" as a set of self-consciously articulated beliefs.[40] Sewell's 1985 essay remains, to my mind, even more helpful for trying to think through this problem.

Goldstone's *Theory and Society* essay began to seem especially problematic to me when I returned to it after looking at his contributions to *Contention*. If these pieces are read in conjunction with one another, what looked at first like a move toward reintegration of ideological factors into a more synthetic approach to revolutions, ends up dangerously close to being simply a new way of marginalizing cultural concerns. What Goldstone gives with one hand (by granting ideology an important place within later stages of the revolutionary process), he takes away with the other (by giving the material roots of state breakdowns pride of place in scientific predictive work). He thus brings culture back into the discussion of revolution but relegates it to a subordinate position, by implying that it is of only minor importance where the key issues of origins and predictability are concerned.

Some of my objections to this approach have already been outlined or hinted at above, but two are worth describing in a bit more detail. The first is that one of the main assumptions underlying Goldstone's remarginalization of culture (the notion that ideological factors tend to become crucially important *after*, but not before, state breakdown occurs) is contradicted by some of the most convincing recent case studies of revolutionary change, including an essay on Eastern European events by Daniel Chirot that Goldstone himself cites in *Contention* . Chirot insists that, to understand the European upheavals of 1989, we need to treat the "great ideological innovation" and mounting moral outrage of the preceding decade as central causal factors. Keith Baker's analysis of eighteenth-century France provides an even more effective illustration of the way in which ideology can act as a driving force during the period leading up to as well as following the breakdown of a state apparatus, by demonstrating that the "structure of meanings in relation to which the quite disparate actions of 1789 took on symbolic coherence and political force, was the creation of the Old Regime."[41]

My second objection to Goldstone's notion that ideological issues are of only peripheral interest to those concerned with prediction, is that in his work it serves as the basis for a vision of "scientific" studies of comparative revolutions that would seem to have no place for some of those who have done particularly interesting work of late on individual revolutions. Where, for example, would the authors of fascinating and controversial recent studies of the gendered dimensions of the French Revolution, and the changing contours of the public and private spheres before and after 1789, fit into Goldstone's teams of "theorists" and "empirical experts"?[42] If these teams are charged solely with searching the world for evidence relating to a specific set of material factors that, when occurring conjuncturally, are thought to indicate that particular regimes are heading into periods of instability, what motivation would participants in these projects have even to read works by these authors?

This is one of the reasons that I am uncomfortable with Goldstone's general claim that students of revolution should emulate their colleagues in the "natural sciences" when trying to determine how to proceed. Another is that I find the very notion that understanding of a topic typically progresses in a linear evolutionary fashion problematic (as of course, do some natural scientists). The problems with an evolutionary view of theory were brought home to me when I found that, in trying to make sense of contemporary crises, the works of earlier generations of scholars (such as Joseph Levenson or, to go back much farther, Emile Durkheim) sometimes proved more valuable (at least in their suggestiveness) than the most "advanced" contemporary models.

I also have problems with Goldstone's vision of the future of revolutionary studies that stem from disciplinary or subdisciplinary orientations and loyalties. Goldstone makes it clear that he is trying to ally himself with those historical sociologists who think that human behavior can be analyzed "scientifically," and that totalizing models can be constructed to explain even the most seemingly chaotic of social phenomena. Many of the recent works on revolution I find most engaging or inspirational, on the other hand, are by people who are skeptical at best about these kinds of positivist assumptions. Not all of them would go as far as Lynn Hunt has in arguing that history should be "treated . . . as a branch of aesthetics rather than as the handmaiden of social theory," or join Charles Tilly in calling for a move away from focusing on revolutions *per se* as a subject of study.[43] Many of them would agree, however, that it may be time to start paying less attention to the pursuit of the perfect model, and direct more of our attention to looking for and making sense of interesting analogies among revolutions that either highlight surprising commonalities, or remind us of the fascinating variability of revolutionary processes.[44]

I do not mean to suggest that there is no point in trying to think of creative ways to get different kinds of scholars who share an interest in revolutions to work together. Goldstone's call for ambitious collaborative projects is welcome, for we all have a great deal to learn from and dispute with each other, as the various symposia that have appeared in *Contention* have demonstrated. We also all have blind spots of one sort or another that people with other areas of expertise can help us correct. Where I differ from Goldstone is in our understanding of the kinds of blind spots that most need to be corrected, and hence the type of collaboration that is in order.

Goldstone's vision of collaboration is one in which comparativists would give area experts guidance about what to look for (thus filling in the theoretical blindspots of these empirical specialists, and helping them see things about "their" country that they have missed). The major problem facing metatheorists, which in his view is a limited ability to scan the world for relevant input, would also be solved by this method. I quite agree with Goldstone that comparativists, who have not immersed themselves in intensive study of a particular country's language and culture, can often bring a fresh perspective to events that occur in that nation. I have frequently been reminded of this in my own work on China, most recently through corresponding with and reading pieces by Craig Calhoun, a sociologist best known for his writings unrelated to Chinese studies, who was in Beijing in 1989.[45] Unlike Goldstone, however, I would stress that collaborative projects should also address the empirical blindspots of area experts (who can benefit from being kept abreast of new developments in the study of specific revolutions other than their own), and the theoretical blindspots of comparativists (who need to be kept abreast of the original theorizing being done by regional specialists, and to be reminded when "old-fashioned" approaches have started to take on new significance in light of current events and research).

I am not sure how this can best be done, but a September 1992 workshop on new approaches to the Chinese and French revolutions, which was held in Bloomington, Indiana, and co-organized by William Cohen and myself, suggests one way to proceed. What we did was simply bring together, for a weekend of free-ranging discussions, a group of approximately twenty scholars whose work focused on one of the two revolutions. We prepared for the gathering by reading samples of one another's work, and then spent much of the weekend holding group discussions on common themes, including the relevance of Skocpol and Goldstone's work for "our" particular revolutions.

No formal presentations of new research were allowed at this workshop, and there was clear agreement that the gathering's proceedings would not serve as the basis for a conference volume of any sort. The weekend did conclude, however, with a consensus among members of the group that a more formal follow-up workshop be held in the future, which would lead to a conference volume. We also agreed that this second workshop should include a wider range of scholars. Most of the participants in the original gathering were historians influenced by the "new" social or cultural history, although the disciplines of sociology, political science, literature, and anthropology were also represented. Our hope is that the follow-up conference will include comparativists, specialists working on other parts of the world, and a larger contingent of non-historians. The Bloomington gathering also indirectly inspired plans for another comparative conference of a similar sort, which will focus on new approaches to the urban dimensions of the Chinese and Russian revolutions, involve a similarly diverse mixture of scholars, and be co-organized by Alexander Rabinowitch and myself.

Neither the original Bloomington workshop, nor the two follow-up gatherings that are still in the preliminary planning stage, takes the kind of model-testing approach to revolutionary studies that Goldstone describes.

174   JEFFREY N. WASSERSTROM

Ideally, the two upcoming conferences will include participation by people who think that a "scientific" approach to revolutions is possible, but the main emphasis will remain on furthering communication across geographical and disciplinary boundaries, and stimulating debate over the relative explanatory value of differing approaches to the revolutionary process.

The value of this sort of approach has already been demonstrated to my satisfaction by a multi-disciplinary NEH-sponsored conference on "Media and Revolution," which was organized by Jeremy Popkin and took place in Lexington, Kentucky, in October of 1992. No new grand theoretical models emerged from this gathering, in which revolutionary upheavals of the seventeenth through late twentieth centuries were discussed. Nonetheless, many participants went away with new ideas concerning how best to approach the countries or topics that concerned them most, and a new appreciation for the various ways in which revolutions have differed from and resembled each other. Whether or not this contributes to the advancement of a "scientific" agenda, it certainly seems like the kind of thing we could use more of, if we want to come to a more sophisticated understanding of the subject of revolutionary change.

NOTES

1   Jack A. Goldstone, "Theories of Revolution: The Third Generation," *World Politics* 32 (April, 1980): 425-443.
2   Jack A. Goldstone, *Revolution and Rebellion in the Early Modern World* (Berkeley: University of California Press, 1991); Randall Collins, "Maturation of the State-Centered Theory of Revolution and Ideology," *Sociological Theory* 11, 1 (1993): 117-128, esp. 118; Andre Gunder Frank, "The World is Round and Wavy: Demographic Cycles and Structural Analysis in The World System, *Contention* 2, 2 (1993): 107-125, esp. 107 and 121. Much more critical reviews include Said Amir Arjomand, "A Demographic Theory of Revolution; or, Sociology as Sorcery?" *Contemporary Sociology* 21, 1 (1992): 3-8.
3   John Foran, "Theories of Revolution Revisited: Toward a Fourth Generation," *Sociological Theory*, 11 (March 1993): 1-20; see also idem.,

"Revolutionizing Theory/Theorizing Revolutions: State, Culture, and Society in Recent Works on Revolution," *Contention* 2, 2 (1993): 65-88.
4   Jack A. Goldstone, "Ideology, Cultural Frameworks, and the Process of Revolution," *Theory and Society* 20, 4 (1991): 405-454; and idem., "Predicting Revolutions: Why We Could (and Should) Have Foreseen the Revolutions of 1989-1991 in the U.S.S.R. and Eastern Europe," *Contention* 2, 2 (1991): 127-152.
5   My major publications include *Student Protests in Twentieth-Century China: The View from Shanghai* (Stanford: Stanford University Press, 1991); and *Popular Protest and Political Culture in Modern China: Learning from 1989* (Boulder: Westview Press, 1992), for which I was a co-editor (along with Elizabeth J. Perry) and a contributor.
6   Nikki R. Keddie, "Response to Goldstone," and Jack A. Goldstone, "Reply to Keddie," *Contention* 2, 2 (1993): 159-170 and 185-189, respectively.
7   Goldstone, "Reply to Keddie," 186.
8   This is also true of Goldstone, *Revolution and Rebellion*, 416-458.
9   Goldstone, "Predicting Revolutions," 127 and 149.
10   Ibid., 130 (emphasis in original).
11   Frank, "The World is Round and Wavy," 109.
12   Goldstone, "Predicting Revolutions," 131.
13   Goldstone, "Reply to Keddie," 186.
14   Along with Goldstone, "Predicting Revolution," see Farrokh Moshiri, "Revolutionary Conflict Theory in an Evolutionary Perspective," in Jack A. Goldstone et al., eds., *Revolutions of the Late Twentieth Century* (Boulder: Westview Press, 1991), pp. 4-36
15   François Furet, *Interpreting the French Revolution* (Cambridge: Cambridge University Press, 1981), translated by E. Forster.
16   William H. Sewell, Jr., "Ideologies and Social Revolution: Reflections on the French Case," *Journal of Modern History* 57, 1 (1985): 57-85.
17   Lynn Hunt, *Politics, Culture, and Class in the French Revolution* (Berkeley: University of California Press, 1984); idem., *The Family Romance of the French Revolution* (Berkeley: University of California Press, 1992), esp. 71-73; idem., "Constitutions, Human Rights, and the Rights of Women in the Atlantic World of the Eighteenth Century," in M'hammed Sabour, ed., *Liberté, Egalité, Fraternité, Bicentenaire de la Grande Révolution Française* (Joensuu, Finland: Joensuu Yliopisto, 1992), pp. 186-204; and Jeffrey N. Wasserstrom, "Was There a 'Family Romance' of the Chinese Revolution?," unpublished paper to be presented

at the American Historical Association meetings in San Francisco, January 1994, as part of a panel on "Gendered Symbols and Revolutionary Political Culture in France, Russia, and China."

18   Elizabeth J. Perry, *Rebels and Revolutionaries in North China 1845-1945* (Stanford: Stanford University Press, 1980); James C. Scott, *Weapons of the Weak* (New Haven: Yale University Press, 1985); Prasenjit Duara, *Culture, Power, and the State: Rural North China 1900-1942* (Stanford: Stanford University Press, 1988), esp. pp. 15-41 and 250-257.

19   Charles Tilly, "The Bourgeois Gentilshommes of Revolutionary Theory," *Contention* 2, 2 (1993): 153-158, esp. 153 and 158.

20   Goldstone, "Predicting Revolutions," 131.

21   Ibid., 130.

22   For citations to specific works by these authors, see the bibliography to Wasserstrom, *Student Protests.*

23   Joseph W. Esherick and Mary B. Rankin, eds., *Chinese Local Elites and Patterns of Dominance* (Berkeley: University of California Press, 1990).

24   Theda Skocpol, *States and Social Revolutions: A Comparative Analysis of France, Russia, and China* (Cambridge: Cambridge University Press, 1979), p. 155.

25   Ibid., xi and 4, my emphasis.

26   Goldstone, "Predicting Revolution," 141.

27   Goldstone, "Ideology," 438.

28   Goldstone, "Predicting Revolutions," 142.

29   Joseph R. Levenson, *Confucian China and Its Modern Fate: A Trilogy* (Berkeley: University of California Press, 1965), book 2, pp. 3-7.

30   One of Elizabeth Perry and my goals in compiling *Popular Protest and Political Culture* was, in fact, to contribute to just this kind of learning process.

31   Jack A. Goldstone, "For China, the Revolution of Modernization is Just Beginning," *Los Angeles Times*, May 24, 1989, section two, 7.

32   In the spirit of disclosure, my inaccurate predictions concerning 1989 can be found in Jeffrey N. Wasserstrom, "Taking It to the Streets: Shanghai Students and Political Protest, 1919-1949" (University of California, doctoral dissertation, 1989).

33   William H. Sewell, "Ideologies and Social Revolutions"; Goldstone discusses this and related critiques, in "Cultural Frameworks," 405-406.

34   Foran, "Revolutionizing Theory," 71; Collins, "State-Centered Theory," 122-123.

35   Sewell, "Ideologies and Social Revolutions," 85.

36   Goldstone, "Ideology," 405, emphasis in original.

37   Ibid., 407-408.

38   Clifford Geertz, "Centers, Kings, and Charisma: Reflections on the Symbolics of Power," in Joseph Ben-David and Terry Nicholas Clark, eds., *Culture and Its Creators: Essays in Honor of Edward Shils* (Chicago: Chicago University Press, 1977), pp. 150-171.

39   Skocpol, *States and Social Revolutions*, 32.

40   Said Amir Arjomand, "Plea for an Alternative View of Revolution," *Contention* 2, 2 (1993): 171-183.

41   Daniel Chirot, "What Happened in Eastern Europe in 1989?," in Wasserstrom and Perry, *Popular Protest and Political Culture*, pp. 215-243, esp. 223; Keith Baker, *Inventing the French Revolution* (Cambridge: Cambridge University Press, 1990), p. 4.

42   Karen Offen, "The New Sexual Politics of the French Revolution," *French Historical Studies* 16, 4 (1990): 909-922; Hunt, *Family Romance*.

43   Lynn Hunt, "Introduction: History, Culture, and Text," in idem., ed., *The New Cultural History* (Berkeley: University of California Press, 1989), p. 21; Tilly, "Bourgeois Gentilshommes."

44   Here I am inelegantly paraphrasing a suggestion that William H. Sewell, Jr., made at a workshop held recently in Bloomington, Indiana, that is described below.

45   Craig Calhoun, "The Beijing Spring, 1989," *Dissent* (Fall 1989): 435-437, is one of several insightful essays of his that draw upon his experiences as an eyewitness.

ANALYZING REVOLUTIONS AND REBELLIONS:

A REPLY TO THE CRITICS

JACK A. GOLDSTONE

It is a rare pleasure to have one's ideas examined by such learned critics as Professors Arjomand, Foran, Frank, Tilly, and Wasserstrom.[1] However, my concepts of revolution have been developing over a series of works, and not all these authors have seen them all;[2] they thus sometimes err in describing my ideas. I attempt here to clarify the worst misunderstandings and provide answers to their more valuable questions. Of course, I start from the belief that we are all seeking to understand a highly complex phenomenon; I admit that every portion of my work is in some ways incomplete, and that further work will be needed before even a partial theory of revolutions (from me or further generations of scholars) can be considered proven; nor is it likely that any theory will be final or complete.

WHAT ARE "REVOLUTIONS?"

"Revolutions" is an almost useless term for scientific inquiry — but nonetheless inescapable. It is much like the term "rocks." Ask geologists what they study, and many will say "rocks." We know roughly what they mean — those hard irregular-shaped objects ranging from pebbles to monoliths that compose the solid surface of the Earth. Ask a geologist for a theory of "rocks," however, and you will get either a laugh, or a patient explanation that "rocks" is not a scientific term, and that rocks come in many kinds with different origins and compositions. Only for the specific kinds (e.g., igneous or sedimentary) or their components (e.g., specific minerals) can one make sound generalizations or find empirical regularities.

"Revolutions" is a term like "rocks;" we know roughly what the term points to — those events involving a disorderly change in governments that punctuate the history of complex societies. However, the actual events are varied in their origins and composition. We cannot escape the word for heuristic and conversational purposes, but we should not pretend that it denotes a straightforward object of analysis. "Revolutions" need to be separated into different types and their varying components before analysis can begin. This is Charles Tilly's point and mine as well. In *Revolution and Rebellion in the Early Modern World* ([hereafter *R&R*] 9-12) I noted that the events we describe as "revolutions" or "revolution-like" have a variety of components that appear in dozens of combinations, and that we cannot generalize about them all. I am thus at a loss for why Tilly believes that I do not recognize "the conclusion to which the reasoning leads: Abandon singular models, recognize the continuity between revolutionary and non-revolutionary political processes . . . seek to examine and explain variability."[3] The very title "Revolutions *and* Rebellions*" pointed out that both revolutionary and non-revolutionary events would be involved in my analysis!

Moreover, my "Manifesto" for comparative history (*R&R* 53) gives equal weight to the detection of "critical differences" and "robust processes." Tilly seems to find fault with my sliding from one to the other, and wants to study only differences. To me, this is like forcing music into separate notes without searching for harmonies. I argue that good comparative history illuminates *both* similarities and differences.

Instead of Tilly's simple directive to abandon singular models and seek variability, let me offer instead a paraphrase of some familiar common wisdom: In the study of revolutions and rebellions, a single model might explain much about a particular kind of event, or a small part of many different events; but no single model will explain much about all kinds of events.

What appears to mislead Tilly and other critics is that they fail to see how my work applies several quite different models. These need to be kept distinct, for each provides the key to a different part of the problem of understanding revolutions and rebellions. These models are (1) the demographic-structural model, which explains much about the causes of a particular kind of event — state breakdown in early modern agrarian-bureaucratic states; (2) the PSI measurement model, which explains a small part of state breakdown — how to analyze and track its development — in many different kinds of states; and (3) the model of ideologies as particular programs built from the elements of broader cultural frameworks, which again explains a small part, this time of the outcomes of revolution — whether or not elite and popular mobilization and state reconstruction can produce fundamental change in the ideological basis of governance.

EXPLAINING EARLY MODERN STATE BREAKDOWNS

As I state in diverse places, I believe it is useful to get away from conceiving "revolution" as a holistic entity. Rather, I see "revolutions" and "revolution-like" events as involving three overlapping stages which may span decades: state breakdown; struggles for power; and reconstruction and consolidation of authority. In revolutions producing fundamental change that last stage is undertaken by new actors with new conceptions of authority and social order; in failed revolutions and rebellions that last stage is undertaken by regime incumbents or their close allies; in successful rebellions that last stage is undertaken by new actors, but with conceptions of authority and social order firmly rooted in the order of the pre-breakdown regime. These are of course ideal types; in some cases, such as the Meiji Restoration, elements of successful rebellion and revolution are combined.

Whereas this view certainly "seeks to examine and explain variability," I admit that most of *R&R* focuses on a single robust process: the impact of population change on relatively inflexible economies, status systems, and administrations. However, that process is presented to explain only a carefully delimited analytical and temporal *part* of the phenomena of revolutions and rebellions, namely the causes of *state breakdown* in *early modern agrarian-bureaucratic states*. Early modern agrarian-bureaucratic states are a fairly special case. These states were sufficiently large, and their economies sufficiently commercialized and market-dependent, that price and income effects could upset stable patterns of taxation and social status on a large scale. However, their technology was sufficiently simple and slow-changing that the range of GNP growth rates that we see in the modern world (from -5% to +10% per annum) was inconceivable. It was only in such states that modest but cumulating changes in population (from -1% to +1% per annum) could, over a few generations, play a determining role in political stability.

Of course, while these cases are limited that does not mean they are not significant, for they include the origins of some of the key events considered to have shaped the modern world. Thus for the important historical puzzle — why did revolutions and rebellions arise in many major Eurasian states in the periods 1618-1660 and 1770-1868, while relatively few such crises occurred in the intervening period? — *R&R* offers a solution, pointing to the vulnerability of early modern institutions to demographic shifts. I never claim that the solution to this particular *historical* puzzle should be taken, by itself, as a general theory of state breakdown in all kinds of states.

Tilly and Arjomand seem to err in thinking that I present the demographic/structural explanation of early modern state breakdowns as a general theory of all revolutions. I don't, and I can only say that those who think I do have not read my work carefully. I *do* make some general statements about state breakdown, however, which I claim are useful in prediction. Let us be clear exactly what those statements are, and what they mean.

EXPLANATION VS. PREDICTION OF REVOLUTIONS

Barometers predict the weather — when pressure is rising the weather will be clear; when pressure is falling the weather will turn stormy. But a barometer certainly doesn't *explain* the weather. Indeed, many weather patterns are too complex to be explained at all in terms of initial causes. And of course, the barometer doesn't predict the weather infallibly, or far into the future; it simply tells you what the current trends portend. That is not useless — virtually every ship and weather station in the world is equipped with a barometer. But it is not "law-like" prediction, deducing precise and invariant outcomes from specific initial conditions.

When I spoke of prediction with regard to revolutions, I meant that my explanation of early modern state breakdown had within it elements — namely the PSI model of political stress — that could be used like a barometer, to predict the coming of state breakdown more generally. To be fully clear, in saying prediction of "revolution" I was using the word in the general heuristic way; I meant only prediction of the onset of state breakdown. I did not mean that one could predict the shape of revolutionary struggles and their outcome from the PSI model. Moreover, the prediction is of the barometric sort — "current trends portend" — not the "law-like" invariant prediction from initial causes that some readers suspect me of offering.[4]

How does this work? *R&R* argued that early modern state breakdowns could be explained from initial causes by starting with population shifts, following their impact on prices, and then detailing the joint impact of population and price changes on three factors — a crisis of state capacities (chiefly fiscal), elite competition and alienation, and popular mobilization potential. The conjuncture of these last three factors, if all present at high levels, constituted a situation of impending state breakdown.

Tilly argues that this last statement is a tautology, simply saying that "state breakdown" is composed of three components. True, it is a tautology; and you can only *explain* state breakdown if you can point to the factors responsible for a rise in the three constituent factors. Population shifts and inflexible institutions constitute the explanation for the early modern states analyzed in *R&R*. In modern states, with their greater power, variety, and industrial complexity, additional factors — including technical change, policy planning failures, and foreign intervention — may affect state capacity, elite loyalties, and popular mobilization potential. However, the tautology, being a tautology, is not bound to any particular cases. It can be used more generally as a tool of analysis and prediction.

How can this be? Tautologies have a respected and valuable place in scientific work. Scientific theories tend to have three parts. One is observations of empirical regularities (e.g. revolutions and rebellions occur more frequently in some eras than in others). Another is models of cause and effect (e.g., population growth in relatively static economies can overwhelm economic, political, and status institutions). A third is tautologies, which form the basis for measurement. For example, Newton's Third Law — Force = Mass x Acceleration ($F=MA$) — is a tautology; it is true by definition. However, it is still extremely useful, for it provides a way to measure the force on an object. If we can measure an object's mass and acceleration, then we know the magnitude of the force acting on it (even though the force may have different causes in different cases). Moreover, if we can measure how mass and/or acceleration are changing over time, we can track how the force is changing over time as well.

My tautology for measurement is as follows: PSI (pressures for state breakdown) = state crisis x elite competition and alienation x popular mobilization potential. If we can identify proxies or indicators for these three factors and measure them, then we can track the pressures for state breakdown (with no claim that the origins of those pressures is the same in every case). The difference between my tautology and the one that Tilly offers is not that mine pretends to be an explanation. It doesn't. The difference — but what a difference — is that my tautology comes with illustrations of how to use it as tool for measurement, rather than as merely a definitional and analytic aid.

To go back to the barometer, although there are various theories of weather systems, one needs neither a full explanation of the source of a particular storm, nor a single theory for the origins of all storms, to use the barometer to see it coming. One only needs to know that low pressure = stormy weather, and a way to measure the pressure. Similarly, I argue that the PSI model can be a useful barometer — when the PSI levels are high, "stormy weather," politically speaking, is just over the horizon.

I illustrate with two cases. In Figure 1, the upper graph is drawn from *R&R*; it indicates that early modern England faced politically "stormy weather" in the mid-seventeenth century, with calmer spells on either side. It is based on combining three data series: a measure of fiscal stress, changes in university enrollments (as a proxy indicator for elite competition), and a measure reflecting primarily changes in real wages (as a proxy indicator for grievances regarding living conditions that might conduce to mass mobilization). The lower graph is drawn from my current work on the state breakdown in the Soviet Union. It also tracks three simple data series, modified to serve as proxies for state fiscal stress, elite competition and alienation, and popular mobilization potential, namely inverse GNP growth per annum, inverse percentage of high school graduates admitted to elite universities, and death rates per thousand (used in lieu of wages to indicate changes in living standards since wages are almost meaningless in the price-controlled Soviet economy), respectively.[5] While I must refer interested readers to that work for detailed justification, the point here is simply illustrative; by tracking the components of PSI and

Pressures for Instability, England

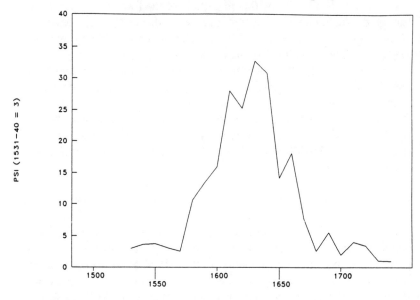

Pressures for Instability, USSR

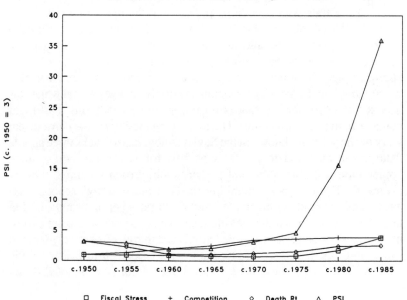

combining them to take a "pressure" reading, one can see that just as in England by 1640 so too in the U.S.S.R. by 1985 political conditions were indicating heavy storms just ahead. The "tautological" decomposition of state breakdown into three separate conditions thus works extremely well as an analytical and measurement tool, even for quite different societies.

What then is the main contribution of *R&R* — the explanation of early modern state breakdowns? Or the analytical definition of state breakdown that allows it to be tracked in a variety of settings? The answer is both, or neither, depending on your needs. For a historian interested in the causes of early modern revolutions and rebellions, the demographic explanation is my main contribution.[6] For a political scientist interested in analyzing or forecasting state breakdowns in other times and places, the analytical decomposition of state breakdown may be more valuable.[7] On the other hand, for scholars interested in yet another topic — how revolutions unfold and produce new regimes — we shall have to turn to a third element of my work, namely the role of elites, ideologies, and cultural frameworks in the process and outcomes of revolutionary situations.

MATTERS OF CULTURE

When critics such as Wasserstrom say they need to bring culture back in, it seems they believe I am excluding culture from affecting anything prior to state breakdown, as if all state breakdowns looked alike and only at a later point are differentiated into revolutions and non-revolutions. That is not true.

My views are grossly misunderstood by treating the assertion that material factors cause state breakdown while cultural factors cause revolution (or conservative reconstruction) as a *temporal separation* rather than an *analytical ordering* of the role of material and cultural factors. The correct interpretation of my theory is that some societies, if they suffer state breakdown, are liable to experience revolutions. Other societies, if they suffer state breakdown, are liable to experience successful rebellions but not revolutions. What distinguishes the two kinds of societies in this regard is their cultural frameworks, which provide the basis for different varieties of ideologies.[8] The differences in culture shape the content of the entire process of pre-revolutionary conflict, state breakdown, struggles for power, and state reconstruction. Yet the factors whose change produces state breakdown in *both* kinds of societies are demonstrably material causes — namely changes in the flow of resources among the state, elites, and popular groups that undermine key institutions.

I make these claims not because I wish to give some meta-theoretical priority to material factors, or because such factors inevitably dominate a "scientific" approach to revolutions. I make these claims about both origins and outcomes because that is simply what I found. That is, I do not know of societies with stable and sound resource flows — states with neither excess debts nor excessive accumulations from corruption; elites with neither highly visible rising *nouveaux riches* nor marginalized elite aspirants; and popular groups with stable incomes and employment opportunities — where cultural or ideological changes have led to state breakdown.[9] Moreover, states with a wide range of cultural frameworks *have* experienced state breakdowns, and in those that I have examined disrupted or altered resource flows were the cause.

Given that there is no empirical correlation between specific kinds of culture, or specific changes in culture, and state breakdown, I do not see how we can claim that culture is a prime *cause* (as opposed to shaping the form) of state breakdown. Since there *is* a correlation between specific kinds of cultural frameworks — eschatological — and revolution in the sense of a fundamental change in the ideological basis of governance, and no correlation between the material causes of state breakdown and this kind of revolutionary outcome, I consider it an equally scientific fact that cultural, *not* material, factors play the main causal role in producing fundamental revolutionary change.

In short, to say that material factors cause state breakdowns while cultural factors determine fundamental change does not deny the role of cultural factors in shaping many aspects of pre-revolutionary conflicts and the revolutionary process. It is simply an observation, based on extensive case examination, that the *causal priority* of material and cultural factors should be analytically distinguished over different *aspects* of revolutions and rebellions.

Some authors may be troubled that my position is inconsistent — how can I stay so close to Marx in favoring material causes (though not class conflicts) for revolutions, but completely oppose Marx in claiming cultural, not material, factors as the prime determinant of outcomes? The answer is that my approach *is* inconsistent with any monocausal simplification of history. I like to believe that it is more consistent with what actually happened in history. That is, if we ask — what factors determined whether or not a state broke down? — the answer is material changes that undermined the stability and effectiveness of institutions. If we ask — what factors determined the content of state reconstruction? — the answer is cultural frameworks that provided the conceptual vocabulary for seeking change. If we ask — what factors determined revolutionary mobilization and revolutionary success? — the answer is both material and cultural factors; material resource flows determine the viability of revolutionaries' organizations and the vulnerability of the state, while cultural factors underly the language and content of revolutionary mobilization.

How then should we combine cultural and material factors in analyzing a problem in the explanation of revolutions? Let us take one of Wasserstrom's concerns: "Why was the collapse of the Qing followed by such a long and chaotic period, during which a complete reversion to the previous political status quo was impossible, and yet those attempting to establish new orders seemed destined to fail;" and moreover, why did the Chinese Communist Party succeed in winning power against the Nationalist Goumindang regime?

In answer to the first part of the question, it should be recalled that a long period of shifting and unstable rule is not unusual following state breakdown.

A comparativist can point out that post-state breakdown consolidation is always problematic, frequently takes decades and reveals a succession of different and short-lived regimes. France after 1792 saw a short-lived republic, a military empire, a restored monarchy, a constitutional monarchy, and another republic and empire, all in the course of six decades. England after 1640 saw a series of religious compromises, a commonwealth, a military dictatorship, a restored monarchy, another round of religious compromises, then a change of dynasty with constitutional reforms, in the succeeding five decades. The "problem" of lasting disorder after 1911 is not unique but a normal part of many revolutionary situations. In several cases a series of regimes have tried to replace a state that broke down but failed to provide solutions to most of the problems that had felled it — problems that persisted beyond the demise of the old regime because they were rooted in the economic and geopolitical context, *not* just in the structure of the old regime itself.

It is clear that the Nationalists inherited not only the territory, but the problems of the fallen Qing regime — an economy that struggled to keep pace with China's population growth and that did not offer the resources to fight off Western and Japanese imperialism. After all, these problems were inherent in China's geopolitical and economic condition, not merely defects of the old imperial regime, and any successor seeking to reconstruct and consolidate state authority would have to deal with them. Why then did the Nationalist's fail, and the Communists succeed?

Wasserstrom, I presume, would be at pains to point out the role of Maoist ideology and peasant culture in mobilizing the peasantry to the Communists' cause. I certainly would insist on including this *element* in the analysis, for I specifically (*R&R*, 421-436) point out that ideologies — usually blending rectification, redistribution, and nationalism — play a key role in marginal elites' construction of winning coalitions that enable their organizations to seize power. However, I could not rest content with Maoist ideology as the *main* explanation for Communist victory — especially since recent research shows that there was not a single Maoist "ideology," but that different ideas guided tactics in different base areas, and at different stages of rural mobilization.[10] Moreover, a critical factor in the fall of the Nationalists was the desertion of elites and workers — intellectuals, professionals, businessmen, officials, soldiers — who were less attracted by Communist ideology than repelled by Nationalist economic and military failures.

I thus suggest that Mao would not have had the opportunity to mobilize the peasantry with his ideology and organization *unless* the Goumindang regime had failed for its part to establish a sound fiscal basis, to gain the loyalty of national and local elites, and to mobilize popular support (or at least create contented passivity) by solving economic and imperialist problems. Thus to explain why the Chinese Communists achieved victory it would be necessary to demonstrate the material bases of Goumindang failure, and the corresponding material bases of the Communists' success — that is, what was their fiscal base, how did they establish elite loyalty and deal with popular economic grievances? My comparative perspective on the roles of material and ideological factors suggests that the *primary* reason for Mao's success would have to lie in the Goumindang failure, and Communist success, in these three material foundations of state-building; without them Communist ideology would not have had a chance to play its role in mobilization and state reconstruction. On the other hand, my comparative perspective equally would argue that many of the key policies implemented by Mao — including the imposition of rural "work-team" structure on the cities, the Great Leap Forward, and the Cultural Revolution — derived not from any material conditions in Chinese society (and here I differ markedly from Skocpol), but from ideological developments in the Communist Party that unfolded in the course of the revolution.

Despite numerous errors of interpretation (e.g., assuming that I give pride of place to origins over outcomes in scientific work on revolutions — I don't, it's just that I've spent more time tackling the origins problem to date; or assuming that I want to marginalize the discussion of culture in analyzing revolutions — I don't, I just find causal priority for material factors in explaining certain issues, while for others I minimize the role of material causes; or, and this is maddening, assuming I give priority to comparativists over area specialists — I don't, I preach mutual dependence and recognize that comparativists need area specialists much more than they need us), Wasserstrom is a perceptive critic. He correctly finds fault with my statement that inconsistent repression makes "rapid revolution" more likely. What I meant was that inconsistent repression makes "the onset of state breakdown likely to develop more quickly," *not* that fundamental change would arrive sooner. I am guilty here of not being clear regarding state breakdown vs. revolutionary outcomes. Even more importantly, Wasserstrom points out that comparativists don't always "scratch" where historians "itch." This observation deserves comment.

COMPARATIVISTS AND HISTORIANS

Wasserstrom is right that there is currently a misfit between the interests of comparativists and historians. This is because a funny thing happened in late twentieth-century European historiography. Having finally freed themselves of the Marxist answer to the question — what caused the great revolutions of European history? — European historians abandoned the question itself. Scholars of seventeenth-century England and eighteenth-century France seem resigned to considering the political crises of those eras to be accidents, due to freak conjunctures of bad weather and bad policy, momentous in their consequences perhaps (or perhaps not), but certainly unremarkable in their origins.[11]

Historians have thus turned from analyzing the origins of these events and seeking explanations for their occurrence to seeking richer descriptions of how they unfolded, how they appeared to participants, and why they developed in particular directions. Clearly for these questions my view of revolutions suggests that matters of culture, ideologies, and elite/popular interaction should take center stage. However, comparativists including myself have done little to develop a full schema for the unfolding and outcomes of revolutions. The bulk of our efforts has been to go back to the question — why do revolutions occur? — grant the demise of the Marxist answer, and seek to develop better explanations. Since historians have moved on to other matters, it is no surprise that they find the current efforts of comparativists less than compelling. And of course, when they look at my work in particular on the origins of state breakdown, in which the effort to find a better answer leads firmly to material factors, they find that their current language and concerns about culture seem comparatively neglected — overlooking the fact that I am working on a problem that they have largely set aside. I do hope, however, that when they tire of semiotic deconstruction of what transpired in the course of revolutions and again rouse themselves to ask *why* these events commenced when and where they did, they will find in recent comparative work a valuable starting point.

Before I lay myself open to further misunderstanding, let me say that in speaking of "comparativists" and "specialists" I am speaking of roles, and not of persons. Many of the best comparativists have also played the role of superb area specialists (Barrington Moore on Russia, Immanuel Wallerstein on Africa), and outstanding area specialists have played the role of excellent analysts of general theories of revolutions (Nikki Keddie, William Sewell, Jr.). Indeed, such scholars humble those of us (on both sides) who find ourselves limited to one role or the other. Moreover, only a fool (and I don't think Wasserstrom is painting me as such) would ignore the comparative implications of more specialized work by scholars such as Sewell and Furet; indeed my treatment of ideology in revolutions begins with Sewell and explicitly builds upon Furet's analysis of the revolutionary process. Any attempts to set priorities between comparativists and area specialists will find no friend in me; in *R&R* (54) I wrote that "A comparative historian does not approach historical scholarship as a miner approaches a mine [i.e. to map it out and pick it over]. Instead, he or she approaches the literature as a historian would, to engage in a conversation about what happened." In that sense I endorse Wasserstrom's view of the way that comparativists and specialists can help fill in each other's oversights as a fruitful way to proceed.[12]

As an example of such a conversation, let me reply to Wasserstrom's query — what did I mean by comparing the Tiananmen Square demonstration to the taking of the Bastille in France? Wasserstrom is right to push me on this — how can I say that June 4 was like July 14, when the latter led quickly to revolution while the former did not?

My answer is that I meant that Tiananmen Square would be seen as a turning point in the history of the Communist regime. Unlike other confrontations that involved mainly intellectuals, such as the Hundred Flowers Movement, or other events that were in some sense orchestrated by the regime, such as the Cultural Revolution, Tiananmen marked the first time that a cross-class coalition involving intellectuals and popular elements acted independently to challenge the regime. The immediate consequence was repression; however, I believe the forces that brought on Tiananmen, namely fiscal problems brought on by the encouragement of rapid growth in a still largely state-controlled economy; elite competition and alienation brought on by the encouragement of private wealth accumulation in a still party-controlled political system; and problems of popular dislocation due to uneven development in a context where the Party maintains responsibility for public welfare, are not passing, but inherent in the policies being pursued by the Party. I therefore believe that these problems will grow, weakening the Party, strengthening the intellectual/professional/business coalition of elites seeking freedom from Party control, and increasing the likelihood of mass demonstrations against the Party. The overthrow of the Communist Party may be years away, and the consolidation of a new regime years or even decades into the future. But in a comparative perspective this is not unusual — the fall of the Bastille took several years to lead to the creation of a Republic against a monarchy much weaker than the Communist regime in China. And even so, republican government was not firmly established in France for decades — less than twenty of the eighty years from 1789 to 1869 in France were years of republican government. Many scholars seem to believe that revolutions "work" rapidly and all at once. If nothing else, comparativists can remind them — despite the heroic myth of revolution — this is not how history works. Given the three possible interpretations of Tiananmen that were possible in May 1989 — (1) that it signalled the end of Communist rule, (2) that it was a passing outburst, like other incidents of protest following a window of liberalization and followed by repression that have marked, but not seriously challenged, Communist rule, or (3) that it marked a turning point in revealing the weakening grip of the Communist regime on society, but one whose full impact would not be settled until yet further conflicts and confrontations occurred — I would still stand by (3), which I offered in my analysis of May 30, 1989 as the most accurate of the three.

That "prediction" was based on my comparative perspective, which suggested that the necessary conjunctural components for state breakdown were growing, but not yet all at high levels. Wasserstrom's comparison of Tiananmen to Russia's 1905 outburst is also, interestingly, an assessment of type (3): that it revealed the weakness, but not the immediate end, of the regime. I used the Bastille day analogy because both the Bastille and Tiananmen Square represented takings of a symbolic central place in the capital city; Wasserstrom may prefer the 1905 analogy because, as we now know, there were disturbances throughout China, and the combination of reform and repression that followed 1905 is more similar to the Chinese response. I am willing to concede Wasserstrom's version of what is basically an agreement between us on the significance of Tiananmen. Other area specialists may disagree, but there a valuable conversation begins.

ARJOMAND'S ALTERNATIVE

Said Amir Arjomand is one of those scholars who deftly combines the roles of area specialist and comparativist. Yet I find less that is useful in his comments. Arjomand's claim that Skocpol's "emphasis on the autonomous role of the state" is "subverted" by my "materialism" is a ridiculous misstatement of my views. In my model state actors, elite actors, and popular actors are all autonomous and potentially divided into competing autonomous factions and groups within each category — with all actors seeking to hold or maintain income, political power, and social status. Population growth does not produce state breakdown by some puppet-like pulling of actors' strings; rather where population growth creates scarcities, and autonomous actors compete intensely for limited or redirected resources, conflict results. Indeed, as I spell out in great detail in R&R (334-343), a major example of the autonomy of the state was evident in Germany in 1848, when improved fiscal institutions allowed the Prussian regime to survive dramatic population pressures that alienated elites and provided a basis for popular actions in much of Germany. The stronger fiscal basis of the state meant that in this case population pressures produced only a mild state breakdown which the regime soon reversed. Not a postulated helplessness of states or other actors in the face of material change, but the emprical facts that institutions that worked effectively when population and prices were stable became ineffective or unreliable when populations grew, and that such institutions were generally slow to change, created the links between changing material conditions and state breakdowns. *R&R* explicitly points out (341-342 and 481-482) that in those cases where state institutions had been reformed to give them unusual effectiveness (as in early nineteenth century Prussia), or states could more readily change their institutions (as in England in 1832), even great population pressures might result in state breakdown being mild or averted.

In addition, Arjomand's claim that I ignore the normative foundations of political order and issues of "legitimacy" stems from his ignorance of my work on contemporary revolutions. That work noted that although fiscal factors were the key to state capacity in early modern agrarian bureaucracies, this is not a sufficient guide to state capacity in general. I therefore replaced fiscal crisis as one of the three determinants of state breakdown by the broader notion of "state crisis." This is defined as a crisis of state effectiveness *and justice*, which combine to create legitimacy, and in which fiscal competence is only one component. I explicitly say "a state crisis should be defined . . . as a situation in which significant numbers of elites and popular groups believe that the central authorities are acting in ways that are fundamentally ineffective, immoral, or unjust. State crises are, in other words, crises of legitimacy."[13] I thus cannot understand Arjomand's premise that state autonomy and legitimacy are excluded from my work. His plea for an alternative view of revolution to correct these failings seems to rest on misreading and ignorance of my actual writings.

His sketch of an alternative seems no more valid. His two ideal types of revolution simply restate old views. Tocqueville and Skocpol argued that revolution most commonly leads to greater centralization of state power (although the anti-Communist revolutions of 1989 so far offer a challenge to this trend). The notion that revolutions involve the expansion of political participation may go back to Aristotle, but it was stated most succinctly in recent years by Samuel Huntington, who wrote: "Revolution is the extreme case of the explosion of political participation."[14] To repeat that revolutions involve centralization of power and/or the expansion of political participation tells us nothing new about why they occur when they do, or what they involve.

This failure is clear in Arjomand's attempt to account for the East European Revolutions of 1989. He points to three factors: (1) "disintegration of the central authority," (2) the challenge of the intellegentsia who "wanted in"; and (3) "loss of legitimacy" due to "economic failure that came to light in the 1980s" which eroded support among both the populace and the administrative staff. I hope I am not the only one who sees the irony in Arjomand's posing an "alternative" theory whose components correspond almost exactly to my analysis of state breakdown as occurring when there is a conjunction of (1) state crisis; (2) elite alienation and divisions; and (3) a rise in mass mobilization potential. This is just wordplay, not a meaningful alternative theory of revolutions.

Most importantly, however, Arjomand does not go beyond this tautology because he does not seem to realize it *is* a tautology. After all, one cannot say that communism fell *because* the central authority disintegrated and the system lost legitimacy. That disintegration and delegitimation *constitute* the fall of communism. It would require much more than Arjomand gives us to begin to explain *why* state disintegration and delegitimation developed in the late 1980s.

Indeed, I am puzzled by scholars who claim to make progress in explaining revolutions simply by saying that regimes perish when they lose "legitimacy." When pressed to explain what *caused* the loss of legitimacy, they often fall back upon the same factors — economic failures, alienation of elites, corruption, administrative inefficiency — that I have cited in explaining revolutions in both early modern agrarian bureaucracies and modern neopatrimonial dictatorships. If "legitimacy" is to be introduced as an aid to explanation, it is necessary to spell out the state actions that both retain and lose legitimacy, and explain what leads state actors to take such actions. Where I have explored legitimacy, I have tried to be precise about legitimacy depending on the state achieving a balance of compliance with elite and popular expectations regarding both performance and procedural norms, and to show how in certain circumstances performance and procedural demands are either frustrated or pitted against each other, resulting in loss of legitimacy. It is precisely because "delegitimated" (i.e. "immoral") states can remain in power if they retain *effectiveness*, which depends on material achievements that sustain a sound fiscal base and administrative loyalty to the regime, that pointing to legitimacy is not sufficient to understand why and when states fall (Wasserstrom is wise enough to point out that the Chinese Communists retention of power after being "delegitimized" by Tiananmen raises this issue).

To return briefly to the issue of material and cultural factors in revolutions, it is precisely because illegitimate states do *not* break down until they lose their effectiveness that I give material factors causal priority in state breakdown. Indeed, I have found that legitimacy can help states survive short period of ineffectiveness; however, any state that fails in performance for a sustained period loses its legitimacy (as Arjomand admits for the Soviet regime). What legitimacy buys a regime is time to fix problems. As I point out in discussing neo-patrimonial regimes, their illegitimacy means that when they do lose their effectiveness they collapse very quickly and thoroughly. In contrast, more legitimate regimes, when they lose their effectivness, may experience decades of attempted reform. Yet if these fail, the state will lose its legitimacy along with its resources.[15] Once a state breaks down, successor regimes must solve the material problems of state reconstruction in order to survive. Yet they must also choose an ideological basis for legitimizing the measures they take for state reconstruction; it is in that choice that cultural factors become critical.

In short, considerations of legitimacy fit well within my overall analysis, and I have moved to incorporate them. I welcome efforts to further this analysis, but simply waving the word "legitimacy" as a talisman to banish complex problems of revolutionary causation is not helpful.

Finally, Arjomand's claim that ideology has disappeared in these revolutions is nonsense. Perhaps *communist* ideology perished, but nationalist ideologies and liberal ideologies were behind these revolutions and are very much alive in the debate over how they will unfold. How Arjomand can claim that nationalism and liberalism are not ideologies, or that they are not active in post-Soviet eastern and central Europe, is simply beyond my ken.

WHAT NEXT IN THE STUDY OF "REVOLUTIONS?"

Wasserstrom and other critics have called for greater attention to culture in the study of revolutions. That is fine, but we need more detailed suggestions for *how* to integrate culture into the analysis of "revolutions" for progress to be made. My own suggestions are roughly as follows: Don't treat culture as an abstract "above the fray" guide to events; treat culture as a *component* of complex situations with political and material components as well, with culture sometimes leading, sometimes reacting to, other elements. Don't treat culture as operating only on one level, particularly "society" as a whole, or as pointing only in one direction; treat culture as something varied that influences different actors in different degrees, and which actors themselves appropriate, develop, and use in creative ways to pursue power, wealth, and status. Recognize that ideologies are double-edged swords that can legitimize *and* delegitimize actors in the same conflict (for example, the Chinese Communists claimed to be the legitimate heirs to the democratic May 4th movement in Chinese history; are they still so legitimated, or does the ideology associated with May 4th now delegitimize the post-Tiananmen Party?).

Do recognize that culture shapes the language and actions of parties in pre-revolutionary and consquent conflicts, and that culture sets the performance and procedural norms that states must meet to retain legitimacy and avoid state crisis, yet grant that material factors affect their ability to meet those norms. And realize that culture sets bounds on the conceivable range of actions and ideologies that elite and popular groups can adopt in response to material change.

My own agenda for research includes more efforts to measure the trends that produced state breakdowns in a wide variety of societies. But it also includes efforts to better understand how elites draw on and use ideology in revolutionary (and counter-revolutionary) mobilization, especially nationalism.[16] It also includes efforts to distinguish those circumstances in which revolutions, rebellions, and/or reforms are more likely to produce genuine democratization from those circumstances in which they are more likely to produce authoritarian regimes.[17] And I particularly encourage students to explore the actions and fate of "hidden" actors in revolutions — families, women, and ethnic minorities.[18]

A general theory of revolutions is clearly a long way off. Perhaps Arjomand's forthcoming two-volume history of revolutions will make a greater contribution; certainly the kind of exchange among historians and comparativists described by Wasserstrom will help. I do not claim to offer such a complete theory; I merely hope that the various parts of such a theory that I have tried to develop will continue to be a part of future debates.

NOTES

This paper was written while the author was a Fellow at the Center for Advanced Study in the Behavioral Sciences. I am grateful for research support provided by NSF grant SES-9022192.
1   Said Amir Arjomand, "Plea for an Alternative View of Revolution," *Contention* 2 (Winter 1993): 171-183; John Foran, "Revolutionizing Theory, Theorizing Revolutions," *Contention* 2 (Winter 1993): 65-88; Andre Gunder Frank, "The World is Round and Wavy," *Contention* 2 (Winter 1993): 107-125; Charles Tilly, "The Bourgeois Gentilshommes of Revolutionary Theory," *Contention* 2 (Winter 1993): 153-158; Jeffrey Wasserstrom, "Bringing Culture Back In: A Critique of Jack Goldstone's Recent Essays on Revolution," *Contention* 3 (Fall 1993): 153-175.
2   Jack A. Goldstone, *Revolution and Rebellion in the Early Modern World* (Berkeley and Los Angeles: University of California Press, 1991); *idem*, "Ideology, Cultural Frameworks, and the Process of Revolution," *Theory and Society*, 20 (1991): 405-454; *idem*, "Deterrence in Rebellions and Revolutions," in *Perspectives on Deterrence*, ed. P. Stern, R. Axelrod, R. Jervis, and R. Radner (New York: Oxford University Press, 1989), pp. 222-250; *idem*, "Revolutions and Superpowers," in *Superpowers and Revolutions*, ed. Jonathan Adelman (New York: Praeger, 1986), pp. 38-48; Jack A. Goldstone, Ted Robert Gurr, and Farrokh Moshiri, eds. *Revolutions of the Late Twentieth Century* (Boulder, CO: Westview Press, 1991).
3   Tilly, "Bourgeois Gentilshommes," p. 158.
4   In logical-positivist models of explanation based on univeral covering laws, explanation and prediction are of course equivalent, since if invariant laws link the the cause and effect one can go backwards (explanation) or forwards (prediction) from the same model. However, historical explanation is not equivalent to prediction, since one is tracing robust processes in *particular* settings, not deducing universal laws. Similarly, prediction by tracking indicator trends — as with a barometer — is not equivalent to explanation, since one is not deducing the effect from initial conditions. Once we set aside simple logical-positivist models of science, explanation and prediction are both still possible, but they are different and independent. For further examples of how scientific reasoning in the *historical* sciences — both natural history (geology, evolution) and human history — need not be tied to logical-positivist "laws," see Jack A.

Goldstone, "Sociology and History: Producing Comparative History," in *Sociology in America*, ed. Herbert Gans (Beverly Hills, CA: Sage Publications, 1990), pp. 275-292.

5   The graph of PSI in England in *R&R* (p. 144) is presented in standard deviation form (mean = 0, st.dev. = 1). I have here restored it to cardinal data form, and normalized both the English and Soviet data to the same scale (PSI in initial period = 3) for ease of comparison. The sources of the Soviet data series are: GNP growth from Anders Aslund, *Gorbachev's Struggle for Economic Reform* (Ithaca, NY: Cornell University Press, 1991), p. 17; University admissions, trend estimated from Murray Yanowitch, *Social and Economic Inequality in the Soviet Union* (White Plains, NY: M.E. Sharpe, 1977), p. 80; death rates from Murray Feshbach and Alfred Friendly, Jr., *Ecocide in the U.S.S.R.* (New York: Basic Books, 1992) p. 5. A full explanation of this analysis is in Jack A. Goldstone, "Testing the PSI model of State Breakdown: An Application to the Soviet Collapse of the 1980s." Paper presented to the Center for Advanced Study in the Behavioral Sciences, January 1993.

6   For an example of how my analysis has been useful to a European historian examining an early modern political crisis I did not analyze, the revolts in the Austrian Habsburg empire, see Karin J. MacHardy, "The Rise of Absolutism and Noble Rebellion in Early Modern Habsburg Austria, 1570 to 1620," *Comparative Studies in Society and History* 34 (July 1992): 407-438.

7   Goldstone, Gurr, and Moshiri, *Revolutions of the Late Twentieth Century*, offers a series of case studies in which area specialists use this decomposition of state breakdown to guide their analyses of modern revolutions.

8   Although I am often referred to as student of Theda Skocpol, and thought to have taken over her often relentless materialism, I was equally a student of S.N. Eisenstadt (visiting Faculty member at Harvard 1976 - 1979), and I am indebted to him for an appreciation of the role of culture in shaping revolutions (see S.N. Eisenstadt, *Revolution and the Transformation of Societies* (Free Press, 1978) and *idem*, "Frameworks of the great revolutions: culture, social structure, history and human agency," *International Social Science Journal* 133 (1992): 385-401.) While I differ from both these mentors, my aims might best be conceived as seeking to combine what is best in both scholars' works.

9   On the general point that new ideologies and cultural frameworks can only emerge if there is a prior shift in resources that provides the

material basis for cultural entrepreneurs to propagate their ideas in contest with the existing institutions' cultural hegemony, see Roberth Wuthnow, *Communities of Discourse: Ideology and Social Structure in the Reformation, the Enlightenment, and European Socialism* (Cambridge, MA: Harvard University Press, 1989).

10   Kathryn Bernhardt, *Rents, Taxes, and Peasant Resistance: The Yangzi Region, 1840-1950* (Stanford: Stanford University Press, 1992); Edward Friedman, Paul G. Pickowicz, Mark Selden with Kay Ann Johnson, *Chinese Village, Socialist State* (New Haven: Yale University Press, 1991).

11   The pioneering texts presenting these views were G. R. Elton, *Studies in Tudor and Stuart Politics and Government*, 2 vols. (Cambridge: Cambridge University Press, 1974) and Francois Furet, *Interpreting the French Revolution*, trans. E. Forster (Cambridge: Cambridge University Press, 1981).

12   Let me also endorse his comments on the exceptional vision of his field. Of all area specialists, I have found China scholars to be the most generous and inviting to this comparativist in exchanging ideas and perspectives. Fred Wakeman, Philip Huang, Liz Perry, Philip Kuhn, Edward Friedman, and G. W. Skinner — distinguished specialists all — have been unstintingly supportive in their reviews, helpful in their criticism, and welcoming to their discussions.

13   Ted Robert Gurr and Jack A. Goldstone, "Comparisons and Policy Implications," in Goldstone, Gurr, and Moshiri, eds., *Revolutions of the Late Twentieth Century*, p. 325. For a more extended discussion of legitimacy in terms of effectiveness and justice, see Goldstone, "Deterrence in Rebellions and Revolutions."

14   Samuel P. Huntington, *Political Order in Changing Societies* (New Haven: Yale University Press, 1968), p. 266.

15   See Goldstone, "Deterrence in Rebellions and Revolutions."

16   Jack A. Goldstone, "The Birth of States, the Birth of Nations," Paper presented at the 1993 American Sociological Association Meetings, Miami, FL.

17   This direction was begun in Gurr and Goldstone, "Comparisons," pp. 343-344.

18   E.g., see the selections in Chapter Six, "Families, Women, and Minorities in Revolutions" of my undergraduate text, Jack A. Goldstone, ed., *Revolutions: Theoretical, Comparative, and Historical Studies*, 2nd rev. ed. (Fort Worth, TX: Harcourt Brace Jovanovich: 1994).

THE WORLD IS ROUND AND WAVY:

DEMOGRAPHIC CYCLES & STRUCTURAL ANALYSIS IN THE WORLD SYSTEM

A REVIEW ESSAY OF JACK A. GOLDSTONE *REVOLUTIONS AND REBELLIONS IN THE EARLY MODERN WORLD* (Berkeley: University of California Press, 1991).

ANDRE GUNDER FRANK

Jack Goldstone's marvelous book is more than just another study of revolutions and rebellions. In addition, it offers a demographic/structural and *cyclical* analysis of economic, political, social, cultural and ideological factors responsible for *state breakdown*. Revolutions are only the straw that break the camel's back, and rebellions fail to topple the state only because structural conditions are not ripe. Goldstone examines these factors in a detailed new and comparative analysis of the English Revolution of 1640, the French Revolution of 1789, the Ottoman crises, and the transitions in Ming China (1500-1650). The Ming Dynasty was in trouble from 1590 onward and came to its end in 1644, four years after the revolution in England. Major army revolts and other political disturbances ravaged and almost undid the Ottoman empire periodically from 1589 to 1633, and again in 1648 and 1667-58. For purposes of further comparison Goldstone also examines *simultaneous* related events in seventeenth-century France and Spain and in eighteenth-century Germany and elsewhere.

Goldstone also makes some comparative excursions into nineteenth-century crises in Qing China, Tokugawa/Mejii Restoration Japan, and again the Ottoman Empire, arguing that "any claim that such trends were produced *solely* by unique local conditions is thoroughly undermined by the evidence" (p.462).

To explain, we may best let Goldstone speak for himself:

My primary conclusion is quite beautiful in its parsimony. It is that *the periodic state breakdowns in Europe, China, and the Middle East from 1500 to 1850 were the result of a single basic process.* . . . The main trend was that population growth, in the context of relatively inflexible economic and social structures, led to changes in prices, shifts in resources, and increasing social demands with which the agrarian-bureaucratic states could not successfully cope.

The four related critical trends were as follows: (1) Pressures increased on state finances as inflation eroded state income and population growth raised real expenses. . . . (2) Intra-elite conflicts became more prevalent as larger families and inflation made it more difficult for some families to maintain their status . . . while creating new aspirants to elite positions. . . . (3) Popular unrest grew, as competition for land, urban migration, flooded labor markets, declining real wages, and increased youthfulness raised the mass mobilization potential of the populace. . . . (4) The ideologies of rectification and transformation became increasingly salient . . . and turned both elites and middling groups to heterodox religious movements in the search for reform, order, and discipline. The conjunctures of these four critical trends . . . combined to undermine stability on *multiple* levels of social organization.

This basic process was triggered all across Eurasia by periods of sustained population increases that occurred in the sixteenth and early seventeenth centuries and again in the late eighteenth and early nineteenth centuries, thus producing worldwide waves of state breakdown. In contrast, in the late seventeenth and early eighteenth centuries populations did not grow, and the basic process and its four

subthemes were absent. Political and social stability
resulted
(pp. 459-60, emphasis in the original, also in quotations
below unless otherwise indicated).

Goldstone himself labels and summarizes: "the present model of
state breakdown, though not Marxist, is nonethless materialist — I claim
that it was changing population/resource balances that led to state
breakdown" (p. 348).

This book's analysis and its author's critiques of other writers tread
on so many people's toes that true believers of every stripe have been and
will be rising to scream in self-righteous self-defense of their respective
but varied received wisdoms and self-evident truths. Therefore, it is not
necessary here also to tread on everybody else's home ground for more of
the same, even if Goldstone also offends some of my own pet peeves.
Idealists will be mortally wounded by Goldstone's materialist analysis.
Marxists will find traitorous, and perhaps treacherous, his negation of
[inter] class struggle as the motor of history in general and of revolution
in particular. Revisionists will feel denuded in the shortcomings of their
own revisions. Specialists, as always, will exhibit their jealousy of
outsiders' comparative analysis and generalists' broader scope, not to
mention Goldstone's better analysis of their own material, by saying it is
not that way in their own backyard. Localists here and there will be upset
to find that the similar things also happened there — all the way across
Eurasia — at the same time as here, and therefore are unlikely to have been
exclusively or even especially due to the unique local conditions which
are so dear to them. Generalists [like me] will complain that Goldstone
still misses the wood for comparing the trees. His comparisons of Ottoman
and Chinese experience as at least equivalent to if not more important than
"classical" British and French ones will offend Eurocentrists, and perhaps
Sinologists and others, in their parochial false superiority. Nor will the
former and perhaps the latter easily accept Goldstone's claim that "the
standard story of the 'Rise of the West' is false" (p.484). Defenders of
various true faiths will reject his observation that "history tells a quite
different story. Revolutions, in general, no more give rise to democracy
than capitalism gives rise to revolutions" (p.476).

Historians will say, "this is not history." Demographers may
quibble with Goldstone's use of data. Economists may have reservations
with his demography and feel attacked by his rejection of the Quantity

Theory of Money, not to mention his denying an important role to American silver in Europe's [and Asia's] 16th century inflation.[1] Sociologists and political scientists will feel discomfort at having Goldstone pull various comfortable old and new revisionist rugs out from under them. Believers in the overriding importance of ideology will not like its being confined to conjunctural and even marginal roles. Ideal ideologists or ideological idealists will feel unhinged by this book's very de jure and de facto challenge to their idealist ideology. If this is not history [or economics, sociology, etc.], so much the worse for history [or whatever discipline]! Concerned and qualified specialists have already begun and will wish to continue examining Goldstone's tour de force over the traditional turf of the English and French revolutions. They will no doubt rise to defend themselves and their respective disciplines by rejecting Goldstone's affronts to their scholarly fields and personal sensibilities.

Instead of dwelling on the above conflicts, this review essay tries to pursue the implications of Goldstone's analysis beyond even his own already wide-ranging concerns. In particular, Goldstone's analysis and arguments about the early modern world are here related to wider concerns in macrohistorical sociology and international political economy as well as, specifically, to world system history over a much longer time span.

We may begin with an important methodological/historiographic difference between Goldstone and others. Goldstone, contrary to most historians and macrosociologists, comparative or otherwise, looks at different places and cases *at the same time*. If the same thing happened not only in Europe but also in West Asia and China at the same time, it behooves us to inquire into possible simultaneous and common causes and at least to be wary of localist explanations. This insight and approach are welcome as a sine qua non of good historical and macrosociological analysis. "The most necessary and the least accomplished contribution of the historian to historical understanding is successively to relate different things and places at the same time in the historical process. The very *attempt* . . . [to do so] is a significant step in the right direction."[2] Attention to simultaneity and horizontal analysis through each time period is also essential for any study of the possible world *system* of which the compared events may only be parts. We can return to this matter below.

Another major departure of Goldstone's book from most western historiography and social science is its emphasis on cycles: "The centuries between 1250 and 1850 show relentlessly *cyclic* patterns" (p. 41). There may or may not be a trend of "progressive" historical development; but even if there is one, it is made up of cycles of accelerations in events followed by renewed retrogressions or at least pauses. Goldstone's recognition and analysis of cycles merit welcome. Attention to cycles of economic growth and decline and their political repercussions have also been central to the understanding of other regions, e.g. Latin America,[3] and of the world [system] history as a whole.[4] As Wallerstein's analysis of the modern world-system progresses from one volume to the next, he pays more and more attention to the importance of its long economic cycles.[5] They are often named after the Russian economist N.D. Kondratieff, according to whom the upswing of the first such cycle began in 1790. Since the time he wrote, in the 1920s, the same cycles have also been identified earlier, however, as we will again note below. Joseph Schumpeter, who studied "Kondratieffs" and shorter cycles in his *Business Cycles* observed "cycles are not, like tonsils, separable things that might be treated by themselves, but are, like the beat of the heart, of the essence of the organism that displays them."[6]

What then *is* the organism or unit that displays these cyclical features we observe? As George Modelski, a political scientist at the University of Washington, observed in my seminar in Amsterdam, before we inquire into cycles we must know what the system is within which these cycles occur. The father of historians, Herodotus, observed that Africa, Asia, and Europe form a single historical unit[y], in which the "imaginary line that separates East from West," as Frederick Teggart called it in 1918,[7] was artificially imposed on the basis of non-existent differences — by "Westerners." More recently, world historians like Marshall Hodgson in "Hemispheric Interregional History as an Approach to World History," William McNeill in *The Rise of the West*, and L.S. Stavrianos in *The World To 1500. A Global History* have emphasized the Afro-Eurasian ecumene in the "eastern" hemisphere of the "old" world as the locus of a one world historical process.[8]

Under the title *"The Rise of the West After Twenty Five Years,"* McNeill recently wrote that "the central methodological weakness of my book is that . . . it pays inadequate attention to the emergence of the ecumenical world system within which we live today. . . . The interactions among peoples living in different landscapes . . . led to the emergence of a cosmopolitan world system between 1700 and 500 B.C."[9] However, the emergence of this "world system within which we now live" can also be traced back at least 5,000 years to 3,000 B.C.[10]

However, for Goldstone, the unity seems to be forged primarily if not exclusively by common underlying climatological-ecological mortality-demographic influences on otherwise separate societies. Any and all these indications of possible unison also deserve attention. We should also go still further to look for political-economic, as well as demographic-migratory and diffusionary-cultural links, which tie all the "separate" units into a single Afro-Eurasian *system*.

This world system did exhibit cyclical swings, and they may well have been demographically influenced. However, even the system-wide cycle phases involved more than demography. Although it happened before the time of his main interest, Goldstone mentions the Black Plague as the best known such demographic event. It came from Eastern Central Asia and arrived in Southern and Western Europe in 1347/8.[11] However, as Janet Abu-Lughod also demonstrates, the world [system] economic crisis actually arrived earlier![12] In Europe and the eastern Mediterranean, but also farther to the east, the economic crisis was already in evidence by 1320, at least a full generation earlier. This economic crisis had already weakened society's economic and political ability to resist the plague before it arrived. It is true that there had already been an important agricultural crisis just before in 1315-17. However, it may be argued that the Eurasian-wide long crisis period or phase in the cycle also began earlier, in 1250-1300.[13]

Thus, the middle of the thirteenth century marked a cyclical departure in Eurasia, as Goldstone himself observes. However, it is disputable that 1250 also marked the beginning or departure of major cycles, as his dating implies. It may be enough for Goldstone just to mention the possible existence of earlier cycles, e.g. in Imperial Rome (p.30), as long as he limits his inquiry to the early modern period. On the other hand, it is not enough for Wallerstein to recognize the cycle back to 1050, but limited only to Europe.[14] For the evidence suggests that 1250 was the turning point from a previous up phase to a down phase and 1050 the beginning of an earlier up phase of a Eurasian-wide cycle, whose origins may, that is should, be traced much further back (See my critique of Wallerstein and his reply).[15]

This same sequence of recurrent phases of economic expansion and contraction in this same world system can be traced back to at least 1700 B.C., and perhaps it can and should also be identified back through the third millennium B.C.[16] These long cycles can be identified first in the "West Asia," as Andrew and Susan Sherrat also do for the second millennium B.C., and then across all of Afro-Eurasia.[17] It is significant that, for instance, Han China, Kushan India, Parthian Persia, and Imperial Rome simultaneously first rose economically and politically from 100 B.C. to 200 A.D. and then again simultaneously suffered economic and political decline from A.D. 200 to 500. So we need not be surprised by Goldstone's mention (p.30) that a plague struck and revisited Rome from the late second century A.D. onward. We could also agree with his footnote reference (p. 487) that Rome's decline "may have been due to similar causes" as the ones he analyzes for other later cases in his book.

However, we can suppose that — and we should investigate whether — these contemporaneous empires, as well as many contemporaneous ones also at *other* times, also rose and fell due to similar causes — and that each contemporaneous set of empires was interrelated. For example, Christopher Beckwith observes that in the short period between 742 and 757 successful political revolts seriously weakened or led to what Goldstone calls the state breakdown of every Eurasian empire, including the Carolingian in Europe, Abbasid in West Asia, Uighur Turkik in Central Asia, and the Tang in China. "Significantly, all seem to have been intimately connected with Central Asia," Beckwith observes.[18] Of course, it may be difficult or impossible to make the same sophisticated structural analysis of these state breakdowns as Goldstone essays. However, fiscal crisis and a balance of payments deficit with its trading partners to the East, indirectly including Han China, did play a significant role in Rome's decline, as the contemporary Pliny and Cicero already observed. Thus, we should not be surprised if Goldstone's analysis could also be extended to the abovementioned and other cases and should welcome any specialists' attempts to do so.

What lies behind these cycles of expansion and contraction at least of "economic" growth rates, and their political consequences? Perhaps demographic changes, due in turn to Eurasian-wide ups and downs in mortality rates, as Goldstone persuasively argues. They could well combine with the above-mentioned long cycles of typically 200 years expansion and two hundred years contraction.[19] Alas, this possibility has not been investigated. However, some archaeological[20] and climatological[21] evidence and analysis is available to combine with demographic evidence to pursue this hypothesis about ecological cycles, as Goldstone also calls them.

Already at the turn of the century, for instance, Ellsworth Huntington wrote *The Pulse of Asia: A Journey in Central Asia Illustrating the Geographic Basis of History* and *Civilization and Climate* to argue the case for ecological determination. "History can never be written correctly until its physical basis is thoroughly understood," Huntington wrote.[22] He found a dry period from 1400 to 1200 B.C., moist conditions from 400 to 500 B.C., greater dryness around 200 B.C., and better conditions when Christ was living. These were followed by renewed desiccation reaching its climax about 650 A.D., improvement until about 1000 A.D., renewed dryness culminating in the thirteenth century, followed by a recovery and then minor fluctuations in climate. Huntington saw climatic degradation as leading to economic distress, political instability, and increased migration. Conversely, he saw "the repeated coincidence between periods of improving climate and periods of cultural progress [which] appears to be due not only to the direct stimulus of climate . . . but to that stimulus combined with a high racial inheritance due to natural selection."[23] Huntington's geographic and climatic determinism, including ideas on character formation, is now mostly discarded but has recently been resurrected by James De Meo.[24] This kind of investigation should be made for all of Eurasia and particularly for Central Asia.[25]

As Goldstone insists, however, it is not demographic changes alone but their relations to political economic sociocultural structure that generates the economic and political cycles we observe. Of course, Goldstone's demographically-based economic, political, and social cycles challenge both the view that history is only linearly progressive and that, at least since early modern times, it is determined by the development of capitalism. If the same demographic changes elicited similar financial/economic consequences and socio-political responses in various parts of Europe and Asia at the same time in the 16th to 18th centuries, the latter can hardly have been due to capitalism and its development or failure to do so.

Goldstone's analysis effectively pulls the rug out from under the "Marxist" and "neo-Marxist" *Eurocentric* interpretations of the uniqueness of the "development of capitalism." Much the same may be said of the "Rise of the West" as seen both by Marxists and their "bourgeois" opponents, Eurocentric all. Beyond Goldstone's correct challenge of the latter's ideological emphasis on "internal" freedom and democracy, there is also the question of the place of the "West" in Eurasia as a whole. As Janet Abu-Lughod persuasively argues, " 'the fall of the East' preceded the 'Rise of the West' " and resulted in a hegemonic shift from East to West.[26] This was at a time of overextension and political-economic decline in various parts of the East — during a period of cyclical economic decline, which was common to several regions and world-system wide.

Goldstone correctly observes in a footnote (p. 485) that "a history of the development of Europe's industrial capitalism that avoids the Marxist and classical economic biases, and takes account of the exogenous cyclic processes of the early modern period, remains to be written." The "Rise of the West," including European hegemony and its expansion and later transfer to the "New World" across the Atlantic, did not constitute a new Modern World Capitalist System as much as it represented a new but continued development and hegemonic shift *within an old world system*, whose cyclical development exerted exogenous influences on both "Europe" and "capitalism" of the most far-reaching importance.[27]

Of course, if similar cycles can be shown to extend farther back through history, the attribution of causality to "capitalism" becomes literally nonsensical. This point was already raised above, but Goldstone's point is even more well taken if the demographic and political economic cycles extend farther back than the supposed origin of capitalism around 1800, 1500, or whenever. The real existence of any such world, and especially world economic, system before recent times is disputed by almost everyone, including probably by Goldstone. He does indeed advance the existence and analysis of Eurasian-wide demographic waves. Nonetheless, early on he says that when he gets to examining the Ottomans, he will show that they essentially lived in a world of their own. In his chapter devoted to the Ottomans, however, Goldstone demonstrates rather the opposite. The Ottomans sat between East and West and maintained competitive and conflictive contact with both. Indeed, that was one of the mainstays of the Ottoman Empire. However, Goldstone does go to some lengths to demonstrate that the economy of Ming and early Qing China was substantially independent from external relations, except to a limited extent with Japan. He assembles monetary data to deny any significant influence of American silver on Chinese, Ottoman, or even much of West European inflation in the 16th century, which he traces instead primarily to grain price responses to demographic and man/land ratio changes. "Thus, the total volume of European trade was never more than just over 1 percent of China's economy, and it was on average only .2-.3 percent" (p. 372). Therefore, Goldstone may wish to part company with me regarding the existence and importance of a world economic system, capitalist or otherwise, in the centuries after 1500, and a forteriori before.

Nonetheless, the question remains what the organism or system is that displays the cyclical waves and how long it or they have been around. For Goldstone, as opposed to Eurocentrists and enthusiasts for or against capitalism, the cyclical organism is limited neither to Europe nor to capitalism. On this score, should any doubt remain in Goldstone's book, he dispels it elsewhere when he says explicitly "this suggests that the motive forces behind the logistic waves lay outside the internal dynamics of world capitalism. . . . Regardless of the precise labor system — whether capitalist [or otherwise] — [in] periods of population growth . . . wealth will be concentrated among owners of land, and real incomes among labor-suppliers will fall, reducing the demand for manufactures. . . . This will happen in societies that are not capitalist in organization, as well as those that are."[28] Thus, not "capitalism" but more basic [world] systemic factors make the socioeconomic organism move cyclically in the many ways that it does.

    Thus, although Goldstone himself does not go so far as to say so, the very idea of capitalism as a separate and useful category, not to mention system, is undermined by his materialist analysis: He shows how many demographic and social structural processes are independent of the forms or institutions of socio-political economic organization, capitalist or otherwise. Yet even without analyzing Goldstone's demographic evidence, we can see that the "differentia specifica" of "incessant capital accumulation" and all of its twelve characteristics identified by Wallerstein[29] and others existed outside the modern-capitalist-world-system as well as long before the dawn of the "the early modern world" around 1500. It is time to replace the ideologically colored interpretations, widely shared from left to right, about the supposed unique characteristics of feudalism, capitalism, and socialism, and of the supposed transitions from one to the next. The material evidence and its analysis, which may differ from but are not incompatible with those of Goldstone, of the continuity of this world system suggests that it is high time to consign all three categories of "system" and the supposed transitions between them to the dustbin of history.[30]

    In the last chapter before his conclusions, Goldstone explicitly treats the role of ideology and culture. Many idealists ascribe virtually all independent determination to these factors by "agency." Of course Goldstone demurs, and also looks at "structure," especially in the generation of the crisis, which has demographic/structural causes. Then however, "both material and ideal factors play a leading role, although they do so in different phases of the process of state breakdown and reconstruction" (p. 465). He finds that ideology and culture do play important and sometimes decisive roles in the resolution of the crisis when one power group replaces another and begins to set up an alternative, partly ideologically guided, régime, albeit still within existing cultural norms. Even so, in the cases examined by Goldstone, the cycle and even the crisis is still marked by much continuity and often by de facto restoration of many features of the ancien regime. This suggests that the role of ideology in shaping the future is limited by material constraints. Herein Goldstone's approach and results offer a sophisticated analysis of "transitions," in which ideological and political forces can play a more significant role in determining the structure of the economic nexus that emerges from the transition. It is also in such periods especially that broad-based social movements intercede in world (and local) history.[31] However, when and what a "transition" is may be subject to dispute. Goldstone (p.43n) quotes a Westerner in turn quoting a Chinese scholar to the effect that "virtually all of China's recorded history (over 2000 years!) [was] a 'transitional age' suspended between two Marxist social formations." But who is to say that these two "formations" were not "transitional" as well? For "a transition is a transition between a transition and a transition."[32]

Goldstone observes that much recent historical analysis had already cut much of the ground out from under the largely ideologically-driven Marxist [and also anti-Marxist] but still Eurocentric interpretations. That is true, but it does not mean that this leaves us with no material analytic base of any kind. Goldstone's and my analyses also rest on material foundations, and so does that of some others, even among neo-classicists he cites, like Douglass North.[33] After all, materialist analysis was not invented by, and is not limited to, Marxism. Indeed, adherents to the latter also demonstrate considerable de facto idealism and ideology.

A major case in point is the insistence, against all the evidence, that the class struggle *between* classes is the motor force of history. Goldstone denies that, and adduces contrary evidence again and again. Alvin Gouldner already emphasized this contradiction between *The Two Marxisms*.[34] One version holds that material economic conditions shape social relations and form consciousness, and the other claims that the class struggle and consciousness thereof drive history. Yet, writing at about the same time and under the revealing sub-title "Towards a Non-Marxian Historical Materialism," the Polish writer Leszek Nowak pointed out that the transition from slavery to feudalism was not generated by interclass slave revolts against their masters, and the transition from feudalism to capitalism was not due to inter-class uprisings by serfs against their lords.[35] In both "transitions", the conflicts and "struggles" were *intra*-class *within* the old and emerging new ruling classes, which responded to underlying economic changes. Slave and serf revolts were at best secondary and supplementary.

As Goldstone demonstrates, in each of the cases he analyzes the important conflicts and struggles were among the existing and emerging *elites*, and not between the "people" and the elites. *"Factional conflict within the elites*, over access to office, patronage, and state policy, rather than conflict across classes, led to state paralysis and state breakdown" (p. 461). Grassroots social movements from below were supplementary in that they helped further destabilize an already unstable state, if only by obliging it to spend already scarce resources to defend itself. Also, popular movements favored the interests of some elite factions against others. "I know of no popular rebellion that succeeded by itself without associated elite revolts or elite leadership in creating institutional change" (p. 11). Moreover, regarding "broad-based elite conflicts, consideration of the *interaction* of demographic, economic, and political relationships is far more fruitful than asserting the centrality of purely class, or purely political, factors" (p. 464). All this would be obvious, if it were not so frequently denied by those whose ideology leads them to claim to know better.

On a related matter, Goldstone is right to say that the French Revolution was not a "bourgeois" revolution and that it did not usher in "freedom": "The Revolution of 1789 had not produced a new world or even a new France. . . . [It] had left largely untouched the fundamental aspects of French life — economic activity, social structure, distribution of population . . ." (p. 298, quoting D. H. Pinkney). The "revolution" did not even bring about much political transformation. In addition to the Thermidor and Napoleon, it was also followed by the revolutions of 1830 and 1848. Moreover, as Goldstone argues persuasively, 1789 itself was the outcome of earlier economic, social, and political conditions, many of which continued thereafter.

The French Revolution, the American "revolution" [which was even less a revolution than the French one], *and* the Industrial revolution [if *it* was one] all were brought on by the long world economic crisis between 1762 and 1790 in what may also be termed a Kondratieff downturn or "B" phase. The American and French "revolutions" additionally were sparked by cyclical economic recessions beginning in 1773 and 1787 respectively. The latter also spelled the doom of the American Articles of Confederation and initiated their replacement by the Constitution. Moreover, according to Goldstone, the economic crisis was world wide, and so were the cyclical recessions within it.[36] Goldstone's analysis also offers a basis for these arguments because of his insistence on the importance of cycles, even if he does not look at Kondratieff cycles, and much less at any before 1790. Josh Goldstein does so and follows the lines of my datings of cyclical turning points, and Modelski and Thompson now suggest that there have been not just Kondratieff's five or Frank's and Goldstein's ten, but at least nineteen K-waves, and that these in turn have been constituent parts of longer one hundred year cycles.[37]

On a related matter, Goldstone questions the importance that "dynastic cycles" in China and elsewhere have traditionally received in both Eastern and Western historiography. There are not only too many counterexamples to Ibn Khaldun's observation of three-generational cycles in dynasties, but the formal survival and/or replacement of dynasties also often obscures the real world economic cycles and political changes of power. Goldstone reviews dynastic survivals that were more in name than in fact, and he contrasts them with dynastic changes, which did not really reflect the real economic and political continuity or situation. An important earlier case in China was that of the Tang Dynasty. Formally, it survived in China until A.D. 907. However, its real power was wrested from it in the abovementioned 742-755 period in which it lost the battle of Talas in 751 and was subject to the An Lu-Shan rebellion in 755.[38]

Finally, Goldstone's analysis of interelite factional conflicts and bottom-up rural *and* urban social movements can also contribute to the analysis of their role in economic cycles. In this book, Goldstone himself is primarily concerned with state breakdown, to which these social movements make relatively minor contributions. That is, Goldstone's [or his publishers?] title and his clarifications notwithstanding, social movements are not the main object of Goldstone's emphasis or analysis here, although they have been elsewhere.[39] Nonetheless, Goldstone in this book makes important contributions to the understanding of social movements. For instance, he signalizes how a population increase also increases the absolute and relative number of young people, who are both more prone to social mobilization and whose leadership has to compete for elite positions in society. He also points to the connections between these two social manifestations of population change.

Goldstone remarks on social movements in Europe, as well as in West Asia and East Asia since 1800, which are also examined in Frank and Fuentes.[40] We sought with varying success to trace them to underlying Kondratieff cycles. These social movements coincided, as hypothesized, with Kondratieff crises periods in the 1830s-40s and since 1967, but also with the Kondratieff economic expansion from the late 1890s to World War I. Goldstone, instead, seeks to trace social movements in relation to the underlying demographic/structural changes.

Social movements coincided in time with labor strikes and other forms of social unrest and rebellion, especially in the 1830s and 1840s. Other social movements certainly coincided with the class (and also national) movements of these same decades, culminating in the revolutionary and reform movements of 1830-34 and 1847-52, centering on 1848.[41] For the first social movements, for instance, Goldstone (pp. 285-6) mentions revolutions or rebellions in England, France, Belgium, Poland and Ireland. During the second period he lists "revolutions or serious revolutionary crises" in France, Germany, Austria, Hungary, Bohemia, Switzerland and Romania. Except in Prussia, "these nineteenth-century crises were full-fledged cases of state breakdown" in which "social protest was absolutely central," certainly in France but apparently elsewhere as well.

Goldstone (pp. 187 ff) notes that the previously mentioned social movements, rebellions, and state breakdowns of the early 1830s and late 1840s ocurred predominantly in the more "traditional" regions of least industrial growth, where population growth had impinged on the carrying capacity of the land. This sociopolitical unrest occurred less in regions of greater industrial growth, which offered more possibilities to absorb population growth. Contrary to the Marxist thesis that stresses industrial capitalist-generated interclass struggle, this regional pattern of social movements and intraclass inter-elite struggle conforms more to demographic/structural crises and explanations.

Goldstone's discussion of social movements is also welcome for other reasons: He shows [1] that they come and go in cycles of their own, and he relates them to wider systemic/structural cycles; [2] that they display much variety and changeability, but they share individual mobilization through a sense of morality and [in]justice, and for survival and identity; and [3] that none of this is new. By implication neither are our contemporary social movements "new." In reverse order, these observations correspond to the first three of the "Ten Theses on Social Movements" of Fuentes and Frank.[42] These movements have always been important but often neglected actors in history, even if — or perhaps because — they often do not lead to state breakdown. Thus once again, Goldstone's guidance for the study of bottom up social movements is also welcome.

In conclusion, we may note that Goldstone (p.23) approvingly quotes the late Joseph Fletcher: "Without a macrohistory . . . the full significance of the historical peculiarities of a given society cannot be seen."[43] Goldstone himself magnificently combines the analysis of structural, cyclical, ecological, demographic, economic, social, political, and ideological factors to contribute to a Eurasian-wide macrohistory of the whole [system], which we need to illuminate and comprehend the peculiarities of its constituent parts. In so doing, perhaps Goldstone shortchanges some external and military dimensions a bit, because he is less interested in international relations than in domestic ones. However, he brilliantly fortifies the ecological base or dimension of the economic leg of the real and analytic economic/ecological, political/military, and cultural/ideological analysis that may be called the "three legged stool" of social analysis, and whose ecological foundation is mostly so spectacularly inadequate in other analyses, including my own.[44]

Thus, historians and social "scientists" alike will long be in Goldstone's debt. We can only hope that they will pay it off by emulating him or, with his valiant help, even go him one better. Is that still possible? Real history will tell! In the meantime, Goldstone's structural analysis has already made an important contribution to the intelligent pursuit of "agency" struggle. In the words made famous by the peoples of the Portugese ex-colonies: A Luta Continua! [The Struggle Continues].

NOTES

1   It is true that Goldstone's documentation and analysis in dispute of monetarist theory appear only briefly in this book and are much further and more persuasively elaborated in Jack A. Goldstone, "Causes of Long Waves in Early Modern Economic History," *Research in Economic History*, Suppl. 6, (Greenwich: JAI Press, 1991).

2   Andre Gunder Frank, *World Accumulation 1492-1789* (New York: Monthly Review Press and London: Macmillan Press, 1978). Also cited in "A Theoretical Introduction to Five Thousand Years of World System History," *Review* June (1990): 155-248, and "A Plea for World System History," *Journal of World History* Vol.II, No.1, Winter (1991): 1-28.

3   Andre Gunder Frank, *Capitalism and Underdevelopment in Latin America* (New York: Monthly Review Press, 1967); *Lumpenbourgeoisie: Lumpendevelopment*,(New York:Monthly Review Press, 1972); *Mexican Agriculture 1521-1630. Transformation of the Mode of Production* (Cambridge: Cambridge University Press, 1979).

4   Andre Gunder Frank, *Crisis: In the World Economy* (New York: Holmes & Meier and London: Heinemann, 1980); S. Amin, G.Arrighi, A.G Frank & I. Wallerstein, *Dynamics of Global Crisis* (New York: Monthly Review Press and London: Macmillan Press, 1982); A.G. Frank "American Roulette in the Globonomic Casino: Retrospect and Prospect on the World Economic Crisis Today" in Paul Zarembka, ed. *Research in Political Economy*, (Greenwich: JAI Press); Barry K. Gills and A.G. Frank, "World System Cycles, Crises, and Hegemonial Shifts 1700 BC to 1700 AD," *Review*, XV, 4 (Fall 1992).

5   Immanuel Wallerstein, *The Modern World-System*. 3 vols. (New York: Academic Books, 1974, 1980, 1989).

6   Joseph Schumpeter, *Business Cycles* (New York: McGraw Hill, 1938).

7   Frederick J. Teggart, *Rome and China: A Study of Correlations in Historical Events* (Berkeley: University of California Press, 1939), p.248.

8   Marshall Hodgson, "Hemispheric Interregional History as an Approach to World History," UNESCO *Journal of World History / Cahiers d'Histoire Mondiale* Vol.I, No.3 (1954): 715-723; William McNeill, *The Rise of the West. A History of the Human Community*, (Chicago: University of Chicago Press, 1963); L.S. Stavarianos, *The World to 1500. A Global History* (Englewood Cliffs: Prentice Hall, 1970).

9   William McNeill, *"The Rise of the West* After Twenty Five Years," *Journal of World History*. Vol. I, No. 1, (1990): 9,12.

10   A.G. Frank, "A Theoretical Introduction . . .", "A Plea. . . ," "Transitional Ideological Modes: Feudalism, Capitalism, Socialism." *Critique of Anthropology*, Vol. 11, No. 2 (Summer 1991):171-188; A.G. Frank and B.K. Gills, "The Five Thousand Year World System: An Interdisciplinary Introduction," *Social Change*, 18, 1 (Spring 1992); A.G. Frank and B.K. Gills, Eds. *The World System: Five Hundred Years or Five Thousand* (London and New York: Routledge, forthcoming), B. K. Gills and A. G. Frank "The Cumulation of Accumulation: Theses and Research Agenda for 5000 Years of World System History," *Dialectical Anthropology* (New York/Amsterdam) Vol.15, No.1, (1990):19-42. Expanded version published as "5000 years of World System History: The Cumulation of

Accumulation" in C. Chase-Dunn & T. Hall, Eds. *Precapitalist Core-Periphery Relations* (Boulder: Westview Press, 1991): 67-111; B.K. Gills and A.G. Frank "World System Cycles, Crises, and Hegemonial Shifts 1700 BC to 1700 AD," *Review*, Binghamton No. 4 (Fall 1992).

11   See also William McNeill, *Plagues and Peoples* (New York: Doubleday, 1977).

12   Janet Abu-Lughod, *Before European Hegemony. The World System A.D. 1250-1350* (New York: Oxford University Press, 1989).

13   A.G. Frank, "A Theoretical Introduction. . . ," "A Plea. . . ," "Transitional Ideological Modes. . . ," *The Centrality of Central Asia.* VU University Press for Center for Asian Studies Amsterdam (CASA), Comparative Asian Studies (CAS) No. 8, (1992); "The Centrality of Central Asia," *Studies in History*, New Delhi, Vol. VIII,No. 1, (Feb. 1992):43-97; B.K. Gills & A.G. Frank "World System Cycles . . ." *Bulletin of Concerned Asian Scholars*, Vol. XXIV, No. 2, April-June 1992.

14   Immanuel Wallerstein, "The West, Capitalism, and the Modern World-System." Prepared as a chapter in Joseph Needham, *Science and Civilization in China*, Vol. VII: *The Social Background*, Part 2. Sect. 48. *Social and Economic Considerations.* Published in French as "L'Occident, le capitalisme el le systeme-monde moderne," *Sociologie et Sociétés*, XXII,1, Avril (1990):15-52. Now in English in *Review*, XV, 4 (Fall 1992).

15   A.G. Frank, "Transitional Ideological Modes: Feudalism, Capitalism, Socialism" and Immanuel Wallerstein, "World System vs. World-Systems," *Critique of Anthropology*, Vol. 11, No. 2 (Summer 1991).

16   B.K. Gills & A.G. Frank, "World System Cycles . . ." and A.G. Frank, "The World System and its Cycles in the Bronze and Iron Ages," (1992 ms.) identifies the cycles back through the 3rd millennium B.C.

17   Andrew and Susan Sherrat, "From Luxuries to Commodities: The Nature of the Bronze Age Trading System," in N. H. Cole, ed., *Bronze Age Trade in the Mediterranean* (Jonsered: Paul Aströms Förlag, 1991). E.N. Chernykh also claims Eurasian wide long economic cycles of expansion and contraction in his *Ancient Mertallurgy in the USSR: The Early Metal Age* (Cambridge: Cambridge University Press, forthcoming).

18   Christopher Beckwith, *The Tibetan Empire in Central Asia* (Princeton: Princeton University Press, 1987), p. 192.

19   B.K. Gills and A.G. Frank "World System Cycles . . ."

20   Klavs Randsborg, *The First Millennium A.D. in Europe and the Mediterranean* (Cambridge: Cambridge University Press, 1991); Kristian Kristiansen, "The Emergence of the European World System in the Bronze

Age. Divergence, convergence and social evolution during the first and second millennium B.C.in Europe" in Jorgen Jensen and Kristian Kristiansen, eds., *Europe in the First Millennium B.C.* (Department of Archaeology, University of Sheffield, forthcoming); and K. Kristiansen *Europe Before History. The European World System in the Second and First Millennium B.C.* (forthcoming).

21   A.F. Harding, ed. *Climatic Change in Later Prehistory*, (Edinburgh: Edinburgh University Press, 1982).

22   E. Huntington, *The Pulse of Asia: A Journey in Central Asia Illustrating the Geographic Basis of History* (New York: Houghton Mifflin, 1907); *Civilization and Climate*,(New Haven: Yale University Press, 1971 [original 1915]); Huntington, *Civilization*, p. 20.

23   Ibid., p. 28.

24   James DeMeo, "Desertification and the Origins of Armoring: The Saharasian Connection. *Journal of Orgonomy* Vol. 21, No. 2, Vol. 22, Nos. 1 & 2, Vol. 23, No. 2. (1987); "Origins and Diffusion of Patrism in Saharasia: Evidence for a Worldwide, Climate-linked Geographical Pattern in Human Behavior. *Kyoto Review*, No. 23, Spring (1990):19-38; "Origins and Diffusion of Patrism in Saharasia c. 4000 B.C.: Evidence for a Worldwide, Climate-linked Geographical Pattern in Human Behavior," *World Futures*, Vol. 30, No. 4, (1991):247-271.

25   A.G. Frank, *The Centrality of Central Asia.*

26   Janet Abu-Lughod, *Before European Hegemony*, p. 338.

27   A.G. Frank "Transitional Ideological Modes . . ."; A.G. Frank and B.K. Gills, "The 5000 Year World System . . ."; B.K. Gills and A.G. Frank, "World System Crises, Cycles . . ."

28   Jack Goldstone, "The Causes of Long Waves . . .": pp. 69,71.

29   Immanuel Wallerstein, "The West, Capitalism . . ."

30   A.G. Frank, "Transitional Ideological Modes . . ."

31   B.K. Gills and A.G. Frank, "Cumulation of Accumulation . . ."

32   A. G. Frank, "Transitional Ideological Modes . . ."

33   Alvin Gouldner, *The Two Marxisms*, (London: Macmillan Press, 1980).

34   Lezek Novak, *Property and Power. Towards a Non-Marxian Historical Materialism* (Dordrecht/Boston/Lancaster: D. Reidel Publishing Company of the Kluver Group, 1983 [translation]).

35   Douglass C. North, *Structure and Change in Economic History* (New York: Norton, 1981), and Douglass C. North and Robert Paul

Thomas, *The Rise of the Western World. A New Economic History* (Cambridge: Cambridge University Press, 1973).

36   A.G. Frank, *World Accumulation.*

37   Joshua S. Goldstein, *Long Cycles. Prosperity and War in the Modern Age* (New Haven: Yale University Press, 1989); George Modelski and William R. Thompson, "Kondratieff Waves, The Evolving Global Economy, and World Politics: The Problem of Coordination," paper persented at the N.D. Kondratieff Conference, Moscow, March 17-19, 1992 and at the International Studies Association Meetings, Atlanta, April 1-5, 1992.

38   A.G. Frank, *The Centrality of Central Asia.*

39   Jack A. Goldstone, "Theories of Revolution: The Third Generation," *World Politics* 32:(1980): 425-453; "The Comparative and Historical Study of Revolutions," *Annual Review of Sociology* 8 (1982): 187-207.

40   A.G. Frank and Marta Fuentes, "Civil Democracy: Social Movments in World History," in S.Amin, G. Arrighi, A.G. Frank & I. Wallerstein, *Transforming the Revolution. Social Movements and the World-System*, (New York: Monthly Review Press 1990), pp. 139-180.

41   Ibid. Also A.G. Frank and M. Fuentes, "On Studying Cycles In Social Movements," paper presented at a Conference on "Social and Political Cycles," Fundación Pablo Iglesias, Madrid, June 18-22, 1992.

42   Marta Fuentes and A.G. Frank, "Ten Theses on Social Movements," *World Development* XVII, 2, February (1989):179-191.

43   Joseph Fletcher, "Integrative History: Parallels and Interconnections in the Early Modern Period, 1500-1800," *Journal of Turkish Studies* 9: (1985): 37-58.

44   B.K. Gills and A.G. Frank, "The Cumulation of Accumulation . . ."

PART THREE

Why Communism Fell in the Soviet Union and Eastern Europe

WHAT WAS SOCIALISM AND WHY DID IT FALL?

KATHERINE VERDERY

The startling disintegration of Communist Party rule in Eastern Europe in 1989, and its somewhat lengthier unraveling in the Soviet Union between 1985 and 1991, rank among the century's most momentous occurrences.[1] Especially because neither policy-makers nor area specialists predicted them, these events will yield much analysis after the fact, as scholars develop the hindsight necessary to understanding what they failed to grasp before. In this essay, I aim to stimulate discussion about why Soviet-style socialism fell. Since answers to the question require understanding how socialism "worked," I begin with a model of this; I then suggest how it intersected fatefully with certain features of the world-system context.

WHAT WAS SOCIALISM?

The "formerly existing" socialist[2] states of Eastern Europe and the Soviet Union differed significantly from each other — for instance, in the intensity, effectiveness, and span of central control, in the extent of popular support or resistance, and in the degree and timing of reforms. I opt nevertheless for a single model of them. The resemblances within socialism were more important than its variety, for analytic purposes, much as we can best comprehend French, Japanese, West German, and American society as variants of a single capitalist system. Acknowledging, then, that my description applies more fully to certain countries and time periods than to others, I treat them all under one umbrella.

For several decades, the analysis of socialism has been an international industry, employing both western scholars and eastern dissidents. This industry has lately received a massive infusion of new raw materials, as once-secret files are opened and translations appear of research by local scholars (especially Polish and Hungarian) into their own declining socialist systems.[3] My own taste in such theories is "indigenist": I have found most useful the analyses of East Europeans concerning the world in which they lived. The following summary, which is subject to revision as new material appears, owes much to that work.[4] Given temporal and spatial constraints, I will compress elements of a larger analytical model.[5] I will emphasize how production was organized and the consequences of this for consumption and for markets, themes that afford the best entry into why Party rule crumbled much faster than anyone expected.

PRODUCTION[6]

Socialism's fragility begins with the system of "centralized planning," which the center neither adequately planned nor controlled. Central planners would draw up a plan with quantities of everything they wanted to see produced, known as targets. They would disaggregate the plan into pieces appropriate for execution, estimating how much investment and how many raw materials were needed if managers of firms were to fill their targets. Managers learned early on, however, that not only did the targets increase annually, but the materials required often did not arrive on time or in the right amounts. So they would respond by bargaining their plan: demanding more investments and raw materials than the amounts actually necessary for their targets. Every manager, and every level of the bureaucracy, padded budgets and requests in hopes of having enough, in the actual moment of production. (A result of the bargaining process, of course, was that central planners always had faulty information about what was really required for production, and this impeded their ability to plan.) Then, if managers somehow ended up with more of some material than they needed, they hoarded it. Hoarded material had two uses: it could be kept for the next production cycle, or it could be exchanged with some other firm for something one's own firm lacked. These exchanges or barters of material were a crucial component of behavior within centralized planning.

A result of all the padding of budgets and hoarding of materials was widespread shortages, for which reason socialist economies are called *economies of shortage*.[7] The causes of shortage were primarily that people lower down in the planning process were asking for more materials than they required and then hoarding whatever they got. Underlying their behavior was what economists call *soft budget constraints* — namely, if a firm was losing money, the center would bail it out. In our own economy, with certain exceptions (such as Chrysler and the Savings and Loan industry), budget constraints are *hard*: if you cannot make ends meet, you go under. But in socialist economies, it did not matter if firms asked for extra investment or hoarded raw materials; they paid no penalty.

With all this padding and hoarding, it is clear why shortage was endemic to socialist systems, and why the main problem for firms was not whether they could meet (or generate) demand but whether they could procure adequate supplies. So while the chief problem of economic actors in western economies is to get profits by *selling* things, the chief problem for socialism's economic actors was to *procure* things. Capitalist firms compete with each other for markets in which they will make a profit; socialist firms competed to maximize their bargaining power with suppliers higher up. In our society, the problem is other sellers, and to outcompete them you have to befriend the buyer. Thus, our clerks and shop-owners smile and give the customer friendly service because they want business; customers can be grouchy and it will only make the clerk try harder. In socialism, the locus of competition was elsewhere: your competitor was other buyers, other procurers, and to outcompete them you needed to befriend those higher up who supplied you. Therefore, in socialism it was not the clerk — the provider, or "seller" — who was friendly (they were usually grouchy) but the procurers, the customers, who sought to ingratiate themselves with smiles, bribes, or favors. The work of procuring generated whole networks of cozy relations among economic managers and their bureaucrats, clerks and their customers. We would call this corruption, but that is because getting supplies is not a problem for capitalists: the problem is getting sales. In a word, for capitalists salesmanship is at a premium; for socialist managers, the premium was on acquisitionsmanship, or procurement.

So far I have been describing the clientelism and bargaining that undercut the Party center's effective control. A similar weakness in vertical power relations emerges from the way socialist production and shortage bred workers' oppositional consciousness and resistance. Among the many things in short supply in socialist systems was labor. Managers hoarded labor, just like any other raw material, because they never knew how many workers they would need. Fifty workers working three eight-hour shifts six days a week might be enough to meet a firm's targets — *if* all the materials were on hand all month long. But this never happened. Many of those workers would stand idle for part of the month, and in the last ten days when most of the materials were finally on hand the firm would need 75 workers working overtime to complete the plan. The manager therefore kept 75 workers on the books, even though most of the time he needed fewer; and since all other managers were doing the same, labor was scarce. This provided a convenient if unplanned support for the regimes' guaranteed employment.

An important result of labor's scarcity was that managers of firms had relatively little leverage over their workers. Furthermore, because supply shortages caused so much uncertainty in the process of production, managers had to turn over to workers much control over this process, lest work come to a standstill.[8] That is, structurally speaking, workers under socialism had a somewhat more powerful position relative to management than do workers in capitalism. Just as managers' bargaining with bureaucrats undercut socialist central power, so labor's position in production undercut that of management.

More than this, the very organization of the workplace bred opposition to Party rule. Through the Party-controlled trade union and the frequent merger of Party and management functions, Party directives were continually felt in the production process — and, from the workers' viewpoint, they were felt as unnecessary and disruptive. Union officials either meddled unhelpfully or contributed nothing, only to claim credit for production results that workers knew were their own. Workers participated disdainfully — as sociologist Michael Burawoy found in his studies of Hungarian factories — in Party-organized production rituals, such as work-unit competitions, voluntary work-days, and production campaigns; they resented these coerced expressions of their supposed commitment to a wonderful socialism.[9] Thus, instead of securing workers' consent, workplace rituals sharpened their consciousness and resistance. Against an official "cult of work" used to motivate cadres and workers toward fulfilling the plan, many workers developed an oppositional cult of *non*-work, imitating the Party bosses and trying to do as little as possible for their paycheck. Cadres often found no way around this internal sabotage, which by reducing productivity deepened the problems of socialist economies to the point of crisis.

The very forms of Party rule in the workplace, then, tended to focus, politicize, and turn against it the popular discontent that capitalist societies more successfully disperse, depoliticize, and deflect. In this way, socialism produced a split between "us" and "them," workers and Party leaders, founded on a lively consciousness that "they" are exploiting "us." This consciousness was yet another thing that undermined socialist regimes. To phrase it in Gramscian terms, the lived experience of people in socialism precluded its utopian discourse from becoming hegemonic — precluded, that is, the softening of coercion with consent.[10]

SURVEILLANCE AND PATERNALISTIC REDISTRIBUTION

Ruling Communist Parties developed a variety of mechanisms to try to obscure this fact of their nature from their subjects, mechanisms designed to produce docile subject dispositions and to ensure that discontent did not become effective opposition. I will briefly discuss two of these mechanisms: the apparatus of surveillance, and redistribution of the social product.

In each country, some equivalent of the KGB was instrumental in maintaining surveillance, with varying degrees of intensity and success. Particularly effective were the Secret Police in the Soviet Union, East Germany, and Romania, but networks of informers and collaborators operated to some extent in all. These formed a highly elaborate "production" system parallel to the system for producing goods — a system producing *paper*, which contained real and falsified histories of the people over whom the Party ruled. Let us call the immediate product "dossiers," or "files," though the ultimate product was political subjects and subject dispositions useful to the regime. This parallel production system was at least as important as the system for producing goods, for producers of files were much better paid than producers of goods. My image of this parallel production system comes from the memoirs of Romanian political prisoner Herbert Zilber:

> The first great socialist industry was that of the production of files . . . This new industry has an army of workers: the informers. It works with ultramodern electronic equipment

(microphones, tape recorders, etc.), plus an army of typists with their typewriters. Without all this, socialism could not have survived . . . In the socialist bloc, people and things exist only through their files. All our existence is in the hands of him who possesses files and is constituted by him who constructs them. Real people are but the reflection of their files.[11]

The work of producing files (and thereby political subjects) created an atmosphere of distrust and suspicion dividing people from one another. One never knew whom one could trust, who might be informing on one to the police about one's attitudes toward the regime or one's having an American to dinner. Declarations might also be false. Informers with a denunciation against someone else were never asked what might be their motive for informing; their perhaps-envious words entered directly into constituting another person's file — thus, another person's sociopolitical being. Moreover, like all other parts of the bureaucracy, the police too padded their "production" figures, for the fact of an entry into the file was often more important than its veracity.[12] The existence of this shadowy system of production could have grave effects on the people "processed" through it, and the assumption that it was omnipresent contributed much to its success, in some countries, in repressing unwanted opposition.

If surveillance was the negative face of these regimes' problematic legitimation, its positive face was their promises of social redistribution and welfare. At the center of both the Party's official ideology and its efforts to secure popular support was "socialist paternalism," which justified Party rule with the claim that the Party would take care of everyone's needs by collecting the total social product and then making available whatever people needed: cheap food, jobs, medical care, affordable housing, education, etc. Party authorities claimed, as well, that they were *better able* to assess and fill these needs than were individuals or families, who would always tend to want more than their share. Herein lay the Party's paternalism: it acted like a father who gives handouts to the children as he sees fit. The Benevolent Father-Party educated people to express needs it would then fill, and discouraged them from taking the initiative that would enable them to fill these needs on their own. The promises — socialism's basic social contract — did not go unnoticed, and as long as economic conditions permitted their partial fulfillment, certain socialist regimes gained legitimacy as a result. But this proved impossible to sustain.

Beyond its effects on people's attitudes, paternalism had important consequences for the entire system of production discussed above and for consumption; here I shift to the question of why consumption was so central in the resistance to socialism. A Party that pretends to meet its citizens' needs through redistribution and that insists on doing so exclusively — that is, without enlisting their independent efforts — must control a tremendous fund of resources to redistribute. Nationalizing the means of production helped provide this, and so did a relentlessly "productionist" orientation, with ever-increased production plans and exhortations to greater effort.

The promise of redistribution was an additional reason, besides my earlier argument about shortages, why socialism worked differently from capitalism. Socialism's inner drive was to accumulate not (as in capitalism) *profits*, but *distributable resources*. This is more than simply a drive for autarky, reducing dependency on the outside: it aims to increase dependency of those within. Striving to accumulate resources for redistribution involves things for which profit is totally irrelevant. In capitalism, those who run lemonade stands endeavor to serve thirsty customers in ways that make a profit and outcompete other lemonade stand owners. In socialism, the point was not profit but the relationship between thirsty persons and the one with the lemonade — the Party center, which appropriated from producers the various ingredients (lemons, sugar, water) and then mixed the lemonade to reward them with, as it saw fit. Whether someone made a profit was irrelevant: the transaction underscored the center's paternalistic superiority over its citizens, i.e., its capacity to decide who got more and less lemonade.

Controlling the ingredients fortified the center's capacity to redistribute things. But this capacity would be even greater if the center controlled not only the lemons, sugar, and water but the things they come from: the lemon trees, the ground for growing sugar beets and the factories that process them, the wells and the well-digging machinery. That is, most valuable of all to the socialist bureaucracy was to get its hands not just on resources, but on resources that generated *other* usable resources, resources that were themselves further productive. Socialist regimes wanted not just eggs but the goose that lays them. Thus, if capitalism's inner logic rests on accumulating surplus-value, the inner logic of socialism was to accumulate *means of production*.[13]

The emphasis on keeping resources at the center for redistribution is one reason why items produced in socialist countries so often proved uncompetitive on the world market. Basically, most of these goods were not being made to be sold competitively: they were being either centrally accumulated or redistributed at low prices — effectively given away. Thus, whether a dress was pretty and well made or ugly and missewn was irrelevant, since profit was not at issue: the dress would be "given away" at a subsidized price, not sold. In fact, the whole point was *not* to sell things: the center wanted to keep as much as possible under its control, because that was how it had redistributive power; and it wanted to give away the rest, because that was how it confirmed its legitimacy with the public. Selling things competitively was therefore beside the point. So too were ideas of "efficient" production, which for a capitalist would enhance profits by wasting less material or reducing wages. But whatever goes into calculating a profit — costs of material or labor inputs, or sales of goods — was unimportant in socialism until very late in the game. Instead, "efficiency" was understood to mean "the full use of existing resources," "the maximization of given capacities" rather than of results, all so as to redirect resources to a goal greater than satisfying the population's needs.[14] In other words, what was rational in socialism differed from capitalist rationality. Both are stupid in their own way, but differently so.

CONSUMPTION

Socialism's redistributive emphasis leads to one of the great paradoxes of a paternalist regime claiming to satisfy needs. Having constantly to amass means of production so as to enhance redistributive power caused Party leaders to prefer heavy industry (steel mills, machine construction) at the expense of consumer industry (processed foods, or shoes). After all, once a consumer got hold of something, the center no longer controlled it; central power was less served by giving things away than by producing things it could continue to control. The central fund derived more from setting up a factory to make construction equipment than from a shoe factory or a chocolate-works. In short, these systems had a basic tension between what was necessary to *legitimate* them — redistributing things to the masses — and what was necessary to their *power* — accumulating things at the center. The tension was mitigated where people took pride in the economy's development (that is, building heavy industry might also bring legitimacy), but my experience is that the legitimating effects of redistribution were more important by far.

Each country addressed this tension in its own way. For example, Hungary after 1968 and Poland in the 1970s gave things away more, while Romania and Czechoslovakia accumulated things more; but the basic tension existed everywhere. The socialist social contract guaranteed people food and clothing but did not promise (as capitalist systems do) quality, ready availability, and choice. Thus, the system's mode of operation tended to sacrifice consumption, in favor of production and controlling the products. This paradoxical neglect of consumption contributed to the long lines about which we heard so much (and we heard about them, of course, because we live in a system to which consumption is crucial).

In emphasizing this neglect of consumption as against building up the central resource base, I have so far been speaking of the *formally* organized economy of socialism — some call it the "first" or "official" economy. But this is not the whole story. Since the center would not supply what people needed, they struggled to do so themselves, developing in the process a huge repertoire of strategies for obtaining consumer goods and services. These strategies, called the "second" or "informal" economy, spanned a wide range from the quasi-legal to the definitely illegal.[15] In most socialist countries it was not illegal to moonlight for extra pay — by doing carpentry, say — but people doing so often stole materials or illegally used tools from their work place; or they might manipulate state goods to sell on the side. Clerks in stores might earn favors or extra money, for example, by saving scarce goods to sell to special customers, who tipped them or did some important favor in return. Also part of the second economy was the so-called "private plot" of collective farm peasants, who held it legally and in theory could do what they wanted with it — grow food for their own table or to sell in the market at state-controlled prices. But although the plot itself was legal, people obtained high outputs from it not just by virtue of hard work but also by stealing from the collective farm: fertilizer and herbicides, fodder for their pigs or cows, work-time for their own weeding or harvesting, tractor-time and fuel for plowing their plot, etc. The second economy, then, which supplied a large part of consumer needs, was parasitic upon the state economy and inseparable from it. It developed precisely because the state economy tended to ignore consumption.

It is clear from what I have said that whereas consumption in our own society is considered primarily a socioeconomic question, the relative neglect of consumer interests in socialism made consumption deeply political. In Romania in the 1980s (an extreme case), to kill and eat your own calf was a political act, because the government prohibited killing calves: you were supposed to sell them cheap to the state farm, for export. Romanian villagers who fed me veal (having assured themselves of my complicity) did so with special satisfaction. It was also illegal for urbanites to go and buy 40 kg of potatoes directly from the villagers who grew potatoes on their private plot, because the authorities suspected that villagers would charge more than the state-set price, thus enriching themselves. So Romanian policemen routinely stopped cars riding low on the chassis and confiscated produce they found inside.

Consumption became politicized in yet another way: the very *definition* of "needs" became a matter for resistance and dispute. "Needs," as we should know from our own experience, are not given: they are created, developed, expanded — the work especially of the advertising business. It is advertising's job to convince us that we need things we didn't know we needed, or that if we feel unhappy, it's because we need something (a shrink, or a beer, or a Marlboro, or a man). Our need requires only a name and it can be satisfied with a product or service. Naming troubled states, labeling them as needs, and finding commodities to fill them is at the heart of our economy.

Socialism, by contrast, which rested not on devising infinite kinds of things to sell people but on claiming to satisfy people's *basic* needs, had a very unadorned definition of them — in keeping with socialist egalitarianism. Indeed, some Hungarian dissidents wrote of socialism's relationship to needs as a "dictatorship."[16] As long as the food offered was edible or the clothes available covered you and kept you warm, that should be sufficient. If you had trouble finding even these, that just meant you were not looking hard enough. No planner presumed to investigate what kinds of goods people wanted, or worked to name new needs for newly created products and newly developed markets.

At the same time, however, regime policies paradoxically made consumption a problem. Even as the regimes prevented people from consuming by not making goods available, they insisted that under socialism, the standard of living would constantly improve. This stimulated consumer appetites, perhaps with an eye to fostering increased effort and tying them into the system. Moreover, socialist ideology presented consumption as a "right." The system's organization exacerbated consumer desire further by frustrating it and thereby making it the focus of effort, resistance, and discontent. Anthropologist John Borneman sees in the relation between desire and goods a major contrast between capitalism and socialism. Capitalism, he says, repeatedly renders desire concrete and specific, and offers specific — if ever-changing — goods to satisfy it. Socialism, in contrast, aroused desire *without* focalizing it, and kept it alive by deprivation.[17]

As people became increasingly alienated from socialism and critical of its achievements, then, the politicization of consumption also made them challenge official definitions of their needs. They did so not just by creating a second economy to grow food or make clothes or work after hours but also, sometimes, by public protest. Poland's Communist leaders fell to such protest at least twice, in 1970 and in 1980, when Polish workers insisted on having more food than government price increases would permit them. Less immediately disruptive were forms of protest in which people used consumption styles to forge resistant social identities. The black markets in western goods that sprang up everywhere enabled alienated consumers to express their contempt for the system through the kinds of things they chose to buy. You could spend an entire month's salary on a pair of blue jeans, for instance, but it was worth it: wearing them signified that you could get something the system said you didn't need and shouldn't have. Thus, consumption goods and objects conferred an identity that set you off from socialism, enabling you to differentiate yourself as an individual in the face of relentless pressures to homogenize everyone's capacities and tastes into an undifferentiated collectivity. Acquiring objects became a way of constituting your selfhood against a deeply unpopular regime.

BUREAUCRATIC FACTIONALISM AND MARKETS

Before turning to why these systems fell, I wish to address one more issue: politicking in the Party bureaucracy. Although this took different and specific forms in the different countries, it is important to mention the issue, for socialism's collapse owed much to shifts in the balance among factions that emerged within the Party apparatus. Even before 1989, researchers were pointing to several forms of intra-Party division.[18] One such division might be that between *ownership* and *management*, another that between the people who oversaw the paperwork of administration and those "out in the field," intervening in actual social life.[19] We might then look for conflicting tendencies based in the different interests of these groups. Such conflicts might arise between the central "owners" or paper-workers, on one hand, who might persist in policies that accumulated means of production without concern for things like productivity and output, and the bureaucratic managers or field-workers, on the other, who *had* to care about such things. Although the power of the system itself rested on continued accumulation, such tendencies if unchecked could obstruct the work of those who had actually to deliver resources or redistribute them. Without tangible investments and hard material resources, lower-level units could not produce the means of production upon which the Party bureaucracy relied. If productive activity were so stifled by "overadministration" that nothing got produced, this would jeopardize the redistributive bureaucracy's power and prestige.

Thus, when central accumulation of means of production began to threaten the capacity of lower-level units to produce; when persistent imbalances between investment in heavy industry and in light industry, between allocations for investment and for consumption, etc., diminished the stock of distributable goods; and when the center's attempts to keep enterprises from meddling with surplus appropriation obstructed the process of production itself: then pressure arose for a shift of emphasis. The pressure was partly from those in the wider society to whom not enough was being allocated and partly from bureaucrats themselves whose prestige and prospects of retaining power depended on having more goods to allocate. One then heard of decentralization, of the *rate of growth*, of *productivity* — in a word, of matters of *output*, rather than the inputs that lay at the core of bureaucratic performance. This is generally referred to as the language of "reform."

For those groups that became concerned with questions of output and productivity, the solutions almost always involved introducing mechanisms such as profitability criteria and freer markets. This meant, however, introducing a subordinate rationality discrepant with the system's inner logic and thereby threatening continued Party rule. Market forces create problems for socialism in part for reasons treated implicitly or explicitly above (recall the contrast between demand-constrained capitalism and socialism's economy of shortage, and socialism's lack of interest in the salability of its products). But more broadly, markets create problems because they move goods *horizontally* rather than vertically towards the center, as all redistributive systems require. Markets also presuppose that individual interest and the "invisible hand," rather than the guiding hand of the Party, secure the common good.[20] Because these horizontal movements and individualizing premises subverted socialism's hierarchical

organization, market mechanisms had been suppressed. Reformers introducing them were opening Pandora's box.

WHY DID IT FALL?

My discussion of socialism's workings already points to several
reasons for its collapse; I might now address the question more compre-
hensively. To do this requires, in my view, linking the properties of its
internal organization (discussed above) with properties of its external
environment, as well as with shorter-term "event history." This means
examining the specific conjuncture of two systems — "capitalist" and
"socialist," to use ideal types — one encompassing the other.[21]

In event-history terms, the proximate cause of the fall of East
European and Soviet socialism was a public-relations gambit by the
Hungarian government on the eve of a visit by President George Bush: the
dismantling of the barbed wire between Hungary and Austria. This enabled
some East German tourists to extend their tour, and thereby — because
Gorbachev refused to support Honecker with Soviet troops — to bring
down the Berlin Wall. We still need to explain, however, the conjuncture
in which Hungary could score its public-relations coup and Gorbachev
could decide to refuse his troops. For that, we must wind up the static model
I have offered and set it in its international context. This includes asking
how socialism's encounter with a changing world capitalism produced or
aggravated factional divisions within Communist Parties.

My discussion of socialism indicated several points of tension in
its workings that affected the system's capacity for extended reproduction.
Throughout their existence, these regimes sought to manage such tensions
in different ways, ranging from Hungary's major market reforms in the
1960s to Romania's rejection of reform and its heightened coercive extrac-
tion. In all cases, managing these tensions involved decisions that to a
greater or lesser degree opened socialist political economies to western
capital. The impetus for this opening — critical to socialism's demise —
came chiefly *from within*, as Party leaders attempted to solve their structural problems without major structural reform. Their attitude in doing so
was reminiscent of a "plunder mentality" that sees the external environment as a source of booty to be used as needed in maintaining one's own
system, without thought for the cost. This attitude was visible in the

tendency of socialist governments to treat foreign trade as a residual sector, used to supplement budgets without being made an integral part of them.[22] Because of how this opportunistic recourse to the external environment brought socialism into tighter relationship with capitalism, it had fateful consequences.

The critical intersection occurred not in 1989 or 1987 but in the late 1960s and early '70s, when global capitalism entered the cyclical crisis from which it is still struggling to extricate itself. Among capitalists' possible responses to the crisis (devaluation, structural reorganization, etc.), an early one was to lend abroad. This enabled recipients to buy capital equipment or to build long-term infrastructure, thereby expanding the overseas markets for western products.[23] The loans became available just at the moment when all across the socialist bloc the first significant round of structural reforms had been proposed, half-heartedly implemented, and, because profitability and market criteria fit so poorly with socialism's rationale, largely abandoned. Instead of reforming the system from within, most Party leaderships opted to meet their problems by greater articulation with the surrounding economy: importing western capital and using it to buy advanced technology (or, as in Poland, to subsidize consumption), in hopes of improving economic performance. Borrowing, then, became a substitute for extensive internal reforms that would have jeopardized the Party's monopoly over society and subverted the inner mechanisms of socialism. Thus, the internal cycles of two contrasting systems suddenly meshed.

The intent, as with all the international borrowing of the period, was to pay off the loans by exporting manufactured goods into the world market. By the mid 1970s it was clear, however, that the world market could not absorb sufficient amounts of socialism's products to enable repayment, and at the same time, rising interest rates added staggeringly to the debt service. With the 1979-80 decision of the western banking establishment not to lend more money to socialist countries, the latter were thrown into complete disarray. I have already mentioned several features that made socialist economies inapt competitors in the international export market. The "plunder" stance toward external economies, the system's fundamental organization *against* notions of salability of its products, the shortage-economy's premium on acquisitionsmanship rather than on sales-manship, the neglect of consumption and of producing to satisfy consumer needs with diverse high-quality products — all this meant that an adequate response to the hard-currency crisis would have catastrophic effects on socialism's inner mechanisms. To this was added the fact that socialist economies were "outdated": as Ken Jowitt put it, "After 70 years of murderous effort, the Soviet Union had created a German industry of the 1880s in the 1980s."[24]

In these circumstances, the balance of power tilted toward the faction within the Communist Party that had long argued for structural reforms, the introduction of market mechanisms, and profit incentives, even at the cost of the Party's "leading role." The choice, as Gorbachev and his faction saw it, was to try to preserve either the Soviet Union and its empire (by reforms that would increase its economic performance and political legitimacy), or collective property and the Party monopoly. He was ready to sacrifice the latter to save the former, but ended by losing both.

While western attention was riveted on the speeches of policy-makers in the Kremlin, the more significant aspects of reform, however, were in the often-unauthorized behavior of bureaucrats who were busily creating new property forms on their own. Polish sociologist Jadwiga Staniszkis describes the growth of what she calls "political capitalism," as bureaucrats spontaneously created their own profit-based companies from within the state economic bureaucracy. Significantly for my argument that socialism's articulation with world capitalism was decisive in its fall, the examples she singles out to illustrate these trends are all at the interface of socialist economies with the outside world — in particular, new companies mediating the export trade and state procurement of western computers.[25] She sees as crucial the factional split between the groups who managed socialism's relations with the outside (such as those in foreign policy, counterintelligence, and foreign trade), and those who managed it internally (such as the Party's middle-level executive apparatus and the KGB).[26] Forms of privatization already taking place by 1987 in Poland and similar processes as early as 1984 in Hungary show the emerging contours of what Staniszkis sees as the reformists' goal: a *dual economy*.[27] One part of it was to be centrally administered, as before, and the other part to be reformed through market/profit mechanisms and selective privatization of state property. The two were to coexist symbiotically.[28]

These forms of "political capitalism" arose in part by economic managers' exploiting the shortages endemic to socialism — shortages now aggravated to crisis proportions. In the new hope of making a profit, "political capitalists" (I call them "entrepratchiks") were willing to put into circulation reserves known only to them — which they would otherwise have hoarded — thus alleviating shortages, to their own gain. As a result, even anti-reformist Soviet and Polish bureaucrats found themselves acquiescing in entrepratchiks' activities, without which, in Staniszkis's words, "the official structure of the economic administration was absolutely unsteerable."[29] Contributing to their tolerance was rampant bureaucratic anarchy, a loss of control by those higher up, rooted in the "inability of superiors to supply their subordinates (managers of lower level) with the means to construct a strategy of survival."[30] Since superiors could no longer guarantee deliveries and investments, they were forced to accept whatever solutions enterprising subordinates could devise — even at the cost of illicit profits from state reserves. Entrepratchiks soon began to regard the state's accumulations much as Preobrazhensky had once urged Soviet leaders to regard agriculture: as a source of primitive accumulation. They came to find increasingly attractive the idea of further "privatization," so important to western lenders.

It is possible (though unlikely) that socialist regimes would not have collapsed if their hard-currency crisis and consequent intersection with capitalism had occurred at a different point in capitalism's cyclicity. The specifics of capitalism's own crisis management, however, proved unmanageable for socialist systems. Without wanting to present recent capitalism's "flexible specialization" as either unitary or fully dominant (its forms differ from place to place, and it coexists with other socio-economic forms), I find in the literature about it a number of characteristics even more inimical to socialism than was the earlier "Fordist" variant, which Soviet production partly imitated. These characteristics include: small-batch production; just-in-time inventory; an accelerated pace of innovation; tremendous reductions in the turnover time of capital via automation and electronics; a much-increased turnover time in *consumption*, as well, with a concomitant rise in techniques of need-creation and an increased emphasis on the production of *events* rather than *goods*; coordination of the economy by finance capital; instantaneous access to accurate information and analysis; and an overall decentralization that increases managerial control (at the expense of higher-level bodies) over labor.[31]

How is socialism to mesh with this? — socialism with its emphasis on large-scale heroic production of means of production, its resources frozen by hoarding (no just-in-time here!), its lack of a systemic impetus toward innovation, the irrelevance to it of notions like "turnover time," its neglect of consumption and its flat-footed definition of "needs," its constipated and secretive flows of information (except for rumors) in which the center could have no confidence, and its perpetual struggle to retain central control over all phases of the production process? Thus, I submit, it is not simply socialism's embrace with capitalism that brought about its fall, but the fact that it happened to embrace a capitalism of a newly "flexible" sort. David Harvey's schematic comparison of "fordist modernity" with "flexible post-modernity" clarifies things further: social-ist systems have much more in common with his "fordist" column than with his "flexible" one.[32]

Let me add one more thought linking the era of flexible specializa-tion with socialism's collapse. Increasing numbers of scholars note that accompanying the change in capitalism is a change in the nature of state power: specifically, a number of the state's functions are being under-mined.[33] The international weapons trade has made a mockery of the state's monopoly on the means of violence. Capital's extraordinary mobil-ity means that as it moves from areas of higher to areas of lower taxation, many states lose some of their revenue and industrial base, and this constrains their ability to attract capital or shape its flow. Capital flight can now discipline *all* nation-state governments.[34] The coordination of global capitalism by finance capital places a premium on capital mobility, to which rigid state boundaries are an obstacle.

This has two consequences for the fall of socialism. First, within socialist countries those groups whose structural situation facilitated their fuller participation in the global economy now had reasons to expand their state's receptivity to capital — that is, to promote reform. Second, the extent to which socialist states controlled capital flows into their countries may have made them special targets for international financial interests, eager to increase their opportunities by undermining socialist states. These internal and international groups each found their chance in the interest of the other. It is in any case clear from the politics of international lending agencies that they aim to reduce the power of socialist states, for they insist upon privatization of state property — the basis of these states' power and revenue. Privatization is pushed even in the face of some economists' objections that "too much effort is being invested in privatization, and too little in creating and fostering the development of new private firms" — whose entry privatization may actually impede.[35]

NO TIME FOR SOCIALISM

Rather than explore further how flexible specialization compelled changes in socialism, I will summarize my argument by linking it to notions of time. Time, as anthropologists have shown, is a fundamental dimension of human affairs, taking different forms in different kinds of society. The western notion of a linear, irreversible time that consists of equivalent and divisible units, for instance, is but one possible way of conceptualizing time and living it. A given cultural construction of time ramifies throughout its social order, as calendars, schedules and rhythms establish the very foundations of daily existence (which is why elites, especially revolutionary ones, often manipulate them) and affect how people make themselves as social beings.

Capitalism exists only as a function of time — and of a specific conception of it. Efforts to increase profits by increasing the velocity of capital circulation are at its very heart. Thus, each major reorganization of capitalism has entailed, in Harvey's terms, "time-space compression": a shrinking of the time horizons of private and public decision-making, whose consequences encompass ever-wider spaces owing to changed communications and transport technology.[37] The inner logic of socialism, by contrast, placed no premium on increasing turnover time and capital circulation. Although the rhetoric of Stalinism presented socialism as highly dynamic, for the most part Soviet leaders acted as if time were on their side. (When Khrushchev said "We will bury you," he was not too specific about the date.) Indeed, I have argued that in 1980s Romania, time — far from accelerating — was being gradually *slowed down*, flattened, immobilized, and rendered non-linear.[36]

Like the reorganization of capitalism at the end of the 19th century, the present reorganization entails a time-space compression, which we all feel as a mammoth speed-up. Yet the socialism with which it intersected had no such time-compressing dynamic. In this light, the significance of Gorbachev's perestroika was its recognition that socialism's temporality was unsustainable in a capitalist world. Perestroika reversed Soviet ideas as to whose time-definition and rhythms were dominant and where dynamism lay: no longer within the socialist system but outside it, in the West. Gorbachev's rhetoric from the mid 1980s is full of words about time: the Soviet Union needs to "catch up," to "accelerate" its development, to shed its "sluggishness" and "inertia" and leave behind the "era of stagnation."

> [By] the latter half of the seventies . . . the country began to lose momentum. . . . Elements of stagnation . . . began to appear. . . . A kind of "braking mechanism" affect[ed] social and economic development. . . . The inertia of extensive economic development was leading to an economic deadlock and stagnation.[38]

Change has suddenly become an "urgent" necessity. These are the words of a man squeezed by the compression of space and time.

Even as he spoke, new time/space-compressing technologies were wreaking havoc on the possible rhythms of his and other leaders' control of politics, as Radio Free Europe made their words at once domestic and international. Soviet leaders could no longer create room for themselves by saying one thing for domestic consumption and something else for the outside world: they were now prisoners of simultaneity. The role of western information technology in undermining socialism was evident in the spread of Solidarity's strikes in 1980, news of which was telephoned out to the West and rebroadcast instantly into Poland via Radio Free Europe and the BBC, mobilizing millions of Poles against their Party. The revolutions of 1989 were mediated similarly.

I am suggesting, then, that the collapse of socialism came in part from the massive rupture produced by its collision with capitalism's speed-up. If so, it would be especially useful to know something more about the life-experience of those people who worked at the interface of these two temporal systems and could not help realizing how different was capitalism's time from their own. Bureaucrats under pressure to increase foreign trade and foreign revenues, or importers of computer equipment, would have discovered that failure to adapt to alien notions of increased turnover time could cost them hard currency. They would have directly experienced time-annihilating western technologies, which effected a banking transaction in milliseconds as opposed to the paper-laden hours and days needed by their own financial system. Did the rise of "profitability" criteria in the command economy owe something to such people's dual placement? Did they come to experience differently their sense of themselves as agents? My point, in short, is that the fall of socialism lies not simply in the intersection of two systems' temporal cycles but rather in the collision of two *differently constituted temporal orders*, along with the notions of person and activity proper to them.

If socialist economies had not opened themselves to capital import and to debt servicing, perhaps their collision with capitalist speedup would have been less jarring — or would at least have occurred on more equal terms. But the capitalist definition of time prevailed, as socialist debtors bowed to its dictates (even while postponing them), thereby aggravating factional conflicts within the elite. Because its leaders accepted western temporal hegemony, socialism's messianic time proved apocalyptic. The irony is that, had debtor regimes refused the definitions imposed from without — had they united to default simultaneously on their western loans (which in 1981 stood at over $90 billion[39]) — they might well have brought down the world financial system and realized Khrushchev's threatening prophecy overnight. That this did not happen shows how vital a thing is a monopoly on the definition of social reality, and it should give pause to those impatient to move beyond capitalism.

NOTES

1   This paper was prepared as a lecture for the Center for Comparative Research in History, Society and Culture, at the University of California, Davis. I am grateful to those who invited me — William Hagen, G. William Skinner, and Carol Smith — as well as to members of the Center's seminar. I also received helpful advice from Ashraf Ghani.

2   Cf. Bahro's "actually existing socialism." Rudolph Bahro, *The Alternative in Eastern Europe* (London: Verso, 1978).

3   See especially Elemér Hankiss, *East European Alternatives* (New York: Oxford University Press, 1990); Agnes Horváth and Arpád Szakolczai, *The Dissolution of Communist Power: The Case of Hungary* (New York: Routledge, 1992); and Jadwiga Staniszkis, *The Dynamics of the Breakthrough in Eastern Europe: The Polish Experience* (Berkeley: University of California Press, 1991) and *The Ontology of Socialism* (New York: Oxford University Press, 1992).

4   In particular: Pavel Campeanu, *The Origins of Stalinism: from Leninist Revolution to Stalinist Society* (Armonk, NY: M. E. Sharpe, 1986) and *The Genesis of the Stalinist Social Order* (Armonk, NY: M. E. Sharpe, 1988); Ferenc Fehér, Agnes Heller, and György Márkus, *Dictatorship over Needs: an Analysis of Soviet Societies* (New York: Basil Blackwell, 1983); George Konrád and Ivan Szelényi, *The Intellectuals on the Road to Class Power: a Sociological Study of the Role of the Intelligentsia in Socialism* (New York: Harcourt, Brace, Jovanovich, 1979); János Kornai, *Economics of Shortage* (Amsterdam: North-Holland Publishing Co., 1980).

5   See my "Theorizing Socialism: A Prologue to the 'Transition,' " *American Ethnologist* 18 (1991): 419-439.

6   This section draws upon Michael Burawoy's discussion in *The Politics of Production* (London: Verso, 1985), as well as the sources listed in note 4.

7   See Kornai, *Economics of Shortage.*

8   See Burawoy, *Politics of Production*, ch. 4.

9   Michael Burawoy and János Lukács, *The Radiant Past: Ideology and Reality in Hungary's Road to Capitalism* (Chicago: Univ. of Chicago Press, 1992), ch. 5.

10   Cf. Burawoy, *Politics of Production.*

11   Andrei Şerbulescu (Belu Zilber), *Monarhia de drept dialectic* (Bucharest: Humanitas, 1991), pp. 136-8.

12   These observations show how fraught is the use of files in assessing fitness for political office (as in the Czech practice of "lustration").

13   Campeanu, *Genesis*, 117-8.

14   Horváth and Szakolczai, *Dissolution*, 77-78.

15   See, e.g., István Gábor, "The Second (Secondary) Economy," *Acta Oeconomica* 3-4 (1979): 291-311, and Steven Sampson, "The Second Economy in Eastern Europe and the Soviet Union," *Annals of the American Association of Political and Social Science* 493 (1986): 120-136.

16   Fehér et al., *Dictatorship over Needs.*

17   John Borneman, *After the Wall* (NY: Basic Books, 1990), pp. 17-18.

18   E.g., Leslie Benson, "Partynomialism, Bureaucratism, and Economic Reform in the Soviet Power System," *Theory and Society* 19 (1990): 92; Burawoy and Lukács, *Radiant Past*, 90-92, 96-100; Campeanu, *Genesis*, 143-157; Horváth and Szakolczai, *Dissolution*, 204-5; Konrád and Szelényi, *Intellectuals*, 153; Jadwiga Staniszkis,

242 KATHERINE VERDERY

"Patterns of Change in Eastern Europe," *East European Politics and Societies* 4 (1990): 80.

19   Campeanu, *Genesis*, 143-157; Horváth and Szakolczai, *Dissolution*, 204-205.

20   Horváth and Szakolczai, *Dissolution*, 48-49.

21   See also Terry Boswell and Ralph Peters, "State Socialism and the Industrial Divide in the World Economy," *Critical Sociology* 17 (1990): 3-34; Valerie Bunce, "The Empire Strikes Back: The Evolution of the Eastern Bloc from a Soviet Asset to a Soviet Liability," *International Organization* 39 (1985): 1-46; Daniel Chirot, "After Socialism, What?" *Contention* 1 (1991): 29-49.

22   Paul Hare, "Industrial Development of Hungary since World War II," *East European Politics and Societies* 2 (1988): 115-151.

23   David Harvey, *The Condition of Postmodernity* (Oxford: Blackwell, 1989), p. 184.

24   Ken Jowitt, "The Leninist Extinction," in Daniel Chirot, ed., *The Crisis of Leninism and the Decline of the Left* (Seattle: Univ. of Washington Press, 1991), p. 78.

25   Jadwiga Staniszkis, "Political Capitalism in Poland," *East European Politics and Societies* 5 (1991): 129-30.

26   Staniszkis, "Patterns," 79-83.

27   David Stark, "Privatization in Hungary: From Plan to Market or from Plan to Clan?" *East European Politics and Societies* 4 (1990): 364-5.

28   Staniszkis, "Patterns," 77-78.

29   Staniszkis, "Political Capitalism," 131.

30   Staniszkis, *Dynamics*, 164.

31   See Harvey, *Condition*, 156, 164, 340-341.

32   *Ibid.*, 340-41.

33   E.g., Eric Hobsbawm, *Nations and Nationalism since 1780* (Cambridge: Cambridge Univ. Press, 1990), pp. 181-183, and Charles Tilly, *Coercion, Capital, and European States, A.D. 990-1990* (Oxford: Blackwell, 1990).

34   Harvey, *Condition*, 164-5.

35   Peter Murrell, "Privatization Complicates the Fresh Start," *Orbis* 36 (1992): 325.

36   "The 'Etatization' of Time in Ceauşescu's Romania," in Henry Rutz, ed., *The Politics of Time* (Washington, D. C.: American Ethnological Society, 1992), pp. 56-7.

37   Harvey, *Condition*, 147.

38   Mikhail Gorbachev, *Perestroika: New Thinking for Our Country and the World* (NY: Harper and Row, 1987), pp. 5, 6.
39   Bunce, "Empire Strikes Back," 39.

NOT THE JUICE BUT THE JUICER:

ON NO-LONGER EXISTING SOCIALISM AND LEMONADE

REGINALD E. ZELNIK

Scholars struggling to keep up with the kaleidoscopic changes now taking place in the Former Soviet Union (FSU) and Eastern Europe are often careful to end their articles with an exact date of submission, lest tomorrow's unexpected events cast a shadow over their scholarship by the date of publication. Gorbachev is unlikely to stay in power — but he stays; he will never allow the wall to fall — but it falls; there will never be a free election while Gorbachev remains in power — but Yeltsin is freely elected President of the Russian Republic; a coup is out of the question — but there's the coup (but wait, it's gone!); the collapse of Soviet power will mean civil war — but there's no civil war, not in Russia, not yet (May 3, 1993); the significance of the referendum is. . . . And so it goes, with the right prediction often based on the shallower analysis, the wrong one on the deeper, as wish and thought, emotion and scholarship, are stirred together into the language of academic ratiocination. One is reminded of the nervous father in a Ring Lardner story, who, lost at the wheel of his car in the forests of New York City, responds to a suggestion from his overzealous son: " 'Shut up,' he explained!"

Wisely, in her thoughtful and thought-provoking essay, "What Was Soviet-Style Socialism and Why Did it Fall?," Katherine Verdery eschews prediction (what comes next, she says in an earlier version, is "anybody's guess") and even avoids much commentary on the present situation; so no need for a date at the end of her article! Instead, she uses the dramatic events of recent years to explore in depth and, I would add, with neither tears nor laughter, the deeper structure of the Communist system, probing as she does so for the underlying causes of its demise, while remaining alert for the non-structural input from human agents. The result is one of the most compelling statements of the problem I have read.

Before reviewing the steps of Verdery's analysis sequentially, I would call attention to her very controlled use of language, specifically her self-conscious effort to deploy a terminology that carries a minimum of ideological or emotional baggage, lest the charged language of the various "camps" that have dominated the Sovietological debate get in the way of clarity. For example, she steers clear of "Leninism," while drawing heavily (and, as always, with generous acknowledgment) on Ken Jowitt's studies of the "Leninist" phenomenon; and she avoids "totalitarianism," neither attacking nor defending the term, though clearly harboring no illusions about the enormous punitive power of the old Communist security apparatus. (For an example of the debasement of language that now surrounds the term, see the May 1 AP report of die-hard communists and Russian ultra-nationalists protesting against Yeltsin's "totalitarian" regime.) None of this is to deny that Verdery's findings will be greeted more warmly in some camps than in others, but it is a strength of her essay, as I hope to show, that it pushes us all in the direction of a different, less loaded, less tendentious (and less tedious) language of analysis.

As suggested by the title, the essay is subdivided into two main problem areas: What was Soviet socialism? and Why did it fail? As to what it was, Verdery, while recognizing the wide variations that existed among the Communist countries of Europe (let alone those of East and Southeast Asia), sensibly uses the Soviet Union as her basic model, the system from which the others, all dating from the post-war period, were derivative. She is also correct in noting that the USSR was the country where the Communist Party had the greatest "legitimacy," by which I think she means that there was the least popular sentiment that the regime was imposed from without, by alien arms. (She might have added that to the extent that Communist legitimacy was revitalized by the patriotic engagements of World War II, at least among ethnic Russians, the same could be said of Yugoslavia, at least among ethnic Serbs.) Hence it is by probing the character of Soviet socialism, the "Ur-socialism" (or the Ur-*existing* socialism) that we can best get to the character of its unwilling progeny.

As an anthropologist, Verdery predictably draws upon the testimony of the natives — she calls this approach "indigenist" — the major source of information about the world in which they lived. But insofar as her purpose is systemic analysis and not merely ethnographic description, this method can take her only so far, especially in light of the many self-contradictory tales these natives tell. She needs some kind of conceptual framework to help her assess the credibility and organize the insights of her informants into a useful pattern, lest she fall into the polemical trap I have observed so many times: the abrupt ending of an argument about the Soviet system by calling on the authority of what natives believe: if *they* call it "totalitarian" (or "democratic"? or "Judeo-Masonic"?), then it must be totalitarian (or as Russians say, If he calls himself a mushroom, we'll put him in the mushroom box!).

The framework Verdery uses in order to pattern and make sense of her ethnographic information about "actually existing socialism" (socialist theory as such is of little interest to her) is provided by the system of centralized planning and distribution and by its points of intersection with Soviet methods of police control. Almost from the outset, though mainly implicitly, she measures that system against the old standard model of Party domination and control, but unlike other critics of that model, she does so not in order to test the limits to which the system was cruel or benign, but in order to uncover its structure, functions, and internal weaknesses and contradictions.

Drawing heavily on the work of Michael Burawoy, Verdery concludes that the centralized planning system was hardly a planning system at all, but rather a system of hoarding, padding, and barter, based on the systemic scarcity of materials and the need for "planners" and production managers to protect themselves from unforeseen shortages; though essentially inefficient, the system was perpetuated by the political center's desire to protect each unit of the system from the consequences of its own inadequacy. Far from being the summmum of economic rationality it proclaimed itself to be, Soviet socialism squandered resources, mainly at the expense of its own citizens.

Paradoxically, however, this inefficient system "worked"; it worked, that is, in the limited sense that for many years, for decades, it managed to provide minimum satisfactions to almost everyone involved in the production process, with only one important reservation. It was important that these producers, from management down to the lowliest production-line worker, not begin to think of themselves as consumers.

For it was the consumer, Verdery argues, who was deliberately excluded from even the meager advantages derived from the system; the consumer was the odd man out (in practice, more often than not, the odd woman), scraping fawningly for what he (usually she) could procure, using bribery, flattery, whatever means were at hand. Of course, as Verdery must understand, the consumer-producer distinction functions at a certain level of abstraction, for in reality the consumer and producer are sometimes one and the same person, in which case what Verdery is talking about is not just a conflict within the hierarchal structure of society, but a conflict within one's self-identity, with satisfaction possible only insofar as people are able to suppress or control their desire for new worldly (no pun intended!) goods, or perhaps more accurately, their desire and capacity to *choose* among such goods.

Within certain limits, Verdery argues convincingly, the worker qua worker benefited from this system. Viewed as a raw material in short supply, the worker (unlike Verdery, I would stress the *skilled* worker here, again mainly male) had to some extent to be pampered by the Soviet manager, kept on hand even when the plant was idle lest he be missing when the plant was working at full capacity. (Analogous practices occurred during earlier stages of the industrial revolution, the capitalist one, that is, including in late nineteenth-century Russia.) This was Soviet full employment, providing an objective point of reference for what Verdery does call, with measured irony, I am sure, a kind of workers' state (as well as for the old workers' joke about the Communist social contract: "we pretend to work and they pretend to pay us"). But however satisfactory this arrangement was to workers in the short or medium run, it was bound to feed their cynicism in the long run, and to promote what Verdery calls "an oppositional cult of non-work." Certainly the failure of miners and other Soviet workers to rally to the cause of a Party-State that had flattered and coddled them so long was in part attributable to the state of affairs that Verdery describes.

If the system of production was loosely held together by a minimally beneficial social contract (including the social safety net that Verdery subsumes under the notion of "socialist paternalism"), its threads were too loose to survive in the absence of a tight political superstructure, what Verdery calls the "apparatus of surveillance." Of course, she doesn't mean the subtle surveillances that Foucault attributes to the internalized discourses of bourgeois society, but a far grosser system of internal espionage ("the production of [personal] files") that kept the Soviet and East Euro-

248 REGINALD E. ZELNIK

pean populations divided and defensive. Although it does no irreparable damage to her basic line of argument, I find Verdery's novelistic emphasis on dossier production (and overproduction), based on the memoirs of a Romanian political prisoner, a little too precious to be useful. What counted in the end (including for her prisoner) was the police's power of arbitrary arrest, with or without a dossier — even whimsically, at the high (or low) point of the Stalinist system; this was the power that gave the dossier system its terrorizing underpinnings.

Where does "society" fit into Verdery's schema? To be sure, she again eschews the dull, conventional, time-worn problematic ("did 'society' exist under the Communist system?" — of course it did), but implicit in the logic of her analysis is the notion that popular expectations were constantly shaping, reshaping, and especially restricting the options available to an otherwise powerful state. This was true not only of privileged workers but even of the average consumers of State paternalism, who, however passive they were trained to be, however dependent on the State for the definition of their needs, nevertheless were able to force the state to design and limit its much beloved productionist goals in order to maintain a minimal storehouse of wearable and edible goods (rarely goodies) — "distributable resources," in Verdery's terms — to pass out among them. This was the lemonade, lemonade socialism (conceptually clearer, I think, than goulash), though the regime's self-esteem and self-definition depended not so much on possession of the lemonade as of the lemons and the juicers.

All this shows in a fresh and insightful way how the system functioned at the level of its political economy, that is, badly, but with the wherewithal for longevity, and where the points of friction and weakness were should the system be faced with tough new challenges and be forced to innovate creatively. The toughest challenge came, according to Verdery, from the outside, but not, as is usually claimed, from Reagan's "Star Wars" project, but from a deeper and more extensive conjunctural confrontation with Western economies ("the conjuncture of two systems"). (Verdery could have integrated the Star Wars factor into her scheme, I believe, but that is another matter.) The pivotal moment came in the late 1960s-early 1970s, when rather than face up to the need for radical reform, with the attendant risk (to put Verdery's complex argument much too concisely) of empowering the Soviet consumer by attending to privately-generated needs and filling them with quality products, the Soviet leadership opted for a strategy of compensating for its deficiencies by entering into friendlier economic relations with the capitalist world, essentially by borrowing large sums of capital with which to shore up a tottering system without remodeling its structure (without perestroika, let us say). Verdery seems to suggest, but is not very clear on this point, that the alternative, an internally driven reform campaign (a pre-Gorbachev perestroika?), would have weakened the foundations of the system and led to its collapse, though at what pace and with what differential outcomes are not explained. Possible alternative trajectories are not sketched in, leaving me with some doubts as to the explanatory power of her provocative notion that socialism's deadly "embrace" with capitalism just at a time when capitalism was redesigning its "temporal order" is what brought about its fall. Was the collision between "capitalist speed-up" and socialism's "messianic time" the necessary condition for socialism's demise, or was an earlier effort to resolve the system's contradictions "internally" just as likely to collapse into a similar endgame? This should be clarified.

In any case it is a matter of historical record, not counterfactual, that the conditions Verdery describes eventually split the Soviet and other Communist parties into reformist and reactionary camps. The same conditions also created, extended, intensified and multiplied non-Party values and desires among the populace, especially for forbidden fruit (not just lemons), and ultimately culminated in Gorbachev's reformist regime, one, I would add, that among its many accomplishments (its failures have been well rehearsed), permitted the historical losers, yesterday's gods, to slip from the stage of power feebly and undramatically, without a Valhalla. As a historian I commend Verdery for introducing contingent "events" — Hungary's decision to lower the barbed wire on its Austrian frontier, and Gorbachev's refusal to rescue Honecker with Soviet troops — into her story. She is of course right that only by grasping the conjuncture within which these events occurred are we able to understand the historical rationality of such decisions, but she is wrong to allot them an equal order of importance or probability. It is hard to imagine something like the Hungarian decision not taking place in Eastern Europe under these circumstances. It is all too easy, however, to imagine a very different, much more adventurous and perilous decision by Gorbachev (or his replacement?), had discussions in the Kremlin taken a different but historically familiar turn. It will surprise me very much if we fail to learn some day, perhaps from archives, that the decision not to use force in East Germany (or elsewhere) was a close call, and came at the end of a bitter, divisive debate. Had the other fork in the road been taken, Verdery might be writing not of why Socialism failed, but of why its escalating internal crisis led to dangerous military adventure (as many Kremlinologists used to predict).

What, if any, is the relevance of Verdery's analysis to the issues raised in Prof. Peter Reddaway's interview (*Contention*, I, 3, 1993), and, at greater length, in his thoughtful pieces in the *New York Review of Books* (most recently in the April 22 issue, but of course with a March 23 dateline at the end)? And beyond the Reddaway argument, in what ways should her analysis help us rethink some of the broader historical and political issues that continue to torment students of the region, especially of the FSU (and, more specifically still, of Russia)? Reddaway's most powerful and impassioned point is, at its base, a plea (to Yeltsin and to his supporters, especially abroad, i.e., here) for modesty and restraint in the pursuit of capitalism, an unfettered market economy, approaches based on "economic shock therapy" (EST). Reddaway draws on his vast knowledge of the Soviet past and the Russian present to suggest a number of economic, social and cultural resistances to an excessively rapid reversal of engines, a time-machine-like movement back to the capitalist future. Recast in Verdery's (and David Harvey's) terms — and I take deliberate liberties at the almost certain risk of rebuttal or denial — Reddaway seems to be saying that the "time-space" compression that Verdery attributes to recent capitalism not only could not be absorbed by the Soviet-type personality, but that the Russian cultural type as it exists today is still so grounded in the personality formation produced by 75 years of hothouse existence under the old system that the best that can be hoped for is a gradual, step-by-step, phase-by-phase movement across political-economic time zones, lest the passengers experience ruptured eardrums or much worse. Or to shift the image somewhat, he in effect reminds us that no astronaut or cosmonaut has been launched into orbit without months and years of preparation in simulated space travel. The people who worked in Verdery's module, though they experienced the impact of powerful new forces, were hardly prepared or even preparing for a rapid ascent into the world of laissez-faire, free markets, and a consumer driven social order, in short — EST.

Thus the Verdery analysis, or at least my own peculiar reading of it, strengthens Reddaway's case, already a credible one, particularly in light of his impeccable credentials as a defender of the victims of Soviet oppression and, as far as I can gather, a defender in principle of market economies, a man with no personal or intellectual stake in the survival or defense of Soviet "Socialism." Even Verdery's explication of the growing role of the "second economy" does little to undermine his case, for far from being a school for free enterprise, as she points out, the second economy has to a large extent been parasitic on the first. (Her important point about the dependency of the super-productive private plot on resources siphoned off [my euphemism] from the collective farm is a telling one.) If consumer demand has increased over time, especially the demand for higher quality Western or Western-like goods, even this change in consciousness, important as it was to the decline and fall of the system, was largely defined as a (negative) dependent variable of the system, that is, as a defiant quest for external markers of non-Socialist identity in the presence of a discredited Communism.

As a historian of Russia I would like to suggest that another dimension of this issue is worthy of exploration in the context of the debate over Russia's readiness for the plunge into a market economy. Deep beneath the Soviet version of the Socialist system described by Verdery there lies a long history of Russian cultural attitudes, the structure of Russian mentalities over a much longer durée than the life of the Soviet system as such. This subject is enormously complicated, and does not lend itself to easy generalization. Many pages of good history have been and will be written about the rise of entrepreneurship during the last decades of Imperial Russia, the appearance on the scene of private corporations, the development of corporate law, the Russian version of the independent farmer (the yeoman if you like him, the kulak if you don't), and many other related phenomena that imply that a market culture was starting to take root. More broadly, many pages have been written, and many more are in the works, that reveal the early signs of an embryonic democratic political culture, grounded in legality (*zakonnost'*), aborning in the womb of the troubled Russian Empire (not to mention other, more "advanced" areas of Eastern Europe). Whether one believes that a more liberal democratic order fosters a freer economy, or that a free economy is the necessary foundation for such a political order, or — closer to the historical truth, I believe — that the two often work in harmony with one another without a clear, one-directional causality (Weber's "elective affinities"), there is plenty of evidence that Russia had the historical wherewithal to progress in these directions.

But while keeping this positive, progressivist picture in mind, we cannot forget that the best of this historical work also reveals the deep and pervasive antipathy to market values that continued (and apparently continues) to survive in the Russian political culture: the anti-capitalism that not only suffused the entire political left but penetrated the liberal center and the right as well; the family-based collectivism of the peasant commune (in no way to be confused with centralist, productionist Commun*ism*, but nonetheless hostile to the values of liberal individualism, including those of the farmer who separated his plot from the commune in the Stolypin era); the powerful egalitarian ethos of industrial workers, still operative even in the mining communities that are supportive of Yeltsin; and the élitist cultural prejudices against the "crass" materialism and consumerism of the West, characteristic of such politically diverse groups and individuals as Herzen, the Slavophiles, the Populists, the anti-democratic right of various shadings, and, to take a contemporary example with superb anti-Communist credentials, Alexander Solzhenitsyn. Although I cannot possibly be sure, even Yeltsin's commitment to the free marketplace strikes me as a recently learned strategic position rather than a positive personal commitment with deep roots in his own past experience. In short, even if and when the thick topsoil layer of "Socialist" experience described by Verdery has been removed, Russians (and many others) will have to confront the enormous challenge of a deeper layer of pre-capitalist, if not anti-capitalist, permafrost.

I do not believe that Peter Reddaway is asking Russians not to face this inevitable challenge, but he is asking them to be realistic and, in a sense, unheroic in the way they go about it, and asking us to allow them to be so. Russia has experienced more than its share of sacrifice and "heroism." While serious economic reform cannot await the full establishment of a new political order, building democratic institutions in a new spirit of negotiation and compromise, pluralism and tolerance, including, above all, the willingness to lose by the rules as well as win by the rules, should be Russia's highest priority. Our part of the capitalist West, which, as Verdery points out, has been going through its own conjunctural pains (a major factor in her explanatory mechanism) may be about to engage in its own redistribution of goods (not lemonade, but vaccines, insurance premiums, and medical assistance) through the avenue of the state, but based on the democratic exercise of political power. How a nation combines the market with its social needs is not the defining element in the characterization of a polity; how it *chooses* to design that combination, the *process* of decision-making, is. Here I find Reddaway too cautious. As he says, it is not in our power to save democracy in Russia (a "grandiose idea"), but we do have a moral imperative to be as supportive of Russia's very fragile democracy as we can be. In the long run, it is more important than the mix of what is sure to be some kind of mixed economy, a mix, after all, that can always be changed and changed again through the democratic process.

AFTER SOCIALISM, WHAT?

THE GLOBAL IMPLICATIONS OF THE REVOLUTIONS OF 1989 IN EASTERN EUROPE

DANIEL CHIROT

Since the start of the industrial era advanced economies, and eventually the entire world, have suffered from a set of recurring problems. Enormous material progress has not eliminated the periodic crises of capitalism; the spread of modern technology has not ended the differences between rich and poor countries, but in many instances has increased them; and within the most advanced societies there continue to be rich and poor people, unemployment, and severe social problems. Capitalism, for all its successes, never brought perfection.

But the European eighteenth century Enlightenment taught modern thinkers that reason could remedy serious problems, and the very progress that created a whole set of typically capitalist problems and crises in the nineteenth century also gave rise to utopian theories based on the wonders of growing scientific and technological prowess. Socialism, in its many forms, emerged from the hopes and projections of European thinkers who sought to harness progress in order to solve social problems. And in the twentieth century, several types of socialism, first of all the Marxist-Leninist version, but also social democracy and several local variants, took power and tried to move many societies closer to socialism's ideals.

Now that adventure seems to be ending. The central idea of socialism, that economies controlled and planned by the "people" acting through their governments can bring about more rapid progress than market driven ones, is in disgrace. The goal of radical egalitarianism is recognized as a vain dream that can only turn into a totalitarian nightmare if attempts are made to enforce it. Destroying old ruling classes and replacing them by a socialist bureaucracy only creates a new ruling class. The fantastic projection of so many intellectuals' dreams onto the industrial working class, which endowed that class with a purity, internationalist selflessness, and rationality no class could ever possess, has been exposed as a sham. In any case, the old industrial working class is in decline in the advanced industrial countries, and it cannot be the dominant class of the future. All of this has meant that "scientific socialism," particularly its Marxist version, has been shown to be neither scientific nor the wave of the future.

The demise of socialism as an ideal marks the collapse of the most long-lived, coherent, and politically successful challenge to capitalism in the nineteenth and twentieth centuries. The only other serious challenger, fascism, is a descendant of the aristocratic-religious opposition to the Enlightenment that also developed in the first half of the nineteenth century, and for most of the second half of the twentieth century, fascism has been in eclipse. But the decline of socialism leaves many of capitalism's problems unresolved and raises a question: what new critical ideology can replace socialist theory? Or might it be, implausible as at that may seem, that there will be no more ideological resistance to triumphant democratic bourgeois capitalism?

To answer these questions, it is necessary to explain why socialism seemed so appealing to so many for so long, and then to explain its startling fall in the last two or so decades.

THE CONTRADICTIONS OF CAPITALISM

The changes that occurred with the start of industrial era ushered in novel problems. We have not come out of that era, and are still subject to its predictable cyclical swings with their attendant difficulties. There was an age of cotton and textile (1780s-1830s), followed by the "second" industrial revolution of railways and iron (1840s-1870s). This, in turn, was followed by the age of organic chemistry and electricity (1870s-1910s), that of automobiles (1920s-1970s), and now by the fifth industrial age of computers and biotechnology. But with each of these changes, similar problems have arisen.[1]

The first set of recurring problems is a function of the loss of competitiveness of certain firms and geographic areas because of changes in technology. Previously successful firms and areas may find themselves bypassed, and well-paid laborers may have to take cuts in pay or become unemployed. To some extent, migration mitigates this problem, and firms or areas with sufficiently balanced infrastructures can adapt and survive. But readjustment always entails suffering, and those caught by such problems are upset and seek explanations. They also seek redress by political means.

Observations he made about the shift from the first to the second industrial age lay behind Karl Marx's theories about the end of capitalism. Pushed to the wall by increasing competition and declining profitability, textile firms in England, and later in the other industrializing parts of Europe, ruthlessly cut costs. Marginal producers, well established artisans who were not using the most modern machinery, and whole regions were ruined. Under such conditions, it was not foolish to believe that capital investment could not, in the long run, provide sufficient profits to sustain industries, and that instead, capitalists had to cut labor costs to the bare minimum.

But the first industrial age gave way to the second, and that to the third, fourth, and fifth. Each time, new technologies were invented which took pressure off the economy by providing new sources of profit, new employment, and a higher level of productivity. Cyclical crises in the past have always ended with capitalist economies at higher standards of living, with higher real wages, and new periods of accommodation between capital and labor. In the long run economic change has been anything but a zero-sum game, though in the short run it may be.

There has been a parallel, second set of problems associated with major industrial shifts. The first industrial period was dominated by England, the most advanced and powerful economy of its day. The accumulated capital and experience gained by England during this age allowed it to dominate the second, railway and iron age, too. But the third age that began in the 1860s and 1870s was different; it was much more highly dependent on direct scientific research. In this respect, England was not particularly progressive. Germany, and even before unification, the German states, tended to support university scientific research much better than the English, and they reaped rewards for this. Also, Germany, like the United States, educated a considerably larger portion of its population than the English or French.[2]

So, Germany and the United States moved ahead of England in this age, and it was particularly the German success that was striking because Germany did not have the immense advantages of enormous resources and cheap immigrant labor possessed by the United States. Also, Germany threatened England's hegemony in Europe much more directly. This problem eventually led to the mad race for empire that dominated international relations in the last part of the nineteenth century, and finally produced World War I.[3]

But the feeling shared by the great and medium powers of the world during that time was based on a thorough misunderstanding of how progress and economic success worked. Just as Marx felt that technological progress in industrial societies had to be a zero-sum game in the end, with the workers losing whatever capital might gain, so did most statesmen, generals, and captains of industry in the late nineteenth century believe that progress and prosperity had to be zero-sum games. Countries that could not protect their markets and sources of raw materials by acquiring colonies had to suffer for it. Many failed to appreciate that education and research were the basis of Germany's strength, not its army and martial bearing.

The aftermath of Word War I was bad enough, but the coincident shift from the third to the fourth industrial age compounded the problem. In the fourth industrial age research and education assumed an ever greater importance, but so did something quite new. Automobiles and the spread of electrical consumer appliances demanded a rapidly broadening mass consumer base. The Great Depression was primarily a failure of demand to keep up with increasing productivity. What would have been required was a highly stimulating macroeconomic policy on the part of the main industrial powers, chiefly the United States, the only country able to go through the transformation of the fourth industrial age in the 1920s. But as we all know, the United States did not follow such a policy, particularly abroad, and this made it virtually impossible for the world economy to adjust to the changes occurring. This is what lies behind Charles Kindleberger's phrase to explain the Great Depression, ". . . the British couldn't, and the United States wouldn't."[4]

In contrast to this, the United States after 1945 refloated the world economy and created the conditions for the greatest economic boom in history. During that time, the fourth industrial age flourished and its benefits spread throughout the advanced Western countries and Japan, and even began to spread into formerly poor countries. But now that age has ended, and the United States is losing the hegemonic preponderance it once had. The transition to the fifth industrial age, while unlikely to be as rocky as some of the past transitions, will not be without its problems. That is what much of the discussion about the decline of the United States is about.

The third problem associated with the industrial era is the problem of backwardness. There have always been more or less advanced parts of the world, but only in the modern era has backwardness become so perilous. Only since the industrialized revolution have the technological advantages of the leading industrial nations given them the potential to dominate the more backward regions so thoroughly. Ever since this perception has come into being, ideological solutions have been proposed.

Socialist theory and ideology were important attempts to understand the nature of cyclical crises in industrial societies, and to offer remedies. Socialism was also a consistent extension of eighteenth century Enlightenment thought. It believed that social and economic difficulties could be solved through the rational application of science. Progress was not only possible, but it could be managed.

In contrast, fascism, which came after socialism, but which inherited some of the opposition to the Enlightenment embodied by the Church and the aristocratic opposition to the French Revolution, sought to overcome the problems of industrial society by rejecting Enlightenment rationalism and substituting for it mysticism, enthusiasm, and "folk" exclusivity.

Fascism and socialism, however, had something in common. They rejected the liberal assumption that the purely impersonal, undirected economic mechanisms of free markets were really capable of solving the economic crises engendered by the industrial age. What socialism tried to overcome by more rational planning and internationalist appeals to proletarian interests, fascism sought to overcome by rebuilding the community's bonds and destroying the crass materialism of bourgeois capitalism. Both aimed to rebuild a sense of supposedly lost social solidarity. In power, both disappointed many of their followers because of the necessary compromises forced on them. But the ideals remained important, both as blueprints for the future and as motivating myths that could energize true believers.

These cyclical problems have been even more acute in backward countries than in rich ones. Poor economies dependent on primary exports suffer greater price depressions in their key exports than do industrial ones during cyclical downturns. They are more dependent on the fate of the world market, especially if, like many colonial economies, they substitute export crops for home grown food. Those backward countries unable to engage in the imperialist games that have resulted from competition between more advanced countries have become their victims. Moderately developed countries have been among the most enthusiastic players, eager to prey on their weaker neighbors. Finally, over time ambitious elites in backward countries have come to feel these problems ever more acutely.

At various times, socialism and fascism have appealed as solutions. Both have promised to be uniquely able to solve the problem of backwardness. Fascism's rejection of a rationality based on economic profits and the lonely individualism of modern liberal society was never far removed from socialism's distrust of capitalist alienation. Fascism relies on some supposedly higher capacity of pre-modern, non-Western ideologies and solidarities to give a society the power to overcome powerful internal and external opponents. Socialism believed that certain classes in power could be more rational than capitalist elites. Ultimately both sets of assumptions were based on faith.

The weakness of socialism today raises important questions. First, why has an ideology which has survived so successfully for over a century, and in one form or another, come to power in over a third of the world, suddenly begun to fail? Secondly, given the persistence of many of the problems that led to its rise, at least in some parts of the world, what will replace it? Finally, what does all this portend for the future of ideology and politics?

THE COLLAPSE OF EUROPEAN LENINISM IN 1989

Socialism not only appealed because it promised to be more rational than capitalism, and less alienating, but also fairer. Rewarding those who happen to be lucky or clever in commerce has never been viewed as legitimate by most people. Modern egalitarian ideologies share this with older agrarian societies from the Confucian East to the Christian West.

To be fair in the late twentieth century, however, requires a high level of productivity. As the material advantages of the fourth, and recently the fifth industrial period increased, it became painfully obvious that centrally planned economies were unable to keep up. Then, the lies and repression which kept their ruling party bureaucracies in power became unbearable, because the fundamental promise that all these sacrifices were going to yield a golden future ceased to be believable. Without knowing much about the continuing problems and contradictions of capitalism, those who lived in societies based on Leninism could only see that instead of unfairness produced by the market there was unfairness caused by shortages and corruption, and that the situation was becoming worse. Whatever flaws the capitalist societies may have had, ordinary people there were better off than in non-market economies.

Much has been written about the inherent inability of central planning and state controlled economies to yield high levels of productivity. The problem results from two basic flaws of socialism, one general, and the other specific to countries that modelled their economies on Soviet, that is Leninist-Stalinist principles.

As János Kornai's work has demonstrated, highly centralized economies run by communist party cadres necessarily produce shortages and bad quality. Because pricing, investment decisions, employment policies, and long term economic goals are set for political rather than market efficient goals, successful performance is not measured through maximization of quality, profits, or consumer satisfaction. The result is a mediocre economic performance. The flood of high quality, technologically superior East Asian electronic consumer goods all around the world, even in relatively poor countries, has made it evident to the entire world that Soviet style economies cannot perform.

In Western Europe, too, some of the same problems, though to a far lesser extent, have appeared in nationalized firms that are subject to political pressures from unionized labor forces and therefore tend toward unjustifiably high wages, overstaffing, and resistance to technological innovation. This is not a concomitant of generous welfare policies, but of socialist ones. Whether in Great Britain, Czechoslovakia, or Tanzania, socialism has demonstrated its inability to deliver the goods, and it is impossible to explain this away any more.

But in specifically Leninist-Stalinist societies, there is a second problem. The successful Bolshevik revolutionaries based their model of economic success on the "high technology" industries of their day, that is, the giant steel mills and chemical plants, the electrification projects, and the huge concentrations of capital and labor in immense factories that characterized the more advanced parts of Germany, Britain, and the United States. These were the showcases of the "third" industrial period. Stalinism forced the Soviet Union to industrialize this way, and in many ways, succeeded. By the last third of the twentieth century, the Soviet Union had become the world's largest early twentieth century economy. By then, however, it was too late. The close attention needed to marketing, the flexibility that allowed new types of production processes to flourish, and the integration of local economies with rapidly evolving international markets that characterized the successful capitalist firms were absent in this model. In the capitalist world, firms that missed these changes, and there were many, failed. In the Soviet Union, and in all its imitators, the identity of managerial and political power added to the closed nature of these economies allowed the outdated model to survive much longer than it should have. No economy oriented to the world market could have maintained the gross inefficiencies exhibited by these systems for so long. Nor would democratic societies have tolerated such failures.

It is not enough to point to these well known economic problems of socialism, particularly of the Leninist-Stalinist kind. After all, there were successes, too, and even today the Soviet Union is a military giant with nuclear weapons and rockets. It has a well educated population, many engineers and scientists, and in certain fields it does not lag far behind the West. In Eastern Europe, the communist regimes that crumbled so quickly in 1989 were ruling over countries with intact armies and police forces, with no starvation or civil disorder, and in several cases economies that were only poor compared to Western Europe, but not to most of the rest of the world. There remain many countries where poverty, corruption, inequality, and injustice are far worse. So why did the East European regimes collapse, almost without a fight, and why is the idea of socialism so generally discredited?

The reason is that socialism, and more specifically Marxism, which became the only generally accepted theoretical base of all forms of socialism, began and is ending as a utopian ideology. There was, first of all, the idea, the word. Almost any other aspect of Marxism could be reinterpreted and adapted to changing realities except the central notion that it was a scientifically correct interpretation of the past, and a guide to a future utopia. If Marxist socialism was no longer a science of history, if it no longer predicted the future, it was worthless.

Stalin certainly understood this, as have other Marxist leaders. This is why the more reality deviated from the ideological promise, the more they had to lie. It was impossible to be openly cynical about Marxism, because that would totally undermine the legitimacy of socialist rule. So, starting in the 1920s, there were lies. Lies were built on lies, and as the gap between reality and the promise became all the more evident, the sensation of guilt and dishonesty spread throughout all Leninist societies.

Timothy Garton Ash's reporting about Eastern Europe in the 1980s captured this sense of the omnipresent lie. For societies increasingly well educated, for intellectuals who could no longer be kept ignorant of reality, it was intolerable. This is what led to the creation, in northern Eastern Europe (that is, Central Europe), of alternate social bonds, to the attempt to build civil social ties that avoided the official state and party institutions.

What Gorbachev did in the late 1980s, in an attempt to improve the economic and technological performance of the Soviet Union, was to suggest that there be more openness and truth. That was the one thing communist regimes could not survive. Underneath, in Eastern Europe, everyone had long known the system was a hoax, and now we know that this feeling was far more prevalent in the Soviet Union than we had thought. What had been brewing in Eastern Europe could now boil over; and in his desperate attempt to revive the Soviet economy by obtaining Western help, Gorbachev calculated that it was no longer worth it to suppress Eastern European discontent. Toward the end of 1989 he made it clear to the more recalcitrant Eastern European communist leaders that they had to change to save themselves because there would be no Soviet intervention on their behalf.

If the moral basis of socialism had not become a hollow shell long before, the political changes of 1989 would not have occurred. But the loss of faith was neither new nor confined to the communist world. Elsewhere, the notion that socialism was somehow the progressive future of the world had begun to disintegrate in the 1970s, and for many of the same reasons. The sense that history was no longer moving in the direction of Marxism, that centralized economic control was not efficient, and that the leading examples of socialism, the communist countries, were no longer trustworthy models was responsible for the startling retreat of socialist ideals throughout the world, a process which has only been accelerated by the events of 1989.

THE GENERAL DECLINE OF THE SOCIALIST IDEAL

Few events of the 1980s dramatized the decline of the left as sharply as those in France. The Communist Party went from being the single largest opposition party, the darling of intellectuals and of reform minded youth, to being a marginal old age home for hacks. To be sure, much of its loss has involved a transfer of political allegiance to François Mitterand's Socialists. But after his first victory in 1981, Mitterand himself has progressively abandoned almost any trace of socialism. After a few years of nationalizations and strengthened central controls over the economy, Mitterand's Socialists have adopted a series of measures, both domestic and in defense and foreign affairs, in line with the much more conservative governments of the other principal Western powers. So, unlike German and British voters, who repeatedly expressed their distaste for socialism and unilateral disarmament, French voters were spared this choice after 1981 by having their Socialists abandon socialism except in name.

In southern Europe the pattern has been similar. The Spanish Socialists have remained in power by abandoning socialism, and the Spanish Communists, as well as their Portuguese counterparts have disappeared as viable political forces. The Italian Communists, for all their clever attempts to distance themselves from Leninism, are on the decline. The Greek left, even before personal scandals brought it down, had abandoned its socialist policies in favor of orthodox free market policies. It was not just domestic politics that caused the decline of the once powerful left in these countries, but especially in France and Italy, the dismal example of Eastern Europe convinced most voters that there must be something wrong.

One of the enduring mysteries of the 1980s was the failure of the German Social Democrats and the British Labour Party to overthrow conservative politicians who lacked inherent popularity or warmth. The reason, simply, was that these two socialist parties refused to shake off their socialism, being less pragmatic, or perhaps less cynical than their French and Spanish counterparts. In the 1990s, that is changing, but in the meantime, young intellectuals and the more active among the discontented have switched from socialism to ecological activism.

Though the fundamental social advances of the welfare state have been preserved in advanced capitalist societies, the idea that public own-

ership of the means of production or tight regulation of market forces are
sound economic policies has been abandoned in all of them, whether
Sweden, New Zealand, Australia, Japan, or others. This has left socialist
parties and intellectuals in a state of confusion and uncertainty about what
to do next.[5]

The situation is more dramatic in most of what used to be called
the "Third World." Look, for example, at the Islamic countries. In the
1950s and 1960s the force of the future, from North Africa to Islamic
Southeast Asia seemed to be inspired by one variety or another of Western
Marxism. Whether it was the Algerian FLN, Nasser in Egypt, the Ba'thists,
or the Indonesian Communist Party and its ally Sukarno, it could be said
that the nationalist, progressive, forward-looking elements in the Islamic
world accepted the notion that rational, scientific social engineering using
Western technology and ways of planning was possible and the best way
of bringing about free, roughly egalitarian societies. Moreover, this seemed
to be the way of catching up to the West, and freeing the Muslim world of
its backwardness and weakness. In other words, the European tradition
was not rejected, but embraced in its socialist form, just as, simultaneously,
imperialism and Western domination were being fought. The opposition
to the socialist Muslim progressives consisted, for the most part, of
seemingly feeble monarchs held up by their imperialist mentors, or of other
old elites holding on to power by corruption and collaboration with foreign
interests.

What a different world it is now! Nasser is long dead. The
greater degree of equality his rule brought about was purchased at the
price of leaving behind a crushingly inept bureaucracy. The regimes
that succeeded his are not socialist, but their failures have only aroused
a right wing Islamic opposition, not a revived left. Elsewhere in the
Arab world Ba'thism degenerated into tyranny in Syria and Iraq, held
in place by terror rather than ideology or solid accomplishments. The
remnants of Ba'thist thought came to be used by Hafez Asad and
Saddam Hussein to justify personal rule by themselves, their families,
and their religious-ethnic minorities. Theirs are centralizing, militaristic police states whose legitimizing principles are nationalism and the
cult of the leader. There is very little difference between their ideologies
and those that characterized Mussolini and the other pre-war European
fascists.[6]

In Iran, as we know too well, the Shah's failed attempt to modernize
his country from above led to a fundamentalist Islamic revolution, not to

a socialist one. It is anti-rational, anti-Western, xenophobic, and it has exterminated the Iranian left far more effectively than the Shah's secret police could have hoped to do. Women and minorities have been pushed back into subservience, and though there is considerable support for this regime, it is almost the exact opposite of what optimistic radical leftists would have hoped to accomplish. But it is not just in Iran that religious fundamentalism is the new voice of radicalism. It is everywhere throughout the Islamic world. Whether in Tunisia, long a bastion of Arab secularism and Westernism, or Algeria, Egypt, and Syria, or further to the east, Pakistan, Malaysia, and Indonesia, the future seems to lie with highly politicized Islamic fundamentalism. The idealistic, radical young have turned to Islam, not to socialism, to protest the serious social problems faced by their societies.[7]

In Africa, the situation is similar. In Mozambique, Angola, Somalia, and Ethiopia, socialist projects exacerbated civil wars and are now in ruins. The prospects for African socialism seemed brighter thirty years ago when Kwame Nkrumah of a newly independent Ghana claimed that his socialist, independent, and progressive regime would show the way for Africa. Nkrumah summarized the elementary misunderstanding so typical of the nationalist intellectuals of his era when he wrote that "capitalism is too complicated for a newly independent country." In fact, socialism is even more catastrophic for very backward societies than it is for semi-developed ones.

The longest lasting African experiment with socialism was Sékou Touré's bloody reign in Guinea. Immediately after his death his heirs were overthrown and his legacy renounced. Benin, another long lasting attempt to create a kind of African socialism, has given up. The Tanzanian economy, after the fairly benign socialism promoted by Julius Nyerere, is also in economic ruin. Even the South African ANC has begun to abandon socialism.

The situation in Latin America is not much brighter for socialism. Cuba's failure to diversify its economy or wean itself from dependency has made a good many Latin Americans skeptical about Marxism's efficacy, and in Cuba itself, produced its first full scale Stalinist purge trials in 1989. In general, the prospects of the left are surprisingly poor for a continent with such abominable social inequality and so many economic problems. Brazil has one of the world's most unequal income distributions, a large proletariat, and many landless peasants, but its left has never been very strong. In Mexico, the ruling Revolutionary Institutional Party which has been in power for decades, finally responded to electoral discontent and has embarked on a policy of privatization, more open foreign trade, encouraging private business, and adhering more closely to International Monetary Fund guidelines. This reverses its longstanding policy of autarkic, government controlled development which led to massive corruption and inefficiency. In Argentina the left has little influence, and politics is a triangular affair among the liberals, the army, and the Peronists, though increasingly, leading Peronistas recognize that a more liberal, rather than the old statist, autarkic path will yield more positive economic results in the long run.

Nor does a guerrilla movement like the Shining Path in Peru, which is more an alliance of angry Maoists (or Fanonists) and drug exporters than Marxist-Leninist revolutionaries, offer much hope. Peru, it should be noted, was utterly ruined by a set of conventionally leftist, and originally very popular, policies followed by Alan Garcia who presided over the country during the late 1980s. Everywhere, conventional free market economic measures, adherence to World Bank and International Monetary Fund guidelines, greater integration into the world market, and more democratic politics are recognized to be the most practical road to salvation. This hardly means that it will be easy, or in some cases even possible to apply such policies, but it does mean that for the time being, even in Latin America, socialist ideology is far weaker than it was a decade ago.

All of these developments in every part of the world have had an effect that goes well beyond local politics. The crisis of socialism is a combination of all that ails it. Hard line Leninists, Maoists, social democrats, and other types of socialists have been affected. What it all adds up to is a loss of faith so severe that it will be many decades, if ever, before socialist ideals can recover the vitality they had until the decade of the 1980s.

IF NOT SOCIALISM, THEN WHAT?

Does this mean, however, that there will be no new anti-capitalist revolutionary ideologies? Does it mean that democracy will become the rule everywhere? To think so would be a mistake because the problems of capitalism have not vanished. Economic cycles and consequent shifts in the balance of economic and political power have not ended. Inequality between and within nations has not been eliminated. New problems that the nineteenth century could not imagine, ecological degradation, migration on an unprecedented scale, and the spread of very dangerous weapons, remain unsolved. The acceleration of the dissolution of traditional family ties, leaving enormous problems in the care of the young and the old, the persistence of unemployment, and continuing tensions between capitalist countries over control of markets are older problems but they persist. Utopia has not arrived. There will continue to be losers in the world.

Firms, industries, regions, or countries that fail to keep up with change will suffer relative, or sometimes absolute, drops in their standard of living. This is what happened to the United Kingdom in the decades after World War II, and what is happening to the United States right now. In very large parts of the globe, most of Africa, much of Latin America, and in South Asia, poverty will continue to grind down the majority of the population. In Muslim societies the continuing failure to catch up to the advanced non-Islamic world will continue to stimulate Islamic fundamentalism and angry nationalism. And now, there will be a whole new set of potential losers, the formerly communist countries that try to adapt to the requirements of capitalism and find that successful transformations to efficiency are neither easy nor rapid.

Losing is not pleasant, and losers, or those who are simply afraid of being left behind, demand dramatic solutions. These cannot easily be answered by advising patience. We have had a number of tragic examples of what these pressures can lead to. The race for colonies in the late nineteenth century, which was irrational from any economic viewpoint, contributed heavily to the arms race that led to World War I. That the Germans, whose superior educational, scientific, and industrial vigor would have made them the predominant country in Europe had they maintained peace, were among the most blind to the reality of their situation only means that statesmen and generals are not necessarily better informed than managers of big firms. Then in the Great Depression of the 1930s, we know that every major country turned to economic nationalism in order to save itself. Fascism and World War II resulted, not a new market equilibrium. What guarantee is there that future economic crises, perceptions about diminishing competitiveness, and fears about drops in the standard of living will not have equally nefarious effects in the future? Will the response be blind trust in the ability of the free market to set things right?

Among young intellectuals, there will always be those trying to discover revolutionary answers. To believe otherwise is to believe in a world with no problems, no angry young people, and no thinkers eager to formulate new programs. The question, then, is what will appeal to them? If not socialism, what?

Fundamentalist Islam is not likely to be imitated outside of the Muslim parts of the world. On the other hand, extreme nationalism, religious fanaticism, and bitter hostility to the rationalizing, liberal, skeptical Enlightenment tradition spread throughout the world by Western Europeans are quite capable of filling the void left by the collapse of socialism. Religious Iran, secular Ba'thist Iraq, and the Peruvian Shining Path might be unwelcome harbingers of a much more widespread phenomenon.

Fundamentalism, whether of the Islamic variety, or of the Christian variety (as seen in the United States or Russia, for example) is much more than anti-foreign xenophobia. It is a denial of the power of scientific inquiry to offer solutions to our problems or an understanding of the physical and human world. It substitutes faith for reason, and devalues the individual's right to make important personal moral and political decisions. There is faith, and the community alone is paramount. Rejection of communal values is viewed as proof of heresy and can only be explained as pollution of the original, pure community by outside forces. Therefore, the "foreign Satans" who threaten the community may be Americans for the Iranian mullahs, Jews for the Russian Orthodox, or abortionists and believers in Darwinian theory for the American religious right. Blaming "outsiders" is not mere scapegoating; it becomes an essential explanation of the source of evil, a theory to explain why God's perfection has not yet been established. And God is not always necessary. Neither Hitler nor Saddam Hussein needed formal religion to develop very similar ideologies and political strategies. The "Arab Nation" or the "Aryan race" can be perfectly adequate substitutes.

In its early twentieth century form socialism was largely immune to, and an effective counterweight to, religious fundamentalism. Later, as communist regimes began to devise fantastic scapegoats to explain their own failures, and to turn socialism into ritualized expressions of community faith, the original belief in the power of individual rationality and science was lost. That is one of the main reasons why communism collapsed in Eastern Europe and is in trouble everywhere it rules. Without the original guiding premise of Enlightenment values, communism turned into one more irrational faith looking for convenient targets to blame for the pollution of healthy communal spiritual values. Everything foreign was suspect. The national genius, exemplified by a living god, Mao, Enver Hoxha, Kim Il-Sung, Ceausescu, Stalin, or Castro, could triumph over all obstacles.

The collapse of the socialist ideal, therefore, has removed an important barrier to many "fundamentalist" revivals. The death of the socialist ideal leaves fundamentalism as the last, best hope for many angry intellectuals in the Muslim world, and in Russia religious, populist, anti-semitism is on the rise.

It is not surprising, therefore, that all kinds of religious, populist local nationalisms are erupting with renewed virulence in many multi-ethnic states, but particularly in ones previously guided by some variety of socialist ideal. Educated elites in such disparate countries as the Soviet Union and India have had little else to turn to in the 1980s.

Socialism also fought populism. The anti-urban, anti-big business, anti-free market egalitarianism in populist doctrines around the world have shared many of the assumptions of religious fundamentalism. In the United States, as Richard Hofstadter's classic research on anti-intellectualism showed, they have always been closely associated. But whether religious or not, populists shared with fundamentalism fear of the "powerful outsider," and emphasized the redeeming virtues of native traditions. In Eastern Europe during the interwar period populists championed agrarian, "original" values over decadent, foreign, urban ones. Populist Argentinian Peronism even had an industrial working class base. Socialists insisted that theirs was a more rational, scientific way of creating egalitarian, fair societies. With the decline of socialism, populism has been liberated of its main ideological enemy.

What fascism provided for populists and those inclined to cultural fundamentalism, but not to any particular religious program, was a theory of how to organize society. Corporatist theory views the most desirable form of social organization as a series of vertical, solidary groups whose potential conflicts can be resolved by a mediating body standing above society. Rather than horizontal, class based alliances pitting workers against capitalists, peasants against landowners, vertical groups are supposed to be more akin to large families, with the superior members being more like paternalistic overseers of the group interest than like impersonal bosses. In fact, communist societies were largely organized on corporatist lines, much more so than the main fascist countries in the 1920s and 1930s, where corporatism was never thoroughly applied.

The demise of the socialist dream will greatly enhance the prospects of a fascist revival. This does not mean that Naziism will return to Germany, or that the Iron Guard will take power in Romania, but that in one form or another, fascism's appeal to nativism, anti-capitalism, and a new moral order will find followers among those frustrated by their world.

Corporatism has never been totally eclipsed. A mild version persists in Japan where it takes the form of social conformism and a rigidly enforced collaboration between key government ministries and large corporations. A harsher kind persists in South Korea, whose social and nationalist ideals are not so different from North Korea's. The idealized Confucianism favored by Singapore's Lee Kuan Yew's, or Indonesia's "Pancasila" are also forms of corporatism.

IDEOLOGICAL PERSPECTIVES FOR THE FUTURE

The collapse of communism and the decline of socialism have already unloosed a number of atavistic forces in Western Europe, notably in France, where a substantial number of former communist voters seem to have moved to the anti-foreign, antisemitic far right. Green parties, at least their radical wings, are often considered "leftist." But they are actually engaged in an anti-Enlightenment project, too. They reject the capacity of science and technology to solve the world's problems, and they dream of a mythical, bucolic past. In the long run they may present a serious challenge to prevailing liberal values. But on the whole, it is unlikely that liberal democratic parties will lose control in Western Europe. On the contrary, the social democrats will continue to abandon what little remains of their socialism and the political stability, international success, and continuing prosperity of the region will insure that anti-liberal movements will remain small. The same is probably true in the United States.

The situation is quite different in the rest of the world. We have already seen what the ideological future of the Muslim world may be. In Latin America and non-Muslim Africa, the decline of the left leaves open the possibility that protest will be channeled increasingly into what Ken Jowitt has called "movements of rage" like the Peruvian Shining Path.[8]

In East Asia, if the moderate corporatism that has prevailed has seemed fairly liberal during the past decades of economic and political success, the situation would change very quickly in case of a world economic crisis. Trade wars would quickly bring about a revival of extreme nationalism and anti-Westernism. Grafted on to corporatist institutions, this would mean the recreation of militaristic fascism. As for China, it is difficult to foresee much beyond the eventual collapse of communism. But if one is to judge from the Russian and East European examples, such a collapse does not mean the quick and automatic adoption of stable liberal democracy.

Because of the continuing turmoil in Central and Eastern Europe and the old Russian Empire, and because this region includes some important, visible, but unstable parts of Europe, it is likely that it will provide some influential models for the rest of the world. If one includes Germany before 1945 in the area of "Central Europe" (the very term was invented by the Germans — *Mitteleuropa*), then one can see how big a role this large area played in providing anti-liberal ideological models to the world. Here fascism reached its most extreme degree. Here communism was incubated and then destroyed. This part of the world, with its rich mixture of ethnicities and religions, has been at once highly advanced and the home of large pockets of economic backwardness. It produced some of the finest examples of the Western Enlightenment in terms of science, philosophy, and the arts, but it also spawned bestial rejections of that same Enlightenment in the twentieth century. As the prototypical "semiperiphery," it embodies all the contradictions of the modern era that have produced revolutionary turmoil in the past, and perhaps in the future. Therefore, it is worth ending with a brief look at what may happen in the former Soviet Empire.

Immediately after the revolutionary year of 1989, a distinct pattern began to emerge in Eastern Europe. In the northern countries, that is, the Central European ones that were Protestant and Catholic, communism collapsed far more thoroughly than in the southern, Balkan ones, or than in Russia. Even within the Soviet Union, a similar pattern emerged, with the Baltic countries taking the lead in trying to end communism.

It may seem odd that such different lands as Serbia (in opposition to Catholic Croatia and Slovenia), Bulgaria, Romania, and Russia, united by little else than their common Christian Orthodox historical tradition, should seem to form a kind of a block. But this should not be surprising. The long history of church-state conflicts in the Catholic and Protestant lands, of the maintenance of some degree of independence by church intellectuals, and the long exposure of these countries to Enlightenment philosophy and science contributed to the greater resistance to communism in Central Europe compared to the Balkans and Russia. Protestant churches in East Germany, and the Catholic Church in Poland provided an institutional base of support for opposition, and for the survival of civil society outside the confines of the party-state. Orthodox churches, on the other hand, have long been purely national, less intellectual, and broken to the dictates of the state. This does not mean that Orthodox cultures lack a tradition of opposition or political instability; it only means that they have much less understanding and appreciation of liberalism.

But too much ought not to be made of such historical differences, because Central Europe also has a rich tradition of anti-liberalism. The fact is that 1989 left all these countries with very similar problems. Converting inefficient, outdated industrial structures into efficient ones is inherently difficult. When industries have workers who, after forty years of communism, have come to think of themselves as a distinct class with rights to job security and good wages, conversion is more difficult. The population feels it is entitled to broad welfare rights. For a decade or two standards of living will not rise, but social expectations will remain far higher than justified by economic reality. In such conditions, privatization of industry (unlike agriculture and small services) is very difficult. States will continue, in most cases, to own and operate most large industries, thus failing to resolve the inherent problems of socialism.

Economic failure, which is virtually guaranteed in Russia and Romania, and highly likely in some of the other East and Central European countries, will make the adoption of liberal democracy problematic. There exists a rich tradition of populist and fascist ideology to use as the basis of opposition. Adam Michnik, one of the heroes of Poland's liberation, phrased it this way:

> The greatest threat to democracy today is no longer communism, either as a political movement or as an ideology. The threat grows instead from a combination of chauvinism, xenophobia, populism, and authoritarianism, all of them connected with the sense of frustration typical of great social upheavals. This is the perspective from which we must view the old conflicts that are now flaring up again in Central and Eastern Europe.[9]

In Poland, Michnik points out, "there are people who hold aliens and foreigners — Russians, Germans, Jews, cosmopolites, Freemasons — accountable for bringing communism to Poland. The most important conflict . . . today is being fought between those who see the future of Poland as part of Europe and those characterized . . . as 'nation-centric' . . ."

Making liberal capitalist democracy work is very difficult. As that quintessential westernizing Central European Karl Polanyi proved, accepting the free market, believing, somehow, that the seeming chaos of competing interests, can produce a workable economic system, was too much for most people to accept.[10] He believed that the revolt against the free market produced those two twentieth century monstrosities, fascism and communism. Writing in the 1940s, he underestimated the power of the United States to revive liberal capitalism, but in the long run, his vision remains troubling. Now, unless there is an economic miracle in Central and Eastern Europe, and in Russia, the same anti-market forces he analyzed are certain to resurface. But this time, there will be no left to fight against the right.

The success of liberalism in the western world does not insure its universal acceptance. It remains an ideology dependent on peculiar cultural histories, on faith in the value of individualism, gradualism, and tolerance. These do not appeal to the impatient, the afflicted, or the angry who will long remain the majority of the world. On the other hand, we should not underestimate the power of liberalism, either, as so many intellectuals have in the past. It survived, barely, the challenges of fascism in the 1930s and 1940s, and of communism from the 1940s to the 1980s. The "Revolutions of 1989" did not mark its final triumph, but it was a triumph nevertheless.

NOTES

1   W. W. Rostow, *The World Economy: History and Prospect* (Austin: University of Texas Press, 1978), pp. 298-348. Also, Daniel Chirot, *Social Change in the Modern Era* (San Diego: Harcourt Brace Jovanovich, 1986), pp. 223-230.

2   Chirot, *Social Change*, 88-90.
3   Paul M. Kennedy, *The Rise of Anglo-German Antagonism 1860-1914* (London: George Allen & Unwin, 1980), pp. 464-470.
4   Charles P. Kindleberger, *The World in Depression* (London: Allen Lane, 1973), p. 292.
5   All these and many other cases are discussed by S.M. Lipset's "No Third Way: A Comparative Perspective on The Left," in Daniel Chirot, ed., *The Crisis of Leninism and the Decline of the Left* (Seattle: University of Washington Press, 1991).
6   Samir al-Khalil, *Republic of Fear: The Politics of Modern Iraq* (Berkeley and Los Angeles: University of California Press, 1989).
7   Emanuel Sivan, *Radical Islam* (New Haven: Yale University Press, 1985).
8   Ken Jowitt, "The Leninist Extinction," in Chirot, *The Crisis of Leninism.*
9   *New York Review of Books*, July 19, 1990 "The Two Faces of Europe," p. 7
10   Karl Polanyi, *The Great Transformation* (Boston: Beacon Press, 1957).

A Singular Collapse: The Soviet Union, Market Pressure and Inter-State Competition

FRED HALLIDAY

INTRODUCTION: NEW LIGHT ON OLD QUESTIONS

The collapse of the Soviet system within the USSR and internationally in the late 1980s, in addition to its manifold implications for global politics and policy, has raised a range of important and unresolved issues, analytically and within social and international theory. The first question is that of explanation, of providing why a political and socio-economic system that was broadly equal to its rival in military terms should have collapsed rapidly and unequivocally, and in the absence of significant international military conflict.[1] No explanation in terms of a single factor is possible, and there is much that will only become clearer with the passage of time. What is being attempted here is a provisional analysis of the causes of the collapse of the communist system, focusing on the international dimensions of this process. The internal weaknesses of the system played a major role in its demise, not least the paralysis at both economic and political levels that characterized it,[2] but an analysis of the international factors is of relevance for several reasons — first, because so much has been said and written about how international competition did contribute to the failure of communism and it is worth now assessing these claims; second, because, despite talk of its "failure," this system did not fall because of internal pressures alone; third, because a discussion of the historical question, why communism collapsed, may cast light on underlying theoretical issues pertaining to interstate and intersystemic competition.

The communist leaderships were engaged in a project that was both national and international: it was international as a result of systemic pressure from other states, but it was also ideologically international, an attempt to constitute a model society on an international scale, and to promote similar movements in other countries. Yet if the overall failure of communism includes its failure to spread worldwide, a better starting point to analyze why the regimes collapsed is the record of internal, top-down transformation which the regimes promoted. The elites in the central committees and politbureaus of the ruling parties sought to transform the societies in accordance with a theoretical blueprint of where socialist society should be going. This project was a failure, not only in reaching its goal, but also because much of what had apparently been achieved was impermanent and superficial. The claims that "developed socialism" or some sort of more perfect society had been reached were false, and so too were the apparently less apologetic claims that these societies were in some implicitly teleological sense "in transition" to a new socio-economic model and represented a permanent advance beyond what capitalism could provide.

This failure is as true for attempts to create a viable and self-sustaining planned economy as it is for those to forge politically viable one-party systems, and for attempts to reform attitudes regarding major areas of ideological importance, notably work, gender, religion, and ethnicity. The simplest explanation of the collapse is to say that such a project was, in an absolute sense, a "failure": this is the conclusion that many in the communist countries now draw, as those who deny the efficacy of "social engineering" have always done. There are, however, reasons to resist this conclusion. In terms of the capacities of states to transform society from above, the record is not so absolute.

First, it is far too early to say how much of the legacy of communist rule will endure and whether some of it may not in fact survive. Second, it is wrong to take as evidence of the failure of communism the emergence of forces that appear to mark a return to pre-communist forms of behavior, since many of these have a character that has been shaped by the very impact of communist transformation — ethnic conflict being an obvious case. Similarly, as many who have analyzed the emergence of Gorbachev have shown, the change in Soviet society is in some respects a product of the achievements of communism — expansion in education and urbanization being obvious contributory factors.[3] Third, even if much or all of what is associated with communist rule does disappear, say in a decade or two, the historical fact of the communist achievement over some decades will remain: this was evident in socioeconomic transformation, the raising of living standards and the implementation of a widespread social welfare system, the sustenance and reproduction of a political system and, not least, a considerable success in the most testing area of all, inter-state competition. It may be that the success of the latter — Soviet victory in World War II, plus four decades of rivalry with the West thereafter — provided part of the illusion of communism's overall efficacy, at home and abroad. However, the record of interstate competition alone would suggest that the characterization of the communist record as a "failure" is simplistic. Such a verdict would have come as rather a surprise to, for example, the 250,000 Germans captured at Stalingrad as it would have to military planners in the Pentagon during the 1970s and early 1980s. The achievement was substantial, even if temporary.

THE NATURE OF COLD WAR

If the events of 1989 signal the end of the Cold War, they make it more possible to address the question of what the Cold War was, and how as one specific instance it pertains to broader conceptions of interstate competition. Despite its apparent distinctiveness, the Cold War has been treated by most writers as merely another chapter in a longer history of international competition. The term "cold war" tended to be used in two ways: one to denote particular periods of intense East-West rivalry, 1947-53, the classic original "Cold War" and, though this is more disputed, the period 1979-84, the "Second Cold War." The other usage denotes not specific periods but the more protracted rivalry of the two systems, capitalist and communist, as it developed after 1945 and originated in 1917.[4]

The academic literature has tended to focus on historical questions pertaining to the first, narrower sense of cold war, of who originated the intensified conflict in 1947 or 1979 and why, and this is the basis of the debate between orthodox, revisionist and post-revisionist historians on the origins of the cold war. Less articulated has been the theoretical debate, on what kind of conflict this cold war in the broader sense was, and what its implications are for international and other social theory. In one view, there was no problem: the Cold War was a strategic rivalry between great powers like any other and susceptible to conventional "realist" analysis. This explanation had several things to recommend it: it had considerable explanatory power; it drew attention to what were undoubtedly points of comparison between historic great power conflicts and the Soviet-American one, most obviously competition for spheres of influence and military power; it provided a way of creating academic distance from the rival ideological claims of both sides to be representing one or other set of universal values; it distinguished itself from the orthodox Marxist view that in some way the Cold War represented an internationalized political conflict, class struggle on a world scale.

Yet it can be questioned how far this conventional description of the Cold War did accord with reality and, not least, how far it can be seen to provide a basis for understanding communism's collapse. One initial novelty about East-West rivalry in the postwar epoch was the role of nuclear weapons, the limits these placed upon direct territorial competition between the core blocs and the peculiarly intense but controlled competition of the arms race. While the two blocs were involved in wars in the Third World to challenge hegemony or take territory in core states of the other bloc, it was not possible. More important, if often overstated by the two competitors themselves, was the fact that the Cold War involved not just relative degrees of power and strategic advantage, but also competition about the way in which society and political systems were to be organized. It involved a drive by both sides to produce a homogeneous world, not just in the conventional International Relations sense of states that performed in roughly similar ways on the international stage, but in terms of internal political and socioeconomic organization. It was heterogeneity in this latter domain that lay at the core of the Cold War and which, for all its strategic and other similarities with great power conflicts of the past, made it distinctive.

What was involved in the Cold War was the confrontation of two societies, including but not solely involving, the United States. Both U.S.-led capitalism and Soviet-led communism sought nothing less than to create worlds in their own image: although, for four decades both were checked by the military and political strength of the other, the endurance of this universalizing drive was evident. Soviet communism gave up its global political aspirations at some point after the mid-1970s — with the collapse of Eurocommunism and the paralysis of Third World socialist and socialist-oriented regimes. Western capitalism did not give up and, with greater resources and determination, sustained its pressure, and in the end prevailed. Nothing bore this underlying nature of the conflict out more clearly than the manner in which it ended. Had the Cold War been a traditional great power conflict alone it could have ended with a truce, negotiated distribution of power and military strength. This was what had existed in Europe after 1945 and what was attempted, without success, in the Third World. Ultimately, the denouement came in the apparently paralyzed, "balanced" core, namely Europe, and as a result of a change of policy at the core. It came because one system was no longer able to sustain itself in the face of the other, and it was as a result of this, of one side in effect collapsing, that the Cold War could be said to have ended.

THE ROLE OF EXTERNAL COMPETITION

It is now possible to address the main question of this analysis, one of both historical and theoretical importance, namely how far and in what ways external competition contributed to the evolution and final collapse of the communist system.[5] As already noted, that system was not destroyed by war, nor was its collapse solely exogenous. Internal factors, most importantly the paralysis of the economies and political systems, played a major part. But external forces, including economic ones, did contribute to the final collapse of 1989. Two kinds of factors conventionally evolved in analysis of interstate competition   "traditional" and contemporary — can be examined: the conclusion will be that, above all, it was neither of these but competition in the fields of perceived economic and ideological performance that determined the outcome.

The cold war was not the first case of international competition between heterogeneous states. The fate of the Ottoman and Chinese empires in the latter half of the nineteenth centuries up to their final disappearances during World War I are two classic earlier instances of this. Here too military competition, administrative reform as a response to interstate competition, and rising dissension within all contributed to the collapse of the weaker system. As in the cold war, the erosion was gradual, not cataclysmic, and involved military, economic and diplomatic dimensions. Yet for all the similarities, the differences between these earlier cases of intersystemic competition and the later cold war are rather greater. At the military level, the Soviet system was far more an equal of its rival than were the Ottoman and Qing (Manchu) empires, and there was no equivalent of the incursions and annexations that preceded the collapse of the latter. Indeed, in the postwar period the Soviet system survived the military challenges at the margin — Korea, Vietnam, even Afghanistan — comparatively well. Economically, the contest was even more different: whereas the Ottoman and Qing (Manchu) empires had been eroded by foreign trade, capitulations, debt and so forth, the Soviet system used interaction with the western economies as a means of retaining power. Loans to, trade with, and investment in, these countries did not weaken, but rather strengthened, the power of the communist states. It was not the "market," in any direct sense, of intervention within these societies and economies, that contributed to their ultimate demise.[6]

INTERNATIONAL FACTORS IN COLD WAR

The other set of international factors often cited are more recent and more singular, those which are commonly held to be responsible for the collapse of the communist regimes, and in particular for the crisis of the USSR, in the late 1980s. These revolve around the argument that in one way or another the pressure that the West placed upon the communist system for the mid-1970s onwards, embodied in the policies of the Second Cold War, was such that the Soviet system could not endure. Breaking this general argument down, three specific factors are often cited: the burden of the arms race, the economic and CoCom technological embargoes, and the anti-communist guerrilla movements in the Third World Soviet allies. On their own, or in some kind of combination, these were, it is frequently argued, the forms of international competition and pressure that brought the U.S.S.R. to its knees.

(I) THE ARMS RACE

Enough is now known for us to be able to outline the history and significance of the East-West arms race. In summary form, its record was as follows: (A) from the late 1940s onwards the USSR and the U.S.A. were engaged in an arms race, conventional and nuclear, involving growing expenditures and a technological race, in which, for all major dimensions except space in the late 1950s, the USA was in the lead, in the technological field, and remained, in most dimensions, in the lead in the quantitative domain;[7] (B) despite this US lead, the relative burden on the USA was significantly less, representing between 5% and 10% of GNP, whereas for the USSR arms expenditure represented between 10% and 20% throughout this period — some Soviet officials now say it was as high as 25%; (C) despite the lack of a direct U.S.-Soviet military confrontation, conventional or nuclear, this arms race represented, in a Clausewitzian sense, a continuation of politics by other means: it reflected a search for an elusive but strategically meaningful measure of "superiority" over the other, it embodied a pursuit by both sides of prestige and status in the international arena, and it constituted a means of pressure on the budget and hence on the state-society relationship within the other bloc.[8]

Given the burden on the U.S.S.R. and its evident inability to compete with the U.S.A., it is frequently argued that it was this which forced the U.S.S.R. into strategic retreat in the mid-1980s. At least three variants of this argument can be noted: an economic one, that the level of expenditure on arms and the diversion of resources to the military sector were such that the U.S.S.R. could not continue to compete, and needed a drastic reduction in military expenditure in order to divert resources for domestic economic reorganization; a technological argument, that it was the continued U.S. lead, acutely represented in the early 1980s by two developments, the strategic defense initiative ("Star Wars") and cruise missiles, which forced the Soviet leadership to realize that it could not continue to compete; and a political argument, that the dangers of nuclear war and the costs involved forced the Soviets to abandon the idea of the world as one divided between two camps, locked in social conflict, in favor of a stress on the common interests of human kind. All three are, in varying degrees, found in the writings of Soviet and Western writers and each must have played a role. Gorbachev himself has consistently evoked the third, political argument. The power of nuclear weapons and the accident of Chernobyl in 1986 certainly served to reinforce this awareness of the dangers of nuclear energy and, by extension, nuclear weapons.

Important as it is, there are reasons to qualify the import of the arms race explanation as the major factor behind the Soviet collapse. Certainly, the economic argument must have considerable force: indeed, the very quantitative figure of 10% or 20% of Soviet GNP being spent on defense understates the qualitative and distorting impact, with the allocation of the best administrative and scientific personnel and of key material resources to this sector. On the other hand, military expenditure at 10% or more of

GNP is far from being an adequate explanation for the failings of the Soviet economy. The very high rate of military expenditure as a percentage of GNP is but another way of saying that GNP itself was rather low — the figures for overall expenditure as between the U.S. and the U.S.S.R. show that in absolute terms the U.S.A. was outspending the U.S.S.R.[9] The focus must, therefore, be as much on the efficiency and allocative mechanisms of the civilian sector as on the claim of the military on GNP: had the Soviet GNP been rather higher and the remaining 80% of the Soviet economy been more efficiently organized, the "burden" of military expenditure would have been less and would, given reasonable efficiency and growth rates, have represented a lower percentage of GNP anyway.

Similar problems arise with the technological argument: the assumption of much analysis of the arms race and of the conventional Soviet approach prior to this was that, more or less, the U.S.S.R. was compelled by the necessities of inter-state competition to match the U.S.A. in qualitative and quantitative terms. Previously, the USSR had imitated U.S. advances — as in the MIRVing of missiles after 1972 and the development of a submarine-launched intercontinental capacity. By the late 1970s this was no longer possible: the challenges of SDI and of cruise missiles were that the U.S.S.R. had no comparable riposte antidote. In particular, it could not compete in the technology of the third industrial revolution. Yet the U.S.S.R. could have produced some countermeasures to these U.S. challenges — a few low flying missiles plus decoys would have done much to invalidate SDI. A policy of what is termed "minimum deterrence" could have made a substantial difference and enabled the U.S.S.R. to escape from its self-defeating pursuit of "rough parity." It was perhaps not so much at the military level as such, but what the new technologies symbolized about the overall retardation of the system, that forced the Soviet leaders into retreat. The third argument relevant to the arms race, the political argument about the threat to humanity of nuclear weapons, has much validity and it is to the credit of Gorbachev that he articulated it more clearly than anyone else: but it does not entail the overall process of political and social change within the U.S.S.R. that has accompanied the adoption of these universal values associated with "new thinking." It is conceivable that the U.S.S.R. would have opted out of the nuclear arms race as previously pursued but insisted on preserving its distinctive political and socio-economic system. To explain the latter involves looking beyond the realm of the arms race and its economic, technical, and political costs.

(II) ECONOMIC PRESSURES

The second set of factors commonly adduced to explain the Soviet retreat is the economic, and in particular the impact on the USSR of Western embargoes and restrictions in the field of high technology. Most postwar discussion of the relationship between trade and security in the East-West context has operated with the assumption that increased commercial interaction between the two blocs would contribute to the stability of the Soviet bloc: the argument, as it developed in the 1970s, was between those who believed that greater trade, by making the Soviet Union more secure, would reduce areas of conflict between it and the West, and those who thought it would encourage combative behavior. If the former view, drawing on theories of "interdependence," was dominant in the early 1970s, it was the latter view that prevailed in the period of the Second Cold War.

On the basis of the partial evidence available, it would appear that economic interaction and pressure of various kinds were a factor in the collapse of the communist system, but that the most important factor was the inability of the centrally planned regimes to make use of the advantages that trade with the capitalist world brought. In the case of certain Eastern European countries — Poland is the most striking example — the opening up to the West in the early 1970s had short-term gains, in terms of availability of consumer goods and investment, but led to a longer-run crisis, with foreign debt and increased pressure on domestic earnings once debt repayment became necessary. The centrally planned economic system could not make use of such external support adequately to develop its own economy, and ended up being trapped by its international commitments. In the case of the U.S.S.R., all the evidence suggests that straightforward commercial interaction with the capitalist world had the effect of strengthening the existing system in the short run: most obviously, wheat imports provided a means of offsetting failures in agriculture. The rise in the price of oil in the 1970s gave the U.S.S.R. a windfall profit for much of the decade: however, as Soviet writers have recently pointed out, the longer-run consequences of these profits were inhibiting, since they enabled the central planners and managers to postpone changes that might otherwise have had to be introduced more rapidly.

The same applied in the field of technology: the record of technological innovation in the U.S.S.R. is by no means as bleak as is often suggested, but there is no doubt that most of the major technological innovations of recent decades originated in the West. Here the U.S.S.R. was at a disadvantage in two respects. It did not make any major innovations itself and was therefore compelled, in the civilian and military spheres, to copy or simply steal new technologies from the capitalist world. The degree of Soviet insulation from the international market was never as great as conventional images suggest: the industrialization of the 1930s relied heavily on capital goods imports from Britain and Germany; the history of Soviet aerospace is one of reproduction of Western planes and technologies. Yet in this pursuit of technological development, the U.S.S.R. was always behind. Even more important, however, it was unable to make proper use of the technologies it did have: there was little interaction between the military and civilian sectors; the system of central planning contained built-in disincentives for innovation and encouraged the use of inefficient and traditional methods of production; political and ideological constraints inhibited the use of information technology throughout the system. The pattern of "conservative modernization" identified as endemic to the centrally planned economies operated in this regard.[10] Hence the third industrial revolution, which began in the early 1970s, outstripped it more than ever.

The factor of economic pressure and its political impact is important even when it comes to the embargoes. Here it has been argued that Soviet behavior in the international arena was affected by Western restrictions, both those of a strictly national security kind, through CoCom, and broader political embargoes announced in the wake of Afghanistan. The former, it was said, would make it more difficult for the U.S.S.R. to compete in the arms race, the latter would act as disincentives for unwelcome Soviet foreign policy actions. Given the degree to which the U.S.S.R. protested about these restrictions, it would seem that their impact was considerable.[11] Yet these pressures in themselves can hardly explain the change in Soviet orientation from the mid-1980s onwards: the U.S.S.R., faced with a dire technological lag in the military sphere, could have made substantial concessions without placing their overall strategy in question; in the short run at least, they did not respond to Western political sanctions by making major foreign policy concessions and were indeed more intransigent up to 1985 than had hitherto been the case. The very same factors that diminished the import of Western commercial and technological impact served to lessen the impact of their withdrawal: the centralized political and economic system could absorb the denial, just as it could inhibit the diffusion, of the new technologies.

(III) EROSION OF THE BLOC

A third major factor adduced to explain the retreat of Soviet power is the cost of supporting its Third World allies, at both the economic and military levels. Soviet writers themselves now complain openly about the costs, economic and diplomatic, of backing Third World allies and have reversed the earlier Khrushchevite view that national liberation and Third World revolutionary movements made a positive contribution to the power of the U.S.S.R.;[12] the concept of "imperial overstretch" would seem to apply here and provide a comparative perspective on the Soviet retreat. The character of Soviet relations with Third World allies, resting on substantial economic subsidies in return for political and strategic rewards, made this set of relationships especially burdensome. For U.S. strategic planners in the early 1980s the weakest link of the Soviet system lay in the Third World, which is why there evolved the doctrine of support for anti-communist guerrilla movements.

On closer examination, however, the pressure of Third World commitments seems different and in some ways smaller than at first sight appeared. The greatest cost to the U.S.S.R. of its Third World commitments was in the diplomatic field, e.g., Soviet support for revolutionary allies and movements worsened U.S.-Soviet relations, and the invasion of Afghanistan provided a means by which the West could for the first time weaken the U.S.S.R.'s relationship with the Third World as a whole. The other factors normally adduced, economic and military, may have been less significant. First, the figures for Soviet "aid" to the Third World comprise a variety of forms of support, including, in the case of the largest commitment, Cuba, major long-term trading agreements: though these gave Cuba far better terms of trade than it could have gotten on the world market (high prices for sugar, low for oil), they were not net transfers in the ordinary sense. There were benefits to the U.S.S.R. — getting sugar and nickel that were paid for in rubles, rather than having to pay in hard currency. In other cases, the Third World ally was able to provide the U.S.S.R. with valuable imports — Afghan gas being one example. Second, despite Soviet overstated claims, the amount of aid was in comparative terms very low — 0.25% of GNP, roughly equivalent to the U.S. record.[13] Politically convenient as it may now be within the U.S.S.R. to blame Third World allies, who certainly were also mismanaging their economies, for the economic woes of the U.S.S.R., this was not a major factor in the economic crisis of the Soviet system.

As with military expenditure within the USSR itself, the focus of criticism must go back to the overall system of planning and production and the inefficiencies it contained, which were, incidentally, reproduced by Soviet aid programs within Third World states themselves. The strategic cost of sustaining Third World allies in the 1980s was certainly rising, but if the purpose of U.S. support to Third World anti-communist movements was to weaken the U.S.S.R. at its weakest point this did not happen. One of the major reasons for Soviet and Western involvement in Afghanistan was the demonstration effect of a ruling communist party being overthrown: the impact on Eastern Europe of Kabul's falling was, both sides believed, potentially enormous. Yet in the end it was not in Nicaragua or Afghanistan that Soviet allies were first overthrown, but in Eastern Europe. It was what happened in Warsaw, Berlin, and Prague that affected developments in Managua, Aden, and Kabul and not the other way around.

COMPETITION: THE EXTERNAL IN PERSPECTIVE

The argument so far has identified two categories of external factors, the traditional-imperial ones and the East-West Cold War ones, which can be considered to have played a role in eroding and undermining Soviet power. While both categories have some explanatory power, we have argued that they alone are inadequate. If this is true, it encourages a reexamination of the reasons for the collapse of Soviet power, at both the historical and the theoretical levels: i.e., a reexamination both of what actually happened, and of how our conception of interstate competition may need modifying in the light of the Soviet case.

What needs explanation is that an international system of states collapsed in the absence of the most evident forms of threat: it was not defeated in war; it did not face overwhelming political challenges from below (Poland being the only, partial, exception); it was not, despite its manifold economic and social problems, unable to meet the basic economic demands of its citizenry. It did not, therefore, "collapse," "fail," "break down" in any absolute sense. What occurred, rather, was that the leadership of the most powerful state in the system decided to introduce a radically new set of policies, within the U.S.S.R. and within the system as a whole: it was not that the ruled could not go on being ruled in the old way so much as that the rulers could not go on ruling in the old way. The question is what it was that led these rulers, who cannot be accused of lacking a desire to retain power or of being covert supporters of the West, to introduce the changes they did.

Two kinds of reason, one endogenous and the other exogenous, seem to have been responsible. They can be termed, in summary form, socioeconomic paralysis and lack of international competitiveness. The internal paralysis was evident in a wide range of spheres: falling growth rates, rising social problems, growing corruption and disillusionment, ecological crises. Not only could the system not go on reproducing the rates of growth and improvement in welfare provision characteristic of earlier phases — the 1930s, the 1950s — but it seemed to have run out of steam in a comprehensive manner. This was increasingly clear not just to the leadership but to the growing body of educated people produced by the system. These phenomena are often referred to in the Soviet literature as "stagnation," yet in many ways this is a simplistic term:[14] it understates the degree to which there was continued progress in some spheres, not least the lessening of political repression; it still contains within it the teleological assumption that the system could, under other circumstances, have continued to grow and develop.

Most important, however, "stagnation" leaves out what was also a major factor in forcing the Soviet leadership, faced with this trend, to introduce change, namely the awareness of the system's *comparative* failure vis-a-vis the West. It is here, in the perceived inability of the Soviet system to catch up, let alone overtake, the West that a central aspect of the Soviet collapse must be seen. It was a failure to compete internationally that, on top of the internal crisis, led to the post-1985 changes in the U.S.S.R.: once begun, an attempt to reform the system the better to survive and compete quickly capsized into an attempt to save the state as such.

The awareness of the system's inability to compete in the 1980s was the final in several stages of such loss of hope. The first, historical, disappointment was that immediately after 1917 when the Bolsheviks realized that their revolution would not be reproduced in Germany. This realization led to a double redefinition of strategy — temporary abandonment of the idea of world revolution, proclamation of the idea that a socialist regime *could* be built in the U.S.S.R. With the victories in World War II and the increase in the number of Third World pro-Soviet allies, it appeared for the 1950s and 1960s as if the initial encirclement of the U.S.S.R. could be overcome concomitant with the development of socialism within the U.S.S.R. itself. The successes of post-war reconstruction and space technology in the 1950s seemed to confirm this: hence the new, secularly optimistic, program of Khrushchev which combined continued rivalry with the West in the Third World with a policy of socio-economic development designed to "catch up with and overtake" the West in two decades. It would seem, difficult as it is to believe now, that this perspective, modified by Brezhnev, dominated Soviet thinking until the early 1980s: there were continued advances in the Third World, the U.S.S.R. attained "rough parity" with the U.S.A. in the arms race, and at home it was official policy to state that the U.S.S.R. was now at a new stage, one of "developed socialism."

The reality was, however, rather different, as each of the major areas of interstate and interbloc competition showed. In the most public and privileged area of competition, the military, the U.S.S.R. was always inferior in numbers and quality, except for its conventional strength in Eastern Europe. If this was the area where the Soviet Union was to compete the most, it was evidently not doing anything like well enough.

The international system created by the U.S.S.R. was also markedly weaker quantitatively and qualitatively than that created by the West. Not only was the international capitalist market far stronger in terms of economic output, technological change, and number of countries included within it, but its degree of integration was greater: despite all the talk of a new socialist "system," one of the paradoxes of planning within the U.S.S.R. and the Soviet international system more generally was its inability to integrate sectors beyond giving them separate, if supposedly coordinated, production targets. In many respects, not least innovation and pricing, it remained dependent on the capitalist system, and ineffectually imitative of it. In the military sphere a similar disparity and qualitative inferiority prevailed in the comparison between NATO and the Warsaw Pact. For all the talk of constituting an alternative world order, the Soviet one was less integrated and much weaker overall.[15]

This failure to compete in international terms would, in itself, have been a major problem, given the fact that underlying East-West rivalry and Cold War was an attempt by both sides to provide a basis for a new international "order," to demonstrate the superiority of the one over the other. But this external blockage, one going right back to 1917 and only obscured by subsequent international triumphs, was compounded by the internal limits of the system in many spheres: the failure to match levels of output in the West, the growing gap in living standards between developed socialist and developed capitalist states and, obscured by rhetoric about "socialist" democracy, the contrast between a substantial degree of democratic success in the West and continuing if less brutal centralized political control in the East. Had the U.S.S.R. been able to rival the West successfully in other spheres, these internal deficiencies, those denoted by "stagnation," might have been concealed the longer: but it was the failure at the international level combined with that at home that forced the leadership to face up to them.

Here we come to a central feature of the collapse: almost impossible to believe as it may now be, it would seem that up to the early 1980s this contrast in internal achievement was hidden from, or at least not recognized by, most Soviet observers, in the leadership or elsewhere. The underlying self-confidence of the Soviet system, a product of the revolution's historic claims and of victory in World War II, seemed to have lasted up to that time; but at some point in the early 1980s it began to erode, first amongst the leadership and then within the population as a whole. The awareness of how people lived in the West and of the enormous gap in living standards produced a situation in which the self-confidence that had lasted from 1917 evaporated in the space of a few short years. The lack of political freedom played its part through Helsinki and Western pressure: but the evidence suggests that it was the economic which played the major role in getting this process going. Once the living standards gap became evident then the residual legitimacy of the communist political system was swept away and that of the alternative system, the Western variant of pluralism, was enhanced.

Here it is worth looking at the mechanism by which this change of attitude occurred. The insulation of Soviet society was both physical— lack of communication, radio jamming, absence of travel, punishment of those who sought contact with the outside world—and psychological— a belief that whatever went wrong, *"u nas luchshe"*—"things are better with us."[16] Those who traveled abroad or had access to comparative data were condemned to silence, even when they realized the truth. Here the change of heart of the leadership, one encouraged by broader awareness in the society, was of pivotal importance and opened the floodgates to popular discontent: the breaking of the secular self-confidence of the top leadership must certainly have been encouraged by the failures of international competition in the military and economic spheres, but it would appear that the very perception of the contrast in living standards, highlighting the reality of internal paralysis in the late 1970s, and the growing military gap associated with the third industrial revolution, played the crucial part. In Gorbachev's case, for example, it would seem that his visits to Canada provided such an occasion: it would only take five minutes in an average Canadian supermarket for the point to become clear, and for the specific experience of shortages and administrative problems he experienced in running the Stavropol region to be set in its decisive, internationalized, context.

Once this change had occurred, then the process of broader awareness followed inexorably. The liberalization of the political system within the U.S.S.R. allowed of greater information about the capitalist world, almost all of it favorable when not uncritical, and for a more negative assessment of the record of the U.S.S.R. It is noticeable too how, in speeches made after 1985, Gorbachev himself would make telling comparisons with the capitalist world, in the field of social indicators — infant mortality, hospital conditions, alcoholism, availability of basic foods — as well as in broader macro-economic and political terms.[17] His own process of self-education seems to have followed such a path: already dissatisfied with socialist performance, he came into office in 1985 apparently believing that the socialist system could reform itself by applying technology in a more intense way, the better to "accelerate" production; but by 1989 he had moved much further on both the economic and political fronts, in the face of the evident inability of the system to reform itself within orthodox socialist political and economic parameters. In other words, the international comparison that had brought him to the point of initiating major reform in 1985 pushed him after 1985 to envisage a much more radical reform of the system. The fact that, through forcing the comparison onto the Soviet public, he had unleashed widespread additional dissatisfaction, only served to confirm this trend.

THREE LEVELS OF INTERNATIONAL COMPETITION

This analysis of East-West competition up to the late 1980s has a number of implications for theories of interstate and intersociety competition in particular. No one analyzing East-West conflict can deny the relevance within it of conventional, interstate, forms of competition — at the military, economic, and political levels. The rivalry of the Soviet and U.S. systems in the postwar period involved a comprehensive competition in which the innovation was not the role of states but rather the way in which this interstate competition developed into new domains — the arms race, on the one hand, the comprehensive mobilization of ideological resources on the other. Given its strong position in the economic field, it was natural that the West should seek to use its economic strength to place pressure on the U.S.S.R. for security reasons: the international political economy of East-West relations was, in essence, one of the uses of economic instruments by the stronger bloc, that of Western states, for political and military ends.

This interstate competition, comprehensive as it was, is not sufficient to explain how, why, and when the communist system collapsed, how the West succeeded in prevailing over the East. We have seen how earlier cases of intersystemic conflict — the Ottoman and Manchu cases — provide at best partial points of comparison: despite some similarities, theirs was fundamentally a very different story. The specifically Cold War instruments of interstate competition — arms race, embargoes, Third World harassment — do not, in themselves, explain why the Soviet leadership took the decisions it did after 1985. To analyze this rivalry it is necessary to take a broader look at East-West conflict as a whole, one that encompasses the competition of systems, i.e. capitalism and "communism," within which state competition plays an important, but not exclusive, role.

In this perspective, it becomes possible to distinguish three dimensions of competition which are interrelated but analytically distinct: the level of activities of states; that of social and economic entities, most notably businesses; and what can, in the broadest sense, be termed the "ideological," the perception of and belief about the political, economic levels and culture of another society. In addressing the question of "how" the West put pressure on the East this tripartite distinction may be helpful. Operating on the first level, Western state action had effects, but it was not the only story. Paradoxically, the ability of Western states directly to put such pressure is now greater than ever before as the linking of economic assistance to socioeconomic change within the U.S.S.R. and Eastern Europe show: *perestroika* has created the conditions for such a socioeconomic intervention by the Group of 7, not resulted from it. In the case of Eastern Europe, Western firms — industrial enterprises, banks — also played a role, especially in dealings with Poland in the early 1970s and in the handling of the Soviet oil output. In the opening up that took place from late 1989 onwards, West German business enterprises have taken a lead,

somewhat coordinated with but separate from, that of the Bonn government itself. It would be analytically misleading either to reduce state policy
in East-West relations to the wishes of multinational corporations, or to
see the latter as acting simply within parameters laid down by or at the
behest of Western states. Their actions are parallel and usually — though
not always — convergent: the generally negative response of sectors of
the business community to political embargoes was evidence enough of
divergence in this regard.

The ideological dimension is, perhaps, of even greater importance:
its role in the collapse of communism and in the East-West rivalry that
preceded it was in some ways decisive. Here capitalism operated not just
through states or firms, but through the society as a whole. What above all
forced the leadership of the CPSU to change course, and what destroyed
the support or acquiesence of the peoples of Eastern Europe and the
U.S.S.R. to communism, was, on top of the difference in political achievement, the perceived contrast in political and economic standards and in
living conditions between East and West. This ideological dimension is
certainly something that states help to promote and regulate, and which
their information and propaganda organs disseminate; it is something that
rests upon political record and on economic performance, on the output
and sales policies of business corporations. But it is something distinct,
encompassing as it does the perception of political system, popular culture,
the media, fashion, and, in broad terms the image of what constitutes a
good life, in the eyes of the leadership and population of the rival system.
Moreover, the dissemination of images pertaining to this is not simply the
result of state or business enterprise decisions: it takes place in an uncoor-
dinated but pervasive way, through television and film, through popular
music, through impressions gained from travel and personal encounter. It
is informal and diffuse, but constitutes the most potent interface between
two societies. The abandonment by the majority of the inhabitants of East
Germany of any belief in a separate socialist way or entity was above all
a product of this encounter: years of exposure to West German images on
television, followed by the direct encounter itself, the *Reiseschock*.

Insofar as this distinction is valid, and the importance of ideological
and perceptual factors in international relations is accepted, then it suggests
another interpretation of the Cold War and its end, and of international
relations more generally. Relations between states retain their importance
and the particular mechanisms of conflict and resource mobilization at any
one time are open to analysis on a contingent basis. The denial of state

efficacy and the premature reduction of its role are as misleading as the insistence that all international relations can be seen, or deemed, to be ones between states. At the same time, international competition involves two other major dimensions: the unofficial and the ideological. The latter has always operated — it would be impossible to follow the history of Christianity, its diffusion and division, without it. But the ideological has a special salience in a world where material well-being, fashion and consumerism together with political freedoms occupy a special role in the constitution of specific societies, and in an international situation characterized by immediate transmission of sound and images. There is clearly a relationship between power in one domain and power in the ideological domain — through control of images and their means of diffusion. Never was Gramsci's conception of hegemony, in the sense of ideological and cultural factors as instruments of domination, so relevant as in analyzing the international system today. If communism surrendered without firing a shot, it was because the instrument of international competition in the late twentieth century was as much the T-shirt as the gunboat.

POSTSCRIPT: THE END OF THE SOVIET UNION

The denouement of the August crisis in the U.S.S.R. has unexpectedly accelerated the process analysed here. A last-ditch attempt to save the old regime only brought forward the collapse of the traditional centers of power, and of the Soviet Union itself: it showed how discredited, and divided, the old centers were and, through their implication in the coup attempt, confirmed that discrediting. Leaders and led no longer believed in the system. The goal of those brought to office by the coup is both to complete the abandonment of the U.S.S.R.'s pre-existing international role and to integrate the remnants, as far as possible, into the political and economic structures of the capitalist West. The victory of the West, promoted at all three levels analyzed above, has now been reinforced.

NOTES

An earlier version of this paper was given at the Economic and Social
Research Council conference, "Structural Change in the West," held at
Emmanuel College, Cambridge, September 1990. I am grateful to Jeff
Frieden, Michael Mann, Perry Anderson and Nikki Keddie for their most
helpful comments on the text.

1   See my "The Ends of Cold War," *New Left Review*, 180(March-
April 1990): 5-23; George Schopflin, "Why Communism Collapsed,"
International Affairs, 66, 1(1990): 3-16.

2   For the argument as to why, on economic grounds, the state
socialist model could not work, despite initial successes and a margin for
reform, see Wlodzimierz Brus and Kazimierz Laski, *From Marx to Market*
(Oxford: The Clarendon Press, 1989).

3   Moshe Lewin, *The Gorbachev Phenomenon* (Berkeley: University
of California Press, 1988), is a lucid overview of the social and economic
preconditions for the breakdown of the Brezhnevite order in the 1980s.

4   Fred Halliday, *The Making of the Second Cold War* (London:
Verso, 1983), chapter 1, on the different meanings of "cold war."

5   Theda Skocpol, *States and Social Revolutions*, (Princeton:
Princeton University Press, 1979), remains a classic discussion of this
question.

6   On the Ottoman background see Roger Owen, *The Middle East in
the World Economy, 1800-1914* (Oxford: Oxford University Press, 1981):
Caglar Keyder, *State and Class in Turkey, A Study in Capitalist Development* (London: Verso, 1987).

7   On the arms race see my *The Making of the Second Cold War*,
chapter 3.

8   This was conventionally known as the "arms race theory of arms
control."

9   U.S. expenditure in 1971 was $120 billions, as against Soviet $94
billions, in 1980 $111 billions as against $107. Total Soviet plus allies
expenditure was only half that of its opponents, NATO plus Far Eastern
allies (China, Japan) expenditure: in 1980 $120 billions for the WTO as
against $243 billions. All data from *SIPRI Yearbook* (Stockholm: SIPRI,
1981), figures in constant 1978 prices. U.S. expenditure was conventionally understated by a number of accounting devices: one calculation was

that the 1980 figure of $127 billions should be adjusted upwards to $223 billions, i.e., from 5.2% to 9.5% of GNP: James Cypher, "Rearing America," *Monthly Review*, 33, 6(November 1981): 11-27.

10   See Brus-Laski.

11   For a Soviet view of the Western embargo see Igor Artemiev "International Economic Security," in Igor Artemiev and Fred Halliday *International Economic Security: Soviet and British Approaches*, (London: Chatham House Discussion Paper, no. 7, 1988).

12   Fred Halliday, *From Kabul to Managua*, (New York: Pantheon, 1989). (UK title *Cold War, Third World* (London: Hutchinson/Radius, 1989), chapter 4, for the rethinking of Soviet policy towards the Third World.

13   According to OECD DAC figures.

14   On "stagnation" see Mikhail Gorbachev, *Perestroika, New Thinking for Our Country and the World* (London: Collins, 1987), chapter 1.

15   On the NATO-WTO comparison see note 14 above. The degree of economic integration between the Eastern European Comecon members was far less than that within the EEC: most trade was on a bilateral, Soviet-East European, basis.

16   Hedrick Smith, *The Russians* (London: Sphere, 1976), gives a powerful evocation of this attitude in the period prior to the collapse of Soviet confidence.

17   Gorbachev's *Perestroika* is replete with calls for the Soviet economy to rise to "world standards," i.e., those of the West.

THE ISLAMIC REVOLUTION THAT OVERTHREW THE SOVIET STATE:

A. BENNINGSEN AND M. BROXUP, *THE ISLAMIC THREAT TO THE SOVIET STATE* (New York: St. Martin's Press, 1983)

A. TAHERI, *CRESCENT IN A RED SKY* (London: Hutchinson, 1989)

M. RYWKIN, *MOSCOW'S MUSLIM CHALLENGE* (New York: M.E. Sharpe, Inc., 1990)

MURIEL ATKIN

For years before the events of 1989-1991, there was a small but highly respected group of specialists on Soviet Muslims who predicted that the Soviet Union was doomed. The key to its undoing, they argued, would be the growing population of Soviet Muslims, whose increasingly militant Islamic identity would lead them to revolt against Soviet oppression. On the one hand, the widespread Western belief in the inherent incompatibility of Christians and Muslims and, on the other, the supposed solidarity of Muslims lent credibility to predictions that the Muslim peoples would bring down the Soviet regime. The numerous counterexamples of greater opposition from historically Christian nationalities, including the Russians themselves, tended to be ignored, as was the well-known revolutionary phenomenon that it is often the "advanced" and prosperous rather than the poor and "backward" people who tend to revolt.

This school's interpretation was widely believed and cited internationally. Its leading proponent was the Russo-French historian, Alexandre Bennigsen (1913-1988), who first made his mark with a seminal series of studies in the field published during the 1960s. Much of his work was done with co-authors, including Chantal Lemercier-Quelquejay and, later, his daughter, Marie Broxup, now the editor of *Central Asian Survey* in Oxford. Bennigsen and Broxup expressed the essence of the school's argument in their 1982 prediction that,

> Soviet Muslims . . . are likely to be influenced by the ideas (perhaps even by the political terrorism and guerrilla methods) adopted from the newly radicalised Middle East. These ideas, ranging from the most conservative religious fundamentalism to the wildest revolutionary radicalism, share one common characteristic: the potential for destabilising Soviet Islam, thereby undermining the stability of the USSR itself.[1]

Another historian who shares some, though not all, of the views of this school is Michael Rywkin of the City University of New York. An Iranian journalist now living abroad, Amir Taheri, carries the "Islamic revolution" argument even further than most other members of this school. A wide variety of other authors joined in the debate from a broad range of interpretive positions.

Now that the Soviet Union has dissolved into separate republics, we have reached a useful juncture for reflecting on predictions about the role militant Islam would play in its demise. All the states which formerly made up the Soviet Union still face immense problems. It is too soon to tell how effectively any of them will cope with those problems or what forms of government they will choose after the initial period of transition to independence. However, one thing is already certain. Islamic radicals did not bring down the Soviet regime. The nationalities which led the opposition to rule by command from the Kremlin were not from the Muslim borderlands in the Southeast but from the European parts of the Soviet Union as well as Christian Georgia and Armenia in the Caucasus. The predominantly Muslim republics sought to preserve the Union until the moment of its collapse. In addition, systemic problems that transcended national lines, compounded by Gorbachev's own shortcomings as a reformer and the blunders of the Communist hard-liners were all instrumental in the collapse of the Soviet state.

This essay will consider how, in roughly the last decade of the Soviet Union's existence, a number of non-Soviet authors interpreted the role of Islam in Soviet politics. The point is not to fault anyone for making a prediction that was not borne out by subsequent developments. Rare indeed is the person who predicted before late August 1991 that the Soviet Union would soon disintegrate. (One of the few who did so, and who more accurately than most anticipated the sources of destabilization, is a former Bennigsen student, Paul Goble, who, during the late Soviet years, was the State Department's leading expert on Soviet nationalities and acting director of Radio Liberty research.)[2] The body of works on Islam's influence on political change in the Soviet Union is too large to permit discussion of all contributors or all the issues they raised. Here I will consider only how a few representatives of varied schools of thought addressed topics which can be grouped under two main headings: the nature of the Soviet Union as a multiethnic state and the centrality of Islam in opposition politics.

Even some of the Soviet specialists who viewed nationality grievances with sympathy did not see the nationalities as a serious threat to the stability of the Soviet system. However, few Soviet experts went as far as one of the best known among them, Jerry Hough, of Duke University and the Brookings Institution. Until the final weeks of the Soviet Union's existence he continued to depict Gorbachev as an adept manipulator of nationality politics who would emerge triumphant from the deepening power struggle. He saw nationality discontents as significant — but only for the way others exploited them. He warned American specialists on the Soviet Union not to be deceived by an alleged cabal of anti-Gorbachev "Moscow radicals," whose desire to undermine Gorbachev's resolve gave them a "vital interest in exaggerating" the costs to the Soviet Union of a crackdown in Lithuania.[3]

Hough argued that the very strength of the nationalist challenge guaranteed its ultimate defeat. By allowing "national unrest [to] run a bit wild at first," Gorbachev cleverly facilitated the release of "much of the pent-up emotional resentment among non-Russians" and "reminded the Russians that democracy would mean national disintegration," so that they would not demand too much political change.[4] The persistence of nationalist activity was something Hough interpreted as proof that the danger it posed was diminishing:

The fact that the unrest has continued for two years may indicate that we are much nearer to the end of the revolutionary burst than we think, at least in republics with the most prolonged unrest. Since May [1990] evidence is multiplying that this is in fact happening in the Baltics and Armenia.[5]

In the end, Hough predicted, nationalists would lose momentum while Soviet citizens would enjoy the benefits of improved economic conditions. At that point, "Gorbachev's obvious strategy is to crack down in order to increase the costs for potential participants [in nationalist opposition.] The logic of the situation suggests that it will be a successful strategy for at least the rest of this decade."[6]

For those who considered nationality relations important in their own right, estimates of the likelihood of an Islamic revolution against the Soviet regime hinged in part on judgments about the nature of that regime. Components of this issue included differences of opinion on the degree of continuity between the Tsarist Russian and Soviet states, whether Russians were predisposed to oppress non-Russian fellow countrymen, and whether Soviet nationalities policy had changed significantly since the days of Stalin and Khrushchev, when national differences were seen as remnants of a bygone era, doomed to extinction. The underlying question was whether the state, regardless of the prevailing ideology of a particular era, was so inflexibly Russian chauvinist that no satisfaction of minority aspirations was possible within the system.

Some critics of Soviet treatment of minority nationalities saw the core of the problem in the Russianness of the regime. In this view, the revolution that overthrew the monarchy did not alter the fact that a Russian political mentality guided rulers in St. Petersburg or Moscow. One emigré from the Soviet Union, Aron Katsenelinboigen, of the Wharton School of the University of Pennsylvania, saw in this an innate desire by Russians to have a strong state regulate their lives:

> What is it in the mentality of the Russians that makes them opt for authoritarianism? . . . It was well-known [sic] that the Russians are much prone to drinking, besotted debauchery, and irresponsibility. Apparently, the Russians themselves are aware of their character defects, and hence crave a strong leader who can save them from harmful temptations and channel their energies toward constructive ends.[7]

Linked to this authoritarianism was alleged to be a key component
of the rulers' mentality, the "Russian idea," a "dangerous" phenomenon
which originated in pre-revolutionary times and revived since the Stalin
era.[8]

Some authors who wrote about Soviet Muslims applied this concept of Russian imperial continuity to link the Muscovites who fought
Tatars since the late Middle Ages with Soviet officials in our time who
made policy regarding the country's Muslim inhabitants. The connection
between the earlier battles and current policy dilemmas lay in the fact that,
in the words of Bennigsen and Broxup, it was "the same Russians" facing
the Muslims in both cases, a judgment shared by Taheri.[9]

Closely related to the Russian continuity argument was the contention that Russianness was sinister. Thus, Katsenelinboigen's discussion of
Russian nationalism could dwell on the small, extremist fringe, with its
pernicious bigotry and authoritarianism and could offer only a perfunctory,
dismissive mention of more moderate, tolerant forms of Russian nationalism.[10] Taheri treated the Russians and their ancestors as unwaveringly
vicious to Muslims. Some of his "proofs" were based not on evidence that
could legitimately be subject to more than one interpretation but on badly
garbled information. Thus, he saw one example of the primordial Russian
enmity towards Muslims in their role in a momentous battle in 1071, when
the Seljuk Turks inflicted a major defeat on Byzantine troops, and thus
began the Turkicization of Anatolia. According to Taheri's interpretation
of this event, "Russian mercenaries" and volunteers went to wage a holy
war against Muslim "infidels" when they fought for the "Byzantine
Emperor Manzikert Romanus at the famous battle of Malazgird."[11] Some
soldiers from Kievan Rus' (there was as yet neither a Russia nor Russians)
did fight on the Byzantine side, but so did other Europeans and also the
Turkic Pechenegs and Oghuzes, for whom the battle was no holy war. The
emperor whom they served so poorly on that day was not Manzikert
Romanus, who never existed, but Romanus Diogenes. (Manzikert was the
Byzantines' name for the site of the battle; Malazgird is its name in the
Muslim world.)

Taheri's readiness to see the worst in Russians appeared also in his
interpretation of the Soviet anticorruption campaign in Central Asia during
the 1980s, with its implicit message that the Muslim nationalities were
more corrupt than others. He reversed that argument and implied that the
Muslims were so unaccustomed to chicanery — in contrast to the Russians
— that "all the words associated with corruption . . . are directly borrowed

from Russian by all the Muslim languages of the USSR."[12] The author's ire at the denigration of the Muslim nationalities in general because of the misdeeds of a few individuals is legitimate. However, he responded in kind with an exaggeration that was also inaccurate. For example, in Tajik, a Central Asian form of Persian, none of the common terms used for economic crimes comes from Russian and some would be readily comprehensible to speakers of Tehran Persian like Taheri. (Such terms include [in their Tajik forms] *duzdi* [theft], *ghorat* [pilfering], *qalbdast* [counterfeit], *hannoti* [speculation] *firebgari* [fraud], and *suiiste'mol az mansab* [abuse of office.])[13]

A similar demonization of Russian/Soviet treatment of Muslim peoples can be found in Bennigsen and Broxup's book, which asserted, à propos of Stalin's deportation of the Crimean Tatars during World War Two, that, "In world history, no 'colonialist' power had ever treated its colonised subjects in such a ruthless way. The only possible comparison outside the Soviet Union is the case of the inhabitants of the Bikini Islands." The authors later made a similar statement regarding the entire period from Muscovite expansion in the sixteenth century to Soviet rule in the twentieth.[14] The ascription of collective guilt to and forced relocation of, a whole people certainly deserves condemnation. Would the Crimean Tatars' suffering have been any less if their treatment were not called unique? By what absolute standard can one rank acts of immense cruelty or the pain felt by the victims? Did the calamities that befell the original inhabitants of the Americas under colonial rule or the Africans enslaved to work in those colonies cause less misery than the Soviet deportation of the Crimean Tatars? Examples of colonial horrors may be found in large numbers in many regions of the world. It is an injustice to all victims to imply that only the worst case — as judged by undefined and probably undefinable criteria — counts. The argument that there was a unique Russian-Soviet continuum of imperial brutality treated as distinctively Russian types of misdeeds that have been far too common around the world.

Other authors drew markedly different conclusions when they examined the relationship between Russian national identity and the Soviet state. Alexander Solzhenitsyn, from his standpoint as a Russian nationalist critic of the Soviet system, repeatedly distinguished between what was Russian and what was Soviet, portraying the latter as alien to Russian traditions. Several Western specialists on Soviet nationality affairs, including Alexander Motyl of Columbia, Roman Szporluk of Harvard, and the aforementioned Michael Rywkin, saw what was Russian and what was Soviet as overlapping but by no means identical. In this view, the regime manipulated Russian themes as a useful tool to enhance its own authority, not for the sake of Russian nationalism.[15]

In fact, a kind of continuity between the Tsarist and Soviet states, which advocates of the anti-Russian perspective underestimated or ignored entirely, lay in the gulf between the perceived self-interests of the rulers and the Russians they ruled. As Szporluk noted, the Tsarist regime, too, manipulated elements of Russianness for its own purposes but defined loyalty in dynastic, not ethnic, terms. Russification was only one tool, and one not used consistently, in hope of ensuring loyalty to the monarchy.[16]

Russian national feeling as it evolved during the Soviet era was a heterogeneous phenomenon, which entailed much more than unquestioning identification with the central government, as John Dunlop, a noted specialist on the subject, argued in amply documented studies.[17] During the last fifteen years or so of the Soviet Union's existence, an increasing number of Russians who thought Russian national interests were important also saw the Soviet system as acting against those interests. The more open political conditions of the Gorbachev era enabled such people to be more active in promoting their views. By that time, as Frederick Starr, a Russian historian and president of Oberlin College, and Szporluk observed, Russian nationalists could be found at various points along the political spectrum. The crude chauvinism of a group like Pamiat' represented only one extreme of the Russian nationalist camp, which also included conventional Soviet loyalists, advocates of democratic reforms, and people with different ideas about what territories ought to be part of the Russian state.[18]

The prominent role played by Russians in opposing the coup attempt by the Communist old guard in late August 1991 demonstrates the fallacy of assuming that the only kind of Russian consciousness of any significance is the kind that equates Russian interests with an authoritarian, imperialist state.

Some of the authors who expected the Muslims to pose the greatest threat to the stability of the Soviet state also saw that state not only as a new version of the Russian Empire but also as essentially unchanging in its policies toward the non-Russians. Therefore, part of the case for predicting a crisis in Muslim-Soviet relations rested on the inaccurate presumption of inflexibility at the center. A book by Rywkin published as recently as 1990 contained a chapter on "The Terminology of Nationality

Politics" that dealt overwhelmingly with the Brezhnev era and made only a couple of perfunctory references to subsequent changes.[19]

Other authors looked at the same subject but saw change, not continuity as a distinguishing characteristic. Martha Brill Olcott, of Colgate University, a former Bennigsen student, noted that by the later years of the Brezhnev era, the central government had begun to reevaluate its stance on nationalities. Although it certainly did not become egalitarian or pluralistic, it eventually deemphasized the old objective of the merger of nationalities into a single one (*sliianie*), to be accompanied by the disappearance of anything that made nationalities distinct. It also tried to shift from the Russian coloration of Soviet patriotism by offering a more inclusive approach to the patriotism of non-Russians as well.[20]

In the Gorbachev era, nationality policy and nationality relations became profoundly different from what they had been a generation earlier. Part of this is attributable to Gorbachev's personal impact. The antagonism provoked by his miscalculations in addressing nationality matters forced the leadership to reconsider the inherited truisms about nationality policy. Several Western specialists on Soviet nationalities, including Olcott, Motyl, and Gail Lapidus, of the University of California at Berkeley, remarked on this shift.[21] As Starr and Lapidus have each pointed out, Soviet society itself was changing in ways that affected nationality relations. The decline in the proportion of Russians in the total population continued. More members of society were city born and bred, better educated, more disenchanted with Marxist-Leninist ideology and the regime's claims to legitimacy, and more desirous of having a voice in public affairs rather than being passive creatures of the state.[22]

The combination of those changes and Gorbachev's political reforms made possible the proliferation of new citizens' organizations, "informals" in Soviet parlance, which were not controlled by the regime and which addressed nationality concerns as well as a host of other issues. In addition, the changing nature of Soviet politics made Communist Party leaders in various republics from the Baltic to Central Asia feel the need to seek public support by adopting some of the nationalist rhetoric of "informals" in their republics. Party leaders in the Caucasus and Central Asia broke the long-standing tradition of the primacy of Party loyalty when they disagreed with their counterparts in neighboring republics over issues pressed by nationalists, such as disputes over land or the treatment of minorities. Soviet nationality relations had ceased to be governed by a single policy issued by command of the central government. In Paul

Goble's felicitous description, nationality policy gave way to ethnic politics; and the nationalities became active participants in the dynamics of this new politics.[23]

Muslim nationalities, like their non-Muslim counterparts, engaged to one degree or another in the new ethnic politics. A central point of debate among observers was whether the fact that they were Muslims determined their identity and politics. The Islamocentric approach of some observers to this encompassed a range of issues, including an assertion of the general superiority of Muslims, the unwillingness to distinguish between religious and national identity, and the insistence that Muslims were, or ought to be, implacably hostile to the non-Muslims of the Soviet Union. The response to the Islamocentric approach should not be that it is better scholarship to denigrate Muslims, only that exaggerations from any perspective produce distortions.

Some of the arguments for the superiority of Muslims in Russia or the Soviet Union involved claims that were highly subjective in implausible ways or simply inaccurate. One such implausible claim was Taheri's assertion that by the Gorbachev era, only the Muslims experienced revitalization, that, "there were two USSRs living side by side: one was young, dynamic, warm, optimistic and Muslim; the other was ageing, grey, cold and uncertain of its ideological beliefs."[24] The widespread growth of citizen involvement in public affairs, the rewriting of history, the greater freedom in literary and artistic expression, the search for an alternative system of values, whether religious or secular, and the ascent of nationalism among many Soviet nationalities in this period do not fit the grim depiction of the non-Muslims' supposed decay.

A more significant aspect of the Islamic-primacy approach was the assertion by several authors that Muslims suffered more under Soviet rule than any other nationality. The Balts and Ukrainians would take issue with Bennigsen and Broxup's argument that "the Muslim territories of the USSR [were] simply the last colonies of a European imperialist state."[25] When Rywkin stated that Soviet nationalities policy "was applied more thoroughly to Soviet Central Asia than elsewhere," he did not explain what criteria he used in making that judgment.[26] Stalin's blood purge of people who came under the slightest suspicion of nationalism in the Ukraine or the Baltic republics as well as in the predominantly Muslim areas is one example of the way Soviet nationalities policy was applied as intensively to non-Muslims as to Muslims.

One of the sharpest differences of opinion between the Islamocentrists and others was over the relation between religion and nationalism. Bennigsen, Broxup, Rywkin, and Taheri contended that the bonds of loyalty Soviet Muslims felt towards their coreligionists outweighed by far their commitment to their separate national identities, which were in any case unwelcome creations of the Soviet regime.[27] As Bennigsen and Broxup put it, "A Soviet Russian remains a Russian, a Soviet Muslim simply a Muslim."[28] Similarly, they blurred the distinction between supranational religious identity and national identity by using such terms as "Muslim nationalism."[29] According to this point of view, Muslims in the Soviet Union as well as outside felt at one with each other and saw the one significant division not between any of their nationalities but between the Muslim community as a whole and non-Muslims.[30]

Yet there were discrepancies even within this school of thought, let alone between it and others. Even Bennigsen and Broxup acknowledged that Soviet Muslims were at times divided along national lines. They saw the Muslim nationalities as competing with each other for jobs and other advantages within the Soviet system and resentful of their competitors. These authors also considered the Uzbeks to be close to becoming "a real 'nation' with strong 'imperialistic' tendencies," to the concern of other Central Asians.[31] They dismissed the significance of these interethnic tensions on the grounds that the Muslims cared less about them than about their antipathy towards the European nationalities of the Soviet Union and predicted that in a few more years Central Asia's Muslims would rally around the Uzbeks as regional leaders.[32] Ironically, Bennigsen himself, in a seminal work written with Chantal Lemercier-Quelquejay and published fifteen years earlier, had argued that the more numerous Muslim peoples had been well on the way to developing separate national identities even before the Russian Revolution and that in Soviet times national identity gained increasing strength among them while the supranational ties of Islam waned.[33]

Advocates of alternative points of view gave greater weight to the significance of national differences among Soviet Muslims. As the power of the central government decreased in the late Gorbachev years and then collapsed, Central Asian leaders espoused regional cooperation among the republics. However, as this author has argued elsewhere, the rhetoric did not match the practical obstacles to such cooperation caused by competition over limited amounts of land, water, funds, and food. Central Asia's Muslims were also divided among themselves along the lines of national cultures. The most strident hostility was between the Turkic-speaking Uzbeks and Persian-speaking Tajiks. Despite the extensive influences these two peoples have exerted on each other during the course of centuries of contact, nationalists in both groups resented what they interpreted as the premeditated hostility toward them by members of the other group.[34] Rumors spread in both republics that unpopular political figures in each really belonged to the dominant nationality in the other.[35] Even an Uzbek nationalist, Muhammad Salik, leader of the Erk movement, described the prospect for the foreseeable future of a unified Turkestan as "impossible," "a political dream," because the division of the region into five republics had real meaning and in each of those republics "a national identity has been formed."[36]

Soviet Muslims were also divided within and across national lines by different perceptions of what Islam meant to them. The Shi'i majority and large Sunni minority in Azerbaijan achieved a modus vivendi but, as noted by Aye Rorlich, a historian of the Turkic peoples of Russia and the Soviet Union, the northern and southern Kirghiz still disagreed strongly on what aspects of Islam mattered most. (The southern Kirghiz, who converted to Islam long before those further north, put more emphasis on religious doctrine.)[37] Even among nationalities in which the differences were not polarized geographically, Muslims varied in such matters as the extent to which they viewed their religion in cultural or spiritual terms, their knowledge about their faith, the balance between dogma and ritual, and the extent and ways in which they were observant.[38]

Interethnic tensions among Soviet Muslims existed not only among the educated city dwellers but also on the grass roots level. This was demonstrated by the incidents of violence between Muslims of different nationalities in Central Asia in the late Gorbachev era. The bloodiest clashes were the 1989 Uzbek attack on Meskhetians (deported from the Caucasus to Central Asia in 1944) and the Uzbek-Kirghiz fighting in 1990. Troubles on a smaller scale broke out between Tajiks and Meskhetians, Tajiks and Uzbeks, and Kazakhs and Daghestanis (from the northeastern Caucasus) in the same period.

Other ties of loyalty divided Soviet Muslims along other lines. These alternative bases of association included locale, tribe, extended family, patron-client networks, and politics. However, a discussion of these important subjects lies beyond the scope of this paper.

A natural corollary of the view that membership in the supra-national world of Islam and alienation from the Russian/Soviet non-

Muslim world were of paramount importance to Muslims was the belief that they were in the past and would be in the future opposed to whoever ruled them from St. Petersburg or Moscow. As regards past attitudes, Taheri carried the argument furthest, presenting all true Muslims of the Tsarist Empire as rejecting any Russian influence. He condemned the *Jadidist* modernizers of the late nineteenth and early twentieth centuries as disloyal to their Muslim brethren and ultimately irrelevant to the masses because their program was influenced by Russian examples (although he ignored the way they drew on Islamic sources as well) and because they were more critical of Islamic traditionalists than of the Russian Empire (although he regarded some of those criticisms as well founded.) This made them, in Taheri's view, "a Trojan horse for Russian political domination of the captive Muslim peoples of the empire in both Tsarist and Soviet times."[39]

In contrast, Taheri cited approvingly other nineteenth-century reformers who sought the renewal of Islam entirely from within and saw the Russians has having nothing to offer. Yet his case for this was weak. For example, he stated that Ahmad Donish, a Bukharan reformer, realized that Russians did not have the answers because he saw their unhappiness when he visited St. Petersburg in 1828. Yet that visit never happened. Donish was born in 1826; the Amir of Bukhara sent him to St. Petersburg in 1857, 1869, and 1874. Moreover, he was not religious and found much to admire in Russian and European culture and technological progress.[40] Taheri saw an exemplar of the right kind of Muslim reformist — one who rejected Russian influence — in Shihabeddin Merjani, an important Tatar nationalist of the nineteenth century.[41] However, Rorlich depicted Merjani quite differently in her study of the Volga Tatars, as someone who indeed favored the revitalization of Islam but who also had positive dealings with Russians through the St. Petersburg Archeological Society, the Russian-Tatar school where he taught, and the Russian professors he came to know. These contacts introduced him to the ideas of Russian reformers and the scientific achievements of the West. He came to see scientific progress as essential for social progress and urged Tatars to learn Russian as a tool for studying science.[42]

The application to recent Soviet politics of the argument that Muslims were unwaveringly hostile to Russians was expressed in the assertion that the Muslims were certain to throw off Soviet rule. With the luxury of hindsight, one can know that this did not happen. The Baltic republics, though small in territory and population numbers, turned out to play a crucial role in challenging the Kremlin's authority, not only because of the intensity with which their nationalist movements pressed their cause but also because of the influence they had on other nationalities, both in terms of setting an example for how far the regime could be pressed and practical aid to other nationalists, including Muslims. Other blows to Soviet authority came from non-Muslim republics as well. The Russian republic challenged the jurisdiction of the central government several times in 1990 and 1991. Georgia, Armenia, and Moldova became increasingly restive under the Kremlin's rule. The December 1991 vote by Ukraine not to be part of the Soviet Union, no matter how much the terms of union were modified, guaranteed the Union's demise. Soon afterwards, the agreement among Russia, Ukraine, and Belarus to establish a loose association among themselves in the form of a commonwealth completed the Union's de facto dissolution.

In contrast, the five Central Asian republics, where a majority of the Soviet Union's Muslims lived, sought ways to preserve the Union until the end. They repeatedly used declarations first of sovereignty, then of independence to bargain for more favorable terms of membership in the Union rather than as a literal preliminary to secession. Their reasons were diverse. To some degree, the prospect of independence was daunting in itself. Furthermore, many Central Asians had hoped that Moscow would provide most of the funding to solve the region's extremely costly economic and environmental problems. Reformers looked to a like-minded central government to curb the authoritarianism of the Communist regimes still in power in all of Central Asian republics except Kyrgyzstan. Those regimes supported the proposed new Union treaty in party because it was Party policy, which they were accustomed to support. Complete independence would also require the republics to establish their own armies. That would not only impose costs the republics could ill afford but also raised the prospect of a disparity of strength between more and less populous republics as well as between any of them and forces beyond the former Soviet border.

Yet some observers argued, even during the changes taking place in the Gorbachev era, that an Islamic revolution was the greatest threat to the Soviet Union's survival. One formulation of this view combined overconfidence in the significance of sheer numbers with the assumption that the alienation of Muslims from non-Muslims *had to be* all important. Thus, Rywkin asserted that "the most important threat" to Soviet rule "is the growing Islam-based modern nationalist spirit" coupled with the rapid population growth of the Muslim nationalities.[43] Therefore,

> The Three Baltic nations . . . now challenge Moscow's rule but they are too small to threaten its security. The most serious control problem is in the Islamic republics, with their large territories, rapidly growing populations, and distinctive way of life, fed by a dangerous combination of racial, national, and religious feelings.[44]

Other prophets of an impending Islamic revolution offered internally inconsistent arguments. In Taheri's version, Soviet Muslims found little to appeal to them in Khomeinism; the revival of Islamic consciousness in the Soviet Union took many forms, rather than being a cohesive movement. In any event, he saw the revival as advocating neither terrorism nor secession from the Soviet Union.[45] Despite that skepticism, he concluded that "Islamic explosions in neighboring Afghanistan and Iran might at any time overspill into the USSR."[46] Bennigsen and Broxup made much of the Sufi organizations' tradition of armed opposition to Russian and Soviet rule and deemed them the "focal point" of growing anti-Russian sentiment and the "only organized opposition to the Communist power." However, the authors also argued that Soviet Muslims knew that their rapid population growth would guarantee that they would win autonomy by the end of the century; therefore most of them did not want a Sufi-led "holy war" against the Kremlin on the grounds that would be "foolhardy or premature action."[47] Oddly enough, having argued that the Muslims knew they would obtain their goals without having to resort to arms, the authors closed the book with the observation that the short-term continuation of the status quo would merely delay the onset of "the final, inescapable, violent crisis."[48]

This paradoxical combination of a denial of the likelihood of an Islamic uprising against Soviet rule and the prediction that it was certain to occur reflected an attitude that underlay much of what was written about the Muslims of the Soviet Union in that country's last years. Proponents of the impending-Islamic-revolution school of thought wanted so strongly to believe that the revolution would happen that they took positions which went much further than their evidence could support. In rare instances, an author overcome this difficulty by making assertions with scant regard for corroborating evidence. More frequently, an author saw in the evidence only what he was predisposed to find, thus denying himself the opportunity to learn something he did not already know or assume. Ironically, some of the evidence which best suited such authors' expectations came from the "enemy" camp, from those official Soviet sources which were most hostile to Muslims. Observers who did not admire the Soviet regime and were mistrustful of Soviet propaganda in some settings practically welcomed pronouncements made with equally polemical intent about the Muslim nationalities.[49] Judgments based on such sources could then be quoted in the central Soviet press to lend credibility to Islamophobic warnings of a fanatical anti-Soviet conspiracy among the country's Muslims.[50]

Some specialists on Central Asia perceived dangers in this uncritical use of sources. People like James Critchlow, a specialist on Uzbekistan, and Guy Imart, a specialist on the Kyrgyz, saw the alarmist reports in Soviet publications as designed to serve ulterior political motives, not as impartial, factual reporting. For example, the scare stories of occult threats could distract people from examining serious domestic problems or could be used to discredit nationalist movements among Muslims in Western eyes and persuade Westerners not to support such movements.[51] However, the readiness to accept at face value Soviet accounts of Muslim extremist conspiracies continued in some quarters through the end of the Soviet era. The demise of the Soviet Union for reasons which had nothing to do with an Islamic revolution has put one set of interpretations to the test. However, the temptation remains to assert much more than one can corroborate.

NOTES

1   A. Bennigsen and M. Broxup, *The Islamic Threat to the Soviet State* (New York: St. Martin's Press, 1983), 117.
2   P. Goble, "Gorbachev's Six Crises," *CEO/International Strategies*, 1 (1990): 47-51.
3   J.F. Hough, "The Logic of Collective Action and the Pattern of Revolutionary Behavior," *Journal of Soviet Nationalities*, 1 (1990): 60, 61.
4   Ibid., 63.
5   Ibid., 62.

6   Ibid., 63-64.

7   A.J. Katsenelinboigen, *The Soviet Union. Empire, Nation, and System* (New Brunswick: Transaction Publishers, 1990), 11.

8   Ibid., 35.

9   Bennigsen and Broxup, *Islamic Threat*, foreword, 9; see also A. Taheri, *Crescent in a Red Sky* (London: Hutchinson, 1989), ix, 34, 77, *et passim*.

10   Katsenelinboigen, *Soviet Union*, 36, 151-53, 157-62, 165.

11   Taheri, *Crescent*, 16.

12   Ibid., 172.

13   Representative of such usage is: A. Shukurov, "Badnafsiyu beori — omili jinoyatkori," *Tojikistoni soveti*, June 9, 1990, 3.

14   Bennigsen and Broxup, *Islamic Threat*, 28-29, 61.

15   A.J. Motyl, *Will the Non-Russians Rebel?* (Ithaca: Cornell University Press, 1987), 41-42; R. Szporluk, "The Imperial Legacy and the Soviet Nationalities," in *The Nationalities Factor in Soviet Politics and Society*, L. Hajda and M. Beissinger, eds. (Boulder: Westview Press, 1990), 12, 15; M. Rywkin, *Moscow's Muslim Challenge*, revised edition (Armonk, NY and London: M.E. Sharpe, Inc., 1990), 123.

16   Szporluk, "Imperial Legacy," 2, 17.

17   J.B. Dunlop, *The Faces of Contemporary Russian Nationalism* (Princeton: Princeton University Press, 1983); idem, *The New Russian Nationalism* (New York: Praeger, 1985).

18   S.F. Starr, "Soviet Nationalities in Crisis," *Journal of Soviet Nationalities*, 1 (1990): 83; Szporluk, "Imperial Legacy," 6, 13; idem, "Dilemmas of Russian Nationalism," *Problems of Communism*, 38 (July-August 1989): 15-35.

19   Rywkin, *Moscow's Muslim Challenge*, ch. 10.

20   M.B. Olcott, "Moscow's Troublesome Muslim Minority," *The Washington Quarterly*, 9 (1986): 74-75.

21   Ibid., 76, 83, n. 15; G.W. Lapidus, "Gorbachev's Nationalities Problem," *Foreign Affairs*, 68 (1989): 92-94, 102-3; Motyl, "The Sobering of Gorbachev: Nationality, Restructuring, and the West," in *Politics, Society, and Nationality Inside Gorbachev's Russia*, S. Bialer, ed. (Boulder: Westview Press, 1989), 156-60.

22   Starr, "Soviet Nationalities," 78-84, 86; Lapidus, "State and Society: Toward the Emergence of Civil Society in the Soviet Union," in *Politics, Society, and Nationality Inside Gorbachev's Russia*, 125-30.

23   Goble, "Ethnic Politics in the USSR," *Problems of Communism*, 38 (July-August 1989): 1-14.

24   Taheri, *Crescent*, 226-27.

25   Bennigsen and Broxup, *Islamic Threat*, 4.

26   Rywkin, *Moscow's Muslim Challenge*, viii.

27   Bennigsen and Broxup, *Islamic Threat*, 135, 137; Rywkin, *Moscow's Muslim Challenge*, 116.

28   Bennigsen and Broxup, *Islamic Threat*, foreword.

29   Ibid., 114; Rywkin, *Moscow's Muslim Challenge*, 85; a similar view is expressed in Taheri, *Crescent*, 183-84.

30   Bennigsen and Broxup, *Islamic Threat*, 109, 137-38; in the same vein, Professor Rywkin depicted all Central Asian Muslims as feeling equally at home in any Muslim-populated area, regardless of nationality, and uncomfortable in any non-Muslim area, *Moscow's Muslim Challenge*, 153.

31   Bennigsen and Broxup, *Islamic Threat*, 138, 140.

32   Ibid.

33   Bennigsen and C. Lemercier-Quelquejay, *L'Islam en Union soviétique* (Paris: Payot, 1968), 28, 33, 215-26.

34   M. Atkin, "Religious, National, and Other Identities in Central Asia," in *Muslims in Central Asia*, J.-A. Gross, ed. (Durham, NC: Duke University Press, 1992), 49-53.

35   D.S. Carlisle, "Uzbekistan and the Uzbeks," *Problems of Communism*, 40 (September-October 1991): 44, n. 56; the author is also indebted to Professor William Fierman of Indiana University for similar information and has heard such a rumor from the Tajik perspective herself.

36   Carlisle, "Uzbekistan," 43.

37   A. A. Rorlich, "Islam and Atheism: Dynamic Tension in Soviet Central Asia," in *Soviet Central Asia*, W. Fierman, ed. (Boulder: Westview Press, 1991), 191, 213, n. 23.

38   Olcott, "Moscow's Troublesome Muslim Minority," 77; idem, "Central Asia: The Reformers Challenge a Traditional Society," in *The Nationalities Factor in Soviet Politics and Society*, 270-71, 276; Atkin, *The Subtlest Battle* (Philadelphia: Foreign Policy Research Institute, 1989), 13-28.

39   Taheri, *Crescent*, 76, 77, 81.

40   K. Hitchins, "Modern Tajik Literature," *Persian Literature*, ed. E. Yarshater (Albany: Bibliotheca Persica, 1988), 455.

41   Taheri, *Crescent*, 82, 257, n. 26.

42   Rorlich, *The Volga Tatars* (Stanford: Hoover Institution Press, 1986), 50-53.
43   Rywkin, *Moscow's Muslim Challenge*, 90.
44   Ibid., 122.
45   Taheri, *Crescent*, xix, 182, 189, 197, and 199.
46   Ibid., 222.
47   Bennigsen and Broxup, *Islamic Threat*, 77, 147, 148.
48   Ibid., 152.
49   Bennigsen and Broxup, *Islamic Threat*, 74, 138.
50   I. Beliaev, "*Islam i politika*," part 2, *Literaturnaia gazeta*, May 20, 1987, 12.
51   J. Critchlow, "Islam in Fergana Valley: the Wahhabi 'Threat'," Radio Liberty, *Report on the USSR*, 1 (December 8, 1989): 15; G.G. Imart, "Kirgizia-Kazakhstan: A Hinge or a Fault-Line?" *Problems of Communism*, 30 (September-October 1990): 9.

CONTRIBUTORS

SAID AMIR ARJOMAND is Professor of Sociology at the State University of New York, Stony Brook. He is author of *The Shadow of God and the Hidden Imam* and *The Turban for the Crown,* and editor of *The Political Dimensions of Religion.*

MURIEL ATKIN is Associate Professor of History at George Washington University. She is author of *Russia and Iran, 1780–1828* and *The Subtlest Battle: Islam in Soviet Tajikistan* and is currently at work on a book on religion, nationalism, and political change in Tajikistan.

EDWARD BERENSON is Professor of History at the University of California, Los Angeles. His most recent book is *The Trial of Madame Caillaux.* He is currently at work on a study of the outcomes of the French Revolution.

DANIEL CHIROT is Professor of International Studies and of Sociology at the University of Washington. He is author of *Modern Tyrants: The Power and Prevalence of Evil in Our Age* and *How Societies Change.*

JOHN FORAN is Associate Professor of Sociology at the University of California, Santa Barbara, and author of *Fragile Resistance: Social Transformation in Iran from 1500 to the Revolution.* He is currently working on the comparative study of Third World social revolutions.

ANDRE GUNDER FRANK is Professor of Development Economics and Social Sciences at the University of Amsterdam. The author of thirty books, his most recent works are *The Underdevelopment of Development* and *Transforming the Revolution: Social Movements and the World-System* (with S. Amin, G. Arrighi, and I. Wallerstein).

JACK A. GOLDSTONE is Professor of Sociology at the University of California, Davis. He is author of *Revolution and Rebellion in the Early Modern World* and co-editor of *Revolutions of the Late Twentieth Century.*

NIKKI R. KEDDIE is Professor of History at the University of California, Los Angeles, and author of several books, including *Roots of Revolution: An Interpretative History of Modern Iran*, and co-editor of *Women in Middle Eastern History*.

TIMUR KURAN is Professor of Economics and King Faisal Professor of Islamic Thought and Culture at the University of Southern California. He is author of *Legacies of Living a Lie*, which examines the cognitive, social, political, and economic consequences of preference falsification.

CHARLES TILLY is University Distinguished Professor at the New School for Social Research and Director of its Center for Studies of Social Change. His most recent books are *Coercion, Capital, and European States* and *European Revolutions*.

KATHERINE VERDERY is Professor of Anthropology at Johns Hopkins University and author of *Transylvanian Villagers: Three Centuries of Political, Economic, and Ethnic Change* and *National Ideology under Socialism: Identity and Cultural Politics in Ceausescu's Romania*.

JEFFERY N. WASSERSTROM is Associate Professor of History at Indiana University and author of *Student Protests in Twentieth-Century China: The View from Shanghai* and the project director for an NEH-funded multidisciplinary collaborative study of the "Keywords of the Chinese Revolution."

REGINALD E. ZELNIK is Professor of History at the University of California, Berkeley, and author of *Labor and Society in Tsarist Russia* and *Law and Disorder on the Narova River*.